The Story of Analytic Philosophy

The Story of Analytic Philosophy: Plot and Heroes is an edited collection of essays looking at analytic philosophy in its historical context. Analytic philosophy has been, for some time now, in a state of crisis—having to deal with its self-image, its relationship with philosophical alternatives, its fruitfulness and even legitimacy in the general philosophical community. This crisis manifests itself both within analytic philosophy, as we can see with the discussions and debates concerning the interpretation of its origins and key players (such as Frege, Russell, Wittgenstein), as well as in its evaluation by philosophers of different bents (such as postmodernists and Continental philosophers).

The Story of Analytic Philosophy: Plot and Heroes presents an obvious and explicit awareness of the crisis by "insiders," with a view to interpreting it. Such an interpretation is accomplished by telling the story of analytic philosophy—that is, by presenting its *raison d'etre* and the motivations, methods, and results of its eminent figures. The "plot," or the theoretics of a philosophical movement, is told by contributors Hacker, Hylton, Sacks, Skorupski and others. Each of the essays falling into this category addresses essential issues such as analysis, style, psychologism, and empiricism. The story of the "heroes," signifying the likes of Frege, Russell, and Wittgenstein, is a well known story, but still worth retelling. Floyd, Friedlander, Putnam and Lurie are some of the philosophers in this collection who examine the story of the heroes in a new light.

The unique position of the collection is its internal critique. The collection is an undertaking by analytic philosophers to assess the challenge posed by changing cultural and philosophical winds.

Anat Biletzki is a senior lecturer in Philosophy. **Anat Matar** is a lecturer in Philosophy. Both teach at Tel Aviv University.

Routledge Studies in Twentieth-Century Philosophy

The Story of Analytic Philosophy

Plot and Heroes

Edited by Anat Biletzki and Anat Matar

The Story of Analytic Philosophy

Plot and Heroes

Edited by Anat Biletzki and Anat Matar

1998

London and New York

First published 1998 by Routledge

Simultaneously published in the USA and Canada
by Routledge
29 West 35th Street, New York, NY 10001

© 1998 Anat Biletzki and Anat Matar, selection and editorial matter;
individual chapters, the contributors

Typeset in Baskerville by Routledge
Printed and bound in Great Britain by Hartnolls Ltd, Bodmin, Cornwall

British Library Cataloguing in Publication Data
A catalogue record for this book is available from the British Library

Library of Congress Cataloguing in Publication Data
Ths story of analytic philosophy: plot and heroes/edited by Anat Biletzki
and Anat Matar.
Includes index.
1. Analysis (Philosophy). I. Biletzki
Anat. II. Matar, Anat.
B808.5.S76   1998   97 –23396
146'. 4–dc21   CIP

ISBN 0–415–16251–3

For Burton Dreben and Michael Dummett

Contents

Part IV An eye to the future

Contributors

Gilead Bar-Elli is Professor of Philosophy, Department of Philosophy, Hebrew University, Jerusalem, Israel.

Yemima Ben-Menahem is Professor of Philosophy, Department of Philosophy, Hebrew University, Jerusalem, Israel.

Anat Biletzki is Senior Lecturer in Philosophy, Department of Philosophy, Tel Aviv University, Tel Aviv, Israel.

Juliet Floyd is Professor of Philosophy, Department of Philosophy, Boston University, Boston, Mass. U.S.A.

Eli Friedlander is Lecturer in Philosophy, Department of Philosophy, Tel Aviv University, Tel Aviv, Israel.

P. M. S. Hacker is Fellow of St. John's College, Oxford, U.K.

Jaakko Hintikka is Professor of Philosophy, Department of Philosophy, Boston University, Boston, Mass. U.S.A.

Peter Hylton is Professor of Philosophy, Department of Philosophy, University of Illinois at Chicago, Chicago, Il. U.S.A.

Yuval Lurie is Professor of Philosophy, Department of Philosophy, Ben-Gurion University, Beer Sheba, Israel.

Anat Matar is Lecturer in Philosophy, Department of Philosophy, Tel Aviv University, Tel Aviv, Israel.

Hilary Putnam is Pearson Professor of Mathematical Logic, Department of Philosophy, Harvard University, Cambridge, Mass. U.S.A.

Ruth Anna Putnam is Professor of Philosophy, Department of Philosophy, Wellesley College, Wellesley, Mass. U.S.A.

J. J. Ross is Professor of Philosophy, Department of Philosophy, Tel Aviv University, Tel Aviv, Israel.

Mark Sacks is Reader in Philosophy at the University of Essex, Colchester, U.K.

John Skorupski is Professor of Moral Philosophy, University of St. Andrews, St. Andrews, Fife, Scotland, U.K.

Preface

It seems beyond argument that analytic philosophy has been, for some time now, in a state of crisis—dealing with its self-image, its relationships with philosophical alternatives, its fruitfulness and even legitimacy in the general philosophical community. Interestingly enough this crisis manifests itself not only in its critical appraisal by philosophers of different bents— i.e. massive attacks by alternative perspectives such as postmodernism or "continental" philosophy (e.g. Derrida, Lyotard, Rorty)—but even within analytic philosophy itself—i.e. in the discussions and debates concerning interpretation of its origins, its essence, and its key players.

"Analytic Philosophy—Past and Future" was the name of a conference which took place at Tel Aviv University in January 1996. Its purported aim was to explore the present state of analytic philosophy in the light of recent research on its origins and current scepticism concerning its future. Papers were presented under three general headings: definition of analytic philosophy, origins and development of analytic philosophy, and future prospects of analytic philosophy. During the course of the conference it became evident that the three "topics" as such are in intricate inter-relationships, that one can barely deal with one without alluding to the others, and that, therefore, such a division of labor is unrealistic, if not outright ludicrous. We therefore, in choosing and putting together the articles for the present volume, turned to a different conception—one which comes out of obvious and explicit awareness of the crisis.

Awareness of a crisis involves understanding the bearer of the crisis. Such understanding can only be accomplished by telling the story of analytic philosophy—that is, by presenting its *raison d'être* and the motivations, methods, and results of its eminent figures. By "plot" we cater to the problematics of theorizing upon a philosophical movement as a whole. By "heroes" we appeal to undisputable contributors to the movement. These—both plot and heroes—may be viewed from either an "internal" or an "external" perspective. That is to say, an internal perspective affords an autonomous view of tensions within the movement, both in the theoretical arena (e.g. analysis of specific key-terms, definition of its main concepts, identification of methods, etc.) and in the perhaps more "concrete" area of hero-interpretation. External discussion is a more comparative and dialogical focus on the contrast between both the theory and the actors, on the one hand, and competing theories (and *their* actors), on the other.

"Internal" and "external" can also be understood differently. One can look upon a philosophical tradition from, as it were, an external viewpoint and describe it, evaluate it, interpret it, or argue with it from a, supposedly, neutral position. However, most of the contributors to this volume are, in that sense, internal participants; they view themselves as belonging to that same tradition—though, sometimes, stretching its borders—even while commenting upon and criticizing it.

It should be emphasized that by "plot" we do not allude to the very voguish notion of "narrative" which necessarily involves historical and chronological renditions of a story-plot. Rather we seek to delve deeply into the plot of analytic philosophy by emphasizing its essence and focusing on its principal themes. Yet we realize that, in some sense, historical roots provide explanatory hinges for these essence and themes. Peter Hacker, therefore, supplies the profound historical background to the movement in Part I with his introductory article "Analytic philosophy: what, whence, whither?"—a synoptic view of a movement, with its optional possibilities.

Then starts the Plot. In Part II, Peter Hylton's "Analysis in analytic philosophy" surveys the meanderings of the concept of "analysis" within analytic philosophy, and the question of the movement's unity. Perusing five different analyses of "analysis" he shows that this one common concept, having given analytic philosophy its name, is variously understood by the protagonists. Jacob Joshua Ross, in "Analytic philosophy as a matter of style," provides a critical examination of Michael Dummett's conception of the origins and essence of analytic philosophy, leading to a conclusion which posits "style" as the definitive criterion of the school—as opposed to other styles of philosophizing. In "Analytic philosophy: rationalism vs. romanticism," Anat Matar challenges the commonly accepted opposition between analytic philosophy and continental philosophy, arguing, instead, that the line should be drawn, rather, between essentially rationalist world-views (which house analytic philosophy), and any romanticist attitude towards philosophy. Mark Sacks does turn to the analytic–continental divide, examining the conception of the ego—the experiencing subject—in both traditions. His chapter "The subject, normative structure, and externalism" supplies both a fascinating "story" and an involved statement. Also involved, albeit in a different manner, is John Skorupski, who in "Empiricism without positivism," presents the logical positivists, the group most identified with the heyday of analytic philosophy, as incoherent; and claims that empiricism, but not in its positivist aspect, may still, perhaps, hold a grain of truth. Finally, Yemima Ben-Menahem's "Psychologism and meaning" brings to the fore the original stumbling-block—psychologism—pointed out by early analytic philosophers, and examines its current relevance. Focusing on James, Frege, and Wittgenstein, she plots the course of psychologism by dealing with some of its outstanding heroes. Not surprisingly plot cannot be told without heroes.

Part III—Heroes—naturally begins with the father (sometimes called grandfather, other times referred to as even a forefather) of analytic philosophy, Gottlob Frege. Juliet Floyd's "Frege, semantics, and the double definition stroke" tells the story of two opposing interpretations of Frege relating him to the "semantical" tradition in analytic philosophy: as the father of a theory of meaning and as having nothing to do with such. Her article exemplifies the paradigmatic style which makes a commentator on a hero an analytic philosopher herself. Talking of paradigms, Gilead Bar-Elli, in "Elimination by analysis," gives a new reading to the philosophical significance of Russell's "On Denoting." Russell's counterpart, G. E. Moore, starts off Ruth Anna Putnam's "Perception: From Moore to Austin," which posits these heroes' aim as an explanation of a knowable world, rather than a foundation for empirical knowledge.

Symptomatic of the condition of crisis is the disproportionate attention conferred on Ludwig Wittgenstein and his spell on the tradition (and, interestingly enough, on other traditions as well). Anat Biletzki—"Wittgenstein: analytic philosopher?"—advances the claim that only the early Wittgenstein deserves the label of "analytic philosopher" with the later Wittgenstein's influence being attributed to a kind of bewitchment inappropriate for analytic philosophy. Yuval Lurie, in "Wittgenstein as the forlorn caretaker of language," presents Wittgenstein—an analytic philosopher?—as an exception to the analytic rule of preferring a scientific conception of philosophy to an artistic one. And, continuing the vein of questioning Wittgenstein's analytic credentials, by embracing his non-analytic character, Eli Friedlander—"Heidegger, Carnap, Wittgenstein: much ado about nothing"—considers the differing relations of Carnap and Wittgenstein to what seems to most oppose them—the concept of "nothingness" in continental philosophy.

Part IV resumes the "whither?" of Peter Hacker's opening article. Hilary Putnam and Jaakko Hintikka supply two very different prognoses of "an eye to the future." Both, perhaps in contrast to the conclusions of the previous writers, see Wittgenstein as a key to the future of analytic philosophy. Putnam, in "Kripkean realism and Wittgenstein's realism," presents the difference between commonsense realism and metaphysical realism as the difference between two basic strands of analytic philosophy today—and points to the pragmatistic choice as preferable. And finally, Jaakko Hintikka—"Who is about to kill analytic philosophy?"—exposes certain (now popular) interpretations of Ludwig Wittgenstein as destructive of the analytic movement itself, and points to a way out of this destructiveness. Both Putnam and Hintikka agree, however, on one thing: if analytic philosophy is not dead it has no choice but to change from within using self-reflection and self-awareness. This book—avoiding dogmatic adherence or attack—hopes to supply internal critique, i.e., an undertaking by analytic philosophers to assess the challenge posed by changing cultural and philosophical winds.

Part I
Introduction

1 Analytic philosophy: what, whence, and whither?

P. M. S. Hacker

INTRODUCTION

Analytic philosophy has been the predominant philosophical movement of the twentieth century. Almost from its inception, it was allied with the spirit of rationality and science, and was dedicated to the overthrow of speculative metaphysics and the eradication of philosophical mystification. Methodologically it was associated with the employment of the new logic as a source of philosophical insight and, somewhat later—after the linguistic turn in philosophy—with a principled and meticulous attention to language and its use. Analytic philosophy flourished in various forms from the 1910s until the 1970s. In the last quarter of the century, however, it has lost its distinctive profile, retaining the name of analytic philosophy largely through its genealogy, the foci of concern which it shares with the antecedent tradition, and its contrastive juxtaposition with certain forms of continental philosophy.

It is surprising to discover that although the terms "analysis," "logical analysis," and "conceptual analysis" were widely used from the inception of the movement to characterize the methods of philosophy advocated, the name "analytic philosophy" became current relatively late. It was used in the 1930s,[1] but does not seem to have caught on. Von Wright (1993: 41, n. 35)[2] has conjectured that it entered currency partly through the postwar writings of Arthur Pap, who published his *Elements of Analytic Philosophy* in 1949, *Analytische Erkenntnistheorie* in 1955, and *Semantics and Necessary Truth: An Inquiry into the Foundations of Analytic Philosophy* in 1958. Certainly it is striking that the two most influential postwar anthologies of writings in early analytic philosophy, Feigl and Sellars' *Readings in Philosophical Analysis* in America (1949) and Flew's *Logic and Language* in Britain (1951), did not invoke the name "analytic philosophy" in either their titles or introductions. The purported successor to Flew's anthology, published in 1962, was Butler's *Analytic Philosophy*.

There is little consensus on how to characterize analytic philosophy. There are numerous books and essays identifying the basic principles and doctrines of logical atomism and Cambridge analysis of the interwar years. There was a veritable flood of publications, including a manifesto, specifying and defending the principles and doctrines of logical positivism. And there was no shortage of writings emanating from Oxford in the postwar years explaining and defending the methods of what Strawson called "logico-linguistic" or "connective" analysis.[3] But a short persuasive answer to the question "What is analytic philosophy?" is hard to find. There is a broad consensus, but not a uniform agreement, on who are to be deemed analytic philosophers. Moore and Russell, the young Wittgenstein, Broad, Ramsey, Braithwaite, early Wisdom, and Stebbing from the Cambridge school of analysis can surely not be excluded from the list, nor can the leading members of the Vienna Circle, such as Schlick, Hahn, Carnap, Neurath, Feigl, Waismann, and affiliates such as Reichenbach or Hempel from the Berlin Society for Scientific Philosophy. In a narrow sense of "analytic philosophy" one might draw the line here. The rationale for this would be the general commitment to analysis, reduction, and logical construction. But it would, I think, be ill-advised for two reasons. First, there are more important continuities than differences between the latter two phases and postwar philosophy.[4] Secondly, most of the postwar philosophers at Oxford, such as Ryle, Ayer, Kneale, Austin, Grice, Strawson, Hart, Hampshire, Pears, Quinton, Urmson, and Warnock thought of themselves as analytic philosophers and characterized their work as conceptual or linguistic analysis and, later, as analytic philosophy. So too did many other philosophers working in what they conceived of as a similar tradition. Many of Wittgenstein's pupils, such as von Wright, Malcolm, and Black would rightly be characterized as analytic philosophers, even though they differed in important respects both among themselves and relative to many of the Oxford figures. And if they are to be included, then so is the later Wittgenstein, whose influence upon Oxford analytical philosophy was second to none.[5] Nevertheless, there is disagreement on how analytic philosophy is most illuminatingly to be characterized. And there has been surprisingly little written on the phenomenon of analytic philosophy as a whole, by contrast with the extensive publications on constituent streams within the flood-waters of this philosophical movement.[6]

CHARACTERISTIC MARKS OF ANALYTIC PHILOSOPHY

An analytic account of analytic philosophy will try to elaborate a list of characteristic marks. The starting points are readily identifiable: however it is to be characterized, the notion of analysis must find a place in the description. So too must the ideas of *logical* and of *linguistic* analysis. But what these amount to is problematic, and whether they suffice, on any single interpretation and in any form of combination, to encompass the analytic movement in twentieth-century philosophy in all its diversity is debatable. It may be that no set of features constitutes characteristic marks of analytic philosophy. For it may be that it is not to be defined by *Merkmale* at all, but is best viewed as a family-resemblance concept. It is also possible that an analytic account is not the most fruitful way to look at the analytic movement.

1 Analysis As its name betokens, analytic philosophy is concerned with the analysis of complexes into their constituents. But different forms of analytic philosophy were produced according to the different conceptions of the complexes which were to be the subject of such analysis. For on some conceptions, it was reality, or the facts of which it was thought to consist, that was to be subjected to philosophical analysis. Accordingly, analysis was thought to disclose the ultimate constituents of the world and the most general forms of the facts of which it consists (Russell); alternatively it was held to reveal the composition of mind-independent concepts and propositions which constitute objective reality (Moore). On other conceptions, it was human thought and language that was the matter of analysis, the upshot of which was supposed to reveal the manner in which the forms of thought and language alike necessarily reflect the structure of reality (the *Tractatus*). On yet others, it was language alone that was to be subjected to analysis, either the logical syntax of the language of science (Carnap) or, in a very different sense of "analysis," ordinary language (Oxford analytic philosophy). Moreover, different kinds of analysis emerged, depending upon whether analysis was conceived to terminate in simple unanalyzable constituents or not. Accordingly, atomistic ontological analysis characteristic of logical atomism with its reductive and constructive aspirations—which aspirations it shared with many of the logical positivists—may be contrasted with the more holistic "connective" linguistic analysis after 1945, which eschewed reduction and logical construction.

It would be absurd to sever the notion of analytic philosophy from the conception of analysis that gives it its name. But the mere concept of analysis characterizes Descartes' metaphysics, with its commitment to the analysis of objects in reality into simple natures, no less than classical British empiricism, with its commitment to the analysis of complex ideas into simple ideas derived from experience. If the idea of atomistic or reductive analysis is the net with which to capture analytic philosophers, it will, to be sure, catch Moore and Russell, but it will also collect philosophers of the heroic age of modern philosophy whom one would not obviously wish to classify as analytic philosophers. And it will exclude the later Wittgenstein and his followers, as well as postwar analytic philosophers in Oxford and elsewhere. Alternatively, one may stretch the notion of analysis to the point of including connective analysis characteristic of postwar analytic philosophy. That may legitimately be done, but only at the cost of robbing the conception of analysis of early twentieth-century philosophy of its distinctive content. The idea of analysis alone is too elastic, capable of too many divergent, indeed conflicting, interpretations to be a useful litmus test by itself.

2   Anti-psychologism in logic   Analytic philosophy is sometimes characterized by reference to anti-psychologism. What analytic philosophy achieved was the severance of logic from psychology and epistemology. Thus Kenny, following Dummett, has argued that

> Frege disentangled logic from psychology, and gave it the place in the forefront of philosophy which had hitherto been occupied by epistemology. It is this fact which, more than any other, allows Frege to be regarded as the founding father of modern analytic philosophy.
>
> (Kenny 1995: 210)

It is true that Frege waged a successful campaign against the infection of logic with psychology. He was not the first in Germany to do so, having been anticipated by Krug, Bolzano, and Lotze. And in Britain, Spencer and Jevons pursued a similarly anti-psychologist line, as did the absolute idealists, from whom the early Moore and Russell derived their anti-psychologism. Indeed, the absolute idealists had been sufficiently successful in disinfecting logic that Moore and Russell felt no need to press the point, and could take it for granted that logic was not a branch of psychology and that the laws of logic are not descriptions of regularities of human thinking. A further aspect of anti-psychologism was the repudiation of genetic analysis as pursued by the British empiricists' investigations of the origins of ideas. This campaign had been initiated by Kant, and it purged philosophy of the futile debate about innate ideas that characterized seventeenth and early eighteenth-century empiricism and rationalism.

It is true that anti-psychologism in logic has been a feature of much of analytic philosophy in the twentieth century. Nevertheless, one should be cautious. It is noteworthy that the later Wittgenstein remarked that "The opinion that the laws of logic are the expression of 'thinking habits' is not as absurd as it seems" (MS 120, Vol. XIV: 12). Erdmann was wrong to think that, *even though it is unintelligible to us*, there might be beings who reason according to a rule of affirming the consequent or who reject the law of identity. But then so too was Frege wrong to concede this ("This impossibility of our rejecting the law in question hinders us not at all in supposing beings who do reject it") and equally wrong to suppose that if there are such beings, then we know that they are wrong and that we are right (Frege 1964: 15). Both psychologicians and anti-psychologicians such as Frege failed to appreciate that the laws of thought partly *define* what counts as thinking, reasoning, and inferring. One cannot mean what we do by "not," "if . . . , then . . . ," "the same" and also repudiate the law of non-contradiction or of identity, or also accept affirming the consequent as a rule of inference. One cannot *reject* the inference rule of *modus ponens* and still be held to be reasoning and thinking. Indeed it is far from obvious whether anything would count as a principled *rejection* of this inference rule. Psychologism failed to do justice to the internal relations between logical truths, rules of inference ("laws of thought"), and thinking, reasoning, and inferring on the one hand and the meanings of the logical connectives on the other. But Fregean and Russellian anti-psychologism suffered from the same flaw. Moreover, psychologism, Wittgenstein argued, was not so far from a truth as it seems:

> The laws of logic are indeed the expression of "thinking habits" but also of the habit of *thinking*. That is to say they can be said to show: how human beings think, and also *what* human beings call "thinking" . . .
> The propositions of logic are "laws of thought" "because they bring out the essence of human thinking"—to put it more correctly: because they bring out, or show, the essence, the technique, of thinking. They show what thinking is and also show kinds of thinking.
> (Wittgenstein 1978: 89f.)[7]

Erdmann was in a sense right to claim that the laws of logic are an expression of how we think, as the rules of chess might be said to be an expression of how we play chess. But he failed to see that they are also partly constitutive of what we call "thinking," as the rules of chess are constitutive of the practice of playing chess (that playing in accordance with *these* rules is what is *called* "playing chess." And Frege's Platonist conception of the laws of logic as descriptions of relations between abstract objects likewise failed to grasp this.

So over-hasty characterization of analytic philosophy in terms of early anti-psychologism may be precipitate. It distorts or even screens out the later Wittgenstein, who had little sympathy with either protagonist. To be sure, he did not conceive of the laws of logic as mere descriptions of how people think and reason. He thought that there was a grain of truth in *both* Fregean anti-psychologism and in Erdmann's psychologism, as well as a heap of falsehood and confusion. But he seems to have viewed the familiar

Fregean form of anti-psychologism (with its Platonist alternative to Erdmann's conception) as the more dangerous or deceptive, presumably because its flaws are less obvious.

Be that as it may, anti-psychologism in logic is both too thin and too negative a characterization of analytic philosophy. And when we turn to the positive conception of logic propounded in this century, we find a proliferation of conflicting views. Frege and Russell (prior to *The Analysis of Mind*), to be sure, eschewed psychologism in logic. Both conceived of the propositions of logic as *generalizations* (neither thought that a proposition of the form "$p \lor \sim p$" is a proposition of logic; rather it is "$(p) (p \lor \sim p)$" that is a proposition of logic). Frege espoused an extreme Platonism, conceiving of the laws of logic as descriptions of sempiternal relations between abstract entities. Russell thought of them as the most general truths about the universe, a priori in as much as they are known independently of knowledge of any particular empirical facts, yet presupposing "logical experience" or "acquaintance with logical objects." The *Tractatus* argued that the propositions of logic are senseless—limiting cases of propositions with a sense, which present (show) the logical scaffolding of the world (1922: 6.124). Logic, the young Wittgenstein argued, is transcendental (1922: 6.13). Members of the Vienna Circle conceived of the propositions of logic as vacuous tautologies, but unlike Wittgenstein, they thought of them as consequences of arbitrary conventions for the use of the logical operators. In short, there is no positive characterization of the propositions of logic which would have commanded the assent of all analytic philosophers—and that is not surprising, for a large part of the endeavor of analytic philosophy in the first half of the century was to explain the nature of the necessary truths of logic and its laws, and the decades-long debate that ensued experimented with many different solutions to the problem.

3 Logical analysis   A corollary of (2) was that analytic philosophy is characterized by displacing epistemology by logic as the foundation of philosophy. Accordingly analytic philosophy is distinguished by the fact that it overthrew the Cartesian model of philosophy which gave epistemology primacy over all other branches of philosophy. This characterization is unsatisfactory. On the Cartesian model, it is metaphysics rather than epistemology which is the foundation of philosophy and thereby also of all knowledge. Cartesian *method* gave epistemic considerations primacy, since the Cartesian objective was the reconstruction of all knowledge upon secure foundations of resistance to hyperbolic doubt. But that motive was likewise the moving force behind Russell's philosophical thought in all phases of his philosophical career, and he similarly invoked the Cartesian method of doubt. Moreover, it cannot be said that members of the Vienna Circle held that logic, in some reasonably narrowly defined sense, is the foundation of philosophy, let alone of all knowledge (since, *inter alia* they denied that philosophy yields any *knowledge* at all). It was not a tenet of philosophers at Oxford after the Second World War, whose interest in logic was limited and who, like the later Wittgenstein, denied that philosophy is a cognitive discipline and that philosophy has a hierarchical structure.

It is, however, true that from its inception twentieth-century analytic philosophy differed from its classical seventeenth-century forbears in eschewing psychological analysis and replacing it with logical analysis. The invention of the new logic by Frege, Russell, and Whitehead both set an agenda for analytic philosophy in the first decades of the century and supplied a method. The agenda was to clarify the nature and status of the propositions and laws of logic, to elucidate the relations between Frege's concept-script or Russell's logical language of *Principia* and natural languages, and to cast light upon the relation of both natural language and the logical calculus to thought and reality. This task was pursued through subsequent decades, and divergent solutions to the questions were offered. The questions preoccupied many (but not all) philosophers of the analytic movement. But their answers are various and conflicting. The method (exemplified by Russell's theory of descriptions) consisted in invoking the apparatus of the propositional and predicate calculi in the endeavor to analyze the subject matter at hand. But, as we have seen, that subject matter was differently conceived by different philosophers at different times, varying from the facts and forms, thought, the language of science, to natural language. And logical analysis thus conceived certainly did not play any role in the work of most Oxford analytic philosophers or of the later Wittgenstein, who held that " 'mathematical logic' has completely deformed the thinking of mathematicians and philosophers, by setting up a superficial interpretation of the forms of our everyday language as an analysis of the structures of facts" (1978: 300). On the other hand, it continued to play a prominent role in the work of Quine, who conceives of the symbolism of modern logic as a canonical notation which will perspicuously disclose our ontological commitments. But Quine, as I shall later argue, was the primary subverter of analytic philosophy.

4 A philosophical account of thought by means of a philosophical account of language It is indeed no coincidence that German philosophers commonly refer to analytic philosophy as "sprachanalytische Philosophie." It is evident that analytic philosophy has been bound up with a sharpened awareness of the relevance to philosophy of close attention to language and its use. That much is platitudinous, and does not distinguish analytic philosophy from Socrates' Way of Words or from Aristotle's methodical attention to "what is said." Attempts to go further, however, are perilous. One such attempt was made by Dummett, who claimed that there are three tenets "common to the entire analytic school" (Dummett 1978: 458). First, that the goal of philosophy is the analysis of the structure of thought; second, that the study of thought is to be sharply distinguished from the study of thinking; third, that the only proper method of analyzing thought consists in the analysis of language.

The claim that the goal of philosophy is the analysis of the structure of thought is unclear. Presumably what is intended is that the aim of philosophy is the investigation of the inner structure of, and the logical relations between, thoughts. Assuming that "thoughts" signify what we think when we think that *p*, it is far from obvious that what we think *has* a structure (save metonymically), any more than what we fear, expect, suspect or suppose when we fear, expect, suspect, or suppose that *p* has a structure. It is the *expression* of thoughts (fears, expectations, suspicions, or suppositions) that can be said to have a structure.

Even if these qualms are disregarded, further worries remain. The fundamental questions of axiology are such as "What is the nature of goodness?," "What are the different kinds or varieties of goodness and how are they related?" or, "What distinguishes ethical goodness and how is it related to moral reasons for action?". The fundamental questions in the philosophy of mathematics are such as "What are numbers?," "What is the nature of the necessity which we associate with mathematical truth?" or "What is the relation of mathematical truth to proof?" Such questions, which could be multiplied within axiology or the philosophy of mathematics and similarly exemplified for any other branch of philosophy, cannot be subsumed (by analytic philosophers alone) non-trivially under the heading of "the philosophy of thought" or be said to be uniquely answered according to analytic philosophy by the analysis of thought.

The thesis that the only proper way to analyze the structure of thought is to analyze language would not have commanded the assent of either Moore or the early Russell.[8] And the later Wittgenstein would surely have denied any sense to the idea that thoughts have a structure. The sentences that are used to express thoughts do, to be sure, have a structure. But a cardinal principle of the later Wittgenstein was to dismiss sentential forms or structures, including the forms and structures of the predicate calculus, as misleading. Forms of words are not misleading because the surface structure conceals something that can be called the deep structure given by the predicate calculus (with further improvements), as he had argued in the

Tractatus, but rather because the surface form does not reveal the use, because sentences with totally different uses may have exactly the same form or structure.[9] The forms of the predicate calculus are no less misleading than the forms of natural language.

5 The linguistic turn
A different characterization of analytic philosophy is also to be found in Kenny and Dummett. Kenny suggests that

> If analytic philosophy was born when the 'linguistic turn' was taken, its birthday must be dated to the publication of *The Foundations of Arithmetic* in 1884 when Frege decided that the way to investigate the nature of number was to analyze sentences in which numerals occurred.
>
> (Kenny 1995: 211)[10]

This suggestion too does not seem helpful. If the context principle signals the linguistic turn in philosophy, then that turn was taken by Bentham in 1816, when he wrote in *Chrestomathia*

> By anything less than an entire proposition, i.e. the import of an entire proposition, no communication can have place. In language, therefore, the *integer* to be looked for is an entire proposition—that which Logicians mean by the term logical proposition. Of this integer, no one part of speech, not even that which is most significant, is anything more than a fragment; and in this respect, in the many worded appellative, part of speech, the word *part* is instructive. By it, an intimation to look out for the integer, of which it is a part, may be considered as conveyed.
>
> (Bentham 1983: 400)

This states clearly what is commonly taken to have first been stated by Frege's dictum that "A word has a meaning only in the context of a sentence" and more perspicuously stated in Wittgenstein's later elucidation that the sentence is the minimal move in a language game (cf. Wittgenstein 1958: §49). Bentham's analysis of fictions, in particular of legal fictions, is, in this sense, an exemplary case of analytic philosophy. For Bentham decided that the way to investigate the nature of obligations, duties, and rights was to analyze or, more perspicuously, to find paraphrastic equivalents of, sentences in which the words "obligation," "duty," or "a right" occur. To this end he devised his methods of phraseoplerosis, paraphrasis, and archetypation. But it would be eccentric to date the birth of analytic philosophy to the publication of *Chrestomathia*.

There is no doubt that the context principle is of great importance in the history of analytic philosophy, as is Russell's theory of incomplete symbols (which was likewise anticipated by Bentham's theory of fictions). By itself, however, it signifies merely one analytic method among others. Moreover, there is no good reason to associate the context principle with the so called "linguistic turn" in philosophy. I shall argue below that the linguistic turn postdates the rise of analytic philosophy, and is to be associated with the *Tractatus* and subsequent developments of analytic philosophy under its influence.

6 The primacy of the philosophy of language   Rightly convinced that a distinctive feature of much twentieth-century analytic philosophy is its preoccupation with language and linguistic meaning, and, I hope, persuaded that analytic philosophy cannot be fruitfully identified by reference to (4) or (5), one might try a further gambit. One might suggest, as Sluga does, that the characteristic tenet of analytic philosophy is "that the philosophy of language is the foundation of all the rest of philosophy" (Sluga 1980: 2).[11] But this too is unacceptable. On the one hand Mauthner, whom one would hardly count as an analytic philosopher, argued that all philosophy is a critique of language. On the other hand, both Moore and Russell explicitly denied that their forms of analysis were concerned with analysis of language, let alone with a subject called "the philosophy of language." We have already noted that the later Wittgenstein held philosophy to be "flat" and denied that any part of philosophy has a primacy relative to any other part. A brief glance at the postwar Oxford philosophers reveals no commitment to the thesis of the primacy of philosophy of language. If Ryle counts as an analytic philosopher of psychology, if Hart counts as an analytic philosopher of law, if Austin, in his investigations of speech-acts, counts as an analytic philosopher of language and, in his investigations of perception or of other minds, as an analytic epistemologist, then it cannot be argued that analytic philosophers in general hold that philosophy of language is the foundation of the rest of the subject.

7 The rejection of metaphysics   It might be suggested that analytic philosophy is characterized by its repudiation of metaphysics. It rejected the intelligibility of synthetic a priori truth, and denied that pure reason alone can attain any knowledge of reality. It is true that the repudiation of speculative metaphysics played a role in some of the phases of analytic philosophy. This was certainly true of the Cambridge analysts of the interwar years, of the Vienna Circle, and of most, if not all, of the Oxford analytic philosophers. But this does not distinguish analytic philosophy from other forms. First, as Wittgenstein remonstrated to Schlick apropos the Manifesto of the Vienna Circle, there was nothing new about "abolishing metaphysics": Hume had waved that banner vigorously; so too had Kant (as far as transcendent metaphysics is concerned) and Comte. Secondly, analytic philosophy in its early phases, viz. the pluralist Platonism of the early Moore and Russell, logical atomism of middle

Russell and the *Tractatus*, and Cambridge analysis of the interwar years were surely committed to metaphysical theses concerning the ultimate nature of reality and the logical structure of the world. They rejected the speculative metaphysics of absolute idealism, only to replace it by various forms of putatively analytic metaphysics of facts and their constituents. The *Tractatus* denied that there can be any metaphysical propositions, insisting that any attempt to state metaphysical truths would necessarily result in nonsense. But this was not because Wittgenstein thought that there are no metaphysical truths; on the contrary—most of the propositions of the *Tractatus* are self-conscious attempts to state such truths, even though *stricto sensu* they can only be shown. Just as Kant had drawn the bounds of knowledge in order to make room for faith, so too the young Wittgenstein drew the limits of language in order to make room for ineffable metaphysics.

Repudiation, indeed passionate repudiation, of metaphysics characterizes above all the Vienna Circle. Young Oxford before and mature Oxford after the war had no more sympathy for metaphysics than the Circle,[12] but did not share its crusading zeal. As Ryle remarked, "Most of us took fairly untragically its demolition of Metaphysics. After all we never met anyone engaged in committing any metaphysics; our copies of *Appearance and Reality* were dusty; and most of us had never seen a copy of *Sein und Zeit*" (Ryle 1970: 10). The later Wittgenstein rejected the aspirations of all forms of metaphysics, though not on the grounds that there are no synthetic a priori propositions or that all necessary truths are analytic.

If the above list of philosophers of the analytic movement is reasonable, then it seems clear that none of the seven features serves to capture all in the net save at the cost of distortion. Nor will any combination of these features into a set of conditions individually necessary and jointly sufficient do the trick. It might be argued that the concept of analytic philosophy should be viewed as a family resemblance concept.[13] What unites philosophers of the analytic school would accordingly be an array of overlapping similarities of method and doctrine, none of which is individually necessary for being an analytic philosopher. This may be defensible. But first, one would capture in one's net a whole host of philosophers, from Aristotle to Hume and Bentham, in addition to participants in the twentieth-century analytic movement. That may be an acceptable price to pay. Pap certainly thought so, remarking that

> A history of analytic philosophy, if it should ever be written, would not have to begin with the twentieth century. It could go all the way back to Socrates, since the Socratic "dialectic" is nothing else but a method of clarifying meanings, applied primarily to moral terms. Again, much of Aristotle's writings consists of logical analysis. . . . It is especially the so-called British empiricists, Locke,

Hume, Berkeley and their descendants, who practiced philosophy primarily as an analytic method. To be sure, much of what they wrote belongs to psychology, but if that is deducted there still remains a conscientious preoccupation with questions of meaning, full of lasting contributions to analytic philosophy . . .

(Pap 1949: vii–viii)

Secondly, family resemblance concepts typically evolve over time, new fibers being added to the rope in response to new discoveries or inventions, to the shifting pattern of concepts and conceptual relations, to perceived analogies and similarities of novel phenomena to the familiar, to new ways of looking at things, and to human needs. The term "analytic philosophy" is a fairly new one. It is a philosopher's term of art. There is no point in trying to follow Wittgenstein's advice apropos family resemblance concepts: "don't think, but look!" (1958: 66), i.e. examine how the expression in question is in fact used. For the term does not have a well-established use that commands general consensus. Here we are free to mold the concept as we please; indeed, arguably not free, but required to do so. The moot question is: for what purpose do we need the notion of analytic philosophy? If its primary use is to characterize a movement and its methods in twentieth-century philosophy, then construing it as a family resemblance concept will arguably rob it of its primary usefulness as a historical category inasmuch as it would collect much more in its net than the analytic movement of our century. Moreover, if we were deliberately to mold it in the form of a family resemblance concept, it would be incumbent upon us to determine reasons why these and these features characterize the family and not those. And that would be no easy task, nor one with respect to which one could hope to attain a ready consensus.

A HISTORICAL CATEGORY: A SYNOPTIC VIEW OF ANALYTIC PHILOSOPHY

Analytic philosophy in the twentieth century had numerous precursors, from Socrates and Aristotle, to Descartes and Leibniz, from Locke, Berkeley, and Hume, to Kant, Bentham, and Frege.[14] Most (but not all) of the threads out of which the tapestry of analytic philosophy was woven can be traced back into the more or less remote past. What is most distinctive about the tapestry are the ways in which the various threads are interwoven and the character of the designs. These altered over time, some threads being either abandoned and replaced by new ones or differently used, and others becoming more prominent in the weave than hitherto, some patterns dominating one period, but sinking into the background or disappearing altogether in later periods. It is, I suggest, as a dynamic historical movement that analytic philosophy is best understood.[15]

It was born in Cambridge at the turn of the century with the revolt against absolute idealism. Moore and Russell took anti-psychologism for granted—in this respect they had no quarrel with their idealist teachers. The main bones of contention were the dependence of the object of knowledge upon the knower, the monism of the Absolute, the coherence theory of truth, the unreality of relations and the doctrine of internal relations. Moore and Russell repudiated idealism—both Berkeleian and Kantian, insisted upon the independence of the object of knowledge from the knower, defended a correspondence theory of truth, rejected the doctrine of the internality of all relations and affirmed the reality and objectivity of relations. Their criticism of the absolute idealists was not based upon empiricist principles, and their methodology was not inspired by fidelity to ordinary language. On the contrary, they embraced an exuberantly pluralist, Platonist realism. In place of the synthesis characteristic of the neo-Hegelian idealism they espoused analysis. Moore conceived of himself as engaged in the analysis of mind-independent concepts, which, when held before the mind, could be seen to be either composite or simple. If composite, the task of the philosopher was to specify the constituent concepts into which the complex concept can be analyzed, and to elucidate how it is related to and differentiated from other concepts. He distinguished between knowing the meaning of an expression, knowing its verbal definition and knowing its use on the one hand, and knowing the analysis of its meaning on the other. He construed knowing the meaning of an expression as having the concept before one's mind, and distinguished that from being able to analyze the meaning, i.e. being able to say what its constituents are and how it is distinguished from other related concepts. According to his official doctrine, it is possible to analyze a concept (or the meaning of a term) without attending to its linguistic expression.

Russell's conception of analysis differed in certain respects. It was rooted in the work of nineteenth-century mathematicians such as Weierstrass, Dedekind, and Cantor, whose writings on concepts pertaining to the calculus, such as continuity and limit, were a model for Russell. Like Moore, he conceived of the matter of analysis as objective and non-linguistic. As his work on the foundations of mathematics proceeded, his conception of analysis became increasingly logical, without however being conceived to be linguistic. The logical language of *Principia* became the primary tool to penetrate the misleading forms of natural language and to disclose the true logical forms of the facts. But the theory of descriptions and theory of types exerted pressure, to which Russell only reluctantly and slowly succumbed, to concede greater importance than he had hitherto done to the investigation of language. The method of analysis of incomplete symbols, of which definite descriptions were one kind, was, like Bentham's theory of fictions, in effect a method of sentential paraphrase. And the theory of types lent itself readily to transformation into a fragment of a theory of logical syntax that owes no homage to reality.

The differences between Russell and Moore were deeper than this. Moore was convinced that we do know innumerable facts with absolute certainty. Any philosophy that challenges these is to be rejected as false, for our certainty regarding such facts far outweighs the certainty of any philosophical argument. We know that the world has existed for a long time, that we have a body, that there exist material things which are independent of our mind, that we often could have acted differently from the way we actually acted, that we do really know many truths, etc. What we do not know is the *analysis* of such facts. We know what these propositions mean, and we know them to be true, but we do not know the analysis of their meanings. The task of philosophy is the analysis of meanings (meanings being conceived to be mind-independent and language-independent entities). Russell's philosophy, by contrast, was a Cartesian quest for certainty. We do not know in advance where that quest will lead us, and there is no reason to suppose that it will leave intact the humdrum certainties that Moore cited. Indeed, he remarked impishly, "The point of philosophy is to start with something so simple as to not seem worth stating and to end with something so paradoxical that no one will believe it" (Russell 1986: 172). Mathematics was Russell's paradigm of certain knowledge, and his investigation into the foundations of mathematics was motivated by the need to vindicate the truth and indubitability of the Peano axioms for arithmetic by deriving them from pure logic. Having executed that task to his satisfaction in *Principia*, Russell turned to the analysis of our knowledge of the external world, hoping to do for empirical knowledge in general what he conceived himself to have done for arithmetic, i.e. set it upon secure foundations. Hence his espousal of Ockham's razor: not to multiply entities beyond necessity (in order to avoid giving hostages to fortune) and his advocacy of the "supreme principle of scientific philosophy": wherever possible to substitute logical constructions for inferred entities. Reduction and logical construction were the hallmarks of his two postwar works, *The Analysis of Mind* and *The Analysis of Matter*. He conceived of philosophy as a form of scientific knowledge, differing from the special sciences only in its greater generality. Its task is the search for truth. To ensure that what is disclosed is true, Cartesian doubt is a primary tool.

The differences between Russell and Moore, as von Wright points out (von Wright 1993: 26–30), represent a duality at the roots of analytic philosophy. That duality later becomes a polarity within analytic philosophy in general, manifest in the differences within the Vienna Circle between Carnap and Schlick, and among Oxford philosophers between Ayer and Austin. These poles can even be held to represent, as Waismann argued (Waismann 1939–40: 265; von Wright 1993: 26), two fundamentally different attitudes of the human mind. The one is primarily concerned with truth, the other with meaning; the one with the enlargement of knowledge, the other with the deepening of understanding; the one with establishing certainty in the face of sceptical fears, the other holding sceptical challenges to pre-existing certainties as definitely rejectable (as Moore argued) or indeed incoherent (as Wittgenstein argued); the one with emulating the achievements, progress, and theory construction of the sciences, the other with the pursuit of clarity as an end in itself.[16]

The first phase of analytic philosophy evolved from the exuberant pluralist Platonism of the turn of the century to the emergence of logical atomism (which constitutes its second phase) of the 1910s. This was in part owing to Russell's attempt to apply the methods of analysis of *Principia* to empirical knowledge in general, and in part to the young Wittgenstein— whose impact upon Russell was both devastating and inspiring—and to the masterpiece he wrote between 1913 and 1919: the *Tractatus*. Four features of the *Tractatus* are noteworthy for present purposes.

First, it brought to its culmination the analytic, decompositional drive in modern European philosophy which originated with Descartes and Leibniz no less than with Locke and Hume. This conception dominated Cambridge analysis of the interwar years, and, in a modified fashion (without the metaphysics of facts and simple objects, and without the independence thesis for atomic propositions) it molded the logical positivist conception of analysis. It also brought to full fruition the metaphysics of logic that had flowered at the hands of Frege and Russell. Within the framework of its metaphysical system, the picture theory of thought and proposition provided the most powerful resolution thus far offered to the problems of the intentionality of the proposition which had dominated philosophical thought since Descartes. It gave a metaphysical explanation of how it is possible for a mental phenomenon, namely thinking a thought, to have a content which is identical with what is the case if it is true, but still to have a content if what is the case is different from its content, i.e. if it is false. Corresponding to this, it explained how a proposition can be false yet meaningful. In general, it explained the intentionality of signs by reference to the intrinsic intentionality of mental acts of thinking and meaning.

Second, it definitively destroyed the Fregean and Russellian conceptions of logic and replaced them with a quite different one. The *Grundgedanke* of the *Tractatus* is that there are no logical constants.[17] The logical connectives are not names, neither of logical objects nor of special logical functions (concepts or relations). Propositions are not names, neither of truth-values nor of complexes. The propositions of logic are neither descriptions of relations between abstract objects nor descriptions of the most general facts in the universe. The mark of a logical truth is not absolute generality, for logical truths are not generalizations of tautologies, but tautologies *simpliciter*. The mark of a logical truth is necessity, and the necessity of a logical proposition is a consequence of a degenerate case of a truth-functional combination of propositions. In a logical proposition elementary propositions are so combined by truth-functional operators as to be true no matter what truth-values they possess. The price paid for such guaranteed truth is vacuity. Propositions of logic are senseless, have zero sense, and say nothing at all about the world. But every tautology is a form of a proof. Although all the propositions of logic say the same thing, viz. nothing, different tautologies differ in as much as they reveal different forms of proof. It is a mark of a proposition of logic that in a suitable notation it can be recognized from the symbol alone. This clarifies the nature of the propositions of logic and their categorial difference from empirical propositions. It also makes clear how misleading was the Frege/Russell axiomatization of logic and appeal to self-evidence to underpin their chosen axioms. Those axioms are not privileged by their special self-evidence. They are tautologies no less than the theorems. They are not essentially primitive, nor are the theorems essentially derived propositions, for all the propositions of logic are of equal status, viz. vacuous tautologies. Therefore there is no such thing as logical knowledge as Frege and Russell supposed, for to know the truth of a tautology is to know nothing at all about reality. Neither logic nor mathematics constitute examples of genuine knowledge a priori. This paved the way for what the Vienna Circle termed "consistent empiricism."

Third, the *Tractatus* articulated a revolutionary conception of philosophy, which molded the future of analytic philosophy. Philosophy, on this conception, is categorially distinct from science (1922: 4.111). There are no hypotheses in philosophy. It does not describe the most general truths about the universe as Moore and Russell supposed, nor does it describe relations between abstract entities as Frege thought. It does not describe the workings of the human mind as the British empiricists and the psychologicians supposed, or investigate the metaphysical presuppositions of experience and describe them in synthetic a priori propositions as Kant thought. There are no metaphysical truths that can be expressed in propositions, for the only expressible necessities are the vacuous tautologies of logic. Any attempt to express metaphysical truths inevitably results in the violation of the bounds of sense. The *Tractatus* itself is the swan song of metaphysics, for its propositions are nonsense. There are no philosophical propositions, hence no philosophical knowledge. Philosophy is not a cognitive discipline. Its contribution is not to human knowledge, but to human understanding. The task of philosophy is the activity of logical clarification (1922: 4.112). This task is to be executed by the logical analysis of problematic propositions, which will, *inter alia*, expose metaphysical assertions as nonsense (1922: 6.53). This conception of philosophy was to be pivotal for both the Cambridge analysts and the Vienna Circle. It constituted, Schlick was later to write, "the decisive turning-point" in philosophy.

Fourth, the *Tractatus* introduced, although it did not complete, the "linguistic turn" in philosophy. This marks a dramatic break with Frege, Moore, and Russell. 'All philosophy," Wittgenstein boldly announced, "is a 'critique of language' " (1922: 4.0031). The turn is manifest in the following claims of the book. (a) The limits of thought are to be set by setting the limits of *language,* i.e. by determining the boundary between sense and nonsense. (b) The positive program for future philosophy is the logico-linguistic analysis of propositions, i.e. *sentences* with a sense. (c) The negative task for future philosophy is the demonstration that metaphysical assertions endeavor to say something which by the intrinsic nature of *language* cannot be said. (d) The key to Wittgenstein's endeavors lay in the clarification of the essential nature of the *propositional sign* (1922: 4.5). (e) The logical investigation of "phenomena," i.e. the application of logic (which was programmatically heralded in the book though not undertaken until "Some Remarks on Logical Form" in 1929) was to be effected by the logical analysis of the *linguistic descriptions* of the phenomena of experience. (f) The elucidation of logical truth, the greatest achievement of the book, was effected by an investigation of *symbolism.* The "peculiar mark of logical propositions is that one can recognize that they are true from the symbol alone, and this fact contains in itself the whole philosophy of logic" (1922: 6.113). I have stressed that the *Tractatus* introduced the "turn," but did not complete it. It was only completed when the linguistic orientation of the book was severed from its foundations in an ineffable metaphysics of symbolism (e.g. that only simple names can represent simple objects, that only facts can represent facts, that a proposition is a fact). This was effected only in the 1930s by Wittgenstein's repudiation of the metaphysics of the *Tractatus* which cut logic loose from any metaphysical and (in Wittgenstein's idiosyncratic use of the term) "metalogical" foundations, and, under his influence, by the Vienna Circle.

In the aftermath of the First World War the stream of analytic philosophy split into two branches, Cambridge analysis and logical positivism.

Cambridge analysis had its source in Moore, Russell, and the *Tractatus*. Although Moore published little, his teaching in Cambridge was influential, and his preoccupation with the sense-datum theory of perception, which was shared by Broad, gave Cambridge analysis one of its distinctive themes.[18] So too did his meticulous style of analysis, and his insistence that the business of philosophy is the analysis of meanings. However, as a result of the linguistic turn, what Moore meant by "meaning" was transformed by the younger generation from an intuitive contemplation of objective concepts into a self-conscious endeavor to analyze the linguistic meaning of expressions. Russell, though no longer at Cambridge, was no less influential. Braithwaite remarked in 1933:

> In 1919 and for the next few years philosophic thought in Cambridge was dominated by the work of Bertrand Russell . . . the books and articles in which he developed his ever-changing philosophy were eagerly devoured and formed the subject of detailed commentary and criticism in the lectures of G. E. Moore and W. E. Johnson.
>
> (Braithwaite 1933: 1)

The *Tractatus*, Keynes wrote in 1924, "dominates all fundamental discussions at Cambridge since it was written" (Wittgenstein 1974: 116). It was a major influence upon the young Ramsey, Braithwaite, and Wisdom. Cambridge analysis moved in the direction of a program of reductionism and logical construction. Some accepted the ontology of facts (though not of simple objects) and sought to analyze the logical forms of facts and to show that certain facts are no more than logical constructions out of others. This program culminated in Wisdom's articles "Logical Constructions," published in *Mind* 1931–3. The viability of logicism remained high on the agenda at Cambridge, where Ramsey bent his efforts to remedying its flaws. At the time of his early death in 1930, he had come to agree with Wittgenstein that it was irremediable. The non-cognitive conception of philosophy appalled the older and appealed to the younger generation. Traditional speculative metaphysics, of which, Braithwaite remarked, McTaggart's *The Nature of Existence* (1927) afforded "an awful example," was repudiated. For Wittgenstein had shown that "we can be certain beforehand that a system professing to derive by logically necessary implications from logically necessary premises interesting empirical propositions is wrong somewhere" (Braithwaite 1933: 23). The revolutionary conception of philosophy introduced by the *Tractatus* inspired the extensive debate in Britain throughout the 1930s concerning the nature of philosophy, the character of analysis, and its relation to logic and language. From 1930 onwards Wittgenstein himself was lecturing in Cambridge and uprooting much of his earlier thought. This turned Cambridge analysis in a different direction, away from classical reductive analysis and logical construction and towards the methods of the *Investigations*, which were to dominate British philosophy after the Second World War.

The second stream of analytic philosophy in the interwar years arose in Vienna, whence it spread to Germany, Poland, the Scandinavian lands, and later to Britain and the U.S. Here Wittgenstein's influence was even greater than in Cambridge prior to 1929, partly no doubt due to his contact with members of the Circle between 1927 and 1936, and partly due to the close attention which the Circle paid to the book.[19] They abandoned logical atomism with its ontology of simple objects and facts, rejected the doctrine of saying and showing together with the attendant ineffable metaphysics, and repudiated the thought that every possible language necessarily has the same logical syntax which mirrors the logical forms of the facts. But they welcomed the claims that the only necessity is logical and that logical truths are vacuous tautologies. They accepted Wittgenstein's account of the logical connectives and the thesis of extensionality. Five major themes characterize logical positivism, all of which were deeply influenced by Wittgenstein, sometimes as a result of misinterpretation.

First, the Circle's conception of philosophy was derived from the *Tractatus*. Philosophy is not a cognitive discipline, and it is wholly distinct from science. Its positive use, according to Carnap, is to clarify meaningful concepts and propositions and to lay the foundations of science and mathematics. Traditional philosophical problems are either pseudo-problems or, after due elucidation, empirical. Philosophy is the elucidation of the logical syntax of the language of science.

Second, the Circle advocated the demolition of metaphysics. Here they accepted the *Tractatus* claim that there can be no metaphysical propositions, while rejecting the idea of ineffable metaphysical truths that can only be shown but not said.

Third, they embraced the Principle of Verification, which derived from discussions with Wittgenstein in 1929/30, and held verifiability to be a criterion of empirical meaningfulness.

Fourth, they aimed to uphold "consistent empiricism," denying that reason can be a source of knowledge that is both synthetic and a priori. The traditional stumbling blocks for empiricism were truths of logic, arithmetic and geometry, and metaphysics. In their view it was the *Tractatus* account of logical truth that rendered consistent empiricism possible. But their account of logical truth, unlike Wittgenstein's, was conventionalist. Where Wittgenstein thought of the truths of logic as flowing from the essential bipolarity of the proposition, the Circle construed them as consequences of arbitrary conventions of symbolism, i.e. as being true in virtue of the meanings of the logical connectives. They accepted Hilbert's conventionalist account of geometry, and thought (wrongly) that Wittgenstein held propositions of arithmetic to be reducible to vacuous tautologies.

Fifth, they adopted the thesis of the unity of science and were committed to a reductionist program of displaying all cognitively significant propositions as deducible from the basic propositions constituting "the given." The thesis goes back to Descartes, the program to Russell, but the thought that all propositions are truth-functions of elementary propositions (the thesis of extensionality) was derived from the *Tractatus*. Assuming elementary propositions to be verifiable in immediate experience, this gave support to the program.

By the mid-1930s opinion in the Circle was polarizing into a Carnap–Neurath wing of orthodox positivism as laid out in the Manifesto and a Schlick–Waismann wing, the latter being deeply influenced by Wittgenstein's later philosophical ideas which were developing in opposition to the *Tractatus*. The intellectual unity of the Circle was starting to crumble under internal criticism. Its physical unity, however, was destroyed by the rise of Nazism. Its primary legacy was in the U.S. after the Second World War, where many of the members of the Circle had settled and molded the shape of postwar American philosophy.

The war brought philosophy to a hiatus. Within a few years after 1945, the main center of analytic philosophy became Oxford. Its leading figures were Ryle and Austin, with a powerful supporting cast in Waismann, Grice, Hart, Hampshire, and Berlin as well as their juniors such as Strawson, Urmson, and later Hare, Pears, Quinton, and Warnock. The dominant influence was the later Wittgenstein, whose ideas, prior to the posthumous publication of the *Investigations*, were conveyed to Oxford by Waismann and Paul, and later by Anscombe. But many notable figures, such as Austin, Kneale, and Grice were impervious to them. Oxford analytic philosophy, unlike the Vienna Circle, was not a "school." It published no manifesto, and cleaved to few orthodoxies. Though Wittgenstein's influence was great, his ideas were assimilated rather than cultivated. Oxford analytic philosophy consisted of diverse and sometimes conflicting views, which only ignorance can subsume under the misleading heading of "ordinary language philosophy."

Nevertheless, some common agreements can be identified. Metaphysics was repudiated. For a while the very term was on the Index. When it was returned to currency by Strawson in *Individuals* (1959), it had been well laundered. For descriptive metaphysics had no pretensions to attain transcendent knowledge or to describe the logical structure of the world. It confined itself to the description of the most general features of our conceptual scheme, i.e. of our language or any language in which a distinction can be drawn between experience and its objects. Thus conceived, descriptive metaphysics was a connective analytical investigation into the most general structural concepts such as objective particular, person, experience, space, and time.

Analysis, as previously conceived, and hence too the programs of reduction and logical construction which had prevailed during the interwar years, were rejected. But the idiom of analysis, now denominated "linguistic" or "conceptual analysis," was retained. What this amounted to was the description, for purposes of philosophical elucidation, of the interconnectedness of related concepts, of their implications, compatibilities, and incompatibilities, of the conditions and circumstances of use of philosophically problematic expressions. Such analysis does not terminate in logically independent elementary propositions, or in simple, unanalyzable names or concepts. It terminates in the clarity that is obtained with respect to a given question when the network of concepts has been traced through all its relevant reticulations. Strawson's term "connective analysis" felicitously indicates the method.

What was subjected to analysis, in this loose and non-reductive sense, was the use of words in sentences. The Moorean conception of concepts was repudiated, and talk of concepts was held to be justified as an abstraction from the use of words. It was not generally held that all philosophical problems are problems *about* language, or that they are all pseudo-problems arising *out of* language, let alone that they are all to be resolved by devising an "ideal language." Few, if any, believed that the apparatus of the predicate calculus provided the key to unlock the puzzles of philosophy, let alone that it constitutes the depth grammar of any possible language. But it would have been generally agreed that a prerequisite for the solution or resolution of any philosophical problem is the patient and systematic description of the use of the relevant terms in natural language where they are at home (which may or may not be the technical vocabulary of a special science).

Although the later Wittgenstein's therapeutic conception of philosophy was not generally accepted—at least not as the whole tale—his insistence that philosophy is discontinuous with science, that it is *sui generis*, a contribution to human understanding rather than an extension or addition to human knowledge, would, with varying degrees of qualification, have commanded wide consensus. Although his idiosyncratic use of the term "grammatical" found no following, his claim that "grammatical statements" are a priori, translated into the Oxford idiom of "conceptual truths," did. Philosophical problems, Ryle remarked, are problems of a special sort, not problems of an ordinary sort about special entities—such as ideas, Platonic senses or concepts, logical or intentional objects. They are not scientific, empirical problems, and cannot be solved by scientific methods or theories.

It was accepted that philosophy is not hierarchical. The supposition that logic is the foundation of philosophy, or that a subject called "the philosophy of language" (the term did not even exist at the time) is the foundation of the rest of the subject was not entertained. No part of philosophy was thought to be privileged or foundational. But the linguistic turn had been taken, and by the 1950s was largely taken for granted. Although the different parts of the subject were not conceived to spring from a common trunk, they were manifestly united by the common character of philosophical puzzlement and common methods of resolution. Philosophy's central concern was with meaning and the clarification of the meanings of expressions, not for their own sake, but for the sake of the resolution of philosophical questions. A primary method was the description of the use of words, not the construction of a theory of meaning on the model of the Davidsonian program that came to dominate Anglo-American philosophy of language in the 1970s and 1980s. By then analytic philosophy was waning.

WHITHER?

The unity of analytic philosophy in the twentieth century is historical. It is a unity in diversity, for there are no defining features that characterize the analytic movement in all its phases. But each phase shares some features with the preceding or concurrent ones. Some of these features have an ancient ancestry, e.g. analysis—on some interpretations of the term, the "way of words," the repudiation of metaphysics. But they were explored in fresh ways or with greater thoroughness and precision than hitherto, and defended with novel arguments. Others were new, e.g. the employment of the new logic as an analytic tool and the non-cognitive conception of philosophy. It is, I suggest, most illuminating and least misleading to employ the term "analytic philosophy" as the name of this intermingling stream of ideas distinctive of our century. And since so many of the ideas do have venerable ancestry, the precursors of analytic philosophy can be relatively uncontroversially identified by the affinity of their philosophies and philosophical methods to one phase or another of this twentieth-century movement. The movement itself is best identified by description rather than by analysis.

I claimed that analytic philosophy waned after the 1970s. I should like to conclude by clarifying this. Each phase of the analytic movement was motivated by a revolutionary fervor. The protagonists passionately believed that they were ridding philosophy of intellectual pretensions, clearing the

Augean stables of accumulated refuse, and putting the subject on a fresh footing. By the 1970s the revolutionary days were over. The spirit of scientific rationality needed no defending. It was triumphant in the technology and in the great theoretical discoveries of twentieth-century science. Complacency set in. The methodological self-consciousness characteristic of the analytic movement in all its phases diminished, for philosophy no longer seemed to be in need of justification. It is a striking feature of late-twentieth-century philosophy that there is no vigorous debate on what philosophy is, and what can be hoped for from it, on what, if anything, are philosophical propositions and how they are related to the propositions of science. The hallmark of much contemporary philosophy, especially philosophy of psychology and philosophy of language (particularly where influenced by theoretical linguistics), is scientism. The *critical* function of the analytic tradition has been abandoned. Philosophy once more is widely thought to be an extension of the sciences, distinguished not so much by its generality (as Russell had conceived it to be) as by its speculative character.

The forces that effected this change were manifold, many extraneous to philosophy. Within philosophy, the major contributor was Quine. His repudiation of the analytic/synthetic distinction does not by itself constitute a decisive break with the analytic tradition, but only with Carnap and logical positivism. For the later Wittgenstein similarly eschewed this terminology, and it played no prominent role among Oxford philosophers.[20] But the wholesale repudiation of *any* distinction between analytic/synthetic, contingent/necessary, and a priori/a posteriori or any *related* distinction does, I think, constitute a decisive break. For with the repudiation of these three distinctions *and any kindred*, the conception of philosophy as *sui generis*, as a critical discipline *toto caelo* distinct from science, as an a priori investigation, as a tribunal of sense as opposed to a plaintiff confronting nature collapses. But it is precisely this metaphilosophical conception that characterizes analytic philosophy—albeit in somewhat different ways—from the post-First World War years onwards, i.e. from the publication of the *Tractatus,* through the Vienna Circle and Cambridge analysis, to the *Investigations,* and Oxford analytic philosophers. Analytic philosophy can happily abandon the analytic/synthetic distinctions as drawn by Kant, Frege, and Carnap. It not only can, but should, view the necessary/contingent distinction as a meet subject for investigation and elucidation rather than as an analytic tool to be relied upon. But if it must also relinquish *any* distinction between a priori questions of meaning and empirical, a posteriori questions of fact (*one* form of which is Wittgenstein's distinction between grammatical and empirical propositions—a distinction between uses of sentences, not between type-sentences) then the status of philosophy as an independent discipline is undermined. And that spells the end of analytic philosophy. It opens the gate to speculative science in the guise of philosophy, without the constraints of observation, experiment, and confirmation.

It might well be argued that Quine harks back to the early, Russellian phase of analytic philosophy antecedent to the *Tractatus*. For his conception of philosophy has affinities with Russell's. If so, why should it not be considered a further development of the movement, which marries early Russell with pragmatism? One cannot swim back in the stream of history. Had a young Quine, rather than the young Wittgenstein, encountered Russell in Cambridge in 1911, the history of analytic philosophy might have been altogether different. But the riverbed of analytic philosophy was decisively shifted by the *Tractatus*—and shifted in a direction inimical to Russell's conception of philosophy, which had no further influence upon the movement. By the time Quine's major work was published in 1960, it was not continuous with the mainstream of analytic philosophy as it had flowed for the previous forty years. It constitutes a decisive break. And although it harks back to Russell in certain respects, Quine does not even accept the Russellian conception of analysis—manifest first in his logicism, then in his reductionism in *Our Knowledge of the External World*, and later in *The Analysis of Mind* and *The Analysis of Matter*.

The widespread acceptance in the U.S. of Quine's attack on the three above-mentioned distinctions was not the only feature of his work to encourage scientism in philosophy. Four others seem to me to merit mention: Quine's ontological turn, his physicalism, his advocacy of naturalized epistemology, and his behaviorism and consequent exclusion of questions of normativity from the philosophy of language. The first diverted attention from the analytic questions of what attributions of existence in various domains of discourse mean—i.e. what it means to claim that there are colors, or that there are mental states, or that legal systems exist, or that there are fictional characters—to putative ontological inquiries as to whether certain "entities" exist, or need to be "posited" for the purposes of science or for the best "theory" about what there really is. Quine holds that the only genuine knowledge is scientific knowledge. Physics, he claims, studies the "essential nature of the world," and the fundamental laws governing the behavior of all that exists are the laws of physics. "If we are limning the true and ultimate structure of reality," we should avoid the intentional idiom since there is no need to posit mental states, and employ only the austere scheme which refers only to the "physical constitution and behavior of organisms" (Quine 1960: 221). Hence too, the ultimate explanations of everything that happens are the explanations offered by physics. Quine's physicalism was a primary inspiration for the scientism of eliminative materialism that emerged in the 1970s and

1980s. His naturalized epistemology "falls into place as a chapter of psychology and hence of natural science" (Quine 1969: 82–83). Hence the analytic investigation of patterns of justification and of the conceptual articulations involved in knowledge claims is displaced by the investigation of how the input of patterns of irradiation results in the output of linguistic and other behavior. Naturalized epistemology in effect reinstates a form of geneticism which analytic philosophy's anti-psychologism had labored to extirpate. His behaviorism and the elimination of normativity from his account of language exclude the investigation of the boundary between sense and nonsense which lay at the heart of analytic philosophy from the 1920s onwards.

Quine's conception fostered the belief that philosophy is continuous with science, concerned no less than science with theory construction. Like science, its goal is to add to human knowledge about reality. Since every conceptual scheme is, if Quine is right, theoretical, involving ontological commitments, ordinary language, it seems to many contemporaries, is merely the pre-scientific conceptual scheme of a culture, useful for the mundane purposes for which it evolved, but committed to a host of misconceived pre-scientific theories. Embedded in ordinary language there allegedly is a pre-scientific physics and psychology. Philosophical theorizing need therefore pay no more attention to the ordinary use of expressions than does physics or psychology. Its aim is neither to disentangle confusions resulting from subtle violations of the bounds of sense nor to describe the articulations of our conceptual scheme, but rather to contribute to our theories about the world.

The trends that were stimulated by Quine received further support from extra-philosophical sources: Chomsky's theoretical linguistics, the growth of computer sciences and artificial intelligence, and the achievements of neuro-physiological psychology—especially in the domain of the theory of vision. Post-behaviorist cognitive science (anathematic to Quine) was born, and analytic philosophy of mind declined. Philosophy of psychology allied itself with the speculations of cognitive science, and the boundary lines between analytic investigations into the articulations of psychological concepts and hypotheses concerning the workings of the brain blurred. Similarly, the boundaries between analytic philosophy of language and theoretical linguistics were eroded.

It is possible to take an apocalyptic view of the decline of analytic philosophy. One might be tempted to think that while Kantian critical philosophy spelt the end of the pretensions of philosophy to attain transcendent truths inaccessible to the sciences, analytic philosophy completed the demolition of the subject by putting an end to the philosophical aim of disclosing synthetic a priori truths, as well as curbing the pretensions of pure reason to attain such truths in the domain of mathematics. By depriving philosophy of any subject matter of its own, has analytic philosophy not brought the subject to an end? It is noteworthy that Schlick's "Turning Point in Philosophy" concludes with a vision of the future in which "it will no longer be necessary to speak of 'philosophical problems' for one will speak philosophically concerning all problems, that is: clearly and meaningfully." Carnap queried what remains for philosophy if all statements that assert something are of an empirical nature and belong to science. "What remains," he replied, "is not statements nor a theory, nor a system, but only a *method*: the method of logical analysis." The positive task of logical analysis, he argued, "is to clarify meaningful concepts and propositions, to lay logical foundations for factual science and for mathematics." This, and only this, will be the "scientific philosophy" of the future (Carnap 1959: 77). But, it might be thought, if Carnap's proper domain for philosophy depended wholly upon his insistence upon the analytic/synthetic distinction, and if Quine successfully demolished that distinction, then "scientific philosophy" merges with science. The turning point in philosophy has led to the terminus of philosophy.

This reaction would, I believe, be misconceived. Whether the waning of analytic philosophy is merely a temporary phase or not, I do not know. But this much seems evident. The analytic tradition left philosophy with two general tasks, which future generations are free to take up. The first is critical. It is the task of resolving conceptual puzzlement and dissolving conceptual confusions, both within philosophy and in other domains of human thought and reflective experience. The clearest articulation of this role of philosophy was given by the later Wittgenstein. Duly elaborated, it gives at least a partial characterization of many major problems of philosophy throughout its history and of one way (or class of ways) of handling them. This is too familiar to require elaboration. It has sometimes been accused of being "negative" and "quietist." It is negative only in the sense that medicine is negative—"merely" restoring a patient to health. And as with medicine, many of the diseases of the intellect which philosophy combats are perennial, recurring generation after generation in different mutations. That this conception of the task of philosophy is anything but quietist is evident in a further feature. For the first time, philosophy has been given a license to intrude itself upon the sciences. For conceptual puzzlement and confusion are not unique to philosophy. The great foes of analytic philosophy in its years of revolutionary fervor—the myth-making of speculative metaphysics, the pretensions of religion to pronounce upon scientific matters, *ipse dixitism* (to use Bentham's felicitous phrase) in matters ethical and political—may have been vanquished, at least *pro tempore*. Rational scientific inquiry and rational social and political thought, within their proper domains, are now largely free of such encumbrances in our culture. But this should not induce complacency. For the enemy is now within the gates. If science is triumphant, it is also a source of mythology and mystification. For every source of truth must perforce also be a possible source of error of two kinds. Against empirical error, the sciences are well armed, difficult though their struggle may be. Against myth-making, conceptual mystification, and confusion they are not. For the difficulties one is up against are not theoretical; the fault is not falsehood or defective theory, but lack of sense. To combat this, analytic philosophy is well suited. It is part of the critical task of philosophy to question not the truth, but the *intelligibility* of, for example, theoretical linguists' talk of an innate language of thought, of a "language gene," or of speakers of a language unconsciously "cognizing" a universal theory of grammar or a theory of interpretation necessary for mutual understanding. It is part of its task to investigate not whether it is true, but whether it makes *sense* to claim, as many experimental psychologists do, that in order for a person to see, the brain has to construct hypotheses, employ inductive logic, infer, construct maps of the visual field, and assign colors to surfaces of objects on the basis of the information available to it. And similar questions for investigation are common in branches of physics and biology, as in economics and the social sciences. Critical analytic philosophy is no extension of science, but a tribunal of sense before which science should be arraigned when it slides into myth-making and sinks into conceptual confusion.

The second task is complementary. It is, in Wittgenstein's idiom, to provide a perspicuous representation of the use of our words or of the grammar of our language (in his idiosyncratic use of the term "grammar") within a given domain of discourse. Or, to use Strawson's language, to give a description of the structure of our conceptual scheme or some fragment thereof. Or, in Ryle's metaphor, to plot, and rectify, the logical geography of the knowledge which we already possess. (There are differences of conception here, but they may be disregarded for present purposes.) The map drawn may be very general, representing, as it were, the view from a satellite—if one's purpose is appropriately general, as Strawson's was in *Individuals*. Or it may represent an eagle's eye-view—more detailed, but only of a selected range of terrain, as was von Wright's in *The Varieties of Goodness*. Or it may focus upon a very specific locality, as Alan White did in *Attention*. But whether one aims to depict the globe, a continent, a country or a county, the task may be undertaken for its independent fascination or for specific purposes related to specific philosophical questions, which, although conceptual (non-empirical), are not necessarily expressions of confusion and conceptual entanglement. Either way, its execution cannot but contribute to eradicating conceptual confusions.

This positive task of philosophy can be completed only in a relative sense. There can be no single map of the conceptual terrain. It depends upon the perspective and purpose of the cartographer. Different maps are called for in response to the different intellectual needs of the times. And although many features of the landscape are stable, inasmuch as there are reasonably permanent structural features of our language and its use, other features change, eroded by rain and wind and subject to occasional volcanic upheavals as our conception of ourself and of the world around us undergoes periodic cataclysmic change.

The critical task of philosophy is indeed Sisyphean. For there is no limit to the confusions into which we may fall. Moreover, as new discoveries occur (e.g. contemporary advances in neuro-physiological psychology), as new theories are propounded (e.g. relativity theory) and new inventions made—whether a priori ones (e.g. the invention of the modern logical calculus) or practical ones (e.g. the invention of the computer)—fresh sources of conceptual confusion and intellectual myth-making arise, novel paradigms of explanation become available and are characteristically applied beyond their legitimate limits, and new questions are brought upon the carpet which are not amenable to the experimental methods and theory construction of the sciences. Those who struggle to reach the mountain top must realize that their achievement may be only for their generation, and relative to the problems that beset their times. Each generation must labor afresh. Those who reach the summit may be consoled with the sharpness of the light and the clarity of the view which they can communicate to their contemporaries, even though they know that clouds may be massing beyond the horizon.[21]

NOTES

1 For example, Nagel 1936.
2 I am much indebted to this insightful essay.
3 Strawson introduced the term "connective analysis" in *Scepticism and Naturalism, Some Varieties* (1985: 25) and elaborated further in *Analysis and Metaphysics, an Introduction to Philosophy* (1992: ch. 2).
4 This, to be sure, is a matter of judgment. As Wittgenstein observed, "When white changes to black some people say, 'It is essentially still the same.' And others, when the colour darkens the slightest bit, say, 'It has changed completely' " (MS 125, under 18/5/1942; my translation). All references to Wittgenstein's *Nachlass* are by von Wright number.
5 Von Wright remarks that "No one could deny that Wittgenstein has been of decisive importance to the development of analytic philosophy, both as author of the *Tractatus* and as author of the *Investigations*. Whether Wittgenstein himself can rightly be called an analytic philosopher is quite another question. Of the *Investigations* one might say that its spirit is alien and even hostile to the typically 'analytic' approach. The *Tractatus*, on the other

hand, may in some ways be regarded as a paragon of the analytic trend in philosophy, especially in the form this trend had assumed with Russell and was later carried forward by the members of the Vienna Circle. The later Wittgenstein exhibits some affinities to Moore" (von Wright 1993: 32). With this I agree. Between 1929 and 1932 Wittgenstein came to repudiate classical analysis altogether. But it is noteworthy that in the "Big Typescript" he wrote: "A sentence is completely logically analyzed when its grammar is laid out completely clearly" (BT 417). Accordingly, "analysis" in philosophy now means giving the grammatical rules for the use of the expression in question, clarifying its manifold connections with related concepts and its differences in respect of others. With this shift the turn from classical to "connective" analysis was effected (see below).

6 I have tried to fill this lacuna, with special reference to Wittgenstein's contribution to analytic philosophy, in a volume entitled *Wittgenstein's Place in Twentieth Century Analytic Philosophy* (1996). The present essay draws extensively upon this source.

7 For a more detailed discussion of Wittgenstein's account of logical necessity in general and his attitude to psychologism and to Frege's anti-psychologism in particular, see G. P. Baker and P. M. S. Hacker (1985: 263–347) from which the above remarks are derived.

8 Although I take it, on authority, that it would have gained the assent of Hamann and Nietzsche (see Philipse 1992: 167).

9 True, in the *Investigations* §664 Wittgenstein introduced the contrast between surface and depth grammar. But the metaphor of depth grammar, which was subsequently to be taken up by generative grammarians, was singularly inappropriate for Wittgenstein's purposes. What he meant thereby was the diametrical opposite of what Chomsky had in mind. The depth grammar of an expression is not something hidden from view to be dug up by analysis (as in the *Tractatus*), but rather something in full view—if one will but look around and remind oneself of the general pattern of use of the expression. A topographical metaphor here would have been more appropriate than the geological one.

10 Here Kenny is following M. A. E. Dummett (1993: 5). The expression "the linguistic turn" was made popular by an eponymous anthology on linguistic philosophy edited by Richard Rorty in 1967, who attributes the phrase to Gustav Bergmann's *Logic and Reality* (1964). It has assumed a significance that goes beyond its originators' intentions.

11 Like Kenny, Sluga, too, is following in Dummett's footsteps. Dummett claimed that "we may characterize analytic philosophy as that which follows Frege in accepting that the philosophy of language is the foundation of the rest of the subject" (1978: 441).

12 Strawson, in *Individuals* (1959), obviously had sympathy for the metaphysical endeavor in a Kantian spirit, and revived the idiom of metaphysics in an analytic mode. But it is merely the letter and not the spirit of metaphysics as traditionally conceived that is here revived. See below, pp, 22f.

13 See Philipse 1992 168.

14 Frege did indeed invent the new logic, defended a Platonist form of anti-psychologism, and practiced the logical analysis of arithmetic. In this sense he was a precursor of the analytic school, as Russell acknowledged. But he did not influence Moore and had little influence on Russell save in respect of his

definition of the ancestral relation (Russell remarked that the definition of numbers to which he was led "had been formulated by Frege sixteen years earlier, but I did not know this until a year or so after I had re-discovered it" (Russell 1959: 70).) Frege did not take the "linguistic turn" in philosophy and he did not extend logical analysis beyond the confines of the philosophy of mathematics to epistemology, metaphysics, philosophy of mind, etc. as Russell did. He patently did not think that the philosophy of language is the foundation of the whole of philosophy (including philosophical psychology, ethics, political and legal philosophy, aesthetics, and the philosophy of religion—about which he wrote nothing). On the contrary, he insisted that "It is the business of the logician to conduct a ceaseless struggle against . . . those parts of language and grammar which fail to give untrammelled expression to what is logical" (1979: 6). The logician must try to liberate us from the fetters of language (1979: 143), to break the power of the word over the human mind, to free thought "from that which only the nature of the linguistic means of expression attaches to it" (Frege 1972: Preface), for "It cannot be the task of logic to investigate language and determine what is contained in a linguistic expression. Someone who wants to learn logic from language is like an adult who wants to learn how to think from a child . . . Languages are not made to match logic's ruler" (Frege 1980: 67f.). It is not natural language which, according to Frege, gives us the key to the analysis of propositions (thoughts) but rather his invented conceptual notation.

15 A similar point could be made about another great movement in European culture, namely romanticism.

16 See Wittgenstein's "Sketch for a Foreword," probably written for the "Big Typescript" in *Culture and Value* (1980: 6f.).

17 This thesis has two aspects, only one of which, i.e. the denial that the logical operators are names of logical entities, is touched upon here. The other is that formal concepts (also denominated "logical constants" by Russell) such as fact, object, concept, proposition, relation are not material concepts, and cannot occur in a well-formed proposition with a sense. Hence Russell's claim, that "There are dual relations" is a proposition of logic describing an absolutely general fact about the universe, is misconceived.

18 Another characteristic theme was induction and probability. The Cambridge stimulus was Keynes' *Treatise on Probability* (1921). Broad, Johnson, Ramsey, Wrench, Jeffreys, and, at the end of the 1930s, von Wright all contributed to the debate.

19 Their weekly meetings for the two academic years of 1924 and 1926 were dedicated to a line-by-line reading of the book.

20   Indeed the sharpness of the traditional distinction was challenged in Oxford by Waismann's six "Analytic–Synthetic" articles in *Analysis* 1949–53, prior to Quine's "Two Dogmas" of 1951.

21 I am grateful to Dr H.-J. Glock, Professor O. Hanfling and Dr J. Hyman for their comments on an earlier draft of this paper.

BIBLIOGRAPHY

Baker, G. P. and P. M. S. Hacker (1985) *Wittgenstein: Rules, Grammar and Necessity*, Oxford and New York: Blackwell.

Bentham, J. (1983) *Chrestomathia*, Oxford: Clarendon Press.

Bergmann, G. (1964) *Logic and Reality*, Madison: University of Wisconsin Press.

Braithwaite, R. B. (1933) "Philosophy," in H. Wright (ed.) *Cambridge Studies*, Cambridge: Nicolson and Watson.

Carnap, R. (1959) "The Elimination of Metaphysics," in A. J. Ayer (ed.) *Logical Positivism*, New York: The Free Press.

Dummett, M. A. E. (1978) "Can Analytic Philosophy be Systematic, and Ought it to Be?" in *Truth and Other Enigmas*, London: Duckworth.

——(1993) *Origins of Analytic Philosophy*, London: Duckworth.

Feigl, H. and Sellars, W. (eds) (1949) *Readings in Philosophical Analysis*, New York: Appleton-Century-Crofts.

Flew, A. (ed.) (1951) *Logic and Language*, Oxford: Blackwell.

Frege, G. (1964) *The Basic Laws of Arithmetic*, trans. M. Furth, Berkeley and Los Angeles: University of California Press.

——(1972) *Conceptual Notation*, Oxford: Clarendon Press.

——(1979) "Logic," in *Posthumous Writings*, Oxford: Blackwell.

——(1980) *Philosophical and Mathematical Correspondence*, Oxford: Blackwell.

Hacker, P. M. S. (1996) *Wittgenstein"s Place in Twentieth Century Analytic Philosophy*, Oxford: Blackwell.

Kenny, A. J. P. (1995) *Frege*, Harmondsworth: Penguin Books.

Keynes, M. (1921) *Treatise on Probability*, London: Macmillan.

McTaggart, J. M. E. (1927) *The Nature of Existence*, Cambridge: Cambridge University Press.

Nagel, E. (1936) "Impressions and Appraisals of Analytic Philosophy in Europe," *Journal of Philosophy* 33.

Pap, Arthur (1949) *Elements of Analytic Philosophy*, New York: Macmillan.

——(1955) *Analytische Erkenntnistheorie*, Vienna: Springer Verlag.

——(1958) *Semantics and Necessary Truth: an Inquiry into the Foundations of Analytic Philosophy*, New Haven: Yale University Press.

Philipse, H. (1992) "Husserl and the Origins of Analytical Philosophy," *European Journal of Philosophy* 2.

Quine, W. V. O. (1951) "Two Dogmas of Empiricism," *Philosophical Review* 60: 20–43.

——(1960) *Word and Object*, Cambridge, Mass.: MIT Press.

——(1969) *Ontological Relativity and Other Essays*, New York: Columbia University Press.

Rorty, R. (1967) *The Linguistic Turn*, Chicago: University of Chicago Press.

Russell, B. (1914) *Our Knowledge of the External World*, Chicago: Open Court.

——(1921) *The Analysis of Mind*, London: Allen and Unwin.

——(1927) *The Analysis of Matter*, London: Kegan Paul.

——(1959) *My Philosophical Development*, London: Allen and Unwin.

——(1986) "The Philosophy of Logical Atomism," in John G. Slater (ed.) *The Collected Papers of Bertrand Russell*, Vol. 8, London: Allen and Unwin.

Ryle, G. (1970) "Autobiographical," in O. P. Wood and G. Pitcher (eds) *Ryle, a Collection of Critical Essays*, New York: Doubleday.

Schlick "Turning Point in Philosophy," in A. J. Ayer (ed.) *Logical Positivism*, New York: Free Press.

Sluga, H. (1980) *Gottlob Frege*, London: Routledge and Kegan Paul.

Strawson, P. F. (1959) *Individuals*, London: Methuen.

——(1985) *Scepticism and Naturalism, Some Varieties*, London: Methuen.

——(1992) *Analysis and Metaphysics, an Introduction to Philosophy*, Oxford: Oxford University Press.

von Wright, G. H. (1993) "Analytic Philosophy: a Historico-Critical Survey," in *The Tree of Knowledge and Other Essays*, Leiden: E. J. Brill.

Waismann, F. (1939–40) "Was ist logische Analyse?," *Erkenntnis* 8.

——(1949–53) "Analytic–Synthetic," *Analysis*.

Wisdom, J. (1931–3) "Logical Constructions," *Mind*.

Wittgenstein, L. (1922) *Tractatus Logico-Philosophicus*, London, Boston and Henley: Routledge and Kegan Paul.

——(1929) "Some Remarks on Logical Form," *Proceedings of the Aristotelian Society*, suppl. vol. ix: 162–71.

——(1958) *Philosophical Investigations*, Oxford: Blackwell.

——(1974) *Letters to Russell, Keynes and Moore*, Oxford: Blackwell.

——(1978) *Remarks on the Foundations of Mathematics*, revised edition, Oxford: Blackwell.

——(1980) *Culture and Value*, second edition, Oxford: Blackwell.

Part II
Plot

Part II

Plot

2 Analysis in analytic philosophy

Peter Hylton

It is a natural enough supposition that philosophical analysis has something to do with analytic philosophy. This supposition can be bolstered by connecting it with two other features which are partially characteristic of analytic philosophy (we shall return to each of these features, in somewhat different form, at the end of this essay). One such feature is the emphasis within analytic philosophy on *clarity*.[1] In part this is no more than a practical matter, an injunction (not, of course, invariably followed) to be clear in one's own writing. In part, however, it is also a theoretical matter: it is supposed that philosophical problems vanish, or become soluble, or at least can for the first time be seen for what they are, if only we write about them with sufficient clarity. The connection with philosophical analysis is that analysis is sometimes thought to be a way, or perhaps *the* way, in which to achieve true clarity. A second feature of (some) analytic philosophy is its emphasis on modern (i.e. post-Fregean) logic—meaning, for the most part, first-order logic with identity. One reason, at least, that logic has been important to analytic philosophy has to do with its use as a tool in philosophical analysis. The two features I have mentioned are connected via the idea that the notation of first-order logic holds out an ideal of clarity.

There is, of course, analytic philosophy which has little or nothing directly to do with philosophical analysis.[2] And not everything which has been called philosophical analysis within analytic philosophy has to do with logic. But still there is, at least at first glance, one clear line of thought within analytic philosophy which looks to a paradigm of analysis that draws on elementary mathematical logic. An example of this is what both Ramsey (1931) and G. E. Moore (1946) called a "paradigm of philosophy," namely Russell's theory of descriptions. Suppose you walk into a classroom and see on the blackboard the words:

1 The King of France is bald.

and under them some combination of words and symbols such as the following:

2 (∃x)[x is King of France & (y) (if y is King of France then x = y) & x is bald].

In that case you have surely walked into a classroom where analytic philosophy was recently practiced (or possibly a branch of linguistics closely influenced by analytic philosophy; or perhaps one of these subjects has been attacked, or discussed historically: at any rate what has been going on there has some close relation to analytic philosophy). This is, again, not to deny that there have been and are analytic philosophers who have not gone in for this sort of analysis. But I do think that going in for it is close to a sufficient, if not a necessary, condition for being an analytic philosopher. I also think—though this is perhaps more controversial—that the idea of this line of thought, which emphasizes analysis in the above sense, plays a significant role in the idea that there is a more or less unified tradition of analytic philosophy.

If all of this is correct, or anyway plausible enough to be going on with, then it must be of interest to those concerned with the project of defining analytic philosophy to know what philosophical analysis is. In one sense it is clear enough what philosophical analysis is: we can point to cases, such as the above, and generally agree that they count as examples—perhaps even as paradigmatic examples. But in another sense it is very far from clear what philosophical analysis is. There is—or so I shall seek to show—very little agreement on a theoretical account of what philosophical analysis is, of what goes on when we pass from a sentence such as 1 (an "unanalyzed" sentence) to a sentence such as 2 (its "analyzed" form).

We started with the idea that some sort of unity might to be given to the idea of analytic philosophy by thinking about philosophical analysis. Careful examination, however, tends to undermine the idea that there is a single notion of philosophical analysis which can play this role. Among those one might be inclined to take as paradigm examples of analytic philosophers whose work draws on mathematical logic—Frege, Russell, Carnap, Quine, say—there is very little agreement about what is in fact happening when we pass from 1 to 2. It is sometimes said that what unifies analytic philosophy is its *method*—meaning, among other things perhaps, that it is characteristic of analytic philosophy to employ philosophical analysis. In a superficial sense this may be true of some (though not all) analytic philosophers—many might agree that some sort of philosophical progress is made by the transition from 1 to 2. But if "method" here is to include also the account that one gives of such transitions, then there is no such agreement, and the unity of analytic philosophy becomes a more difficult, though perhaps also more interesting, issue.

I shall begin, as I have indicated, by talking about how various philosophers conceived of philoscphical analysis.

FREGE

The case of Frege, to take that first, is unclear. The very unclarity here is, I think, instructive. On the one hand Frege does speak as if thoughts (*Gedanken*) are made up of parts in some literal sense, so that philosophical analysis would presumably be a process of decomposing a thought into its constituent parts—or at least of displaying it, in a perspicuous fashion, as made up of those parts. Thus he says: "If a name is part of the name of a truth-value, then the sense of the former name is part of the thought expressed by the latter name." (Frege 1964: 90). And in the essay "Logic in Mathematics" he says: "thoughts have parts (*Gedankenbausteinen*) out of which they are built up. These parts, these building blocks (*Bausteinen*), correspond to groups of sounds, out of which the sentence expressing the thought is built up . . . " (Frege 1979: 225). Again, in the opening paragraph of "Compound Thoughts" he insists that we can "distinguish parts in the thought corresponding to parts of a sentence, so that the structure of the sentence can serve as a picture of the structure of the thought" (Frege 1984: 390); rather similar remarks occur elsewhere, in "Negation" (1984: 373–389), for example.

On the other hand, there are other passages that undermine this straightforward picture. The sentence just quoted from "Compound Thoughts" is immediately followed by one which inserts a crucial qualification: "To be sure, we really talk figuratively when we transfer the relation of whole and part to thoughts; yet the analogy is so ready to hand and so generally appropriate that we are hardly bothered by the hitches that occur from time to time." Why should Frege hesitate or qualify at this point? The answer, at its most general, is that his fundamental method of analysis—on which his philosophy is to a large extent based—is that of function and argument, and at least on the face of it the function–argument analysis does not fit well with the part–whole metaphor. Indeed it is clear that *in general* there is a conflict rather than a fit; the value of a function for a given argument does not in general have as parts either the function or the argument, and is certainly not a whole made up of the function and the argument. Absurdities quickly follow from the other view: the number four would have to be a whole made up of the number two and the *square of* function; and also a whole made up of the numbers five and one and the subtraction function; and also the numbers three and one and addition;

and so on indefinitely. Nor is this kind of absurdity confined to the mathe-matical case. If one thinks of *father of* as a function mapping people onto their fathers, then clearly the value of this function for a given argument does not contain the argument and the function.

Of course the fact that this holds for functions and arguments in most cases does not settle the matter. It could be that the realm of sense consti-tutes an exception to the general rule, that in this special case the value (the sense of a sentence, say) does contain both the argument (the sense of a name, say) and the function (the sense of the concept-expression). And, as we have seen, there are places where Frege writes as if this were so. But there are reasons for his hesitation. One says that the thought expressed by a simple subject–predicate sentence may be analyzed in Fregean fashion into function (a concept, in this case) and argument (an object). This way of talking about the matter, however, is loose. Strictly speaking, the thought cannot be analyzed into the relevant function and the relevant object, for the function applied to the object yields not the thought but the truth-value of the sentence. Rather, the sense of the function expression and the sense of the name of the object must be the relevant bases of analysis. This requires us to think of the sense of a function expression as itself a function, and it is not clear either that this is correctly attributable to Frege or that it is coherent in Fregean terms. There is also another difficulty, suggested by the example given above of the number four. It is by no means clear that a given thought can be analyzed into a unique and determinate set of function(s) and argument(s). It seems, for example, that the thought expressed by our simple subject–predicate sentence may be analyzable into a (first-level) function and object; but it will also be analyzable into a first-level func-tion and a second-level function applicable to the first-level function. If this is correct, then which analysis is the appropriate one may depend on what inference we wish to explain: a given thought will play a role in indefinitely many inferences, and some may demand one analysis, others a different and incompatible analysis. On this picture there is no one correct analysis: analysis is relative to inference.

This should leave us, I think, uncertain to what extent a Fregean can think that the process of analysis articulates structures which are there, in the *Gedanke*, objectively and independent of us. The realist tenor of almost all of Frege's language makes it natural to suppose that he would hold that such structures are objective; but a closer examination of his views might lead us at least to hesitate in making this attribution.[3]

RUSSELL

The status of analysis in Frege may be unclear. In Russell, however, and in G. E. Moore, we get a very definite view.[4] The talk of parts and wholes, which for Frege was a persuasive metaphor, seems to be taken literally by both Russell and Moore; philosophical analysis is then like chemical analysis, a process of breaking the complex down into its simpler (and, in the end, absolutely simple) constituent parts.

In 1900, not long after his rejection of idealism, Russell announced the new view with characteristic directness and force (and, one might add, overstatement): "That all sound philosophy should begin with an analysis of propositions is a truth too evident, perhaps, to demand a proof" (Russell 1900: 8). Here Russell's emphasis is on the idea that analysis will show us that many propositions (or, in some versions, all propositions) are relational. This is in opposition to what he took to be the idealist view that all propositions are of subject–predicate form; in his eyes the analysis of propositions provides all at once a devastating and quite general refutation of idealism. (This estimate seems to me too sanguine, a point I have discussed elsewhere.)[5] In service of this idea, however, very little analysis takes place, since the propositions that Russell is chiefly concerned with are, so to speak, relational on the face of it. His insistence is that they really are as they appear.

In spite of Russell's 1900 statement, his initial emphasis on analysis (before 1905, say) is not so much on the analysis of *propositions* as on the analysis of those ideas or concepts of which a proposition may be made up. Here a somewhat different sense of analysis seems to be in play—analysis as a retail philosophical method, rather than as a wholesale anti-idealist argument. Analysis of this sort, or definition, as Russell often calls it, relies completely on the part–whole analogy. Thus Russell says: "Definition, as is evident, is only possible in respect of complex ideas. It consists, broadly speaking, in the analysis of complex ideas into their simple constituents" (1900: 18). In *The Principles of Mathematics* (1903) a similar picture is put forward. Here, however, the exposition is somewhat complicated by the distinction that Russell draws between mathematical and philosophical definition. The former requires only that we give (roughly) necessary and sufficient conditions for being the object we are concerned with; the latter, however, is more demanding: "philosophically, the word *definition* . . . has, in fact, been restricted to the analysis of an idea into its constituents" (1903: 111).

Very similar ideas occur in Moore's *Principia Ethica* (1903); indeed the point is made even more dramatically. Moore also uses the word "definition," rather than "analysis," but he goes to considerable pains to make sure that we do not think that he is concerned with "the expressing of one word's meaning in other words" (Moore 1903: 6); definition in *this* sense, he says, "can never be of ultimate importance in any study except lexicography" (Moore 1903: 6). He is concerned, rather, with "definitions which describe the real nature of the object or notion denoted by the word, and which do not merely tell us what the word is used to mean" (1903: 7). Moore's example here is defining horse. The English word "horse" is of no interest to Moore here. What he's concerned with is definition in a "much more important" (1903: 7) sense, in which a definition of horse tells us "that a certain object, which we all of us know, is composed in a certain manner: that it has four legs, a head, a heart, a liver, etc., etc., all of them arranged in definite relations to one another" (1903: 7). Now one might think from this that Moore's preferred sense of definition applies only to physical objects which can be decomposed into parts. But in fact he applies this idea quite generally. Immediately following the sentence just quoted he says: "It is in this sense that I deny good to be definable. I say that it is not composed of any parts, which we can substitute for it in our minds when we are thinking about it."

Although I do not wish to dwell on the case of Moore, it is perhaps worth noting that in one way, at least, his conception of analysis never altered. He always held that what he was analyzing was not a verbal expression but an abstract entity, a concept or proposition, which is. He makes this absolutely explicit, in typical Moorean fashion, in his reply to C. H. Langford, in the Schilpp volume (Schilpp 1942: 660–7). On p. 661, for example, he says: "When I have talked of analyzing anything, *what* I have talked of analyzing has always been an idea or concept or proposition, and *not* a verbal expression." For Moore, at least, what is analyzed is always a structure that lies behind our words and gives them meaning; the purpose of analysis is to reveal this structure, to make apparent what would otherwise be hidden.

In discussing Russell and Moore here I have emphasized the literalness with which they take the part–whole analogy. More fundamental, perhaps, and more important for our concerns here, is that they never doubt that in philosophical analysis they are getting at structures which are really there, underlying our discourse. Philosophical analysis consists of making explicit what was always already there, previously unrecognized. We might call this the *realist conception of philosophical analysis.*

This central guiding idea survives intact as Russell modifies the conception of philosophical analysis in other ways. The clearest way in which the conception shifts is that, beginning with "On Denoting" (1905), he shifts the emphasis from the analysis of concepts to the analysis of propositions. In *The Principles of Mathematics* he had generally assumed that the structure or form of a sentence generally corresponds to the structure of the proposition which it expresses (see especially 1903: 42). Although this assumption was not one which he always maintained in practice, still the theory was that it would hold at least in most cases. One of the revolutionary changes brought about by "On Denoting," and by the developments which it sparked, was the idea that the form of the sentence will in general *not* be a good guide to the form of the proposition, the underlying logical form. Thus "On Denoting" argues that a sentence containing a definite description expresses a proposition whose logical form is that of an existential quantification; soon almost all sentences containing proper names were thought of in the same way. (Along the same lines, Russell comes to think that the only complexity is that of propositions, or, later, facts; this, however, takes us away from our main focus.)

A second line of development, independent of the theory of descriptions, is also relevant. This development is epistemological. From his rejection of idealism onwards, Russell thought of knowledge of anything outside the mind as being a matter of a direct, presuppositionless, and unmediated relation between the mind and the object—a relation he called *acquaintance*. At first the notion of acquaintance was what one might call a dependent variable: whenever Russell's theorizing made it convenient to suppose that we have direct knowledge of something, he simply made that supposition—he just accepted, often tacitly, that we are in fact acquainted with that thing. Thus the doctrines put forward in *The Principles of Mathematics* seem to imply that we are acquainted with chimeras, Homeric gods, and everything we seem able to name. Beginning in 1904 or 1905, however, Russell turns his attention increasingly onto the notion of acquaintance, and increasingly limits the sorts of things that he is willing to say we are acquainted with. Before long the objects of acquaintance narrow down and sort into categories: on the one hand, sense-data, immediately given in sense-perception; on the other hand, abstract objects, not in space and time. Russell also thinks—though he changed his mind on this point later—that each of us is acquainted with his or her own mind or self. The relevance of acquaintance to analysis comes via Russell's insistence that we have not reached the correct analysis of a sentence, have not made explicit the underlying proposition, unless we can show that the proposition is composed entirely of elements with which we are acquainted. This functions as an epistemological constraint on the notion of analysis. Most of our sentences, however, clearly do not consist of words which refer to entities with which we are acquainted (on Russell's narrowed view of acquaintance). So given the epistemological constraint, almost all of our sentences must express propositions whose constituents and structure are concealed rather than revealed by the sentences themselves.

The two shifts in Russell's view of analysis, that represented by "On Denoting" and that introduced by Russell's increasing epistemological concerns, do not constitute a retreat from the realist conception. Indeed, the emphasis on the idea that the ultimate constituents of propositions must be entities with which we are acquainted seems if anything to reinforce the realism. (The increasingly epistemological bent of Russell's thought makes it clear that analysis, on his view of it, uncovers a structure which has psychological reality. Each element into which a proposition is analyzed corresponds to a psychological act of acquaintance.) There is, however, a shift in the sorts of entities with which Russell is concerned. The various logical forms which a proposition may have are seen as entities in their own right, and increasingly as the objects of interest. Philosophical analysis is still concerned with finding the entities of which a given proposition is composed, but it is also, and primarily, concerned with finding the logical form of the proposition, and with identifying the various logical forms which propositions or facts may have.[6]

Philosophical analysis, for Russell, thus comes increasingly to be concerned with logical forms; he also comes to think that philosophical analysis makes up the greater part of philosophy. By 1914, indeed, he clearly implies that philosophy simply *is* philosophical analysis. Philosophy, he insists, must have its own subject matter, and this subject matter is logical forms.[7] Russell comes to identify philosophy with logic (or with part of logic). "Philosophy," he says, "becomes indistinguishable from logic" (1918: 111); or, again: "every philosophical problem, when it is subjected to the necessary analysis and purification, is either found to be really not philosophical at all, or else to be, in the sense in which we are using the word, logical" (1914: 42). But he does not mean by this that philosophy is to be identified with mathematical logic, in our sense. The claim that philosophy is logic is possible only because of a stretching of the idea of logic. Logic, Russell says, is divided into "two not very sharply distinguished portions." The first is the familiar subject which proves theorems and so forth. The second, however, is logic in the sense in which logic can be identified with philosophy. In this sense, logic "is concerned with the analysis and enumeration of logical *forms*, i.e. with the kinds of propositions that may occur, with the various types of facts, and with the classification of the constituents of facts" (1918: 112; cf. 1914: 67).

So at least according to Russell's statements in 1914, philosophy consists of analysis. Analysis, in turn, is largely concerned with logical forms, though also with classifying the various constituents of propositions. The epistemology of this process, so to speak, relies on the notion of acquaintance, i.e. on the idea of a direct and presuppositionless relation between the mind and various non-mental entities, including logical forms and other abstract entities. The process of analysis is complete when one has found the actual constituents, and the actual form, which underlie what is expressed by any given sentence; the philosopher knows that he or she has done this because the final list of constituents are all objects of acquaintance (and in fact, presumably, all objects with which the philosopher is actually acquainted).

WITTGENSTEIN

Wittgenstein's *Tractatus Logico-Philosophicus* (1922) on its surface, and at least for most of its length, puts forward a view of philosophical analysis which is in many ways a starker and more clear-cut version of Russell's—except that the epistemological component is wholly absent. The world is made up of facts; complex facts are truth-functional compounds of simple facts, each of which is composed of simple objects in some definite arrangement. Language has a real structure, hidden by its superficial structure; the real structure of language exactly mirrors the structure of reality. Every sentence that expresses a fact is—though it may not appear to be—a truth-functional compound of elementary sentences; an elementary sentence is made up of simple names in some definite arrangement. Sentences express facts because at the level of elementary sentences and elementary facts language comes in contact with the world: the simple names in an elementary sentence are the names of the simple objects in the corresponding fact, and the way that the objects are arranged in the fact is the same as the way in which the names are arranged in the sentence. To give the complete analysis of a sentence would, accordingly, be to display the relevant elementary sentences in the relevant truth-functional arrangement.

This picture is, as I say, the one that the *Tractatus* appears, for most of its length, to put forward. The qualifications are needed here because, of course, the last few sentences of the book undermine all that has gone before by declaring it to be nonsensical. Seen in one way this is simply a matter of internal consistency: according to the doctrines of the *Tractatus*, all sentences—all signs which are meaningful—must be analyzable into truth-functional combinations of elementary sentences, which are in turn simply combinations of elementary names. It is, however, very hard to think that the sentences expressing the doctrines of the *Tractatus* itself could meet these requirements; so if the doctrines of the *Tractatus* are true then they cannot be expressed, so the sentences which (apparently) attempt to express them are nonsensical.[8] Similarly, we can think of this radical step as the result of thinking through what is implicit in Russell's 1914 view of philosophy (and even, perhaps, in the theory of types). If philosophy is to consist of philosophical analysis, as Russell sometimes says, how can it contain the sorts of assertions that Russell puts forward? (How, in particular, can it contain the assertion that philosophy is to consist of philosophical analysis?)

Wittgenstein holds that *all* philosophy—including the apparent view of the *Tractatus*, but also including all other philosophy—is nonsense. Where does this rejection of all philosophy leave philosophical analysis? This seems to me unclear; perhaps he is not rejecting the idea, or the process, of such analysis; perhaps he might think, under some circumstances, that there was some point to replacing sentence 1 with sentence 2. What is clear, however, is that he wholly rejects *any* philosophical gloss that may be put on the process, any story that may be told about what we are up to when we engage in philosophical analysis. In particular, in spite of much of the rest of the book, its final remarks—if we take them fully seriously—amount to a rejection of what I called the realist conception of philosophical analysis: the idea that philosophical analysis uncovers structures which exist quite independently of us, and which underlie our discourse and make it possible.

Russell's conception of philosophical analysis was based on a metaphysical account of the structure and constituents of propositions, and of our knowledge of those elements. Wittgenstein argues not just against Russell's account, but against anything comparable, against the viability of the sort of enterprise that Russell is engaged in, the sort of enterprise which attempts to uncover a hidden reality. Yet, in spite of Wittgenstein's arguments, it seems that Russell's enterprise has results which one might be reluctant to surrender—the monumental achievement embodied in *Principia Mathematica* (whatever precisely that work achieved); the tantalizing idea, put forward in *Our Knowledge of the External World*, of doing something analogous for empirical knowledge; and smaller-scale clarifications such as that given by the theory of descriptions. How can the world be made safe for these ideas, without our having to commit ourselves to anything comparable to Russell's metaphysics?

CARNAP

This is the sort of question that confronted Carnap, who was greatly influenced by Frege, by *Principia Mathematica* and by *Our Knowledge of the External World*. He was also greatly influenced by Wittgenstein—but was not willing to give up everything that might go under the name of philosophy. How can we do philosophical analysis—how, indeed, can we do philosophy at all—without making metaphysical claims? Carnap, like Russell, does not think that philosophy is in the business of making claims which are empirical in the sense of being answerable to sensory experience. He follows

Wittgenstein, however, in rejecting all non-empirical claims as nonsensical. So for him the question is even more pressing: how can we do philosophical analysis without making any claims at all?

Carnap seeks to lay rest to these doubts by taking very seriously the idea that the subject matter of philosophy is language. His answer to the question about the nature of philosophical analysis depends on the idea of alternative languages, among which we may freely choose. He would gloss the step from 1 to 2 very roughly like this. We begin with a certain language—ordinary colloquial English, say—which contains sentences of the form of 1. The philosopher sees that for certain purposes English may be inconvenient or misleading, precisely because it contains sentences of that form (it may, for example, encourage fruitless metaphysical worries about how a sentence can be meaningful if it contains an apparent referring expression which does not in fact refer to anything). The philosopher therefore formulates another language, identical to English except that sentences of the form of 1 are introduced as abbreviations for sentences of the form of 2.

Two further points are important to Carnap's picture of philosophical analysis, and of philosophy itself. One is the status of claims about one or the other language. The philosopher will, of course, make such claims. He or she will say, for example, that in English definite descriptions are primitive expressions, whereas in the alternative language—English*, let us call it—definite descriptions are introduced by abbreviation. Carnap cannot allow that such claims are empirical—for he does not wish to assimilate philosophy to empirical linguistics. But neither, it seems, can he allow that they are non-empirical, for then they appear as metaphysical. How can the philosopher's (apparent) claims be both non-empirical and non-metaphysical? Carnap denies that the philosopher's utterances are genuine claims at all: they are to be analytic—empty of content but not meaningless. The philosopher, on this view, deals with languages not as actually existing phenomena—languages in that sense are the province of empirical linguistics. The philosopher's concern is rather with artificial languages, thought of in the first instance as sets of semantical and syntactical rules.[9] Such rules may be set up in order to correspond to an actually existing language (as a piece of pure mathematics may be devised in order to model a physical phenomenon); the language which is of concern to the philosopher, however, is defined by its rules and not by how the speakers of the language act (as the mathematics is governed by mathematical rules, not by the physical phenomenon). Now the philosopher's (apparent) claims about any given language simply follow from the rules of that language. In Carnap's terms they are analytic; they simply explicate what is already contained in the rules, and do not add any new knowledge, either of the empirical sort or of the supposedly metaphysical sort. Like the truths of logic, on Carnap's account, they are neither empirical nor metaphysical because they are not *claims* at all.

The second issue that arises from the sketch we gave of Carnap's picture is the status of the various possible languages—English and English*, in our example. According to Carnap's view, it is not part of the philosopher's task to *legislate*, to mandate the use of this or that language. The philosopher does not say that this or that language is the *correct* language. This is a crucial point. If there is a question of correctness here, then what could make one language correct, and others not? Presumably something like the idea that the first language corresponds to the real structure underlying thought and discourse, but it is precisely this talk of the real underlying structure of all language that Carnap dismisses as metaphysical. In sharp contrast with Russell (and perhaps, though the case is less clear, with Frege), Carnap rejects such claims as nonsensical. Along with this, he gives up any idea of the *correct* language, or even (more modestly) the correct way of analyzing a given sentence or idiom. If such things are not a matter of correctness then they must be, on his view, a matter of free choice. The only sorts of criticism which are legitimate are that a given language has not been clearly explained, or the purely pragmatic point that a given language may not be as convenient for a given purpose as some other language is. This is the position enshrined in Carnap's principle of tolerance:

> *In logic there are no morals.* Everyone is at liberty to build up his own logic, i.e. his own form of language, as he wishes. All that is required of him is that, if he wishes to discuss it, he must state his methods clearly, and give syntactical rules instead of philosophical arguments.
>
> (Carnap 1937: 52)

Carnap's tolerance about choice of language is supported by the idea that there is a clear distinction between what goes on within a language and what goes on when we shift from one language to another. Changes in our beliefs, that is to say, are of two sharply distinct kinds. Changes which involve change of language he calls *external*. Here there are no criteria of correctness, for all such criteria are part of some language. This, of course, is why tolerance is the appropriate attitude. We have no criteria of correctness that could give us a basis on which to say that this language is correct and that one incorrect; all we have are pragmatic considerations, such as that one language may be more or less convenient than another for this or that purpose. Carnap's view, however, is not one of universal tolerance; it is not the position of the epistemological anarchist for whom anything is as good as anything else. For internal changes—those which do not involve change of language—there are clear standards of correctness, laid down by the language. Carnap's position thus seems to require that there be a clear distinction between internal changes and external changes, and that the epistemological statuses of the two kinds of change are quite distinct.

It is worth noting that the internal–external distinction here is essentially another form of the distinction between the analytic and the synthetic: those changes which involve change of mind about a previously analytic sentence are changes of language, since the analytic sentences are (more or less) constitutive of the language; those changes which involve only synthetic sentences, however, are internal.

Let us recapitulate the picture of analysis which emerges from Carnap's work. The analysis of a given kind of sentence—for example the analysis of sentences of the form of 1 into sentences of the form of 2—should, strictly speaking, be understood as the replacement of one language by another, perhaps different from the first in only a single very minor respect. There is here no claim that one language is correct and the other not; there is merely a linguistic proposal: that we should, for such and such purposes, use the second language rather than the first. There is thus no thesis, no claim made which must be either empirical or metaphysical. Nor is any genuine substantive claim made when the philosopher tells us the result of using this language rather than that. There we have only the analytic consequences of the rules of the proposed language; since they are analytic, they make no genuine claim.

This picture is completely antithetical to the realist conception of analysis which we saw in the work of Russell. There is no talk of underlying structure, of the real form (logical form) which makes thought and language possible, and which is concealed by the superficial structure of our language. Yet in spite of this antithesis, not everything changes. In particular, Carnap could follow Russell in analyzing type-1 sentences into type-2 sentences. The step from 1 to 2 may remain exactly the same. What is said about the step, however, its philosophical gloss, and the philosophical commitments which it is taken to have, change completely.

QUINE

Carnap's picture of analysis is part of a conception of philosophy which aims to avoid what he took to be Russell's commitment to metaphysics. That picture, however, has commitments of its own. On the one hand there must be a class of analytic sentences, sentences which can be asserted but do not make genuine or substantive claims to knowledge. On the other hand, there must be a clear and epistemologically significant distinction between shifting from one language to another and modifying one's beliefs within a particular language. Both of these points are forms of what came to be a philosophical monolith: the analytic–synthetic distinction. Quine of course rejects this distinction, at least in every form that will do significant philosophical work; Quine would, accordingly, reject Carnap's gloss on philosophical analysis.

Philosophical analysis, or something closely resembling it, nevertheless survives in Quine's philosophy. Examples of analysis or paraphrase are legion in *Word and Object* (1960), especially past the more obviously philosophical high jinks of the first two chapters. Section 53 of that book is titled "The ordered pair as philosophical paradigm"—surely a conscious echo of Ramsey's description of Russell's theory of descriptions. The accolade is now applied to a different example, but still there is the same idea that philosophical analysis—the transition from one mode of expression to another, to put it at its most neutral—is an example of philosophy at it best. What story does Quine have to tell about such a transition, what philosophical gloss does he put on it? As one might expect, he has no truck at all with the realist conception which we saw in Russell: talk of underlying structure, directly accessible perhaps to the eye of the mind, does not meet his standards of scientific rigor. Nor, of course, does he adopt Carnap's talk of a free choice of this language or that.

Let us see just what Quine says about this example, which he claims is typical:

> We do not claim synonymy. We do not claim to make clear what users of the unclear expression has unconsciously in mind all along. We do not expose hidden meanings, as the words "analysis" and "explication" would suggest; we supply lacks. We fix on the particular functions of the unclear expression that make it worth troubling about, and then devise a substitute, clear and couched in terms to our liking, that fills those functions.
>
> (Quine 1960: 258–59)

Here analysis (or "analysis") seems to be a relatively casual affair, with no metaphysical commitments. One finds, for whatever reason, one mode of expression clearer than another, yet able to fulfill all of the purposes that one had in using the second; accordingly, one uses the first. There is nothing more to it than that.

An earlier passage in *Word and Objects* is also illuminating. Quine speaks of paraphrasing or analyzing a sentence, *S*, into a sentence *S'*. He emphasizes that we should not expect, or even desire, that the two be synonymous. He goes on to say of *S'*: "Its relation to S is just that the particular business that the speaker was on that occasion trying to get on with, with the help of *S* among other things, can be managed well enough to suit him by using *S'* instead of *S*. We can even let him modify his purposes under the shift, if he pleases" (1960: 160). Here it appears that some cases of paraphrase may be completely *ad hoc*; there is no suggestion that the one mode of expression is capable of fulfilling all of the functions filled by some less clear mode. Rather it may just be that on a particular occasion we find we can use a different expression, and still achieve what we want to achieve just as well, or better. Put like this, it would seem difficult to disagree. On the other hand, what Quine says here seems to amount to little more than the injunction: if a particular way of putting things is on a particular occasion unhelpful, if it does not seem to facilitate smooth and accurate communication, for example, then try to find some other way of talking which will do better. This is good advice, no doubt, but it is hard to think that analysis, understood in this minimal sense, could be the heart of philosophy. We have moved a very long way from Russell's idea of analysis as the royal road to philosophical truth, or even Carnap's view that the construction of alternative languages is the philosopher's distinctive contribution to knowledge.

CONCLUSION

I do not wish to suggest that this sketch of various accounts of analysis within analytic philosophy is exhaustive. Another idea worth mentioning arises out of the Chomskyan revolution in linguistics. It is based on the idea that the reality underlying our discourse, and making it possible, is not a reality of abstract objects but rather of mental entities and structures, quite unlike anything of which we are ordinarily conscious (these mental entities or structures may also be asserted to have a neurological reality, i.e. to be instantiated, in some way, in the brain). This is clearly a very different conception of philosophical (or linguistic) analysis, and draws on a rather different set of techniques and paradigms (although the extent of the overlap is perhaps surprising).

Nor do I wish to claim that the line of development I have sketched—from Russell to Carnap to Quine—corresponds in any unproblematic fashion to the movement of the spirit of the age, or even the movement of the spirit of analytic philosophy. There is no tidy dialectical progress here. In the line of development I sketched, the conception of philosophical analysis becomes less and less metaphysical. Russell's metaphysical presuppositions are rejected by Carnap (and, one is tempted to say, Wittgenstein's metaphysical presuppositions in the *Tractatus* are rejected by Wittgenstein in the *Tractatus*). Carnap then puts forward a conception of analysis which appears as non-metaphysical only because it draws on other assumptions (essentially one form or another of the analytic–synthetic distinction). These assumptions are in turn rejected by Quine, who puts forward a view of analysis which seems to carry with it no particular theoretical commitments—but also, for the same reason, to have no very general significance. This story, however, is not the only one that there is to be told. In particular, there is also a story to be told about the revival of a version of the realist conception of analysis. Perhaps this conception, the view of philosophy as getting at the abstract structures underlying our discourse, has never completely gone away since Russell advanced it; yet this view certainly seems to have gained greater prominence over the last twenty-five years. (It is plausible to suppose that the revival of the realist conception of analysis, and of the metaphysics that goes along with it, is due to the decline in popularity of Carnap's anti-metaphysical views. Insofar as this was in turn the result of Quine's criticisms of Carnap, it is one of the nicer ironies in the history of philosophy). There is also, no doubt, a more dismal story to be told about those who have no particular gloss to put on the transition from 1 to 2, no philosophical account of it to offer, yet assume such a move *must* be of philosophical significance.

These various philosophical positions are less my concern than is the fact of their variety. They are all stories about philosophical analysis and what it does and why it matters. Their variety suggests to me, at least, that while the notion of philosophical analysis may bring a certain kind of unity to a central core within analytic philosophy, it is unity of method only in a superficial sense—the unity of a practice, but not of the account of the practice (a unity of method, if you like, but not of methodology, of the *logos* of the method).

This superficial unity of method among some (not, of course, all) analytic philosophers does, I think, show us something about analytic philosophy. It has often been remarked, and no doubt correctly, that analytic philosophy is particularly concerned with language (this idea relegates the work of Russell before 1905, and perhaps also the work of Frege, to pre-analytic philosophy: but this conclusion may seem acceptable). Emphasizing philosophical analysis gives us some idea of the specific ways in which analytic philosophers, as contrasted to other philosophers, have been concerned with language. (Herder, for example, might also be described as "particularly concerned with language"; yet clearly his concerns are very remote from those that we think of as characteristic of analytic philosophy.) The subject matter of philosophical analysis is typically a single declarative sentence; and analytic philosophers have often been concerned with sentences taken one by one, with understanding exactly what claim each is making about the world. More significant, I think, is the way in which philosophical analysis directs our attention to the (actual or potential) misleadingness of unanalyzed language. This idea I take to be closely related to that of philosophical analysis; for many analytic philosophers, it is the misleadingness of language that gives rise to the need for analysis.

The idea that language misleads us is, I think, an important theme in analytic philosophy.[10] Like the technique of philosophical analysis itself, however, this idea is compatible with quite divergent philosophical opinions. To take one obvious example, it is an idea that can be employed to express both metaphysical and the anti-metaphysical tendencies. The metaphysician may say that language is misleading because it conceals the real structure of our thought or (in some deeper sense) language, and that this real structure will show us the form of the world. It is in this spirit that Russell says in 1918 that the theory of symbolism is important, largely for the negative reason that if we are not aware of symbols we will mistakenly think about them rather than about the real subject matter of philosophy, because the symbols are tangible and the real subject matter very abstract and elusive. In this context he famously says that a good philosopher is one who manages to think about the real subject matter of philosophy "once in six months . . . for a minute," whereas "[b]ad philosophers never do" (1986: 166). Here we have the view that there is a real subject matter, and real problems, lying behind or beneath our language.

The anti-metaphysician may equally think of language as misleading, but in very different ways and to very different ends. Here a characteristic view is that there are no genuine philosophical problems, but that the illusion of such problems is created by the structure of our language, or by the language we use in doing philosophy, or by our confused reflections on the structure of our language. The idea here is that language is deceptive, in one way or the other, and that philosophical problems arise because we are deceived by language—they arise, as the author of the *Tractatus* says, "from our failure to understand the logic of our language" (4.003). It is perhaps in this spirit that the author of the *Philosophical Investigations* speaks of philosophy as "a battle against the bewitchment of our intelligence by means of language" (§109).

Philosophers may emphasize the misleadingness of language while varying in other important ways. As I have already indicated, one powerful line of thought within analytic philosophy has been impressed by the fact that (to put it neutrally) elementary mathematical logic—a fragment of the logic of Frege and of Russell—has the capacity to give us great insight into (some aspects of) the inferential powers of our assertoric sentences. Logic gives us insight into the structure of our language and our thought (or at least the illusion of such insight). This I take to be a fact of the greatest significance for analytic philosophy. It is, I suspect, because of this that the invention of mathematical logic is so closely associated with a philosophy that puts language at the centre of its concerns. Within analytic philosophy, however, there are also those who react against the idea that the use of logic to schematize our ordinary language is philosophically useful:

most obviously, the so-called "ordinary-language" school of philosophy. Both Carnap and J. L. Austin were concerned with language, and both were opposed to metaphysics, but these similarities go along with very deep divergences.

As I hope is clear from what I have said, I do not think it possible or useful to give a strict definition, with necessary and sufficient conditions, for being an analytic philosopher.[11] Our understanding of the idea proceeds from certain paradigmatic figures and works and ways of conceiving philosophical problems. In all of this we have, as Wittgenstein said of games, overlapping strands, rather than one (or two or three) continuous threads (Wittgenstein 1953: §67). In this figure, the idea of philosophical analysis may be thought of as representing one such strand; it is, however, a strand that is itself made up of various fibers. The present essay is no more than the beginning of an attempt to trace out some of the complexities of these issues.

NOTES

1 See Hart (1990).
2 I say *directly* here because much work which has no evident connection with analysis takes seriously those who do emphasize this method; this is an important but indirect connection.
3 For correspondence about the topics of this section I am grateful to T. G. Ricketts.
4 I should say that I speak here of Russell in the period between his rejection of idealism and the time when Wittgenstein came to have a significant influence on his thought, say the period 1900–1914, though I think that the Russellian ideas I shall discuss survived at least until 1918.
5 See Hylton (1990), esp. ch. 4, Part 2.
6 I speak here loosely of "propositions or facts" because for our purposes the distinction is not crucial. At some point between 1906 and 1910 (exactly when is, I think, unclear), Russell gave up the idea that propositions are genuine entities; from that point on the notion of a fact comes to play a central role in his thought, whereas it had before been a very subsidiary notion. To be completely accurate, we should speak of the logical forms of propositions in discussing Russell's thought before that point, and of the logical forms of facts in discussing his thought after that point.
7 See Russell (1914), esp. p. 27.
8 I do not mean to imply here that it is Wittgenstein's view that the doctrines of the *Tractatus* are true but nonsensical, or that he would think that such a status is a possible one at all. On the contrary, I think that that view distorts Wittgenstein's thought. My point is merely that one way to see why one might think the doctrines of that book to be nonsensical is to begin, dialectically, as it were, by assuming that they are true.
9 In the period during which he wrote *The Logical Syntax of Language* (1937), Carnap held that syntactical rules alone are needed; later he came to think

that semantical rules are also required. For our purposes, however, this is not a significant point.

10 Here I am indebted to a conversation with Leonard Linsky.

11 See also Hylton (1995).

BIBLIOGRAPHY

Carnap, R. (1937) *The Logical Syntax of Language*, London: Routledge and Kegan Paul.

Frege, G. (1964) *Basic Laws of Arithmetic*, trans. M. Furth, Berkeley and Los Angeles: University of California Press; cf. *Grundgesetze der Arithmetik, begriffsschriftlich abgeleitet*, volume 1, Jena: Verlag Hermann Pohle, 1893.

——(1979) *Posthumous Writings*, Oxford: Basil Blackwell; cf. *Nachgelassene Schriften*, Hamburg: Felix Meiner Verlag, 1976.

——(1984) *Collected Papers*, Oxford: Basil Blackwell. ("Compound Thoughts," original publication in *Beiträge zur Philosophie des deutschen Idealismus*, III, 1923–6: 36–51; "Negation," first published in *Beiträge des deutschen Idealismus*, I, 1918–19: 143–57.

Hart, W. D. (1990) "Clarity," in D. Bell and N. Cooper (eds) *The Analytic Tradition*, Oxford: Basil Blackwell.

Hylton, P. (1990) *Russell, Idealism, and the Emergence of Analytic Philosophy*, Oxford: Oxford University Press.

——(1995) Review of Michael Dummett's *Origins of Analytical Philosophy* (Cambridge, Mass.: Harvard University Press, 1993), *The Journal of Philosophy* XCII, 10.

Moore, G. E. (1903) *Principia Ethica*, Cambridge: Cambridge University Press.

——(1946) "Russell's 'Theory of Descriptions,' " in P. A. Schilpp (ed.), *The Philosophy of Bertrand Russell*, Evanston, Ill.: The Library of Living Philosophers.

Quine, W. V. O. (1960) *Word and Object*, Cambridge, Mass.: MIT Press.

Ramsey, F. (1931) *The Foundations of Mathematics and Other Logical Essays*, London: Kegan Paul.

Russell, B. (1900) *A Critical Exposition of the Philosophy of Leibniz*, London: George Allen and Unwin; new edition 1937.

——(1903) *The Principles of Mathematics*, Cambridge: Cambridge University Press; second edition, London: Allen and Unwin, 1937.

——(1905) "On Denoting," *Mind*, NS 14: 479–93.

——(1914) *Our Knowledge of the External World*, London: Allen and Unwin; revised edition, 1926.

——(1918) "On Scientific Method in Philosophy," in *Mysticism and Logic* London: Longmans, Green and Co.

——(1986) Lecture I on "The Philosophy of Logical Atomism," in John G. Slater (ed.) *Collected Papers of Bertrand Russell*, Vol. 8., London: Allen and Unwin.

Schilpp, P. A. (ed.) (1942) *The Philosophy of G. E. Moore*, Evanston and Chicago: Northwestern University.

Wittgenstein, L. (1922) *Tractatus Logico-Philosophicus*, New York: Harcourt, Brace and Co.

——(1953) *Philosophical Investigations*, London: Basil Blackwell.

3 Analytical philosophy as a matter of style

J. J. Ross

Michael Dummett has recently published an absorbingly interesting book on the *Origins of Analytical Philosophy*, based on a series of lectures he gave at the University of Bologna in 1987. I should like to offer a few comments concerning his account of the movement, concentrating not so much on his version of its origins, as on his views on some of its contemporary manifestations. The moral that I shall seek to draw from these comments will share something with one of Dummett's main themes in the book, namely, the need to bridge the gulf between phenomenology and analytical philosophy. But whereas Dummett suggests that communication can and should be established by going back to common origins and rejoining hands at the point of divergence, I shall argue that we must look ahead, instead, to a common arena of problems, where the styles of approach will matter less than the actual solutions which will be offered and discussed. I believe that one such arena already exists and has been provided by the field of cognitive studies, especially where these overlap with what has come to be called "the philosophy of mind."

While arguing this point, I shall be concerned to take up Dummett's idea that analytical philosophy has a particular style. I shall seek to ascertain what, in his opinion, this style might be and contrast it with what others have said regarding the style of analytical philosophy.

I

In view of Dummett's own previous research into the writings of Frege, it was quite predictable that for him Frege should have emerged as the great hero of the analytical revolution, and that a large part of what was said in those lectures should have concerned Frege's distinctive views regarding truth and meaning, and the relation between thought and language. Much attention is also paid there to the relation between Frege's ideas and the legacy of Brentano and Husserl. Though he specifically regards the "linguistic turn" as the starting point of analytical philosophy proper, and thinks the crucial step was taken by Wittgenstein in the *Tractatus Logico-Philosophicus* of 1922, he regards Frege, Moore, and Russell as the preparers of the ground (Dummett 1994: 127). It is therefore more than a little surprising that although he has much to say about Frege, he says very little indeed about the work of Moore, Russell, or even of Wittgenstein. The reason for this turns out to be Dummett's opinion that though Russell and Moore were important predecessors, neither was a true source of analytical philosophy. In his view,

> the sources of analytical philosophy were the writings of philosophers who wrote, principally or exclusively, in the German language; and this would have remained obvious to everyone had it not been for the plague of Nazism which drove so many German-speaking philosophers across the Atlantic.
>
> (1994: ix)

It was Gilbert Ryle who, he says, opened his eyes to this fact in his lectures on Bolzano, Brentano, Meinong, and Husserl. Dummett excuses himself from dealing with the contributions of Russell and Moore both because, he says, "this ground has been fairly well worked over," and also because Russell and Moore sprang from a very different philosophical milieu. With regard to the exposition of Wittgenstein's ideas, Dummett has little directly to say in these lectures; he tends to take Wittgenstein's ideas for granted as something that the reader or hearer will have already known. He does concern himself with the difference between the views of Donald Davidson (whom he regards as following a line close to that of Frege) and those of the later Wittgenstein (Dummett 1994: 14–21), and with the implications of Wittgenstein's new advice regarding how linguistic investigation is to be undertaken, i.e., by examining our use of statements in the language (Dummett 1994: 162–6). He indicates his general sympathy with this latter view of Wittgenstein, in several places in these lectures, in spite of his respect for the truth-conditional theory maintained by Davidson. But he ends the lectures by indicating that in his opinion "these general ideas [of Wittgenstein] can be vindicated only by a plausible sketch of a systematic account of a language in terms of just those ideas" (1994: 166), and he feels that this has yet to be done. So it turns out that Dummett's book really does concentrate on the *origins* of the analytical movement, much more than offer an exposition of the "linguistic turn," in either of Wittgenstein's versions.

II

More interesting are Dummett's views regarding the present and the future of analytical philosophy, and it is just at this point that he introduces the notion of analytical philosophy as possessing a characteristic style. He considers the new trend of some writers, such as the late Gareth Evans, who reverse the priority of language over thought and maintain that language can only be explained in terms of antecedently given notions of different types of thought, considered independently of their linguistic expression. Dummett is impressed by Evans' idea that the acquisition of information is a more fundamental concept than knowledge, since information is acquired without one's necessarily having a grasp of the proposition which embodies it (Dummett 1994: 186). But since Dummett believes that what distinguishes analytical philosophy from other schools is precisely the "linguistic turn" taken ever since Frege, which, according to his view, is based on the notion that a philosophical account of thought can be attained only through an account of language, this would seem to imply that Evans was no longer an analytical philosopher. Dummett clearly finds such a conclusion unpalatable, since, as he says, the three pillars on which Evans' posthumous book, *The Varieties of Reference*, rests are Russell, Moore, and Frege, who were surely eminent representatives of analytical philosophy. So he removes his discomfort by suggesting, concerning Evans, that "it is only as belonging to this tradition—as adopting a certain philosophical style and as appealing to certain writers rather than to certain others—that he remains a member of the analytical school" (1994: 4–5). It is thus clear, then, that for Dummett, while the "linguistic turn" remains pivotal for analytical philosophy, there is such a thing as a distinctive philosophical style which characterizes analytical philosophy which, together with an appeal to the writings of certain philosophers who are canonical within the movement, will permit us to include as analytical philosophers even those who reject what was, in his opinion, its most fundamental idea.

I find this rather amusing. I do not know why it should be so important for Dummett to retain Gareth Evans and Christopher Peacocke as part of the analytical school when it is clear to some readers that in many ways these, and other contemporary thinkers, have moved beyond anything that could be retained of the once-accepted doctrines of the "linguistic turn." It might be more appropriate to refer to them and to many other contemporary philosophers (such as Tyler Burge, Daniel Dennett, Keith Donellan, David Kaplan, David Lewis, Robert Stalnaker, Stephen Stich, etc.) as "post-analytical" philosophers. Nor is it so obvious to me that this "linguistic turn" is the sole or even the main part of the "revolution in philosophy" which once was said to be the characteristic feature of the new moves in Austrian, English, and U.S. philosophy, from the end of the nineteenth century until the 1960s of the twentieth century which we nowadays refer to as "analytical philosophy." That it was an important part is certain—the centrality of the writings of Wittgenstein would have been sufficient to guarantee that. That it was the main part, so much so, that Frege should be regarded as the only source—the *only* "grandfather" of analytical philosophy (Dummett 1994: 171)—with Bolzano as the great-grandfather and Russell and Moore as more like uncles (or even "possibly great-uncles") of the analytical movement, may well reflect the Dummettian bias which places Frege and his ideas at the center of things. (How strange and unusual it would be, by the way, that this creature—analytical philosophy—should have only one grandfather, when all other such creatures have two!) But there are grounds for regarding the notion of "analysis," which gave the movement its name, as being more connected with the sorts of philosophical techniques which were practiced by G. E. Moore, as well as by Bertrand Russell, at one stage in his career, than with anything directly connected with Frege.

Elsewhere in the book (1994: 128–9), Dummett has a slightly different account of the way Evans and Peacocke might be said to belong to the analytical tradition, even after they have rejected what he regards as its fundamental axiom (that the analysis of thought must be undertaken through the analysis of language). Dummett suggests that although they no longer give the same fundamental place to language, they still treat the philosophy of thought as the foundation of philosophy, so that the general architecture of the subject remains essentially the same for them as for those who still adhere to the fundamental axiom. I find this suggestion somewhat lame and want to argue that this would make Evans' connection to the analytical school even more problematic. For if it is the concentration on the philosophy of thought that is now to be regarded as constitutive of the analytical tradition, it will be very difficult to say wherein the analytical turn in philosophy was really different from the epistemological tradition in modern philosophy from Descartes to Kant. It will be recalled that Richard Rorty, in his *Philosophy and the Mirror of Nature*, which is indisputably and expressly a work of "post-analytical" philosophy, had already pointed out the very similar careers transversed by modern philosophy of the epistemological turn and analytical philosophy of the linguistic turn. Dummett would probably wish to say that Frege's non-psychologistic account of thoughts as the contents of propositional attitudes is what brought about his revolution in philosophy and challenged the primacy held since Descartes by the theory of knowledge (1994: 184–5), and that this anti-epistemological attitude is retained in the work of

Evans and Peacocke. So that this is what distinguishes their approach to the theory of thought from that of the epistemological philosophy from Descartes to Kant. Dummett is probably right about this anti-epistemological approach in Evans and Peacocke. But since their treatment of the notion of thought touches upon the sort of topics that have been raised by Chomsky and a great many contemporary philosophers whom he has influenced, and since Chomsky has pressed the view that philosophy of thought is part of the philosophy of mind, so that meaning has to do with something very complicated that goes on in the brain (1994: 187–8), it will prove very difficult to disentangle, once and for all, questions of the philosophy of thought from questions of traditional epistemology. And, in any case, since followers of Chomsky and followers of the Frege/analytical tradition now discuss their differences in the same public arena, is it so easy to categorize what the first are doing as non-analytical philosophy while maintaining that the second are continuing to do analytical philosophy proper?

III

It is worth noting that Dummett's account of what was revolutionary in analytical philosophy (i.e. that thought is to be analyzed by language) is very characteristic of Oxford philosophy. This was precisely the point made in the series of talks given by a distinguished group of Oxford lecturers (A. J. Ayer, W. C. Kneale, P. F. Strawson, G. A. Paul, D. F. Pears, G. J. Warnock and R. A. Wollheim) in the Third Program of the BBC which appeared in book form as *The Revolution in Philosophy* with an Introduction by Gilbert Ryle. But here the move was also attributed to an Oxford contemporary of Frege, F. H. Bradley, who appears, therefore, as what Dummett might have regarded as the second missing "grandfather" of the analytical school. According to Ryle (1967: 6–8), both Frege and Bradley were rejecting the same false associationist psychology which made terms prior to propositions, and maintaining that thought or judgment is a functional unity possessing distinguishable features but not composed of detachable pieces. In the hands of both Frege and Bradley it was intrinsic to thought to be true or false or to have "objective reference," and it was meanings such as these which Moore's analyses were meant to be analyses of, which Russell's atoms were atoms of, etc. Perhaps Dummett prefers to disregard the part played in the story by Bradley, etc. because he was not particularly enamored (he says) of Oxford philosophy, which in the years immediately after the Second World War, when he was a student at Oxford, was enormously self-confident and insular.

In the Introduction to another collection of articles, published round about the same time (1966), entitled *British Analytical Philosophy*, written mostly by a younger group of Oxford philosophers and edited by Bernard Williams and Alan Montefiore, we find a somewhat different account of the style of analytical philosophy. After drawing attention to the fact that to recognize some philosophical writings as "existentialist" (the collection was originally intended for a continental audience) was to recognize a specific style and type of concern rather than a ready isolable body of doctrine or the relation to some great philosopher to whom the movement owed its leading ideas and its name, the Introduction goes on to argue that this was still more obviously true of the kind of philosophers included in their collection. It was no mere accident, says the Introduction, that differences between schools at this time should express themselves not so much in doctrine as in method.

> It is in certain styles and methods of thought, certain types of questions and certain sets of terms and ideas for discussing them, that the unity of existentialist thought, for example, most obviously appears, and similarly with the essays collected in this book. They are all examples of methods of philosophical discussion that have been most influential in Great Britain and elsewhere in the English-speaking world since the war, and which (it is fair to say) remain so.
>
> (Williams and Montefiore, 1966: 2)

No explanations are immediately offered about what is meant by the "styles" and "methods" which are here being attributed to analytical philosophy. In fact it is pointed out that the range of styles and subject matter included in the collection show that the analytical style is nonetheless compatible with considerable variety in both philosophical interests and general belief. The editors therefore excused themselves from attempting to give a general account of this type of philosophizing and regarded the collection as illustrating this style by showing it in action. But the Introduction nonetheless went on to suggest, very generally, that the continental style was caricatured as speculative, metaphysical, and either obscure in utterance or possessing the special sort of clarity that goes with ambitious rationalism, whereas the British style was caricatured as being empirical, down-to-earth, and sober in expression. Behind the caricature, according to the Introduction (Williams and Montefiore 1966: 5), there lay a genuine disagreement about what constitutes seriousness in philosophy: British philosophy was self-consciously academic and placed emphasis on the colleague rather than the master. It therefore rejected the dramatic style which sought striking examples to heighten the intensity of what we see and feel, which was more customary in continental philosophy.

It may be doubted whether this account really offers much illumination regarding the style of *analytical*, rather than that of *British*, philosophy. But perhaps it is characteristic, in some way, of a certain group of British analytical philosophers, the so-called Oxford analytical school. It was to this school, and especially to such philosophers as Gilbert Ryle and John Austin, who were the guiding figures of this school in the years when he was a student at Oxford, that Dummett reports himself to have been opposed. He regarded the influence of Ryle as negative in teaching his students to disregard Carnap, and that of Austin as positively harmful in pushing people in the wrong direction. Dummett reports that, like Elizabeth Anscombe and Philippa Foot at the time, he felt himself to be an outsider, unsympathetic to Oxford "ordinary language" analysis, and, though critical, more respectful of Quine, who was visiting Oxford in the early 1950s, than anyone else in Oxford (Dummett 1994: 167–70). Clearly Dummett thinks more of the post-Carnapian philosophy in the U.S., as represented by Quine and Davidson, who were the inheritors of what was once called "ideal language analysis," than he thinks of the Oxford school of "ordinary language analysis."

IV

Those of us who were students at the same period in Cambridge, and who were more exposed to the Wittgensteinian legacy as continued by John Wisdom, were taught (like Dummett) to suspect the new "ordinary language analysis" which Oxford was trying to spread. But for us the legacy of the analytical school was supposed to be summed up in the "metamorphosis of metaphysics" (a phrase coined by Wisdom) rather than in the "revolution in philosophy." The main liberating move of the later Wittgenstein, in pointing philosophical investigation in the direction of the detailed analysis of ordinary usage (which, according to Wisdom, was the basis of Moore's technique long before Wittgenstein had worked out the whys and wherefores), was to get us to realize that we must learn to free ourselves of being misled by the insidious traps created by the too-hasty philosophizing based on the forming of a wrong picture of what was sometimes implied in the vagaries of ordinary language usage. So philosophy was largely therapeutic. However, Wisdom thought (as did Friedrich Waismann, then at Oxford) that the metaphysical eccentricities of the philosophers could sometimes reflect insights which were beneficial in getting us to understand things better than before. When Peter Strawson of Oxford went on to argue that there was now once more room for system-construction in philosophy, in which we would try to base ourselves on a more generalized and systematic attempt to distinguish and describe the logical features of our concepts and speech-forms, using the same data and methods as those of therapeutic analysis, Wisdom pooh-poohed and argued that this would be a betrayal of Wittgenstein's view that ordinary usage was perfectly all right as it was. And Strawson did admit that the system-builder was indeed inspired and supported by the post-Carnapian ideal-language techniques being practiced in the U.S., which he regarded as complementary, and not necessarily opposed, to the sort of examination of ordinary usage being pursued in English philosophy. But perhaps many of us could have been excused when we felt that the bottom had now fallen out of analytical philosophy altogether. And we were not surprised when, in the 1960s and 1970s, all sorts of statements of traditional and sometimes ancient philosophical positions reappeared in the market of ideas, which were written in the new idiom and style of analytical philosophy. Perhaps, in retrospect, Wisdom's ideas, and his interpretation of Wittgenstein, were still too close to the reaction against the logical positivism of A. J. Ayer and the Vienna Circle which the later philosophy of Wittgenstein represented.

V

In fact many people never quite got over the fact that from the 1950s there was a growing chasm between analytical philosophy and logical positivism. In his final lecture in *The Revolution in Philosophy* series, G. J. Warnock found it necessary to say "I should like to say in very plain terms that I am not, nor is any philosopher of my acquaintance, a logical positivist. This is worth saying, obvious though it must be in the light of this series of lectures, because there has seemed to be a current belief that logical positivism is somehow the official doctrine of contemporary philosophy" (1967: 124). Down to the present day (forty years after Warnock's statement!), many critics of analytical philosophy assume that at least some of the ideas of the Vienna Circle must still be retained by anyone who claims to be an analytical philosopher. But nothing is further from the truth. Although his *Tractatus* was adopted by the Vienna Circle as a sort of official Holy Script, Wittgenstein himself was never a positivist. At the time, he shared with them something like the verifiability theory of meaning, the rejection of metaphysics as nonsense, the conventionalist interpretation of logic and mathematics, and the view that the only legitimate task of philosophy was logical analysis. But he differed from them in his belief that though one cannot say anything sensible about the existence of the metaphysical subject, or religion, or of good and evil, these formed part of what he called "the mystical," which was perhaps more important to man than anything else. Whereas Carnap thought metaphysics was like a sort of music produced by people of no musical ability, the early Wittgenstein considered it a valiant attempt to say the unsayable. The experience itself was beyond words. From the late 1930s until the 1950s most philosophers, including the former positivists themselves, began to realize that their doctrines were untenable without serious modification. And in the meantime, since 1933, Wittgenstein himself had moved away from his previous picture theory of meaning and was already discussing with his students at Cambridge the new ideas, centered round the notion that meaning was based on use rather than on truth-functionality, which formed the basis of his posthumous *Philosophical Investigations*.

Dummett says he finds it difficult to assign a clear coherent doctrine to the Vienna Circle. The rigorous interpretation of verificationism which holds that if one does not have a procedure for deciding the truth or falsity of a statement then it must be meaningless was far too restrictive. So the positivists tried to weaken the principle. But if one says that one does not have to have a ready procedure for verification, then one must give up classical logic, since the law of excluded middle can only hold for those statements which one does know how to verify or falsify. However the Vienna Circle were unshakably convinced that classical logic was correct— it was central to their whole conception of logic and their talk of tautologies in the manner of the *Tractatus*. So he concludes: "I therefore cannot see how their views hang together" (Dummett 1994: 189–90). While he clearly regards the Vienna Circle episode as a dead-end and an aberration (just as he seems to regard the Oxford ordinary language period of his student days as an unfortunate dead-end), Dummett clearly regards the later views of Carnap, and certainly the techniques he bequeathed to his U.S. followers such as Quine and Davidson, as part of the living tissue of analytical philosophy which continues the revolution which Frege set in motion.

VI

Perhaps Dummett has over-stressed one aspect of Frege's influence—the ideas from which there developed the doctrine of the priority of language to thought—at the expense of another aspect of Frege's influence, namely the ideas regarding the character of logic and predication, which led to the development of mathematical or symbolic logic in the earlier writings of Bertrand Russell, which, in turn, eventuated in the classic work of Russell and A. N. Whitehead's *Principia Mathematica*. It was the notion that the new symbolic logic permitted the formulation of our thoughts in a more precise and exact manner than that to which we were accustomed in any of the natural languages, that stimulated the idea that we could analyze what was really being asserted or argued only by recourse to symbolic logic. Hence the commonly accepted assumption, during the earlier part of the century, that Russell's "theory of descriptions" was the very paradigm of philosophical analysis. It was this, we may recall, that led to Wittgenstein's idea of "logical form," and the subsequent logical atomism of Russell, as well as Wittgenstein's *Tractatus* theory of meaning as "picturing." We have no need to recount here Carnap's development of some of these ideas which led to the notion of "ideal-language analysis." But this has bequeathed to analytical philosophy, until the present day, a whole class of philosophical writings, in books and articles, which make a point of using symbolic logic to set out their arguments. The "ordinary language" philosophers we mentioned above were never much impressed with Russell's logicism. They found support for their attitude in Wittgenstein's retreat from his earlier views during the later 1930s, and his later attitudes regarding the nature of language and logic. They took heart in 1950 with the publication of Strawson's "On Referring" in which he rejected Russell's "theory of descriptions." Gilbert Ryle's *Concept of Mind*, which appeared at about the same time, was written in a racy entertaining English style, and had no recourse to anything but the analysis of concepts in ordinary language. It was, for all that, "linguistic philosophy," inasmuch as the argumentation consisted largely of making explicit references to distinctions that were already embodied in the English language. J. L. Austin's technique was a much more subtle extension of the same thing. He concerned himself with very fine distinctions in the meaning and use of certain English expressions. He was of the opinion that no distinction embodied in everyday speech could safely be overlooked, and sought illumination through the careful examination of subtle nuances of meaning which others might dismiss as trivial. The Introduction to the Williams and Montefiore anthology was therefore prepared to admit (1966: 8–9) that some of his writings in this style (which he himself called "linguistic phenomenology") might well be untranslatable into other languages, even though they thought that similar distinctions would probably be discoverable in other developed natural languages. The style of writing of the Oxford philosophers who concentrate in this way upon the usages of ordinary language is distinctive, and sometimes one feels that valuable distinctions have been revealed. But the avoidance of technicalities has seemed to many critics to be in the nature of a self-imposed handicap. Dummett was not the only one who felt that this mode of analytical philosophy had outstayed its usefulness. This probably explains the growing influence of the U.S.-style of analytical philosophy upon the younger generation of British philosophers during the last two decades.

VII

This influence started with Quine, whose style of philosophizing, after he had emerged from concentration on purely logical issues and began to broach more substantive and original themes ("On What There Is," 1948 and "Two Dogmas of Empiricism," 1951), became more literary and reminiscent of the best writing of the leading American pragmatists such as William James and John Dewey. The departure from the highly technical style of Carnap was as noticeable as his dissension from some of the latter's radical empiricistic views. Quine's *Word and Object* (1960) was hailed as a major contribution to the philosophy of language. This emergence of the philosophy of language as one of the central concerns certainly reflected what had been happening in analytical philosophy in general. But Noam Chomsky's work in the 1950s and Quine's work in the 1960s moved philosophy in the U.S. into directions which stood sometimes in stark contrast to what was happening in Britain. When in 1970 Saul Kripke addressed the problem of reference in his lectures on *Naming and Necessity*, and offered a theory which has affinities with the views of John Stuart Mill in the nineteenth century, he was regarded as breaking new ground largely because of the implications he drew for problems in epistemology, metaphysics, the philosophy of science, and the philosophy of mind. This was strengthened by the writings of Donald Davidson, whose innovative views on the philosophy of mind, the theory of action, and metaphysics attracted much attention and has been very influential in Britain as well as the U.S. Thus, there has been, in the last two decades, a multifaceted debate, centering partly on the philosophy of language, and partly on the philosophy of mind. But has this all been "analytical philosophy?" Some of the problems are the same, and some of the modes of argumentation have been common. But whereas there was a feeling in the 1960s, and even the 1970s, that there had been a revolution and that philosophy was now fundamentally different from what it had been in the past, that feeling no longer seems so prominent.

VIII

We mentioned earlier Dummett's view that the views of Quine and Davidson had contributed to keeping the living tissue of the analytical movement in the spirit of the revolution which Frege had brought about. But is the analytical school in philosophy really still alive? Warnock already wrote in 1967 that the "contemporary philosophy" (a term he obviously preferred to the expression "analytical philosophy") of his day was not a dogmatic, restrictive body of doctrines at all, but a common pursuit of illumination in certain fields. He added:

It is tiresome, though perhaps natural, that academic subjects tend to be thought of in terms of rival schools and groups, with rival heroes and leaders; let us avoid this habit altogether if we can, but if we cannot, at least let us avoid inflicting on the present the obsolete classifications of the past.

(Warnock, in Ryle 1967: 124)

If this was so then, it is all the more so today. So what can we make of Dummett's claim that Evans is still a member of the analytic school "as adopting a certain philosophical style and as appealing to certain writers rather than to certain others?"

IX

Though, as we have seen, it is very difficult to define what this style might be, I believe there is a point to what Dummett says. This was brought home to me at a weekend seminar I attended some months ago, when I had occasion to listen to a lecture concerning the philosophical work of the French philosopher Emanuel Levinas, who has since then passed away. I found the method of presentation of ideas mystifying and the terminology and allusions to the works of other philosophers (Descartes, Hegel, and Rosenzweig) esoteric. There was definitely the feeling of a distinctive mode of philosophizing which was meant for the inner circle of adherents. And the writers appealed to as part of the pantheon would most certainly not have included Wittgenstein, Quine, Davidson, or Dummett. Yet Levinas was an "existentialist" philosopher who was educated in the phenomenological school and was in fact a pupil of Husserl. Could communication have been established between Dummett and Levinas by going back to the point of divergence, when the thought of Frege and Brentano was taken one way by Husserl, and a different way by Russell, Wittgenstein, and Quine? I doubt it. The whole *problématique* that concerned Levinas, in the article referred to by the lecturer, had no connection with anything in which Dummett might have been interested. Only if there had been a common question which concerned them both would Levinas and Dummett have been able to compare their respective answers, collate their reference to common authorities, of the past or the present, and to agree or disagree. Even if, as I understand, both Levinas and Dummett might have found themselves to share, in common, a profound religious commitment, I do not think that their methods of defending their respective views would have had much in common.

X

As we have noted in passing, there are many literary and rhetorical styles of doing analytical philosophy. Wittgenstein's own style, like that of Nietzsche and Schopenhauer, tended to be aphoristic and epigrammatic, when it was not technical and mathematical. The more prosaic style of his lecture notes, as in the *Blue and Brown Books*, clearly do not show him at his best. If the Williams and Montefiore Introduction is correct, he was, unsurprisingly, not a British philosopher at all. Was he ever really an "analytical" philosopher? It would be strange, indeed, if one of the main figures in the analytical pantheon turned out to be a non-analytical philosopher! Russell had a luminous and deceptively clear prose-style when writing most of his philosophical works. Carnap favored a highly technical presentation. Coming closer to our own time, there are the writings which are written in the scientific mode, with many references and footnotes, and detailed bibliographies at the end. And then there are the type of articles written by some contemporary British philosophers who eschew all foot-notes and references to other philosophers. There are those who make much use of logical symbolism, and pursue the aim of "exact" philosophy, and there are those who prefer a conversational style with literary graces and references, and avoid terminology wherever possible. Do all these really have anything in common? Perhaps sometimes there are allusions to snippets from Wittgenstein or Frege, or other modish key-phrases such as "possible worlds," etc. But, if anything, these literary works have at most an attenuated "family resemblance" (note this modish key-phrase!) to each other. So what makes them part of "analytical" or "post-analytical" philosophy?

XI

I want to suggest that the style that now characterizes (post-)analytical writing is so broad that it includes all other schools as well—provided only that they are writing for fellow professionals. Perhaps Ryle was right after all when, in his introduction to *The Revolution in Philosophy*, he pointed out that since the end of the nineteenth century philosophers have become secular and academic, contributing to their own profes-sional journals.

> This new professional practice of submitting problems and arguments to the expert criticism of fellow craftsmen led to a growing concern with questions of philosophic technique and a growing concern for ratiocinative rigour. Eloquence will not silence rival experts and edification is not palatable to colleagues. Nor is the span of an article or a discussion-paper broad enough to

admit of a crusade against, or a crusade on behalf of, any massive "Ism". Philosophers had now to be philosophers' philosophers.

(Ryle 1967: 3–4)

Ryle went on to suggest that "analysis" was a suggested answer to the question asked by practitioners of other academic disciplines regarding what the subject matter of philosophy might be. If Ryle was right about this— and I suspect it is at least part of the story—then Russell's essay on "The Scientific Method in Philosophy" turns out to be one of the most important founding documents of the new analytical school, for it was precisely here that Russell argued for the piecemeal approach to philosophy which could ensure progress.

XII

The later philosophy of Wittgenstein has clearly provided a stimulus for the further development of post-analytical philosophy of a productive scientific sort by its growing concentration on the philosophy of the mind. With the development of the computer and the dawn of the age of artificial intelligence, together with the call for computer translation which encouraged the Chomskyan revolution in linguistics and the growth of cognitive science, at least one arena of inter-disciplinary work has been established where philosophers of all persuasions may offer their contributions. Some of them (such as Evans and Peacocke) have indeed drawn their inspiration from the Frege/analytical tradition. Others have looked for enlightenment elsewhere. And it is not surprising, therefore, that some, such as Hubert L. Dreyfus, have been inspired by the phenomenology of Husserl. There is indeed hope that the gulf between analytical and phenomenological styles of philosophy will be overcome. And so, it is to be hoped, will also the divide between continental and Anglo-American philosophy, together with the still greater divide between the departments of philosophy and the departments of linguistics at some of the continental universities.

BIBLIOGRAPHY

Dummett, Michael (1994) *Origins of Analytical Philosophy*, Cambridge, Mass.: Harvard University Press.
Evans, Gareth (1982) *The Varieties of Reference*, ed. J. McDowell, Oxford: Clarendon Press.
Kripke, S. (1980) *Naming and Necessity*, Oxford: Blackwell.
Quine, W. V. O. (1948) "On What There Is," reprinted in *From a Logical Point of View*, Cambridge, Mass.: Harvard University Press (1953).

——(1951) "Two Dogmas of Empiricism," reprinted in *From a Logical Point of View*, Cambridge, Mass.: Harvard University Press (1953).

——(1960) *Word and Object*, Cambridge, Mass.: MIT Press.

Rorty, Richard (1980) *Philosophy and the Mirror of Nature*, Princeton, N.J.: Princeton University Press.

Russell, Bertrand and Alfred N. Whitehead (1911) *Principia Mathematica*, Cambridge: Cambridge University Press.

——(1917) "The Scientific Method in Philosophy," in *Mysticism and Logic*, London: Allen and Unwin.

Ryle, Gilbert (1949) *The Concept of Mind*, London: Hutchinson.

——(1967) *The Revolution in Philosophy*, A. J. Ayer *et al.* (eds), London: Macmillan.

Strawson, P. F. (1950) "On Referring," *Mind* LIX: 320–44.

Warnock, G. J. (1967) *The Revolution in Philosophy*, A. J. Ayer *et al.* (eds), London: Macmillan.

Williams, B. and Montefiore, A. (1966) *British Analytical Philosophy*, London: Routledge and Kegan Paul.

Wittgenstein, L. (1922) *Tractatus Logico-Philosophicus*, London, Boston and Henley: Routledge and Kegan Paul.

——(1953) *Philosophical Investigations*, New York: Macmillan Publishing Co. Inc.

——(1958) *Blue and Brown Books*, Oxford: Blackwell.

4 Analytic philosophy: rationalism vs. romanticism

Anat Matar

We tend to think in dichotomies, so it seems. In twentieth-century philosophy, the worn-out dichotomy is that between analytic and continental schools of thought. However, this dichotomy seems to me misleading, especially since it blurs a much more important one—that between rationalist and romanticist attitudes towards philosophy. It is only by noting this latter distinction that we may correctly assess the presuppositions underlying the analytic tradition. Analytic philosophers always took the rationalist framework for granted: whether they reacted against Kant or Hegel, Brentano or Mill, their battles were invariably conducted on purely rationalist ground. Indeed, analytic philosophy is often seen (at least by its practitioners) as expressing the rationalist frame of mind with the utmost clarity. But, ironically enough, it seems to present-day romantics[1] that when the distinction between rationalism and romanticism is itself formulated using analytic methods, it exposes some severe—indeed, fatal—problems within analytic philosophy. Moreover, since the latter is taken as paradigmatic to rationalism, these problems point to the futility of the rationalist attitude in general. Hans Sluga's book on Frege (1980) may serve as an example of such a line of reasoning, telling the story of the ascendance and decline of analytic-qua-rationalist philosophy by tracing its evolution until what Sluga takes to be an unavoidable crisis. However, stories are written from particular perspectives, and a story-teller detecting an unavoidable crisis in a philosophical tradition is of necessity located outside it. My own perspective is that of an insider, believing that it is only to romanticist eyes that analytic philosophy, or rationalism in general, seems destined to fail. Although the romantic criticism is sometimes justified, and analytic philosophy may gain some important insights by considering it—this criticism is by no means destructive. On the contrary: it may help analytic philosophers reassess their own perspective and understand it better.

THE ROMANTIC

Let us sketch, with the help of Crane Brinton's essay on romanticism in the *Encyclopedia of Philosophy* (1967), a brief picture of the romanticist attitude, in order to compare it later to the rationalist one. Brinton starts by noting that his endeavor is "the despair of a rigorous semanticist," and by admitting that "the typical romantic will hold that he cannot be typical, for the very concept of 'typical' suggests the work of the pigeonholing intellect he scorns." Nevertheless, it is possible to extract from his essay four interrelated characteristics of romantic philosophers.

- Insisting on the uniqueness of the individual, they resist generalization, concentrating instead on the particular case. Their objection to generalization is closely linked to their disbelief in "abstract ideas" and the "rational organization of man and society," hence they ridicule the "world of reason and common-sense calculation," the "meddling intellect," and "the philistine, the literal-minded ordinary man."
- Romantic philosophers tend to emphasize the role of the ineffable in philosophy. Revolting against "the dullness, the narrowness of rationalism, they strive for *etwas mehr*, for the infinite." Brinton points to Herder and Schopenhauer as exemplifying these two characteristics, but he also classifies Nietzsche with the romantics, despite his use of "romantic" "as a term of reproach." Nietzsche, he writes, "shared all the romantic hatreds for the shopkeeper's world of grubbing common sense and above all had the romantic's desire for *etwas mehr*." On the same basis, emphasizing the primacy of aesthetic experience over the role of reason in gaining understanding, I would also count Heidegger among the romantics, despite his admonition to the contrary.
- Generally speaking, however, it is not easy to associate so called "professional philosophers" with romanticism as a broad cultural movement, since until fairly recently philosophy itself has been largely conceived as the rationalist's exclusive territory. Much more suitable for representing the romantic spirit are, according to Brinton, "the popularizers, the essayists, the preachers." These (e.g. Carlyle, Emerson, Ruskin) stress the "exaltation of intuition, spirit, sensibility, imagination, faith, the unmeasurable, the infinite, the wordless—or at least, the noblest sounding words." In accordance with all the above, "poetry, the novel, and history are the great romantic literary genres," much more than traditional philosophical styles. In accordance with this, a romantic philosopher favors revealing philosophy in art and literature, rather than regarding it as an autonomous discipline.
- The fourth romantic characteristic is resistance to the philosophical obsession with "permanent principles." Romantics emphasize

"continuity, the continuity of life and flow, growth, development; a process . . . always denatured, indeed destroyed, by the dividing analytical mind." They therefore favor the kind of change which is "a product of time, not a product of the planning, present-bound intellect."

Having this rough characterization of romanticism at hand, I shall attempt to give an account of the rationalist stand regarding the above four points. Such an account will, I believe, mark the differences between rationalists and romantics in general, and between analytic philosophers and their (post)modern critics in particular.

My discussion of each point begins at Kant's criticism of Herder on a related issue, thus classifying Kant among the rationalists. As Brinton rightly remarks, Kant always thought of himself as "firmly enlightened," but "a romantic seedling" may nevertheless be detected in his views: Kant's distinction between the phenomenal and the noumenal, between discursive and intuitive certainty, or between the knowable and the unknowable realms, are sometimes viewed as such "seedlings."[2] The issue is one of interpretation, of course; to me it still seems appropriate to regard the noumenal as a way of legitimizing a certain form of our "craving for generality," and the synthetic–a priori as an explicit, dogmatic, and very rationalist adherence to a normative dimension, threatened by naturalistic and other eliminative tendencies.

"CRAVING FOR GENERALITY"

Let us start by deliberating on the conflict between the rationalist emphasis on generalizations and the romantic concentration upon particulars. In his *Ideas on the Philosophy of the History of Mankind*, Herder justifies his tendency towards particulars on the basis that "each human individual has the measure of his happiness within him." Kant, quoting these words, replies: "But as far as the value of their existence itself is concerned—i.e. the reason why they are there in the first place, as distinct from the conditions in which they exist—it is in this alone that a wise intention might be discernible within the whole" (1970: 219). The most *fundamental* question, that is, deserves treatment in a more universalistic spirit.

Romantics, we said, resist the appeal to "abstract ideas," insisting on "the uniqueness of the individual." They combine a particularistic perspective with the contention that philosophical "theories," or "abstractions" entail some version of the distinction between appearances and "what is really true of the world"—a distinction which expresses a futile attempt to touch an unreachable "thing in itself."[3] This attempt is futile either because there is no sense to such a "fantastical" realm, or because it offers itself solely to an aesthetic experience, immanently resisting any formulation in words.[4] The contrast between rationalist and romantic outlooks is thus captured as one between those reaching for a mythical hidden foundation and those insisting that in philosophy nothing is hidden; this latter contrast, in turn, is seen as that between a *scientific* disposition to look for theories and a conception of philosophy as *purely descriptive*. But are these identifications just?

To rationalist eyes they betray a total misunderstanding, since one can—and sometimes ought to—ask *fundamental* questions and answer them in a "theoretical" way which emphasizes unity and ignores differences, without necessarily invoking "hidden structures," let alone inexpressible ones. The romantic mistake might be detected in disregarding a crucial ambiguity in our use of the distinction between "how things are in themselves" and "how they appear to us." As Michael Dummett points out, this distinction

> bifurcates into two quite different, though related, distinctions: that between what is true of the world and what only appears to be, but is not actually, true of it; and that between what may be called an absolute and what may be called a relative form of description.
>
> (Dummett 1993: 389)

While the first distinction involves a transcendent reality showing that common sense is misleading, the second acknowledges the legitimacy and correctness of both particular and general descriptions. "A description in relative terms may, in itself, be perfectly correct," Dummett adds, "but, *in reflective moods*, and to a considerable extent, for practical purposes, we prefer a description in absolute terms." By evading the first distinction, rationalists *avoid* taking the particular as illusory—a step that would compel them to render the general, or absolute, in terms of a hidden, mystical realm of Platonic forms. The second distinction, on the other hand, simply aims at a description of a coherent network of relations between our concepts, clarifying what seems to be confused and leading us to a greater understanding of ourselves.

Believing such a general outlook to be inevitable and important—especially wherever *fundamental* questions are concerned—rationalists regard the romantic declarations that in philosophy "nothing is hidden," since it is "purely descriptive," as over-simplifications, betraying an idleness, acquiescence, and a lack of curiosity. They are, then, *dogmatically* immune from the romantic criticism in this respect. A typical example of such a reaction to romanticist tendencies is Frege's emphasis on the urgency of his inquiry into the essence (or meaning) of Number:

> So free from all difficulty is the concept of positive whole number held to be, that an account of it fit for children can be both scientific and exhaustive; and

that every schoolboy, without any further reflexion or acquaintance with what others have thought, knows all there is to know about it. The first prerequisite for learning anything is thus utterly lacking—I mean, the knowledge that we do not know. The result is that we still rest content with the crudest of views. . . . The concept of number . . . has a finer structure than most of the concepts of the other sciences. . . . My object . . . is to awaken a desire for a stricter enquiry.

(Frege 1953: iii ff.)

Rationalists regard the very distinctions romantics draw between "immediate" and "hidden," "descriptive" and "explanatory" or "theoretical," as doubtful. They do not aim at a scientific theory, or explanation, but at a *description* of, *inter alia*, what appears directly to us, in "human life-with-perceptions"; but since theirs is a *philosophical* description, it must be systematic. They do not strive to reveal a *deep* structure, but rather to formulate an *articulate and clear* one. The result is not a theory involving "hypotheses" about an existing "underlying" layer, but a systematic and perspicuous representation of notions we all share. To use Ramsey's words: "In philosophy we take the propositions we make in science and everyday life, and try to exhibit them in a logical system. . . . Essentially philosophy is a system of definitions, or . . . a system of descriptions of how definitions might be given" (Ramsey 1931: 321). Such an approach is characteristic of rationalists in general and is shared by many prominent analytic philosophers.[5]

EXPRESSING THE INEFFABLE?

It is now the romantics' turn to protest, for the rationalist response seems to evade the radical nature of their criticism. Their complaint did not merely suggest that *alongside* our "absolutist" philosophical outlook there are other forms of knowledge, in which the particular case is indispensable. Rationalists may happily admit that. Rather, the romantic point is exhaustive: not much room is left for *any* meaningful "theoretical" philosophy. Indeed, the very notion of a *philosophical statement* is under attack, since such a statement either aims in vain at expressing the ineffable side of knowledge, the Sublime, or is simply shown to be devoid of any sense.

Rationalists, on the basis of their quest for overall clarity, reject this line of reasoning. It is itself, after all, based on purely philosophical statements, and hence relates to them, practically, as having explanatory power. Truths which are inexpressible cannot have such a power.[6] The ineffable is necessarily useless for philosophical judgments, since "here the only thing considered . . . is that which influences . . . *possible consequences*. Everything necessary for a correct inference is fully expressed . . . *nothing is left to guessing*" (Frege 1972: 113). Such a reply discloses the depth of the abyss separating romantic and rationalist conceptions of the nature of philosophy. In the particular case of analytic philosophers, a debate on metaphilosophical issues consists in a debate on language; this abyss must, then, reflect radically different views of meaning. Let us now examine two of its manifestations.

Family resemblance and vagueness

Kant, in his review of Herder's *Ideas on the Philosophy of the History of Mankind*, criticizes Herder's extensive use of analogy:

> The reviewer must confess that he does not comprehend this line of reasoning from the analogy of nature. . . . What can the philosopher then adduce in support of his assertion except despair of ever finding the answer in any knowledge of nature, and an enforced decision to look for this answer in the fertile field of the poetic imagination? And this will still be metaphysics, indeed highly dogmatic metaphysics, however much our author, in keeping with the current fashion, rejects this implication.
>
> (Kant 1970: 208f.)

The issues of analogy, family resemblance, and vagueness are absorbing, since there has been a radical development in rationalist thought about them. While earlier analytic philosophers like Frege insisted on strict definitions and on the total annihilation of vagueness—it being a defect of natural language—latter-day rationalists are inclined to admit that at least certain vague concepts are indispensable, and that it is sometimes wrong to force a common definition on evolving concepts. This new attitude is in line with the one emphasized above, of avoiding adherence to some external realm of Platonic pure essences:

> But let's not forget that a word hasn't got a meaning given to it, as it were, by a power independent of us, so that there could be a kind of scientific investigation into what the word *really* means. . . . It is wrong to say in philosophy we consider an ideal language as opposed to our ordinary one.
>
> (Wittgenstein 1958b: 28)

Modern rationalists hence introduce a new content into the notions of definition and grammar. Indeed, "sometimes philosophy should clarify and distinguish notions previously vague and confused . . . but in so far as our past meaning was not utterly confused, philosophy will naturally give that, too" (Ramsey 1931: 321). Vague terms are not necessarily "utterly confused," and not every notion is amenable to strict definition. Nonetheless, this concession to romanticism does not amount to a total withdrawal from the rationalist pursuit of a general and explicit surview of the connections within our conceptual scheme.

This new approach is precisely what seems impossible from a romantic standpoint. Frege's insistence on sharply defined terms is not captured as a step in the development of our thinking about the essence of language—but as an *essential* feature of analytic-qua-rationalist philosophy. Frege starts by demanding identity of content in different occurrences of an expression; but

> If the expression is to occur in sentences serving to express the premises or conclusions of inferences, it must have reference. In whatever way our terms have been introduced, something *else* is necessary—the realm of reference must have certain characteristics—if logic can be brought to bear on sentences containing those terms.
>
> (Diamond 1991: 175f.)

The demand for precision and clarity is hence intimately connected with the significance of sameness and repetition; but then it must presuppose some Platonic realm for logic to capture—a realm *external* to it, determining identity. Moreover, the futility of sentences expressing "thoughts proper" entails that of a distinction among vague terms—separating those which are confused and are in need of clarification from other vague terms which are in order as they are. "Family resemblance" is not an innocent and interesting feature of language; it shows the crucial role the *unique* and *different* play in language, manifesting that no external realm may tell right from wrong in our use of language. A romantic reading of Wittgenstein's remarks on rule-following stresses, in this vain, the openness inherent to language, and the inferiority of definitions and theories compared to practice, to actual cases.[7]

However, there is another reading—a rationalist reading—of the same Wittgensteinian point. In their interpretation of the relevant passages in *Philosophical Investigations*, Baker and Hacker (1985) emphasize primarily the conceptual connections between such indispensable concepts as "regularity," "sameness," "rule," and, of course, "language." In order that we may be able to judge a unique application as incorrect, i.e. that openness not turn into anarchy, we must legitimize at least the gist of Frege's demand for sameness of content in different contexts of utterance. The idea of sameness is grammatically linked to those of language and meaning. Indeed, as Frege himself declares, "in applying the same symbol to different but similar things, we actually no longer symbolize the individual thing, but rather what [the similars] have in common: the concept" (Frege 1972: 84). But the question remains: how can we tell that our decision upon "sameness" is correct? What may serve as our criteria? Are we necessarily led to admit an external, let alone Platonic, realm?

Lack of criteria

One way of presenting the controversy over the question whether philosophical statements "can be said" is by noting that whereas rationalists treat these statements as capable of conveying some kind of truth, romantics deny this capability. Empirical statements, say the latter, are capable of being true or false in virtue of some external criteria. There is something (viz. the actual length of a table) that makes the statement "this table is one meter long" true (or false). When we come to assess the capability of philosophical statements to express truth, the following dilemma must hold, then: either there is an external realm making philosophical statements true, or there isn't. If there is, we must ask what this realm consists in, how we come to know anything about it, and what makes our statements about it true or false. Since rationalist philosophers are no naturalists, the realm determining the truth or falsehood of their statements cannot be the empirical one, and hence, insisting upon the idea that philosophical statements have content, they are led, allegedly, to admitting a mystical transcendent realm. On the other hand, refusal to accept such a bogus realm of reference leads directly to the second horn—the claim that *there is no* external realm making philosophical statements true. Logic is applied to language "internally." In this case, the whole notion of content—or truth—seems unfit for philosophical statements. What these statements aim at expressing is, as it were, *nothing*. It is now left for us to decide how to interpret this "nothing," i.e. whether philosophical statements are nonsense *tout court*, or alternatively "important nonsense," trying to express the inexpressible, the ineffable.

Analytic philosophers are naturally prone to suffer most from the above criticism, being so explicit about what makes a statement meaningful or meaningless. It is mainly for this reason that the downfall of analytic philosophy is so strongly identified with the demise of rationalist philosophy in general. Present-day romantics believe to have shown, on the above basis, the inadequacy of a chain of rationalist icons: conceptual notation, analysis, category clashes, the demand for sharpness, grammatical elucidation, and so on.[8]

What can rationalists reply to this attack on the significance of their own statements? What is their way out of the above dilemma? Two ways, amounting perhaps to a single one, come to mind. Choosing the first horn, rationalists may indeed acknowledge an "external realm" which makes philosophical statements true: our use of language. Common use, i.e. daily linguistic practice, serves as the missing criterion. It is a systematic representation of this realm that the philosopher may be seeking.

The second way out of the dilemma is that of denying it altogether, by appealing to a somewhat Kuhnian conception of science, according to which even empirical statements are not true or false in virtue of some independent reality external to them. When science is no longer captured as *representing* anything outside it, a distinction drawn between "legitimate" empirical statements and "illegitimate" conceptual ones, on the basis of the existence (or non-existence) of *external* criteria, evaporates. In other words, when the representationalist picture is forsaken *in toto*, it is no use attacking conceptual or grammatical discourse in particular for not expressing truth external to it. It might be argued that such a new picture is immanently anti-rationalist, being intrinsically holistic, and thus leaving no room for a privileged class of "philosophical" statements. This conclusion is too hasty, though, since the distinction required for this privileged class is not the classical epistemological one, assuming a layer of "raw" data and an organizing scheme. Rather, it is a linguistic distinction between grammatical (conceptual, criteriological) and empirical discourses—a distinction without which language would be impossible.[9] What characterizes philosophical or logical discourse in particular is that *it does not even pretend to represent anything external to itself*, for "the logical principle of truth is consistency of the understanding *with its own laws*" (Kant 1885: 10). As Kant already observed, despite the fact that logic is—

> not a general Art of Discovery, nor an Organon of Truth; . . . not an Algebra, by help of which hidden truths may by discovered . . . it is useful and indispensable as a criticism of knowledge; or for passing judgment on the common, as well as the speculative reason, not for the purpose of teaching it, but in order to make it correct and consistent with itself.
>
> (Kant 1885: 10)

This may sound like another version of the "internal" picture endorsed by romantics—the one that makes philosophical statements meaningless—for the distance between logic and language seems to have vanished. Indeed, in order to avoid a naturalistic, empirical reading of the first rationalist reply suggested, we should omit this distance there too—thus manifesting how close these two replies are. The above reasoning shows, however, that an internal discourse does not amount to nonsense. Insisting upon the grammatical–empirical distinction, we see how it is possible for Kant—and for other rationalists—to endorse a more positive conception of philosophy. It is important to note that wherever a systematic account is involved, a certain distance from ordinary use is inevitable. The way is hence paved to a critical approach, such as the one mentioned by Kant, above. It is also the basis of Ramsey's criticism of "Wittgenstein's view that all our everyday propositions are completely in order and that it is impossible to think illogically" (1931: 325).

Many analytic philosophers, especially in Britain, adopted, in practice, such solutions to the romantic dilemma. The works of Ramsey, Austin, Strawson, Ryle (earlier and later), Dummett, and Hacker, among others, and despite the huge differences among themselves, presuppose at least the gist of these solutions. For all these philosophers, philosophy is, literally speaking, not nonsense; it is not only meaningful, but is capable of expressing truth, despite the lack of external criteria.[10]

AUTONOMY OF PHILOSOPHY

We have seen earlier, in our discussion of "family resemblance," that Kant objects to relinquishing a philosophical treatment to "poetic imagination." Indeed, one of his more poignant remarks concerning Herder's book is the bad effect his "poetic eloquence" had on the essence of his writings, substituting allegories for truths, and using metaphors and poetic images which conceal the body of thought. In an ironic style, Kant declares (1970: 215) that he does not intend to consider whether "instead of neighbourly excursions from the region of philosophic language into that of poetic language, the limits and provinces of both are not at times completely disregarded" by Herder.

R. G. Collingwood, a paradigmatic rationalist, mentions the genuine resemblance between philosophy and poetry and explains its sources (1933: 212f.). He continues by citing the most crucial difference. As opposed to the poet, he says:

> The prose writer's art is an art that must conceal itself, and produce not a jewel that is looked at for its own beauty but a crystal in whose depths the thought can be seen without distortion or confusion; and the philosophical writer in especial follows the trade not of a jeweller but of a lens-grinder.
>
> (Collingwood 1933: 214)

These words manifest a further theme endorsed by rationalists and often attacked by romantics: the uniqueness of philosophy. According to rationalists, philosophy should not be conceived in continuity with other disciplines: neither with literature, literary criticism, and the social sciences, nor with natural science. Philosophical discourse is—as we have seen in the previous section—captured as the only one dealing with thought in itself. It is hence a kind in itself, and should be kept pure and autonomous.

Anti-psychologism, a famous mark of analytic philosophy, is a facet of this attitude. Indeed, its pronounced aim is to wave off as irrelevant anything which is not "objective," and to keep itself within the boundaries of "what is subject to laws, what can be conceived and judged, what is expressible in words" (Frege 1950: 35). This is how intuition is ruled out as instrumental to philosophical explanation, since "what is purely intuitable is not communicable." Any other form of ineffable knowledge is dismissed in the same vein.

However, it should be recognized that objectivity is not the sole motivation behind anti-psychologism. Frege's determination "always to separate sharply the psychological from the logical, the subjective from the objective" has usually been read as identifying psychologism's fault with its subjectivity. Such an identification ignores the fact that Frege excludes from philosophical discourse supposedly-objective science as well. For Frege, as for every rationalist philosopher, philosophy—or what is commonly called "logic" by him[11]—is *purely conceptual.*

> All sciences have truth as their goal; but logic is also concerned with it in a quite different way from this. . . . To discover truths is the task of all sciences; it falls to logic to discern the laws of truth . . . [O]ne can very well speak of laws of thought, too.
>
> (Frege 1967: 17)

Psychologism ensues when "the expression 'law of thought' is interpreted by analogy with 'law of nature' "—hence its fault is its scientism no less than its subjectivism. Anti-scientism is, indeed, a dogma—not of empiricism in particular, but of any rationalistic philosophy. This dogma is clearly stated by Wittgenstein in the *Tractatus*: "The word 'philosophy' must mean something which stands above or below, but not beside the natural sciences" (4.111) And despite the differences between early and later Wittgenstein, it recurs in the *Philosophical Investigations*:

> If the formation of concepts can be explained by facts of nature, should we not be interested, not in grammar, but rather in that in nature which is the basis of grammar? . . . But our interest does not fall back upon these possible causes of the formation of concepts; we are not doing natural science; nor yet natural history, since we can also invent fictitious natural history for our purposes.
>
> (Wittgenstein 1958a: 230)

Wittgenstein's anti-scientism stems from his rationalist idea of philosophy as a conceptual investigation of a realm of possibilities; and this idea must take for granted a dichotomy between normative and descriptive discourses. Against this background—the autonomy dogma—Quine's mistake in looking for explanations or justifications for the concept of analyticity is evident. In order to explain such normative notions as definition, necessity, or meaning, we cannot but use notions of the same breed, otherwise we leap into an erroneous scientism. Hence any such explanation should inevitably result in some kind of circularity. From a rationalist perspective naturalism is not an acceptable starting point at all; neither is any attempt at reducing philosophical (or conceptual) jargon to *any other* vocabulary.

Note that "normative" here does not suggest involving moral and political considerations. Indeed, another consequence of the rationalist insistence on the autonomy of philosophy is the tenet that philosophy is hierarchical. The presumption that it is necessary (let alone possible) to investigate metaphysics, logic, or grammar without paying any attention to ethical, or political, factors, is adopted by many rationalist philosophers—in particular those of the analytic school. This fact seems astonishing, especially when we reflect on the deep and authentic political involvement of some of them. What is the source of this presumption, then? The answer lies in identifying the autonomous character of philosophy with its being *foundational*—not in the epistemological sense, but in the sense that a methodological, metaphilosophical clarification of the aims, limits, and provinces of philosophy must be distinct from, and prior to, any specific philosophical inquiry, including a moral and political one. This assumption recurs throughout rationalistic literature. When it comes to analytic philosophers, it takes the form of a defense of analysis, clarification, or theory of meaning, as prior to any particular move even in philosophy itself. It is also one of the reasons for dismissing the term "theory" for this foundational inquiry, for "what precedes every formulation of a theory cannot itself be a theory" (Schlick 1932/3: 88).

PERMANENT DEVELOPMENT?

The notion of foundation leads us directly to the last point on our list separating romantics from rationalists—the question of change and development. The idea of foundation carries with it almost inevitably a picture of stable, motionless principles—a picture totally opposed to the romantic desire to see everything changing, developing, and growing naturally.

However, the genuine difference between romantics and rationalists regarding this issue is much harder to delineate than the former ones. The historical dimension was, indeed, introduced into philosophy by the romantic Herder, but was later taken up by many Enlightenment thinkers, and remained an important ingredient in the philosophies of subsequent rationalists. In his famous essay "An Answer to the Question: 'What is Enlightenment?'," Kant exhibits very clearly an awareness of the importance of change:

> One age cannot enter into an alliance on oath to put the next age in a position where it would be impossible for it to extend and correct its knowledge . . . or to make any progress whatsoever in enlightenment. This would be a crime against human nature, whose original destiny lies precisely in such progress.
>
> (Kant 1970: 57)

From Hegel onwards, the historical component was absorbed by many rationalist philosophers. Analytic philosophers in general do not emphasize it, but are much more aware of it than it is usually acknowledged. Frege, for example, accompanies his justification of a conceptual notation with a genuine dialectical insight:

> It is impossible, someone might say, to advance science with a conceptual nota-
> tion, for the invention of the latter already presupposes the completion of the
> former. . . . Research into the laws of nature employs physical instruments; but
> these can be produced only by means of an advanced technology, which again
> is based on knowledge of the laws of nature. The [apparently vicious] circle is
> resolved in each case in the same way: an advance in physics results in an
> advance in technology, and this makes possible the construction of new instru-
> ments by means of which physics is again advanced. The application [of this
> example] to our case is obvious.
>
> (Frege 1972: 89)

This view is echoed in Dummett's following words:

> Linguistic habits alter, and our responsibility is to present habits rather than to
> ancient custom. But, in our constant endeavour to make explicit to ourselves the
> workings of our language, we seek also to sharpen meaning, to propose firmer
> connections or even new ones. We know that, with the passage of time, some of
> these connections will loosen, and new ones will begin to form: we do not seek
> to legislate for all future time, only to introduce enough rigidity at critical points
> to serve our present purposes in evaluating, revising, or simply conferring clarity
> on what we say.
>
> (Dummett 1973: 626)

It seems, then, that the romantic accusation that rationalists ignore history and change is unjust. However, there is still a crucial difference in the procedures for introducing change into philosophical accounts. Rationalists claim that in dismissing the universal, absolutist, or theoretical dimension, romantics do not leave room for theory to *criticize practice*, and hence are liable to comply with *every change* occurring *arbitrarily* throughout history. Renouncing any stable criterion and emphasizing the evolving, "family resemblance" essence of language and thought, they must yield, without qualification, to general custom, "for general custom has a power of justifying what is done, just as fashion can give the cachet of beauty to the most detestable mode" (Frege 1952: 141). Thus from a rationalist perspective it seems that change, for romantics, is never *progress*; for it is only natural and gradual, complying with reality, instead of being the result of "meddling" critical thinking. Such a criticism is hinted, implicitly, in the above quotes from Frege and Dummett, but it is obvious and explicit in Kant's criticism of Herder's historicist tendencies. Kant does not criti-cize Herder's idea of progress—the historical dimension he introduces into the philosophical sphere—but rather its *source*, its *motivating power*. As Kant sees it, for Herder, "all cultural advances are simply the further transmission and casual exploitation of an original tradition; and it is this, rather than its own efforts, that man has to thank for all this progress towards wisdom" (Kant 1970: 218). For Kant, on the other hand, *reason* provides us with a goal, thus enabling us to conceive of a deliberate and not merely arbitrary change:

> The philosopher would say that the destiny of the human race as a whole is *incessant process*, and that its fulfillment is merely an idea—but in every respect a very useful idea—of the goal to which . . . we have to direct our endeavours.
>
> (Kant 1970: 220)

Romantics regard their acceptance of practice as the only sane behavior, free from superfluous and meaningless doubts. As a result, they sometimes portray the rationalist, insisting on some abstract "goal" or "rigid points," as unhappy, since "the world does not meet conditions he lays down" (Diamond 1991: 10). However, romantics may also deny the rationalist accusation, establishing certain contingent factors as directives, overlooking their temporary and culture-dependent nature. These factors direct our judgments and help us to criticize ongoing practices; but eventually, they are vulnerable themselves, open to future criticism.[12]

How far removed is this reaction from the rationalist conception stated above? The differences are almost invisible. We started with symmetrical accusations: romantics blaming rationalists for neglecting the historical dimension; and rationalists accusing romantics of quietist conceptions of change. It turns out, however, that the distance between the two might be smaller than they imagined.

CONCLUSION

The principal moral we learn from examining the fourth point of divergence is that we should be very careful with the slogans used by either rationalist or romantic. As a good rationalist, I believe that this moral can be generalized.

There is certainly a genuine difference between the rationalist and the romantic points of departure. What I find absorbing, though, is that sometimes both sides advance similar accusations against each other—and these accusations only read differently according to their targets. Romantics are accused of being mystical since they allegedly accommodate obscure notions as the ineffable in their views. Rationalists, on the other hand, are blamed for precisely the same sin, since they "must adhere" to enigmatic Platonic realms. While rationalists accuse romantics of striving for a suspect *etwas mehr*, they themselves appeal to what may be seen as a dubious "universal dimension." And lately, rationalists and romantics have accused each other of misconstruing the concept of language, on the basis of an absurd account of the role of rules as determining meaning.

The rationalist/romantic debate is thus easily led to empty rhetoric. Diamond's portrayal of the rationalist as "unhappy" may serve as an example: what could be gained by such a portrayal of the rationalist character? The only merit seems to be the gross distortion accompanying it:

> That ethical spirit is shown in [Hawthorne's] story in relation to the doing of evil. The story is a kind of ethics by geometrical construction: extend the lines [of this unhappy character] far enough and it destroys life, goodness, beauty.
> (Diamond 1991: 10)

There is a perfectly good reason for refusing to use such slogans as if they were convincing arguments, and for adopting a more constructive approach. Rationalists may do more by way of admitting into their philosophies a constantly changing essence of essence, by reconsidering the degree of autonomy philosophy is entitled to, and by developing a convincing account of the criteria for their own statements.

Romantics, on the other hand, should admit the inevitability of systematic and explicit philosophical pictures. This conclusion is inescapable. Romantic objections to rationalist ways of thinking are well-argued and are far from being merely intuitive; they are based on implicit metaphilosophical assumptions whose status is questionable. The criteria on which they base their arguments are themselves neither empirical nor innocently commonsensical. In short, the romantic position is no less dogmatic than that adopted by rationalists. This is already acknowledged by Kant, in his criticism of Herder's view: "This will still be metaphysics, indeed highly dogmatic metaphysics, however much our author, in keeping with the current fashion, rejects this implication" (Kant 1970: 209). However, there is no symmetry here. Indeed, precisely like the rationalist stand, the romantic position "contains positive theories of the nature, method, and limitations of philosophical thought"; but unlike its rival, "[I]t is both inconsistent, or false to its own professed principles, and—intentionally or unintentionally—dishonest, because applying to others a form of criticism which in its own case it will not admit" (Collingwood 1933: 140f.)[13]

In a new philosophical vision rationalists should reconsider the degree of autonomy philosophy is entitled to, and find more satisfying ways of embodying contingency, change, and vagueness into their metaphysics and theories of meaning. However, these romantic themes must find their home *within* a rationalist framework, admitting the meaningfulness of philosophy and the inevitability of generality. I can think of no better candidate for developing such a vision than analytic philosophy.

NOTES

1 As I see it, we are, at present, carried by strong romanticist currents in philosophy. Cavell, of course, comes immediately to mind, but I am thinking also of Rorty, McDowell, and Diamond—just to name a few.
2 For an exposition of typical rationalist criticisms of these distinctions see Hylton (1993: 457).
3 "As philosophers . . . we make those discriminations to reflect beliefs that some of the appearances are and others are not caused in certain ways by things not themselves appearing directly to us; the appearances are merely manifestations of something *else.*" This is linked to "the idea that in our thought about the real we mean something totally independent of what has actually to be watched out for in human life-with-perceptions" (Diamond 1991:68).
4 Both these options are acknowledged by Cavell (1988: 53) as romantic; he labels them "animism" and "sublimity," respectively.
5 Even philosophers disagreeing about almost anything else. Compare, e.g., the emphasis on unity and system in philosophy in Russell (1912: 154) and in Strawson (1992: 9).
6 "What cannot be said, cannot be whistled either." Or, less cryptically, if philosophy is nonsense, we must "take seriously that it is nonsense, and not pretend . . . that it is important nonsense!" (Ramsey, 1931: 321)
7 See, e.g., Cavell 1990, ch. 2, "The Argument of the Ordinary."
8 Cora Diamond's interpretations of Frege and Wittgenstein and her persistent criticism of present-day analytic philosophers are based on such arguments. See Diamond 1991, esp. chs 1–6. A connection of the ineffability issue with the way romantics conceive of the absolute point of view mentioned in the previous section is made in 1991: 58.
9 See Wittgenstein 1969: §§ 5, 82, and 88 (and indeed, *passim*), for a defense of this view of language.
10 This is true even of the author of the *Tractatus*, who informed us in its Preface that "the *truth* of the thoughts communicated here seems to me unassailable and definitive" (original emphasis!). Compare with Austin (1962: 1): "The only merit I should like to claim for [what I say here] is that of being true."
11 As it is by Kant, Hegel, and other rationalists.
12 I take this to be the basic idea of Rorty (1989), for example.
13 Collingwood's criticism is directed against any kind of sceptical position.

BIBLIOGRAPHY

Austin, J. L. (1962) *How to do Things with Words*, Oxford: Oxford University Press.
Ayer, A. J. (ed.) (1959) *Logical Positivism*, New York: Free Press.
Baker, G. P. and Hacker, P. M. S. (1985) *Wittgenstein: Rules, Grammar and Necessity*, Oxford: Basil Blackwell.
Brinton, C. (1967) "Romanticism," in P. Edwards (ed.) *The Encyclopedia of Philosophy*, vol. 7, New York: Macmillan.
Cavell, S. (1988) *In Quest of the Ordinary*, Chicago: The University of Chicago Press.
——(1990) *Conditions Handsome and Unhandsome*, Chicago: The University of Chicago Press.

Collingwood, R. G. (1933) *An Essay on Philosophical Method*, reprinted 1995, Bristol: Thoemes Press.

Diamond, C. (1991) *The Realistic Spirit*, Cambridge, Mass.: MIT Press.

Dummett, M. (1973) *Frege: Philosophy of Language*, London: Duckworth.

——(1993) *The Seas of Language*, Oxford: Oxford University Press.

Frege, G. (1950) *The Foundations of Arithmetic*, trans. J. L. Austin, second revised edition, 1953, Oxford: Basil Blackwell.

——(1952) *Translations from the Philosophical Writings of Gottlob Frege*, P. Geach and M. Black (eds.), third edition 1980, Oxford: Basil Blackwell.

——(1967) "The Thought: A Logical Inquiry," trans. by A. M. and Marcelle Quinton, in P. Strawson (ed.) *Philosophical Logic*, Oxford: Oxford University Press.

——(1972) *Conceptual Notation and Related Articles*, trans. T. W. Bynum, Oxford: The Clarendon Press.

Hylton, P. (1993) "Hegel and Analytic Philosophy," in F. C. Beiser (ed.), *The Cambridge Companion to Hegel*, Cambridge: Cambridge University Press.

Kant, I. (1885) *Kant's Introduction to Logic*, trans. by T. K. Abbott, London: Longmans, Green and Co.

——(1970) *Political Writings*, ed. by H. Reiss, trans. by H. B. Nisbet, second enlarged edition 1991, Cambridge: Cambridge University Press.

Ramsey, F. (1931) *The Foundations of Mathematics*, London: Routledge and Kegan Paul. Quotes taken from excerpts reprinted in Ayer (1959).

Rorty, R. (1989) *Contingency, Irony, and Solidarity*, Cambridge: Cambridge University Press

Russell, B. (1912) *The Problems of Philosophy*, Oxford: Oxford University Press.

Schlick, M. (1932/3) "Positivism and Realism," *Erkenntnis* III. Reprinted in A. J. Ayer (1959).

Sluga, H. (1980) *Gottlob Frege*, London: Routledge and Kegan Paul.

Strawson, P. F. (1992) *Analysis and Metaphysics*, Oxford: Oxford University Press.

Wittgenstein, L. (1922) *Tractatus Logico-Philosophicus*, trans. C. K. Ogden, London: Routledge and Kegan Paul.

——(1958a) *Philosophical Investigations*, trans. G. E. M. Anscombe, Oxford: Basil Blackwell.

——(1958b) *The Blue and Brown Books*, Oxford: Basil Blackwell.

——(1969) *On Certainty*, Oxford: Basil Blackwell.

5 The subject, normative structure, and externalism

Mark Sacks

INTRODUCTION

For a variety of reasons, although the analytic tradition was responsible for the introduction to philosophy of a field called "philosophy of mind," the topic of the experiencing subject has not been of primary concern within that tradition. Activity in contemporary philosophy of mind has tended to flow, sometimes circle, studiously around the issues of consciousness and the nature of the experiencing subject. Recently these central issues have begun to be addressed, but only in the confinement of cognitive science or philosophy of mind narrowly conceived. The result is an approach to consciousness as a scientific phenomenon. However valuable it may be, that approach is distinct from, and still leaves untouched, the question of the philosophical conception of the individual experiencing subject, and in particular the question of whether the individual subject has rational autonomy.

But of course not engaging in such questions about the subject is not tantamount to not having a position on the matter. And certainly the analytic tradition would have looked very different had it studiously avoided any default assignment of views regarding the philosophical conception of the self. The neglect is only of sustained explicit preoccupation with the issue. Implicitly, and in consequence of that neglect, the analytic tradition has worked, by and large, with what we might call an *egological* conception of the subject. An egological conception, as I shall be using the term, is meant to be distinct, by definition, from what is referred to as "Cartesian individualism." Unlike Cartesian individualism, which is specifically a semantic thesis, the egological conception is concerned rather with the nature of the subject that employs semantics. The egological conception regards the subject as one whose core normative structures are autonomous, independent of contextual features—and so, primarily, attributes rational autonomy to the subject. (The relation between

Cartesian individualism and the egological conception will emerge in due course.)

It seems to me not only descriptively true, but also unsurprising—given the general realist and logicist orientation of the early analytic tradition—that this egological view of the subject became the default within analytic philosophy. The egological self is conducive to a realist or objectivist view. This is so in two senses. First, such a view of the self is conducive to a sharp dichotomy between the self and everything other than it, which is then set apart as an independent object domain. Second, and this is the primary concern here, such a view of the self is conducive to the expectation of convergence on what counts as rational thought, what counts as a good reason, or as an end worth pursuing. The link between an egological self and there being objective rules for the direction of the mind is obviously not one of entailment (pluralist individualism is a possibility). Nor is it the case that not adhering to such an egological conception of the self would imply the absence of any such convergence (cf. reference to Hegel below). The link is simply that to accept this conception is to render the subject independent of environmental features, such that the individual can be stripped of all contextual coloration to reveal what it essentially is: and where that is possible, there is room for the hope that so stripped, all normal human minds would be seen to be functioning identically, to be running the same programs, so to speak.

Now it will readily be recognized that such a self is at the heart of Enlightenment philosophy. And it is of particular relevance that the Kantian Copernican revolution relies heavily on just this assumption of an egological subject. On the Kantian view, at the level of the fundamental faculties of the mind, any individual, just insofar as they are human and are functioning properly, will function in the same way. This conception could be preserved as a more or less unattended default within the analytic tradition, in part precisely because that tradition was not deeply involved in questioning the basis of Kant's transcendental idealism, or much concerned (in part because of this lack of involvement) with a reflexive turn to the nature of the self. Even when that tradition did turn to the problems with Cartesian individualism, the issue of the egological subject was not so salient as to lead to general recognition of the impact of those developments upon it.

It is of course precisely insofar as it retained the default assignment of the egological self that the analytic tradition can, in this respect, look naive or undeveloped from the perspective of other traditions that did not shy away from discussion of the subject in the same way. This is perhaps particularly so from the perspective of that tradition in German philosophy concerned with the critique of reason, for which the question of the appropriate philosophical conception of the subject was, since Kant, consistently at the centre of philosophical concern. The fact that between these two traditions there is today room to detect convergence on matters relating to the topic of the subject is therefore all the more interesting.

THE REJECTION OF THE EGOLOGICAL CONCEPTION OF THE SUBJECT OUTSIDE THE ANALYTIC TRADITION

While it will be helpful to narrow the comparison here to developments within German philosophy, it is important to note that the threat to the egological subject has come to be widely accepted across the "continental" tradition. Thus Honneth, for example, can talk of the conclusion being widely accepted in philosophy today that the classical notion of subjectivity is destroyed (Honneth 1995b: 262). These "self-evident" conclusions (ibid.), the result of the "century-long" reflexive attention to the subject, are not at all *self-evident* within, and are in marked contrast to, dominant working assumptions made within the analytic tradition, in which the egological subject survived more or less intact by escaping critical attention. In consequence, from the point of view of the analytic tradition, some of the questions into which other philosophy has been led after "the fall of the subject," have seemed rather alien. One of the things I wish to bring out is that in fact the agenda facing the analytic tradition today is not that different. But it will be helpful first to say a bit more about the course that the critique of the egological self took, at least within the German tradition.[1]

Perhaps the most prominent alternative to the traditional egological model of the self derives from Hegel, and can be thought of as *dialogical* or sociological. The self emerges, as does the reflexive consciousness of its identity, only within a social context of intersubjective recognition, the encounter and interaction with others structures the identity of the subject and guides self-consciousness of it. This Hegelian dialogical model runs counter to the Enlightenment ideals for which the egological model was so well suited. After all, on the Enlightenment view it is the naked individual, stripped of all features and standards that depend on socio-cultural context, who can stand back and assess the order of things, and can do so as any other free-thinking agent would. On the dialogical model there *is* no such naked, core individual such that they could step back from all socio-cultural structuring as a free thinker. That conception turns out, ironically, to have been an unnoticed fictional construct at the heart of the Enlightenment project; stripping away all cultural and historical layers does not reveal any naked kernel of the subject, or at best reveals only a brute animal subjectivity that does not have the content with which to engage in any substantive thought or judgment. There is no stepping critically outside all inherited "horizons of significance," to use Taylor's phrase (Taylor 1989). But while this much is true, it is not the case that this Hegelian model also counts against the objectivity of reason and convergence of rational conduct that was encouraged by the egological model. The reason for this is that the objective structure of thought, on at least one reading of Hegel, has simply been displaced: there is still a blue-print that imposes constraints on rational thinking, a program for the direction of the mind, only now rather than being individualistic and context-independent, it is rooted in the socio-historical space across which individuals range.

The full-blown Hegelian alternative to the egological conception of the subject does, however, appear to involve some pretty heavy metaphysical machinery—at least as heavy as the baggage carried by the egological model—with some significant anti-Enlightenment consequences. Put crassly, whereas on the egological model the individual is fully empowered to structure society, on this dialogical model society (in some form) is fully empowered to structure the individual.

Both models came to be widely rejected in contemporary non-analytic philosophy, and by certain elements related to the Frankfurt School in particular. This reaction was in part motivated on purely philosophical grounds which should be familiar to those working within the analytic tradition. Such metaphysical hypotheses, be it the egological or the Hegelian sociological model, no longer seemed sustainable. The rejection of what are essentially uncritical dogmas, and the philosophical systems constructed upon them, betokens a shift from a metaphysical to a post-metaphysical orientation. Such rejection of metaphysics is of course not new, dating back at least to Kant. It is simply more pervasive and rigorous: pointing out for example that Kant himself, for all his rejection of metaphysics, still held on to what was basically a dogmatically accepted metaphysical model of a given egological self as the fixed basis of his purportedly universal critique of reason.[2] But the pervasiveness of this contemporary rejection of metaphysical models that transcend the empirical has to do with the fact that the reaction against metaphysics, at least in Germany, was in part also political.

The Hegelian appeal to a fixed metaphysical system that is not up for revision, and which structures the individual and dictates which socio-historical moves are possible, and to which the individual must be true, is as we have seen a clear reversal of the Enlightenment priority of the free-thinking individual over society. The politically conservative nature of any such Hegelian appeal to metaphysical systems that govern social progress and the possibilities of individual human action is clear, and perhaps particularly in Germany in this century the dangers of it all the more palpable. But the egological model does not escape the charge of being politically conservative. The appeal to a fixed subject, which is not up for revision and to which one must be true, can be seen to serve as a politically and intellectually conservative measure, imposing limits on human freedom. Reason, logic, fundamental taxonomies, possibly values, all then become structural features from which we cannot depart without deviating from the normal, which now means—from our true nature. Such a self can be seen as a fiction, the endorsement of which is a fake philosophical, but real psychological and political imposition on the human freedom to revise and modify the world without any a priori limitations. Seen in this light, the Enlightenment individual paradigmatically conceived of on the egological model, is not more free, but is simply the internalization of the authority to which adherence and subservience are required. By being brought within the subject, the authority of those structures is set up as inalienable. Moreover, the conservative constraint involved might be thought to be all the more pernicious for not being as obvious in the case of the egological model as it is in the Hegelian dialogical or sociological model.

It is in part in consequence of this too that there has been a move among philosophers—and again here Critical Theorists fall in with a much broader trend—to distance themselves from any residual metaphysical impositions. On the one hand they have rejected anything like the Kantian egological subject, the transcendental structure of the mind that is the source of synthetic apriori judgments. On the other hand, they have equally rejected the Hegelian metaphysical system of intersubjective constitution. Instead, philosophers like Habermas, Honneth, and others have turned to a (maximally) metaphysically purged form of Hegel's dialogical model of the subject. This naturalized Hegelian account has led these philosophers to a renewed interest in the American pragmatists, and in particular in George Herbert Mead. The idea is that the dialogical model, the account of subjectivity in terms of intersubjective recognition, allows for the right understanding of the intimate connections and interdependencies that obtain between individuals, and between the individual and his or her society, in a way that the simple egological model, with its stark opposition between the isolated thinking subject and the juxtaposed objective world does not. But at the same time, by avoiding the Hegelian metaphysical system, it avoids the subjugation of human freedom to an imposed metaphysical order. The promise is that we will have an adequate understanding of the nature of the subject and its place within a normative structure, without restricting the scope of possible variation by the imposition of a Hegelian grid (from without) or an Enlightenment one (from within).

The details of this dialogical account of subjectivity need not concern us at this point.[3] The relevant point is that with the rejection of the Enlightenment egological conception of the (substantial) subject, and the avoidance of any Hegelian metaphysical interpretation of the dialogical alternative conception, we are left with a self whose nature and normative constraints are entirely context-dependent, where the context itself—given a consistently post-metaphysical orientation—lacks any non-contingent normative structure. There is now no normative structure, whether within or without the subject, that transcends local intersubjective set-ups. The horizons of normativity are exhaustively set by contingent socio-historical processes. In particular there is no rational subject that outstrips and can neutrally evaluate all local norm-sustaining practices. To assume that there is some such subject is in fact to impose normative canons on all localities on the unsustainable pretence that those canons of rationality themselves have something more than a local legitimacy. It is on this sort of view that the Enlightenment emerges as a form of cultural imperialism.

The pluralism, this indexing of *all* normative structures to local contexts, that results from the naturalized intersubjective model of the subject, can be captured by talking in terms of rigid normative structure. On the Enlightenment egological conception of the self, normative structures of rationality, say, could be taken as rigid, i.e. as being the same across all possible local contexts. On the alternative under consideration, normative structures lose that rigidity. Normative structures become fragile; nested within a local context and, as we might put it, they do not travel well. We are left with the intersubjectivity *and* the contingency of all normative structure.

Now many of those who endorse the naturalized intersubjective model of the subject are inclined to welcome these consequences as being suitably non-conservative. After all, there is now no imposition of normative order on the individual, either from within or from without, that cannot in due course (whether of space or of time) be overturned. But there is reason to think that this liberal optimism is misplaced. This is something to which we can return later. For the moment we can leave the story here.

THE DEMISE OF THE EGOLOGICAL CONCEPTION WITHIN THE ANALYTIC TRADITION

We can leave the story there, in order to point out that in fact within the analytic tradition too there have been developments—not the same ones as in the context we have been canvassing—that suffice to put pressure on the received egological model, leading to the same consequences just outlined. But, importantly, (a) within the analytic tradition these pressures have not been clearly perceived to bear on the egological model, and that model is still the dominant default, and (b) it is difficult to see how the analytic tradition can survive intact the consequences that follow from the demise of the egological subject.

Regarding (a): that the pressures in question were not perceived is, in some cases, simply because they were such as *could* be held at arm's length.[4] But there are also pressures on that conception which, although not yet fully acknowledged as such, cannot be kept at arm's length. These are pressures that arise from within developments that are so central to the analytic tradition that they are ultimately inescapable.

One source of pressure on the analytic tradition's implicit conception of the subject emerged relatively early in the history of the tradition, with Wittgenstein's comments about meaning in the *Philosophical Investigations*.[5] Plato's theory of forms decisively freed the individual from being essentially indexed to, grounded in, any one socio-historial context. The individual, by having independent access to language and thought, was cut loose from social context, in much the same way, structurally, that centuries later natural rights were a reaction to, and an emancipation of the individual from, a system of defining social (feudal) roles and entitlements. In both, the human being was assured standing as a significant individual, with normative structures, quite apart from any grounding in social context. Wittgenstein, in rejecting the Augustinian individualist picture, is in effect threatening that independence of the individual from society. Despite the mythical conception taken up by the Enlightenment, throwing off social constraints and still remaining a language user would in fact be impossible.

Now the impact of the Wittgensteinian considerations on the conception of the egological subject has not been lost on those concerned with this issue outside the analytic tradition.[6] Within the analytic tradition it has not been so readily recognized. This is all the more noteworthy given that, thanks to Kripke (1982), the problem has not been left as something internal to Wittgenstein's thought, and of interest only to so-called "Wittgensteinians." Given Kripke's forceful generalization of the impetus towards the intersubjective paradigm, and the wide exposure that his treatment has had, it comes to seem peculiar that the pressure thus put on the egological conception of the subject could pass by relatively unnoticed in the analytic tradition.

Part of the explanation for this might be simply that the issue of the egological subject is indeed implicit in, rather than an item on, the agenda of the analytic tradition. But it might also be thought that the appeal to intersubjectivity is required only for the working of semantic and linguistic rules, and that this leaves in place the notion of an underlying rational individual, whose very capacity for rational processing and reason explain the capacity for, and so have priority over, any effective social interaction or intersubjective recognition.[7] But this thought, which would serve to salvage the egological conception, does not in fact survive the full impact of Kripke's treatment (or of Wittgenstein's). If Kripke is right, then all rule following, on pain of paradox, requires the constraints of a social context. But clearly, being rational, just is abiding by certain very fundamental rules. So we cannot hold on to the idea of the naked individual—taken privately—as already being a rational thinker.

It might be thought that the individual taken on their own already has a *propensity* to engage in rational thought, even though this can be actualised only upon socialization, and that this explains why individuals of the same species equipped with the same propensities end up converging on canons of rationality subsequent to socialization.[8] And in this sense we could then still hold on to there being an underlying egological core. But this would in fact still miss the full force of the intersubjective impetus both Kripke and Wittgenstein identify. It might be right to say that the individual brings with them a certain propensity to behave in certain ways. But whether that propensity counts as a propensity to be rational, or indeed to follow any system of rules, will depend entirely on what—in part dependent on the propensities to behave that others have—comes to count as rational subsequent to socialization. Once socialized, we can say of a given person by way of retrospective judgment that before socialization they had the propensity to be rational. But *without* socialization that propensity that the individual might have to behave in certain ways cannot count as a propensity to be *rational*, since there is as yet nothing that counts as being rational, or as being any other kind of normative (rule-governed) structure. Talk of the naked individual already having a prototypical normative structure is simply confused about the extent of the connection between normative and social structure. Fully understood, the insights about rule-following leave no room to talk of *any* normative structure at the level below the social.

Propensities to behave are, *as such*, no more propensities to be rational than they are to be irrational. Norms of rationality, and hence the rational subject, are established only at the level of, and so are indexed to, the conventions and practices of the community. And they might therefore in principle be different in different social or socio-biological set-ups (which does not mean, of course, that in any of these set-ups what counts as rationality is a matter of choice). The propensities of what we might regard as an abberant individual would count as rational in a community of sufficiently like-minded others. All of this can be seen to lead from the heart of the analytic tradition to the emphasis on intersubjectivity and the fundamental contingency of our core normative commitments, which is just what we have seen to result generally from the displacement of the egological subject in favour of a naturalized (or post-metaphysical) inter-subjective paradigm.

This pressure on the traditional egological conception of the subject is not confined to this development within analytical philosophy. Equally, if not more significantly, that conception comes under pressure from the debate about semantic externalism.

We can confine attention here to two early moves in the debate which are still central. Putnam (1975) first introduced the case for externalism, arguing that in the case of certain terms, particularly *de re* terms, or those that have an indexical element, what goes on in the head under-determines meaning, so that it is not possible to think of the subject as having command of their language and thought independently of the contribution of the world. Moreover, the external contribution is not just of the object world, but also of other speakers, in the form of experts to whom the relatively uninitiated will defer in the use of certain terms. All this already threatens the isolation and self-sufficiency of the Cartesian subject to be at home alone with their thoughts. But the case is restricted: it applies only to certain thoughts—those with a *de re* element—and even then there remains a well-defined mental content, narrow content, which the subject taken in isolation can retain (it is just that that narrow content is not sufficient to determine meaning). The idea is that there is a fixed internal content, that remains the same in any two individuals that are in identical physical and behavioural states. One way of putting this is to say that there is still a notion of narrow content that supervenes on the indi-vidual person's physiological states. While this might not be enough to secure meaning, it is enough to secure an individualist conception of mental content.

Now this is precisely what does not survive the extension of the exter-nalist case pushed forward by Burge, McDowell and others. On this view it is not only the structure of *de re* attitudes that introduces the appeal to social and physical factors beyond the individual. As long as that was all, we can carry on thinking in terms of a two-component model of proposi-tional content: narrow belief content, which is individualistic, and a second component, the *res*, which in varying might vary the propositional content without varying the narrow content that is applied to it. But on Burge's view even oblique contexts, which provide the contents of psycho-logical states, and which are purported to be *narrow* content, essentially require appeal beyond the individual. In effect this means that externalism applies all the way in: there is no longer any preserved domain of narrow content, over which the subject is an authority. Psychological states and mental content do not supervene on physiological states of the individual.

This means that the subject, taken on their own—without appeal being made to the social or physical context in which they are embedded— cannot authoritatively detect changes in his or her belief contents, and so cannot be said strictly speaking to know what his or her beliefs are.

These consequences have not gone unnoticed in the literature on externalism. Davidson (1987), for example, is concerned with them—in a way that he says externalists by and large have not been (1987: 50)—and attempts to resolve the seeming conflict between externalism of the sort advocated by Burge and others and the strong Cartesian intuition that we can know, with first-person authority, what we are thinking.[9] In a subsequent paper, partly responding to Davidson, Burge (1988) is explicitly concerned to show how externalism regarding individuation of thoughts is compatible with allowing that the subject has direct, immediate knowledge of his or her own thoughts. Burge identifies a sense in which I can be said to know what I believe: Whatever the content of p is, once it is non-individualistically fixed for the first-order belief, it is available for use in a reflexive second-order judgment—if I have a belief that p, I can also state that I know what it is that I believe, namely: p. But that does not in any way deny that I might have only the foggiest grasp of the content of p. I know what I think in the sense of being able to specify the content, but not necessarily in the sense of being able to comprehend it. This technical sense in which I can know what I believe has nothing to do with comprehending, or being able to explicate authoritatively what one believes. Burge concedes this readily:

> One clearly does not have first-person authority about whether one of one's thoughts is to be explicated or individuated in such and such a way. Nor is there any apparent reason to assume that, in general, one must be able to explicate one's thoughts correctly in order to know that one is thinking them.
>
> . . . One should not assimilate "knowing what one's thoughts are" in the sense of basic self-knowledge to "knowing what one's thoughts are" in the sense of being able to explicate them correctly—being able to delineate their constitutive relations to other thoughts.
>
> (Burge 1988: 78)

Thus the sense in which Burge establishes the compatibility between externalism and knowing what one's beliefs are serves only to emphasize the extent to which the sense relevant to the egological conception of the subject has indeed been undermined. If externalism is right, I may have (and know that I have) a belief that p, but that does not mean that I am in a position to identify or explicate comprehendingly the content of my belief, or to track whether and what changes there have been in its content. This leads back to the relevant sense in which it remains the case that, given externalism, I cannot strictly speaking claim to know what my beliefs are. And to the extent that the individual does not know what his or her thoughts are, whether they have changed, or consequently how they might stand in relation to other thoughts that that individual or some other has, it seems pretty clear that he or she cannot count as engaging in autonomous rational deliberation.

It might be thought that regardless of the particular thought contents processed (which may be conceded to be externalistically determined) there are nevertheless formal structures of thought processing which any individual will abide by. But the relevant distinction between formal processing structures on the one hand, and the thoughts processed on the other, is difficult to maintain. There is good reason to consider that the individuation of inferential patterns between thoughts is as much a matter of concept application as is the individuation of the thoughts processed: Both reduce to the application of rules. And if the concepts governing the use of terms like "arthritis" (or for that matter "gold") are externalistically determined, then it is difficult to see why exactly the same would not hold with regard to the concepts governing the use of terms like "modus ponens." The distinction between a privileged class of formal concepts and other merely material concepts is difficult to uphold, at any rate in such a way as would make the former resistant to exter- nalism and the latter not. And if it is said in response that by "formal structures of thought processing" nothing other than a biological mecha- nism is meant, then we are back with the problem of how normativity can arise from that alone, for all the reasons that the rule-following con- siderations bring out.

Now it is true that semantic externalism is not universally accepted— although for some time now there has been a clear sense that internalists are fighting with their backs to the wall.[10] But taken together, the two developments—semantic externalism and the rule-following considera- tions—are significant enough to pose a severe challenge to the received egological model and any associated default ideals. What emerges is a view whereby the individual subject, considered in isolation from social and physical context, cannot properly know what his or her beliefs or desires are, is no authority on their content or relation to other thoughts, cannot tell whether or not they have changed, cannot use language or more gener- ally follow rules and (in consequence of all this) cannot engage in rational deliberation, or indeed be said to be rational in any sense. Far from being an independent agent that applied itself to the social fabric, the subject would seem instead to be a construct in the wider social and physical context. We have here, in other words, a striking push towards a non- egological view of the subject of just the sort that we saw arising in non-analytic philosophy as a reaction against the egological conception.

Now something of this shift was clearly stated by Burge himself in his early work on the subject (Burge 1982: 116–18). He recognized that it is a consequence of his externalism that traditional psychology is mistaken in taking the individual subject as the unit of explanation; instead, he says, the unit of psychological explanation should be the wider social context, with the individual being approached only indirectly, via that context. Burge (1982) explicitly mentions Hegel, as the philosopher whose conception of the individual in relation to society perhaps posed the right non-individualist model. In the present context, this should precisely begin to echo the parallel move towards a naturalized Hegelian view in contemporary non-analytic German philosophy.

Nevertheless, within analytical philosophy the debate has not really developed on the basis of a clear identification that what is at issue is the egological conception of the subject; the threat to the egological conception of the subject has not been placed squarely at the focal point of the discussion.[11] Perhaps because of the dominant concern in this tradition with linguistic meaning rather than with the thinking subject, the case against "Cartesian individualism" has been taken as a semantic thesis that can somehow be taken on board alongside the default assumption of the egological subject, as if the former did not undermine the latter.[12] But it is not only that the pressure on the egological conception of the subject has not been fully appreciated it is also not appreciated that the conception that has come under pressure, and is only illegitimately retained, in fact serves to sustain a presupposition of the analytic tradition itself. This remains to be seen more fully.

It is worth noting first that within the analytic tradition, the demise of Cartesian individualism was not greeted as a threat, at least not to anything essential to the analytic tradition. For one thing, the move towards semantic externalism was a move away from the importance of interiority, and is broadly supportive of the latent behaviourism that has proved attractive to philosophy of mind in the analytic tradition. Second, there is a sense that semantic externalism shows Cartesian scepticism to be simply incoherent. It turns out that, understood aright, there is no way that the individual could be as it is, and yet not be embedded in a social and physical context—so raising the question is not a genuine philosophical (as opposed to psychological) possibility. This might be thought of as a de-transcendentalized Kantianism. Third, insofar as externalism is right, meaning and value are not things that are confined to the individual, leaving him or her in confrontation with an alien and possibly unresponsive external reality. If externalism pertaining to meaning can be extended to value and reason, then the individual, his or her society, and the external world, are together a unitary domain within which meaning, value, and reason obtain. There is then no room for worry about the applicability of our values or reasons to the external world—all are elements internal to the domain of meaning. This latter move is of course that attempted recently by John McDowell, and can be seen to be a natural extension of his earlier externalism about meaning.[13] McDowell, who defends a form of what he calls "naturalized platonism," in fact explicitly connects this move with a (naturalized) Hegelianism. He ends with an appeal (however loose) to Gadamer. Here the two lines we have traced, which have so far been kept apart, come together.

CONSEQUENCES OF DECENTERING THE SUBJECT

We have seen that in both a non-analytic context, and in the analytic tradition, there has been convergence on a naturalized Hegelianism, and that in both—albeit for different reasons—there has been some enthusiasm over this reorientation. It is now time to say why it is that in both cases this enthusiasm seems to be misplaced. This will also bring out the reasons for thinking that in the analytic tradition the reorientation with regard to the egological subject threatens one of the presuppositions of the tradition.

The move that we have been considering, away from an egological conception of the subject, towards a naturalized Hegelianism, can and in some quarters has been taken to have a liberating nature. There is no longer any non-empirical imposition on the individual: neither from without (reason at large) nor from within (the Enlightenment reasoning self). This liberation from the imposition of all authority was seen to invite radical pluralism, an absence of any distinctive human essence which could not be overcome. These consequences can readily be regarded as an affirmation of freedom and liberalism. It is this optimism that seems to be misplaced, for reasons that are familiar from the discussion of communitarianism. If the self, or at least the substantial self, is an intersubjective construct all the way down, the individual cannot transcend his or her socio-historical setting. There remains no trace of the Enlightenment self that can step out of any community in which it is embedded, taking its critical capacities with it, to make an independent judgment about that community. The norms of critical judgment would themselves have been left behind. There are, as we might put it, only inherited horizons of significance, indexed to contexts from which they were inherited. Now if this is the situation, then far from being liberal, the picture threatens to be extremely conservative. With reason itself a product of a particular tradition, there is ultimately only the authority of tradition. We have the inversion of the Enlightenment order: rather than tradition being subservient to reason, reason is subservient to tradition. This can be captured by saying, simply, that there are then only traditional societies. The liberation from fake metaphysical structures might be appropriate, but the post-metaphysical fall-out should not be thought to deliver any liberation. We end up with the unchallenged authority of tradition, with subservience of the individual to the contingent order that wholly defines him or her.

Now the same considerations that reveal this conservative predicament into which the naturalized intersubjective paradigm leads, also reveal the unacceptable impasse into which the demise of the egological subject leads the analytic tradition. Perhaps the egological subject, while being the default, is not *itself* a presupposition of the analytic tradition, so that there is no immediate reason why the demise of this conception of the subject should be of concern. But there is one conception at least that seems crucial to the analytic tradition. This is the conception of reason and rationality as having validity that is not merely historically or culturally grounded. This is in fact an extension of the anti-psychologistic approach of this tradition. Canons of rationality and reason should not be the product of any one tradition; which of course is not to deny that perhaps rationality and reason are such that they are always at work only within a tradition. That is, perhaps—trivially—one cannot think outside any tradition, but that is not to say that one's thought structures and contents are entirely a product of, and valid only within the horizons set by, a given tradition. The analytic tradition can readily accept the former, but seems at odds with the latter. Yet it is precisely the latter that threatens after the demise of the egological subject, which is brought about from within the analytic tradition by various forms of externalism.

Insofar as the individual taken on his or her own cannot be said to follow rules at all, and all normative structure essentially first arises at the intersubjective level, canons of rationality and reason would again seem to be normative structures grounded in the mode of social organization. And given naturalism about the possibilities of social organization, that would seem to suggest further that rationality and reason inherited the contingency of the social structures that grounded them, such that different social structures might bring with them, and impose on their constituent individuals, different normative structures. Rationality and reason then become fragile, entirely internal to a tradition, localized to one way of going on, in just the sense that undermines their presupposed universality. That canons of rational thought—like logic—are not locally or historically indexed is recognizable as a central tenet of the analytic tradition; one that was, it would appear, sustained by the default egological conception of the subject.

Here it is appropriate to consider the move that McDowell has recently attempted.[14] He accepts that a human being cannot single-handedly come to possess the normative structures in question. He sees canons of rationality as essentially linked to a culture, a tradition, an educational process, as those structures within which alone the human being is inducted into the space of reasons, meaning. Our question then arises, how can any such view avoid that space of reasons into which the individual is socialized, being locally indexed, such that alternatives are available in other traditions with their different acculturation processes. One answer would be to think that there is a necessary structure or ordering of the world, so that different societies were in fact nothing other than different stages of one and the same necessary development of anything that can count as a society. However that Hegelian metaphysical view is not the one that McDowell takes—any more than anyone else in the analytic tradition. McDowell's view is rather that what rules out such indexing of rationality and reason to a culture such that alternatives to them are possible in other cultures, is that those normative canons are not in fact constituted by the culture to which they are indexed. Traditions and cultures do not constitute rationality and the space of reasons, they simply function as the enabling conditions for the development of what is in fact second nature to the human animal. Given that acculturation serves to bring out what is already latent in this animal, and simply could not develop on its own, in isolation, it follows that there will be that latent structure common to all human cultures.

But this way of establishing the objectivity of reason and rationality in the face of the rejection of egological models of such normative structures seems to be a case of McDowell wanting both to reject the cake and eat it. After all, we are here once again attributing to the human being, qua individual animal, a well-defined determinate normative structure, which becomes explicit only in some cultural context or another. This appears to commit McDowell to holding both that the space of reasons gets going only within the intersubjective structure, and that the individual is already constrained by it prior to any socialization. Quite apart from the internal tensions within McDowell—who would now appear both to deny that normativity is individualistic and to assert that it is[15]—this would be to revert to the very position that has been seen to come under pressure from within the analytic tradition.

Now it could be said that McDowell is not committed to anything as strong as that the individual human animal, pre-socialized, is already the bearer of a *normative structure*. That would perhaps introduce the tension just alluded to into his position. But possibly all he needs to say is that it is a biological fact about normal humans, as they happen to be, that upon socialization a second nature will develop such that however different the social contexts and educational practices within which the process of maturation takes place might be, there will always be a common rational core. All normal humans will then have the latent compulsion to a core rationality, in the way that all normal human beings have, say, two kidneys. Now some such appeal to hypothetical biological structure might be our best bet. But, barring metaphysical appeals to an underlying form, whether Platonic or Aristotelian, any such biological facts—even if they could in principle sustain some such core rationality—are themselves merely contingent (not all humans have two kidneys), and there would be no objective sense in which any deviations or changes in them could be said to be deviations from the *correct* form, except relative to some socially endorsed norm. There are two distinct problems here. Regarding the latter, the idea was for biological form to underpin the social nesting of normativity, not the other way around. Second, apart from that, any core rationality underpinned by such biological facts is a merely contingent feature that cannot be said to inhere rigidly in human second nature. McDowell seems to be conflating his naturalized Platonism, which is all he can justify, with Aristotle's immanent Platonism, which is what he wants, but which brings in individualist metaphysical assumptions that he cannot defend. Confined to the former, the space of reasons, which encompasses the individual and his or her world, cannot be universalized as the space applicable to any and all acculturated human beings.[16]

It might turn out that some biological grounding, on top of intersubjective constraints, is as much as we could hope for. But it should be clear from what has been said that given the contingency of biological form in the absence of non-empirical underpinnings, such grounding falls significantly short of the conception of rationality as an ahistorically given normative structure.

CONCLUSION

It would seem that without the egological model that has come under pressure (and without an alternative Hegelian or other metaphysical conception of the social or biological sphere), reason and rationality cannot function in the way that the basic orientation of the analytic tradition would have them function. For present purposes, this shows the sense in which the demise of the egological subject should perhaps not be seen as just another twist in the tale of the analytic tradition, but rather as a threat to one of the presuppositions of that tradition.

Probably more important than this, however, is the more general problem identified: that across traditions, the disintegration of the egological model in favour of naturalistically conceived intersubjective models poses a challenge to our Enlightenment trust in rationality and reason.

NOTES

1 For a partisan introduction to this history of the theory of the subject, see Henrich (1992). See also Dews (1995), for a detailed survey of relevant moves in the debate between Tugendhat, Habermas, and Henrich.

2 This criticism of Kant is not new, and dates back to Kant's near contemporaries.

3 It is perhaps worth noting that the obvious problem—what might be called the boot-strapping problem—has not gone undiscussed in the literature. The question is how intersubjective recognition can ground the identity and self-consciousness of the subject. After all it would seem that in order to have such intersubjective recognition there must already be an active subject, minimally aware of itself in order to recognize as relevant those other items in the world that are like it in central respects (intersubjective recognition is to be set up between subjects, not between a subject and his object-world), but that seems to require as a presupposition of the process precisely what is supposed to be the product of that process. (For an entry point to that discussion, see Dews 1995). There is no need to enter into that discussion here, beyond pointing out that we can in fact avoid the problem by upholding a distinction between a rudimentary subject, comprising only a brute responsive capacity, which precedes intersubjective construction, and the substantial subject which results only from it.

4 Some of the relevant discussions might have come from philosophers who, like Rorty, could be regarded as no longer directly relevant to the mainstream of the analytic tradition; others, for example discussions of the self in communitarian literature, while clearly within the mainstream, could be, and largely have been, left in the confinement of political philosophy.

5 I have argued elsewhere (Sacks 1990), on different grounds, that it is possible to regard the analytic tradition as having run its course in the route from the early to the later Wittgenstein. In both cases, the idea is that there has been a delayed recognition, in the analytic tradition, of the impact on it of Wittgenstein's later work.

6 See, e.g., Wellmer (1991), in particular pp. 64–71; McCarthy (1992: 252); or Habermas (1987 vol. 2: 16–22). Indeed it is largely this strand of Wittgenstein's later thought that explains why he has been so readily taken up as central to traditions other than the analytical, thereby constituting a natural bridge between traditions.

7 It might also be thought that the most basic preferences, values, and patterns of perceptual salience remain egological, and that it is only the articulation of them that requires resort to intersubjective processes. In fact it can be argued that even these cannot in fact be coherently attributed to the egological subject. This extension of the case is more thoroughly Wittgensteinian, and is not brought out quite so strongly in Kripke's treatment. For present purposes we should perhaps leave aside this further strand of the case against the egological conception.

8 Something of this sort seems to be held by McDowell (1994), to which we will return below.

9 Davidson's own diagnosis of where the externalists go wrong, and his suggested way back to first-person authority, seem not to do justice to the force of the case from externalism to denial of individual authority; in particular, that it does not necessarily rely on the myth that thoughts require mysterious mental objects (1987: 63–4). Davidson's own proposal also seems to rest on the curiously blatant non-sequitur that "unless there is a presumption that the speaker knows what she means, i.e. is getting her own language right, there would be nothing for an interpreter to interpret" (1987: 64). That would seem simply to beg the question against externalism, and the non-individualist model. There might be a normative structure to interpret, but not an individualistically defined one: all that we need for interpretation is that there is something that the speaker means, not that the speaker knows what this is. It is perhaps therefore not suprising that Burge does not simply endorse Davidson's proposal.

10 Even Fodor, while still insisting that a Language of Thought is necessary, and that without individualism there is no explanation of the causal efficacy of propositional contents, has been forced to make significant concessions to externalism. Concessions such as that although there is narrow content, we cannot say what it is (Fodor 1987: ch. 2); Fodor (1995) goes still further.

11 Which is continuous with Davidson's (1987) identification of a lack of concern within the externalist literature with the consequences for first-person authority about our beliefs (cf. 1987: 50, and 46).

12 This is one point at which the lack of contact between traditions promoted a blindness to the implications of developments within one of them. Had philosophers in the analytic tradition been reading contemporary German philosophy, they would not so easily have remained unappreciative of the fact that their rejection of Cartesian individualism promised to have more than merely semantic implications.

13 McDowell (1994). Some have seen tension between McDowell's earlier endorsement of semantic externalism, and his appeal to the space of reasons expanding to include the natural world; see Wright (1996).

14 Although this cannot be developed here, the problems with this move are also relevant to Habermas' attempt to sustain the universality of reason in a post-metaphysical setting.

15 The *denial* explains our being able to have knowledge of the world; the *assertion* explains why rationality and the space of reasons are not fragile nestings within one tradition or another.

16 It could be universalized as the space of reasons applicable to any and all acculturated human beings, *as human beings were at a certain historical/biological location*, but that is precisely to see rationality as historically indexed, and does not sustain the kind of rigid normative structure or rationality that is germane to the analytic tradition.

BIBLIOGRAPHY

Burge, T. (1979) "Individualism and the Mental," in P. A. French, T. Vehling, and H. Wettstein (eds) *Midwest Studies in Philosophy, Vol. IV: Studies in Metaphysics*, Minneapolis: University of Minnesota.

——(1982) "Other Bodies," in A. Woodfield (ed.) *Thought and Object*, Oxford: Clarendon Press.

——(1986) "Cartesian Error and Perception," in Pettit and McDowell (1986).

——(1988) "Individualism and Self-Knowledge," *Journal of Philosophy* 85, 11: 649–63. Page references are to the reprint in Cassam (1994).

——(1989) "Individuation and Causation in Psychology," *Pacific Philosophical Quarterly* 70, 4: 303–22.

Cassam, Q. (ed.) (1994) *Self-Knowledge*, Oxford: Oxford University Press.

Davidson, D. (1987) "Knowing One's Own Mind," *The Proceedings and Addresses of the American Philosophical Association*, 60: 441–58. Page references are to the reprint in Cassam (1994).

Dews, P. (1995) "Intersubjectivity and the Status of the Subject: Jürgen Habermas and Dieter Henrich in Debate," in his *The Limits of Disenchantment: Essays on Contemporary European Philosophy*, Cambridge: Polity Press.

Fodor, J. A. (1987) *Psychosemantics*, Cambridge, Mass.: MIT Press.

——(1995) *The Elm and the Expert*, Cambridge, Mass.: MIT Press.

Habermas, J. (1987) *The Theory of Communicative Action*, trans. Thomas McCarthy, Vols 1 and 2, Boston: Beacon Press.

——(1992) *Postmetaphysical Thinking*, Cambridge, UK: Polity Press.

Henrich, D. (1992) "The Origins of the Theory of the Subject," in Honneth *et al.* (1992).

Honneth, A. (1995a) *The Struggle for Recognition—The Moral Grammmar of Social Conflicts*, Cambridge, UK: Polity Press.

——(1995b) "Decentered Autonomy: The Subject after the Fall," in his *The Fragmented World of the Social: Essays in Social and Political Philosophy*, Albany: State University of New York Press, pp. 261–71.

Honneth, A., McCarthy, T., Offe, C., and Wellmer, A. (eds) (1992) *Philosophical Interventions in the Unfinished Project of Enlightenment*, Cambridge, Mass.: MIT Press.

Kripke, S. (1982) *Wittgenstein on Rules and Private Language*, Oxford: Blackwell.

McCarthy, T. (1992) "Philosophy and Social Practice: Avoiding the Ethnocentric Predicament," in Honneth *et al.* (1992).

McDowell, J. (1986) "Singular Thought and the Extent of Inner Space," in Pettit and McDowell (1986).

——(1994) *Mind and World*, Cambridge, Mass.: Harvard University Press.

Mead, G. H. (1934) *Mind, Self and Society*, ed. with an Introduction by Charles W. Morris, Chicago: University of Chicago Press.

Peacocke, C. (1992) *A Study of Concepts*, Cambridge, Mass.: MIT Press.

Pettit, P. and McDowell, J. (eds) (1986) *Subject, Thought and Context*, Oxford: Clarendon Press.

Quine, W. V. (1969) *Ontological Relativity and Other Essays*, New York: Columbia University Press.

Sacks, M. (1990) "Through a Glass Darkly: Vagueness in the Metaphysics of the Analytic Tradition," in D. Bell and N. Cooper (eds) *The Analytic Tradition*, Oxford: Blackwell.

——(1997) "Transcendental Constraints and Transcendental Features," *International Journal of Philosophical Studies*, 5.

Taylor, C. (1989) *Sources of the Self*, Cambridge: Cambridge University Press.

Tugendhat, E. (1986) *Self-Consciousness and Self-Determination*, trans. Paul Stern, Cambridge, Mass.: MIT Press.

Walzer, M. (1983) *Spheres of Justice: A Defence of Pluralism and Equality*, Oxford: Blackwell.

Wellmer, A. (1991) "The Dialectic of Modernism and Postmodernism: The Critique of Reason since Adorno," in his *The Persistence of Modernity, Essays on Aesthetics, Ethics, and Postmodernism*, trans. D. Midgley, Cambridge, Mass: MIT Press pp. 36–94.

Wittgenstein, L. (1952) *Philosophical Investigations*, Oxford: Blackwell.

Wright, C. (1996) "Human Nature?," *European Journal of Philosophy*, 4: 235–54.

6   Empiricism without positivism

John Skorupski

EMPIRICISM AFTER KANT

In the period between the death of Kant and the end of "analytic philosophy" (understood as a movement, an organic development of ideas)[1] the two leading versions of empiricism were that of Mill and that of the logical positivists. They had in common the empiricist doctrine that no informative assertion about the world is a priori. They agreed in rejecting Kantian epistemology, in particular the claim that if knowledge is possible there are synthetic a priori propositions. But in their view of the status of logic and mathematics they differed sharply. Mill took logic and mathematics to consist of informative universal truths and denied that they are a priori; the positivists held logic and mathematics to be a priori and denied that they contained informative truths. That is the best-known difference between them. However the doctrine that logic and mathematics are exact and a priori because they are analytic was not peculiar to the logical positivists. It was a cornerstone of the analytic tradition as a whole, in all its phases (empiricist and other), and so the low esteem in which the Millian doctrine was held in that tradition's heyday is easily understood.

To put the two empiricist traditions on a level footing, some brief remarks about Mill's case for his doctrine will be necessary. However the eventual aim of this discussion is to raise another, though not unconnected, issue. If the analyticity of logic and mathematics is a cornerstone of analytic philosophy in general—from its beginnings—the famous dichotomy of linguistic stipulations and factual sentences is a cornerstone of Viennese analytic philosophy in particular. It partitions the sentences of a language into those that express *rules* of that language, decisions about how to use words, and those which obtain a factual content within the framework provided by such linguistic stipulations or rules. I want to suggest, contrary to this Viennese tradition, that empiricism cannot coherently accept the dichotomy as exhaustive. It must also make room for sentences which express normative propositions—propositions which are not factual but *are*, nevertheless, judgable contents.

Such a conclusion leads, in one way, closer to Kant: it recognizes that epistemology needs two cross-cutting distinctions. As Kant held that there must be informative a priori propositions, so this view holds that there must be informative normative propositions. But it is not Kantian. It remains empiricist in that it retains the doctrine that no factual proposition can be guaranteed as irrefutable by evidence. Moreover it can be Millian in including mathematics and logic itself within the factual domain—that is an issue for further study. One might describe the resulting empiricism as neo-Millian and quasi-Kantian. Since it must reject what is perhaps the deepest positivist doctrine—that all cognitive content is factual—one might also describe it as empiricism without positivism.

MILL'S EMPIRICISM ABOUT LOGIC

First, then, some remarks about Mill's radical empiricism. In the *System of Logic* he distinguishes between "verbal" and "real" propositions, and between "merely apparent" and "real" inferences. The assertion of a purely verbal proposition conveys no information about the world; likewise, a merely apparent inference moves to no new assertion—its conclusion has been literally asserted in its premises. There can be no philosophical puzzle about how a verbal assertion or a merely apparent inference is justified, for there is nothing there to justify. In contrast, all real assertions and inferences must in the end be grounded on data and methods of induction.

If we take the notion of a verbal inference as basic, a verbal proposition will be the corresponding conditional of a verbal inference. An inference is verbal if and only if the set of propositions constituting the conclusion is a subset of the set of propositions constituting the premises. This approach fits with Mill's understanding of the logical connectives. He assumes that to assert a conjunction, *A and B*, is simply to assert *A* and to assert *B*. He defines *A or B* as *If not A, then B, and if not B, then A*; and he takes *If A then B* to mean *The proposition B is a legitimate inference from the proposition A*. Effectively the logic of propositions is for him the logic of negation and inferability.

About generality Mill is not very clear. But it fits with much of what he says to treat a universal proposition like "All fathers are male parents" as a license to infer—"Any proposition of the form '*x* is a parent' is legitimately inferable from the corresponding proposition of the form '*x* is a father.' " Then, for example, "The proposition 'Tom is a parent' is legitimately inferable from the proposition 'Tom is a father' " is a substitution-instance of this schematic form, and we can stipulate that a universal proposition is verbal if and only if all its substitution instances are verbal.[2]

Given Mill's definitions of the connectives, certain deductive inferences, for example from a conjunction to one of its conjuncts, will be verbal. But, Mill holds, the laws of contradiction and excluded middle are real—and therefore a posteriori—propositions. He takes it that *not A* is equivalent in meaning to *It is false that A*; if we further assume the equivalence in meaning of *A* and *It is true that A*, the principle of contradiction becomes the principle of exclusion—as he puts it, "the same proposition cannot at the same time be false and true." "I cannot look upon this," he says, "as a merely verbal proposition. I consider it to be . . . one of our first and most familiar generalizations from experience" (*System of Logic*, CW VII: 277).

He makes analogous remarks about excluded middle, which turns—on these definitions—into the principle of bivalence, "Either it is true that P or it is false that P." So the principles of bivalence and exclusion are on his view real—"instructive"—propositions.

To this semantic analysis Mill adds an epistemological argument. If logic did not contain real inferences, all deductive reasoning would be a *petitio principii*, a begging of the question—it could produce no new knowledge. If valid deductions are all verbal then the conclusion of any valid deduction is asserted in the premises. To know that the premises are true is to know that each proposition asserted in the premises is true. Hence, since the conclusion is one of those propositions, it is to know the truth of the conclusion. Yet deduction clearly produces new knowledge. So logic must contain real inferences:

> Logicians have persisted in representing the syllogism as a process of inference or proof; though none of them has cleared up the difficulty which arises from the inconsistency between that assertion, and the principle, that if there be anything in the conclusion which was not already in the premises, the argument is vicious.
>
> (*System of Logic*, CW VII: 185)

It is one of Mill's strengths that he recognises the full depth of the difficulty and does not brush it aside. "It is impossible," as he quite rightly says,

> to attach any serious scientific value to such a mere salvo, as the distinction drawn between being involved by *implication* in the premises and being directly asserted in them.
>
> (CW VII: 185)

THE A PRIORI

Mill's demonstration that logic contains real propositions and inferences did not suit twentieth-century Viennese empiricists—but it need not shock an intuitionist or a Kantian. If a Kantian accepted it he would simply be facing up to the full consequence of the idea which underlies Kant's narrower conception of analyticity, that of containment of the concept of the predicate in the concept of the subject. In accepting it as the full consequence he would, it is true, have to revise his view of logic as a purely formal discipline, in the sense intended by Kant. That is, he would have to concede that logic itself is synthetic a priori; specifically, that bivalence and exclusion are not purely formal principles but themselves rest on some form of intuition. Within the Kantian framework that in turn would force the conclusion that logical truths, like other synthetic a priori truths, are restricted to the domain of phenomena; but this is hardly a disaster for critical philosophy as such.[3]

Thinkers of an intuitionist-cum-Kantian stamp were the opposition Mill had to deal with. He thinks their arguments for the doctrine that there are real propositions whose truth is "perceived *a priori*" are "reducible to two" (*System of Logic*, CW VII: 231, 233).

The first simply points to the fact that we consider ourselves to have grounds for accepting certain propositions in mathematics and logic not on the basis of inductions from experience but by appeal to "intuition"; that is to say, to our experiential imagination—to what we can imagine as experienceable. Since we are prepared to endorse them on this basis alone it seems that they must rest on a priori properties of pure imagination, and not on facts discovered by actual experience. Mill replies that while we are indeed often justified in basing geometrical claims, for example, on intuition, the fact that that *is* a justifiable mode of reasoning in geometry is a posteriori. The reliability of experiential imagination as a guide to real possibilities is itself an empirical question.

The second argument Mill considers turns on the Kantian point that "Experience tells us, indeed, what is, but not that it must necessarily be so, and not otherwise." Since we do have insight into the necessary truth of certain propositions, that insight cannot be based on experience and must be a priori. But Mill rejects any metaphysical distinction between necessary and contingent truth; like Quine he thinks the highest kind of necessity is natural necessity. The only other sense of "necessary truth" he is prepared to concede is "proposition the negation of which is not only false but inconceivable."

> This, therefore, is the principle asserted: that propositions, the negation of which is inconceivable, or in other words, which we cannot figure to ourselves as being false, must rest on evidence of a higher and more cogent description than any which experience can afford.
>
> (*System of Logic*, CW VII: 237—38)

In response Mill dwells at length on associationist explanations of inconceivability. But elsewhere he makes the underlying epistemological basis of his reply clear:

> even assuming that inconceivability is not solely the consequence of limited experience, but that some incapacities of conceiving are inherent in the mind, and inseparable from it; this would not entitle us to infer, that what we are thus incapable of conceiving cannot exist. Such an inference would only be warrantable, if we could know *a priori* that we must have been created capable of conceiving whatever is capable of existing: that the universe of thought and that of reality, the Microcosm and the Macrocosm (as they once were called) must have been framed in complete correspondence with one another. . . . That this is really the case has been laid down expressly in some systems of philosophy, by implication in more, and is the foundation (among others) of the systems of Schelling and Hegel: but an assumption more destitute of evidence could scarcely be made . . .
>
> (*An Examination of Sir William Hamilton's Philosophy*, CW IX: 68)

It needs to be shown that what we are "incapable of conceiving cannot exist." And furthermore it must be shown to be true a priori. In short the nub of Mill's argument lies in the impossibility of providing any model of a priori knowledge about the world which is consistent with that knowledge being *about the world*: about something distinct from the knowing itself and to which the knowing must conform if it is indeed knowledge. But the denial of exactly this ontolological conception of knowledge of the world, that is, the denial that knowledge must in every case conform to its object, was Kant's "Copernican revolution." Kant holds that there are framework features of our knowledge to which every object must conform; his transcendental-idealist interpretation of those features is inconsistent with the naturalistic view that we knowing subjects are straightforwardly a part of the world we know. In contrast, naturalism is Mill's most fundamental commitment. On this point at least, that naturalism is incompatible with the possibility of a priori knowledge about the world, Mill and Kantian idealists could agree. Their disagreement, of course, is about whether without synthetic a priori knowledge any knowledge is possible at all.

Mill's critics in the nineteenth century urged that it was not, and it is to this fundamental criticism of a Millian or any other kind of strictly carried through empiricism that I want to come. But it will be useful, in more ways than one, to come to it by way of examining the claim that Mill's treatment of logic is "psychologistic."

PSYCHOLOGISM

I take "psychologism" to consist in one or both of two views:

1   that laws of logic are simply psychological laws concerning our mental processes; or
2   that "meanings" are mental entities, and that "judgments" assert relationships among these entities.

They are both explicitly rejected by Mill. He holds that logic is the most general empirical science, 'universally true of all phænomena" (*An Examination of Sir William Hamilton's Philosophy*, CW IX: 380–1). Since logic's laws are "laws of all phænomena" and phenomena are all we know, "we are quite safe in looking upon them as laws of Existence" (CW IX: 382). The laws of logic are, Mill accepts, also laws of thought in the sense that they are principles in terms of which we cannot but think. Or rather, we violate them often enough in our thinking but we never do so knowingly, for "knowingly to violate them is impossible" (CW IX: 373). As we have already seen, however, Mill denies that their standing as laws of existence can be deduced from the fact that they codify laws of thought. To prove that "a contradiction is unthinkable" is not to prove it "impossible in point of fact" (CW IX 382). And it is the latter, not the former, claim which is required to vindicate "the thinking process." "Our thoughts are true when they are made to correspond with Phænomena" (CW IX: 384)—if

> there were any law necessitating us to think a relation between *phænomena* which does not in fact exist between the phænomena, then certainly the thinking process would be proved invalid, because we should be compelled by it to think true something which would really be false.
>
> (CW IX: 383)

Turning to (2), above—the view that meanings are mental entities and that "judgments" assert relationships among these entities—we find that stringent criticism of precisely this is a central feature of the *System of Logic*. Mill calls it "Conceptualism." He considers it

> one of the most fatal errors ever introduced into the philosophy of logic; and the principal cause why the theory of the science has made such inconsiderable progress during the last two centuries.
>
> (*System of Logic*, CW VII: 89)

Conceptualists confused judgments with the contents of judgment, that is, with propositions.

> They considered a Proposition, or a Judgment, for they used the two words indiscriminately, to consist in affirming or denying one *idea* of another . . . the whole doctrine of Propositions together with the theory of Reasoning . . . was stated as if Ideas, or Conceptions, or whatever other term the writer preferred as a name for mental representations generally, constituted essentially the subject matter and substance of these operations.
>
> (CW VII: 87)

Against Conceptualism Mill insists on the

> difference between a doctrine or opinion, and the fact of entertaining the opinion; between assent, and what is assented to . . .
>   Logic, according to the conception here formed of it, has no concern with the nature of the act of judging or believing; the consideration of that act, as a phenomenon of the mind, belongs to another science.
>
> (CW VII: 87)

> propositions (except sometimes when the mind itself is treated of) are not assertions respecting our ideas of things, but assertions respecting the things themselves.
>
> (CW VII 88)

Taking logic as a set of truths, then, Mill's view of it, like his view of mathematics, is universalist and empiricist. Geometry formulates the laws of physical space, arithmetic the laws of aggregation—and logic the laws of truth itself. Indeed if one takes a universalist view of logic and combines it with rejection of Kant's Copernican revolution then Millian empiricism can appear inevitable. "Our thoughts are true when they are made to correspond with Phænomena" (CW IX: 384)—so how *could* we know that they are true other than by inductive evidence which shows that they correspond with Phænomena? And that includes our logical thoughts, since they too are true when they are made to correspond with Phænomena.

It is from this universalist and empiricist standpoint, and on its behalf, that Mill criticizes what he sees as the three main attempts to vindicate the aprioricity of logic.[4] "Conceptualism," which we have already considered, is one of these. He seems to take Kantian views to be a form of Conceptualism. The other two views he calls "Nominalism" and "Realism."

The Nominalists—Mill cites Hobbes as an example—hold that logic and mathematics are entirely verbal. Mill takes this position much more seriously than Conceptualism. Indeed he refutes it in extensive detail. He argues that Nominalists are only able to maintain their view because they fail to distinguish between the denotation and the connotation of terms, "seeking for their meaning exclusively in what they denote" (*System of Logic*, CW VII: 91). In contrast Mill's distinction between real and verbal propositions, and the consequent demonstration that logic and mathematics contain real propositions, is grounded on his doctrine of denotation and connotation.[5]

Nominalists and Conceptualists both hold that logic and maths can be known non-empirically, while yet retaining the view that no real proposition about a mind-independent world can be so known—but both are confused. What if one abandons the thesis that no real proposition about a mind-independent world can be known a priori? The Realists seem to do that—they hold that logical and mathematical knowledge is knowledge of universals existing in a mind-independent abstract domain; the terms that make up sentences being signs that stand for such universals. This is the view Mill takes least seriously. But new versions of it were fundamental in the first, Fregean and Moorean/Russellian phase of analytic philosophy, and the semantic analysis of logic was their main source.

It is anachronistic, no doubt, to ask how Mill himself would have reacted to these new Realisms. Still, one can distinguish between a semantically and an epistemologically driven realism. The semantically driven version holds that we are justified in accepting the existence of abstract entities, particular or universal, if the best semantic account of the propositions we have reason to hold true is one which postulates the existence of such entities. The epistemologically driven view is an attempt to account for the *epriiricity* of certain propositions. It holds that such propositions are true because they correspond to facts about language-independent abstract entities. We have knowledge of those facts by virtue of some faculty of non-empirical intuition and that is why the knowledge is a priori. Proponents of the first view (Quine for example) can seek to defend it without resorting to the epistemology propounded by the second and indeed without acknowledging the possibility of a priori knowledge at all.

Mill was a nominalist in the contemporary sense—he rejected abstract entities. It is hard to say, given how little he knew of the difficulties this view faces, how deep his commitment to it was. What is clear is that he was mainly concerned to reject realism as an account of the possibility of a priori knowledge. It is the rejection of *that* possibility which is central to his philosophy.

EPISTEMIC NORMS

A self-serving historical story among analytic philosophers holds that empiricism pre-Vienna peddled a confused "psychologistic" account of the apriolicity of logic. It is certainly false of the leading empiricist in the period after Kant and before Vienna. Frege, unlike Husserl, was clear about that. What Mill rejected was the tenet that logic itself is a priori.

But the question remains, can epistemology dispense with the a priori altogether, as Mill seems to think it can? At this point the idea that Mill's *System of Logic* is psychologistic in some much broader sense returns. The psychologism, in this broader sense, would not be about deductive logic—but about fundamental norms of reasoning, whatever they might be. For what epistemological account can Mill offer of these? How, at *this* point, can he respond to the Kantian claim that the very possibility of knowledge requires that there be a priori elements in our knowledge? Even if we accept his inductive account of logic and mathematics, must we not accept that the principles of induction, whatever they may be, are themselves a priori?

Mill holds that the only fundamentally sound method of reasoning is enumerative induction, generalization from experience. Other methods must in one way or another be based on it. This inductivism puts great strain on his empiricist epistemology of logic and mathematics—for example, when it leads him to suggest that the principle of exclusion is "one of our first and most familiar generalizations from experience" (see page 110 above). One may well argue that if it is to be plausible, empiricism needs a more capacious cognitive armory, one which allows for the conservative-holist and hypothetical elements in our knowledge which Quine has stressed.

But this is not the central issue at stake. Consider an optimal account of inductive logic, perhaps different to Mill's. The question then is, are the canons which appear in this account a priori, or if not, how are they established? We can apply to them Mill's own distinction between verbal and real propositions. They must emerge as real. Does he not therefore have to be a universalist about them? That is, does he not have to consider them as founded on maximally general truths about the world? And does that not provide a case against viewing them as a priori? Yet how else could we know them—and hence know anything? This is one central thrust of the Kantian critique of empiricism.

Mill is not interested in inductive scepticism. He says that we learn "the laws of our rational faculty, like those of every other natural agency," by "seeing the agent at work." We bring our most basic reasoning dispositions to self-consciousness by critical reflection on our practice. Having examined our dispositions, we reach a reflective equilibrium in which we endorse some and perhaps reject others. We endorse them as sound norms of reasoning. But what kind of epistemology can Millian empiricism offer for these epistemic norms?

Mill's favored canon of inductive logic, enumerative induction, serves as well as any other to highlight this issue. We can distinguish between that canon itself—which is a normative proposition—and a factual claim. The normative proposition is

i Enumerative inductions—on appropriate premises—defeasibly warrant belief in general propositions about the world.

This proposition is topic-neutral and applies to all domains of inquiry. The factual proposition is ii Enumerative inductions—in some specified or in all domains of inquiry—frequently yield general propositions which are not refutable by counter-examples (or yield them increasingly as time goes on, etc.).

(ii) is itself a general proposition, or a class of general propositions, about the world. Thus—granting (i)—we may acquire a warrant to believe it by a second-order enumerative induction, in some specified domain for which we have sufficient confirming instances. Equally, since induction is defeasible it is possible—granting (i) again—that a second-order induction will justify us in *disbelieving* (ii) in some or all domains. In the first case, induction is internally self-vindicating in the domain. In the second case, it is internally self-undermining. By induction we come to realize that induction is not to be relied upon. The normative proposition, (i), remains correct but the warranting force of inductions is defeated.

Mill is aware of these points and quite rightly very impressed by the fact that "the inductive process" has turned out to be largely self-vindicating. He also highlights the fact that enumerative induction is differentially reliable in different domains. But he does not make the mistake of thinking that induction itself can produce the sole justification of (i). That would indeed open him to Kantian critique. He accepts that an epistemology of induction must endorse (i) as primitively normative and not seek to derive it from (ii). In other words his universalism about deductive logic does not extend to a parallel universalism about inductive logic. On the other hand he does not claim that (i) is analytic, or in his terms, verbal.[6] He refuses to treat (i) as a priori but he thinks we are entitled to accept it just because it is a primitive and stable feature of our practice of inquiry.

But this way of grounding (i) involves a transition from a psychological to a normative claim. Is that the real truth in the allegation that Mill's system of logic is "psychologistic"? How can one defend such a transition from Mill's own criticism of the a priori school and without making concessions in the Kantian or transcendental idealist direction?

EMPIRICISM AND NORMATIVITY

The answer is to take quite seriously the status of enumerative induction (or whatever principles of induction we agree to be primitive) as a *fundamental norm*, and to develop an epistemology of such norms which will be consistent with empiricism. One must sharply distinguish the epistemology of fundamental norms from that of factual propositions. The epistemology of norms is dialogical: it is the epistemology of reflection and discussion. Warrants for fundamental normative assertions are defeasible by further discussion and reflection but not by empirical evidence. On the other hand factual assertions, just because they picture states of affairs, are always open to refutation by empirical evidence. And further, in the case of a factual proposition there is the simple possibility that there may not be enough evidence to pass a verdict, however long and expensive the inquiry. The point arises from the very idea of a world within which we are situated—Mill's "macrocosm." We interact epistemically with other objects in it but there are inevitably limitations on our possible epistemic interactions. In the case of normative propositions no such point applies. The metaphysics of the normative domain provides no basis for the idea of fundamental normative propositions which we could never be justified in recognising as true. My grounds for asserting a normative proposition turn in the first instance on what I'm spontaneously inclined to think, do, or feel. I can be corrected by further reflection and discussion, and this generates a distinction between what seems to me to be true and what is true: it underpins the status of normative claims as genuine judgments. Corrigibility also generates the same distinction in the case of factual propositions; but whether I am justified in asserting a factual proposition turns on whether I am appropriately linked to what it asserts to be the case. Grounds for holding that I am not so linked are grounds for holding that I am not justified in asserting the proposition. Such a notion of breakdown of evidential linkage simply does not apply in the case of fundamental normative propositions.

This is a view of normative claims which one might describe as cognitivist but irrealist. It does not hold that there is something which *makes* normative propositions true or false, or correct or incorrect—in the realist's correspondence sense. In particular, a normative proposition is not *made true* by some fact to the effect that verdicts on it would ideally converge. That is not its truth condition: it has no non-trivial one. One can legitimately seek a comprehensive truth-conditional semantics which includes normative sentences within its remit, but it should be understood minimalistically. It employs minimalist or nominal notions of truth, reference, and predication, even though stronger notions are applicable to some of the terms and sentences with which it deals.

If this view is defensible we can formulate Mill's empiricism as follows: any *factual* proposition is refutable by evidence. Mill needs two distinctions, not just one, a distinction between the normative and the factual and a distinction between the verbal and the real. He must concede that fundamental normative propositions are real propositions but he could argue that they are not factual, so that the question of providing them with inductive support drops away.

To argue in this way is to go well beyond anything Mill says. And it raises a variety of further questions. For example: if empiricism is developed in this way what argument remains for Mill's extremely parsimonious view of the fundamental epistemic norms? Can we not apply a distinction analogous to that between (i) and (ii) in the preceding section to logic—or indeed arithmetic and geometry? Considered as sciences these are bodies of strictly universal propositions about the world. But may we not also hold that there are fundamental logical or mathematical norms which stand to these strictly universal propositions as (i) stands to (ii)? The thrust of Mill's empiricism could still survive as the claim that any such primitive logical or mathematical norms are defeasible in just the way that (i) is. (So they lie "behind" logic, since logic itself, like any science, is formulated in universal terms. The relation between logical norms and truths of logic is something that an approach of this kind must clarify in detail.) Empiricism becomes the thesis that all fundamental epistemic norms are empirically defeasible in this way. Inquiry cannot show any such norms to be incorrect; but it can defeat their warranting force by showing that the universal factual propositions which correspond to them (of logic, arithmetic, or geometry) are false. The inquiry is itself guided by those selfsame default norms which it may eventually defeat.

If Mill has to endorse these two distinctions, between the real and the verbal and the normative and the factual, have we not pushed him into the Kantian camp? What difference is there between conceding that there are real normative propositions and conceding that there are synthetic a priori propositions? The difference is that saying a fundamental normative proposition is "a priori" would add nothing to saying that it is normative and fundamental. Classically, the distinction between the a priori and the a posteriori is a distinction *within* the factual. Because it is, Kant is led into transcendental idealism's constructive view of the knowing subject and its limitative doctrine that synthetic propositions cannot be asserted to hold of "things in themselves." (So while in one sense all synthetic propositions, including the a priori ones, are factual, in another *none* of them are "really" factual—none correspond to the world as it absolutely is.) In contrast, the distinction between the normative and the factual requires no such constructivism or limitative doctrine and no extra-scientific distinction between noumena and phenomena. In that sense it remains compatible with the only sort of naturalism that a Millian in ethics and epistemology need defend.

But if this kind of empiricism is not a form of transcendental idealism, it certainly also differs greatly from the empiricism of Vienna. Viennese empiricism is radically positivistic in the following sense. It acknowledges the significance only (i) of *statements* about the world (that world—the only world—which is the object of science) and (ii) of *non-assertoric* stipulations, decisions, prescriptions, expressions of attitude. "There is only language and the world"—and a language is nothing but a set of rules, contents of decisions or stipulations, so "There are only facts and decisions."

What drives this view is the doctrine that all cognitive or judgable contents—all propositions—are factual. This is the pure essence of metaphysical realism. Positivism issues from combining it with empiricism. There is a strong dynamic towards that combination already implicit in metaphysical realism, as the discussion above of Mill's responses to arguments for the a priori illustrates. But that combination is indeed incoherent. There are various ways of arguing for this conclusion. The nineteenth-century way was neo-Kantian or more strongly idealist; though there was also, towards the end of the century, a Platonistic counter-revolution against both positivism and idealism. Logical positivism was in turn a revolution against this counter-revolution. Not unnaturally, therefore, it has affinities with neo-Kantianism.[7] These are worth investigating in detail, but I do not myself think that a genuinely common philosophical spirit is revealed by them. The tenet that there are only facts and decisions is fundamental to logical positivism but quite alien to Kant.

Let me say, as a final remark, that the incoherence of this tenet seems to me the main moral of Wittgenstein's rule-following considerations. I am not asserting that he meant to draw that moral, at any rate in quite that way. Clearly the question of the normativity inherent in rule-following preoccupied him, but he may not have come to a clear view of it, or if he did, it may not be possible to establish certainly what it was. At any rate the point is this. When I apply a predicate, F, to a given case I make a judgment which may be correct or incorrect. The judgment is that, given the conventional rule governing the use of F it is correct to call this F. It seems that Wittgenstein does take it as a genuine judgment, not a decision, but it also seems that it cannot be represented as picturing any state of affairs. It neither expresses a decision nor is it factual: it is irreducibly normative and so it runs up against the dictum that "There are only facts and decisions."[8] Rule-following presupposes the inherently dual cognitive capacity of judging facts and acknowledging norms. If there are rules, the dichotomy of facts and decisions is not exhaustive.

If such thoughts are correct then positivism, which combines the view that all propositional content is factual with the view that all factual propositions must be justified empirically, is incoherent. But that does not show that empiricism, even a naturalistic empiricism like Mill's, is incoherent. It only shows that positivism is.

NOTES

1   One might say it ended in the 1950s or 1960s, with Wittgenstein's *Philosophical Investigations*, which belonged to it but also pointed beyond it, and with the growing influence of Quine's work, which had a similarly pivotal role. I have argued that the analytic movement should be seen as an aspect of modernism (Skorupski 1990–91, 1993). Quine and Wittgenstein belong to it inasmuch as they subscribe to one of its fundamental ideas—that "there is only language and the world" (see section above on psychologism). In contrast subsequent developments in philosophy of mind and cognitive science resume the interest in the nature of concepts and judgments, understood as psychological items, which characterized nineteenth-century naturalism. For critical discussion of these developments see Dummett 1993.

2   A Millian empiricist about logic faces vital questions about what account to give of universal instantiation and modus ponens. These issues—connecting as they do with the Millian theme that "all inference is from particulars to particulars"—generate a drive towards treating conditional and universal propositions as normative which is distinct from the reasons for distinguishing normative and factual which are considered on pp. 117–20. I shall leave them out of consideration in this discussion.

3   It does, of course, put in question the philosophical rationale for Fregean logicism. But Frege's philosophical impulse (and connectedly, his conception of analyticity) is no more Critical than it is empiricist.

4   The misconception that Mill's view is psychologistic seems to trace back to a passage in the *Examination* quoted by Husserl (1970: 90): "Logic is not the theory of Thought as Thought, but of valid Thought; not of thinking, but of correct thinking. *It is not a Science distinct from, and coordinate with Psychology. So far as it is a science at all, it is a part, or branch, of Psychology; differing from it, on the one hand as the part differs from the whole, and on the other, as an Art differs from a Science. Its theoretic grounds are wholly borrowed from Psychology, and include as much of that science as is required to justify the rules of the art*" (*An Examination of Sir William Hamilton's Philosophy*, CW IX: 359. The section quoted by Husserl is italicized). But Mill is not here repudiating his view that logic rests on completely universal empirical truths. It's rather that he takes the logician to be concerned not with the scientific task of discovering such truths (since they are so obvious) but with the task of advancing the art of thinking by formulating, on the basis of those truths, the most helpful rules of reasoning—drawing on the psychology of thought to do so. The art of the logician borrows from the science of the psychologist because promoting clear thinking is a psychological question. For a fuller discussion see Skorupski 1989: ch. 5, Appendix.

5   The Nominalists, he says, treat arithmetical equations as proper-name identities. He agrees that *proper-name* identities are in a certain sense verbal but he holds that the names flanking the identity sign in an equation typically differ in connotation.

6   In this respect he differs from Strawson (1952: 261).

7   These have been highlighted by Michael Friedman (see for example Friedman 1991) and by Alberto Coffa (1991), though the latter's account also emphasizes the realist strand in nineteenth-century thinking about logic represented by Bolzano and Frege.

8   I spell this out a little further in Skorupski 1996. Some other aspects of the

contrast between Millian and Viennese empiricism are also developed in Skorupski 1995.

BIBLIOGRAPHY

Page references to the writings of Mill are to *The Collected Works of John Stuart Mill* (33 volumes), John M. Robson, General Editor, Toronto: University of Toronto Press, 1963–1991. They are given as follows: CW I: 15, for *Collected Works*, Volume I, page 15.

Coffa, A. (1991) *The Semantic Tradition from Kant to Carnap: To the Vienna Station*, Cambridge: Cambridge University Press.

Dummett, M. (1993) *Origins of Analytical Philosophy*, London: Duckworth.

Friedman, M. (1991) "The Re-evaluation of Logical Positivism," *Journal of Philosophy* 10.

Husserl, E. (1970) *Logical Investigations*, trans. J. N. Findlay, London: Routledge and Kegan Paul.

Skorupski, J. (1989) *John Stuart Mill*, London: Routledge.

——(1990–91) "The Legacy of Modernism," *Proceedings of the Aristotelian Society* 91:1–19.

——(1993) *English-Language Philosophy 1750–1945*,Oxford: Oxford University Press.

——(1995) "Empiricism: British and Viennese," in J. Hintikka and K. Puhl (eds) *The British Tradition in 20th Century Philosophy, Proceedings of the 17th International Wittgenstein Symposium,*Vienna: Hölder-Pichler-Tempsky.

——(1996) "Why did Language Matter to Analytical Philosophy?," *Ratio* Special Issue "The Rise of Analytic Philosophy," 9:269–83.

Strawson, P. F. (1952) *Introduction to Logical Theory*, London: Methuen.

7 Psychologism and meaning

Yemima Ben-Menahem

Words convey meaning and information. Words also affect us in various ways: they comfort or offend, make us blush, laugh and cry, make us happy or sad. How are these effects related to the meanings of the words? In some cases a simple answer suggests itself. It could be held, for example, that the words "I love you" convey to the addressee that he or she is loved, and since being loved is a basic need, the satisfaction of which typically brings happiness, they make the loved one happy. The merit of the simple answer is that it keeps the meaning of the words (the expression of love) at a safe distance from the causal effects these words may have (making the beloved happy). In this respect this answer seems to be in harmony with a long tradition that sharply distinguishes causal connections from connections in language, and strives to cleanse the theory of meaning of any trace of psychologism. The simple answer, however, is not always fully satisfactory, for at times we may need to refer to the effect of what is said to elucidate its meaning; we may need to find out what certain words do to us to decide what they mean. Thus, listening to what someone tells me, I can grasp an implicit intention to flatter or offend, and use this clue to interpret what has been said differently than I would have otherwise. In such cases it is hard to say whether the offense or flattery is, in this particular context, part of the meaning of what is said or just its intended causal effect. But in so blurring the distinction between the meaning or content of speech, on the one hand, and its effects, on the other, we seem, prima facie at least, to be making concessions to a psychologistic conception of meaning. The question addressed in this chapter is whether this is indeed the case, that is, whether this sort of an effect-oriented examination of meaning is in fact guilty of psychologism. Rather than turning to it directly, however, I deal with it via examination of James's and Wittgenstein's conceptions of meaning. I begin by tracing the development of the notion of psychologism from Frege to Wittgenstein.

From its inception, the analytic tradition conceived of psychologism as a temptation to be overcome, or worse, as an enemy made all the more dangerous by its tendency to elude detection. Heated battle against psychologism is a recurring focus in the thought of Frege and Wittgenstein.

Frege, the first to urge that the theory of meaning be purged of psychologism, lays down three basic principles, *Grundsätze*, in his introduction to the *Grundlagen*:

> es ist das Psychologische von dem Logischen, das Subjective von dem Objectiven scharff zu trennen; nach der Bedeutung der Wörter muß im Satzzusammenhange, nicht in ihrer Vereinzelung gefragt werden; der Unterschied zwischen Begriff und Gegenstand ist im Auge zu behalten.
>
> (Frege 1884: x)

That is, first, "always to separate sharply the psychological from the logical, the subjective from the objective"; second, "never to ask for the meaning of a word in isolation, but only in the context of a proposition"; and third, "never to lose sight of the distinction between concept and object."

Although it seems from the structure and context of the first principle that the two distinctions, that between the psychological and the logical, and that between the subjective and the objective, are closely related for Frege, or even taken by him to be identical, it is by no means self-evident that this should be so. Why should the psychological be identified with the subjective? Frege's clarification of the connection between his first and second principles also elucidates what he means by psychology:

> In compliance with the first principle, I have used the word "idea" always in the psychological sense, and have distinguished ideas from concepts and from objects. If the second principle is not observed, one is almost forced to take as the meanings of words mental pictures or acts of the individual mind, and so to offend against the first principle as well.
>
> (Frege 1884: x)

For Frege, then, the link between the two distinctions is that the psychological pertains to mental pictures or other occurrences within individual minds, and as such must be non-communicable, and therefore subjective. We can borrow Putnam's famous saying to paraphrase Frege: "meanings just ain't in the head" (Putnam 1975: 227). Ironically, Putnam used it to argue against a mentalistic theory of meaning he ascribed to Frege. Thus conceived, psychologism is a much more specific error than linking philosophy with psychology: it represents a theory of meaning based on private ideas, a theory Frege rejects because it threatens the objectivity of language, and, since language is our handle on thought, the objectivity of thought as well. For Frege, the objection to subjectivism is primary, while psychologism is rejected only insofar as it attempts to base a theory of meaning on non-communicable entities. It must be emphasized that in denying the objectivity of ideas, Frege does not deny their existence.[1] Quite the contrary—we have ideas, which by their very nature are subjective, and for that reason differ from meanings, the communicable and objective content of thought. It is not the existence of ideas or mental pictures that he rejects, but their potential relevance for a theory of meaning.

As far as the rejection of psychologism is concerned, throughout his life Wittgenstein remained a faithful disciple of Frege. He too saw in psychologism one of the most serious confusions theories of meaning could be susceptible to. Indeed, Wittgenstein went further than Frege in this respect, viewing Frege's theory of meaning as itself infected with psychologism. Though the strategies he utilized varied from the earlier to the later writings, he outdid Frege in his efforts to liberate the theory of meaning from what he perceived as psychologism. In his earlier period, he objected to Frege's notion of sense, which had an epistemic aspect—how the referent is grasped or given to us. For Wittgenstein, purging the psychological calls for abolishing the epistemic as well. Thus, although Wittgenstein uses *Sinn* and *Bedeutung* in the *Tractatus*, he deviates significantly from Frege's use of these terms: as is well known, for him, names have no sense, and propositions, no reference. As Dummett puts it, Frege's theory of meaning is strongly realistic, but, in light of its epistemic aspect, not purely realistic. By contrast, Wittgenstein's theory in the *Tractatus* is both purely and strongly realistic (Dummett 1973: 589). Thus, to provide a more consistent rejection of psychologism than Frege did is one of the key motivations for the theory of meaning advocated in the *Tractatus*, some of the distinct characteristics of which, such as the senselessness of tautologies, are direct responses to this challenge.

The objection to psychologism is just as strong in Wittgenstein's later writings. While Frege's second distinction, that between the objective and the subjective, cannot be made in the Fregean way, for reasons that will become obvious in a moment, the first distinction, that between the logical and the psychological, sometimes framed in these terms, but also transformed into the distinction between grammar and psychology, permeates Wittgenstein's writings. Time and again he insists that one remark or another is grammatical, or logical, rather than psychological. Clearly, the project of constructing a *theory* of meaning is given up in the later writings in favor of unsystematic but meticulous description of use. But the basic conviction that psychology, insofar as it attempts to look into the mind, makes no positive contribution to this detailed description, or worse, is a source of possible confusion, is as pronounced in Wittgenstein's later conception of meaning as it is in the *Tractatus*.

In one respect, however, Wittgenstein's later thought involves a more thoroughgoing critique of psychologism than that of the *Tractatus*. The *Tractatus*, we saw, makes no use of epistemic considerations in its theory of meaning. Yet it seems conceivable that one could hold on to the *Tractatus* theory of meaning while nonetheless accepting the existence of "ideas" as Frege did—that is, admitting their existence, but rejecting their role in a theory of meaning. However, in his later writings, Wittgenstein launches a direct attack on the possibility of radical subjectivity. Although the precise meaning of the argument against private language is still debated in the literature, it is generally agreed that, for Wittgenstein, the difficulty with private ideas is not merely, as it was for Frege, that they are imprisoned in the individual mind and cannot be communicated, but rather, that the very existence of a radically subjective idea or impression, seems doubtful. Hence, Wittgenstein can no longer be satisfied with the Fregean formulation of the objection to psychologism in terms of the irrelevance of the subjective to meaning theory. If, for Frege, the objection to psychologism is an objection to a particular theory of meaning, for Wittgenstein it is furthermore an objection to a fundamental confusion in the philosophy of mind.

Let us now turn to William James, who is not usually taken to be an analytic philosopher, though he did have considerable influence within the analytic tradition, and who seems to have been guilty of psychologism without suffering any pangs of conscience. When James wants to argue against a philosophical creed he finds unattractive, he first asks himself what the view in question means to its believers. Thus, when arguing against what he calls absolutism (the precise characterization of which in conventional terms is problematic if James is right, but which is generally understood as an essentialist, teleological view of the world) he asserts:

> What do believers in the Absolute mean? . . . They mean that since, in the Absolute finite evil is "overruled" already, we may, therefore, whenever we wish, treat the temporal as if it were potentially the eternal, be sure that we can trust its outcome, and without sin dismiss our fear and drop the worry of our finite responsibility. In short, they mean that we have a right ever and anon to take a moral holiday, to let the world wag in its own way, feeling that its issues are in better hands than ours and are none of our business.
>
> The universe is a system of which the individual members may relax their anxieties occasionally, in which the don't-care mood is also right for men, and moral holidays in order,—that . . . is part, at least, of what the Absolute is "known as", that is the great difference in our particular experiences which its being true makes for us, that is its cash value when it is pragmatically interpreted.[2]

(James 1955: 58)

As the last sentence indicates, James takes himself to have provided an elucidation of the meaning of the belief in question, thereby illustrating his pragmatic method of analyzing the meaning of a belief in terms of the difference it makes in our lives. The strategy seems to be a good one insofar as it strives to do maximal justice to the view James opposes, but at the same time, this type of clarification of meaning appears to be patently psychologistic. Not only does it refer directly to feelings and experiences such as fear, worry, and responsibility, but it also seems, overall, to conflate the meaning of a belief with its psychological effects, taking the latter to explicate the former. The question is whether, in construing this as psychologism, we are using the term in the same sense it is used within the analytic tradition. Would Frege and Wittgenstein object to James's conception of meaning on the grounds that it is psychologistic?

Given his characterization of psychologism discussed above, Frege cannot fault James on this score. James, Frege must concede, does not try to depict the mental representation of the absolute in the minds of its proponents, but rather, the manifest difference it makes in their lives. James's conception of meaning lacks the systematic structure a theory of meaning should, according to Frege, possess, but subjective mental representations play no role in it. It cannot, therefore, be deemed psychologistic in his sense. The same seems to hold for Wittgenstein. Not only does James characterize meaning in terms of manifest differences in our lives rather than in terms of mental images, he also seems uncommitted to the view that mental images exist. Being neither subjective nor mentalistic, his conception should not be seen by Wittgenstein as psychologistic.

We have, however, limited ourselves unduly to one sense of the notion of psychologism, and failed to attend to another. James is indeed innocent of psychologism in the subjectivist sense of the term, but the impression that he is nonetheless putting forward a psychologistic conception of meaning is based on the fact that he understands the belief in question in terms of its effects on the believer's life. Is Wittgenstein's critique of psychologism also directed against psychologism in this latter sense?

Wittgenstein alludes to James critically in a number of places, and yet, he seems to have found some of James's ideas quite agreeable. Specifically, James's approach to meaning as making-a-difference, exemplified in the above characterization of absolutism, has its parallels in Wittgenstein:

> Actually I would like to say that . . . the *words* you utter or what you think as you utter them are not what matters, so much as the difference they make at various points in your life. . . . *Practice* gives the words their sense.
> (Wittgenstein 1980a: 85)

It is by no means coincidental that this remark occurs in the context of discussing religious belief. Neither James nor the later Wittgenstein conceive of meaning in terms of a systematic semantic theory, be it a semantics of truth conditions, assertability conditions or what have you.

Both allow for characterizations of meaning that vary from one utterance and context to another. They would agree that "God listens to our prayers" should not be construed along the lines of "Susan listens to Robert" despite the sentences' structural similarity. It is only in analyzing the meaning of profoundly significant creeds, myths, and philosophical positions, that James has recourse to the difference they make to one's life. He explicitly denies that this method of interpretation is either required or adequate in simpler cases. Thus, it is certainly not the case that more conventional criteria of meaningfulness and truth, such as verifiability, or even correspondence with the facts, have no room in James's pragmatism.[3] His point is, rather, that in some cases, conventional criteria are insufficient or inapplicable, and must therefore be supplemented by a more general inquiry into the overall impact of the belief in question on our lives. The commonly held view that James was merely trying to replace one semantic theory with another, ascribing to a single consequence-oriented term, "satisfaction," the role earlier ascribed to "correspondence," is seriously flawed. Like Wittgenstein, James undertakes a more radical critique of traditional semantics, illustrating the complexity and context-dependence of linguistic practice by a variety of examples. Assessing the value or truth of what he calls a "world-formula," a context in which neither correspondence nor verifiability is available, is precisely where "making a difference" is a relevant parameter.

> There can *be* no difference anywhere that does not *make* a difference elsewhere—no difference in abstract truth that does not express itself in a difference in concrete fact and in conduct consequent upon that fact, imposed on somebody, somehow, somewhere, and somewhen. The whole function of philosophy ought to be to find out what definite difference it will make to you and me, at definite instants of our life, if this world-formula or that world-formula be the true one.
>
> (James 1955: 45)

A superficial similarity with the verifiability principle of meaning has misled many. James has himself contributed to the confusion by representing pragmatism as a kind of empiricism. In fact, the two principles differ widely on what counts as "making a difference." The logical positivists demand empirical import whereas James has in mind any difference to human lives. Metaphysical, moral, or aesthetic beliefs which cannot be verified and which are thus, according to logical positivism, devoid of cognitive meaning, may well be significant on James's conception. The positivist dream is to eliminate metaphysics in favor of science; James's hope is that "science and metaphysics would come much nearer together, would in fact work absolutely hand in hand" (James 1955: 46). For the logical positivists, metaphysical beliefs have only emotive meaning, for

James the very dichotomy between the emotional and the cognitive, is, like that between fact and value, obsolete.

A similar attitude can be found in Wittgenstein. He too has occasionally been read as a verificationist, a reading presumably supported by his impatience with traditional metaphysics and various other "wheels turning idly." But for Wittgenstein, as for James, the idle wheel is not the traditional anathema of empiricism—the unobservable—but, rather, words that have lost contact with our lives. He urges that words which retain such contact be respected.

> It is true that we can compare a picture that is firmly rooted in us to a superstition; but it is equally true that we *always* eventually have to reach some firm ground, either a picture or something else, so that a picture which is at the root of all our thinking is to be respected and not treated as a superstition.
>
> (Wittgenstein 1980a: 83)

Further, when we encounter what appears to be incomprehensible, we should not, according to Wittgenstein, dismiss it as meaningless, as the logical positivists cheerfully do, but make a sincere effort to understand:

> I say to myself: "What is this? What does this phrase say? Just what does it express?"—I feel as if there must be a much clearer understanding of it than the one I have. And this understanding would be reached by saying a great deal about the surrounding of the phrase. As if one were trying to understand an expressive gesture in a ceremony. And in order to explain it I should need as it were to analyse the ceremony. E.g., to alter it and shew what influence that would have on the role of that gesture.
>
> (Wittgenstein 1980b: 34)

> The question is really: are these notes not the *best* expression for what is expressed here? Presumably. But that does not mean that they aren't to be explained by working on their surrounding.
>
> (Wittgenstein 1980b: 36)

The metaphor of the surrounding of an expression, the connection between understanding an expression and understanding its role in a particular context, the importance of noticing the difference this expression makes, are aspects of the understanding of meaning that James, no less than Wittgenstein, was eager to draw to our attention.[4]

But the similarity between James and Wittgenstein runs deeper. Not only do they agree on the importance of the surrounding, and of differences impacting on one's life, they both seek a view of language that respects the *autonomy* of linguistic practice. Admittedly, "autonomy" might be misleading when referring to the views of philosophers who acknowledge the interrelations of, and analogies between, language and non-linguistic practice. The following passage may clarify what I have in mind. In discussing the problem of the nature of necessary truth, Wittgenstein compares it to that of free will.

> This is analogous to an ethical discussion of free will. We have an idea of compulsion. If a policeman grabs me and shoves me through the door, we say I am compelled. But if I walk up and down here, we say I move freely. But it is objected: "If you knew all the laws of nature, and could observe all the particles etc., you would no longer say you were moving freely; you would see that a man just cannot do anything else". But in the first place, this is not how we use the expression "he can't do anything else." Although it is *conceivable* that if we had a mechanism which would show all this, we would change our terminology—and say, "He's as much compelled as if a policemen shoved him." We'd give up this distinction then, and in that case, I would be very sorry.
>
> (Wittgenstein 1976: 242)

Although this incidental remark comes nowhere near James's impassioned, some would say extravagant, plea for indeterminism (James 1956), it is nevertheless non-traditional in a strikingly similar way. Traditionally, the existence of deterministic causal chains leading up to our actions is thought to have direct bearing on whether the customary distinction between freedom and necessity can be maintained. Soft determinists, as well as libertarians and hard determinists, are interested in such causal chains, the former emphasizing that they include agents' wishes and reasons. Wittgenstein and James, on the other hand, hold that the problem of free will has to do with the role of the notion of freedom in our lives, not with its ontology. Wittgenstein concedes that ordinary linguistic practice can be sensitive to scientific change, but does not consider such sensitivity necessary or even desirable. On this point he is in agreement with James.

The relative autonomy of language *vis à vis* physics, revolutionary as it might seem in the context of the problem of free will, is so natural for Wittgenstein that he hardly bothers to argue for it. This explains why the problem of free will can serve him as a helpful analogy for that of necessary truth, which he finds more difficult. But it is the autonomy of language *vis à vis* psychology that is his main focus, and it is in this context that we should look for enlightenment on his critique of psychologism. At times, he explicitly links physics and psychology:

> If we can find a ground for the structures of concepts among the facts of nature (psychological and physical), then isn't the description of the structure of our concepts really disguised natural science; ought we not in that case concern ourselves not with grammar, but with what lies at the bottom of grammar in nature? Indeed the correspondence between our grammar and general (seldom mentioned) facts of nature does concern us. But our interest does not fall back on these *possible* causes. We are not pursuing a natural science; our aim is not to

predict anything. Nor natural history either, for we invent facts of natural history for our own purposes.

(Wittgenstein 1980b: 46)[5]

But he also sharply distinguishes the case of psychology from that of physics, and on this point clearly differs from James:

> The confusion and barrenness of psychology is not to be explained by calling it a "young science"; its state is not comparable with that of physics, for instance, in its beginnings. For in psychology there are experimental methods and *conceptual confusion*.

(Wittgenstein 1972 II: 232)

What are these conceptual confusions and how are they related to the problems Wittgenstein is concerned with? One phenomenon he finds both interesting and troubling is the tendency to be misled by pictures—to reify such mental entities as meanings, intentions, experiences, feelings, and so on. For example, discussing "seeing as," he shows that it is misleading to think of the seeing of aspects as an "inner experience" we "have," an occurrence which takes place "in the mind," regardless of our ability to describe it in language:

> Would it be conceivable that someone who knows rabbits but not ducks should say: I can see the drawing as a rabbit and also in another way, although I have no words for the second aspect"? Later he gets to know ducks and says: "That's what I saw the drawing as that time!" Why is that not possible?

(Wittgenstein 1980b: 70)

Similar questions trouble Wittgenstein with regard to intending, expecting, remembering, and other "psychological" terms. Here the distinction between grammar and psychology is crucial.

> What does it mean when we say: "I can't imagine the opposite of this?" . . . Of course, here "I can't imagine the opposite" doesn't mean: my powers of imagination are unequal to the task. These words are a defence against something whose form makes it look like an empirical proposition, but which is really a grammatical one.

(Wittgenstein 1972 I: §251)

The defence, we must remember, is not against a certain manner of speaking, but rather against a tendency to reify such modes of speaking, or use them as the basis for philosophical theories: "What we 'are tempted to say' in such a case is, of course, not philosophy; but it is its raw material" (Wittgenstein 1972 I: §254). There is another area in which similar temptations provide further raw material of this kind. Mentalistic reification, Wittgenstein maintains, is as common, and as misleading, in the mathematical context as it is in the psychological. Just as ordinary discourse should not be understood in terms of mental representations or inner experiences, so too mathematical discourse should not be understood in terms of either Platonic or mentalistic reification of mathematical objects. Hence "An investigation is possible in connection with mathematics which is entirely analogous to our investigation of psychology" (Wittgenstein 1972 II: 232).

Another problem related to psychology that deeply concerns Wittgenstein is the tendency to confuse the meaning of an expression with the causes of its use. The distinction between causal connections and connections in language is related to a more general distinction, fundamental in the later writings, between explanation and description. Typically, explanations are given from an "external" point of view, while descriptions arise from "within" a shared practice or form of life. Explanations are hypotheses, usually causal hypotheses, and as such introduce new theoretical elements, that are not part of the explained phenomena, entailing projection, induction, uncertainty, and so on. Descriptions, on the other hand, "only correctly piece together what one *knows*" (Wittgenstein 1993: 121), and are typically concerned with internal rather than external relations.

Wittgenstein warns against any blurring of, or insensitivity to, this distinction. "When I wrote 'proof must be conspicuous' that means causality plays no part in the proof" (Wittgenstein 1993: 133). He often reminds us that he is uninterested in the causes of linguistic phenomena— "they *might* be associations from my childhood, but that is a hypothesis" (Wittgenstein 1972 II: 216)—and that even where a causal explanation exists, it does not speak to the problem at hand: "The purpose of this paragraph . . . was to bring before our view what happens when a physiological explanation is offered. The psychological concept hangs out of reach of this explanation" (Wittgenstein 1972 II: 212). Or, "The existence of experimental methods makes us think we have the means of solving the problems which trouble us, though problem and method pass one another by" (Wittgenstein 1972 II: 232).

Wittgenstein is particularly critical of Freud and his followers, whom he sees as making "an abominable mess" in this regard (Moore 1993: 117). Freud should not have modeled psychology on physics:

> Freud was influenced by the 19th century idea of dynamics—an idea which has influenced the whole treatment of psychology. He wanted to find some one explanation which would show what dreaming is.
>
> (Wittgenstein 1978: 48)

And he should have been more careful in drawing conclusions:

The fact is that whenever you are preoccupied with something . . . which is a big thing in your life—as is sex, for instance—then no matter what you start from, the association will lead finally and inevitably back to the same theme. Freud remarks on how, after the analysis of it, the dream appears so very logical. And of course it does.

You could start with any of the objects on this table—which certainly are not put there through your dream activity—and you could find that they all could be connected in a pattern like that; and the pattern would be logical in the same way. One may be able to discover certain things about oneself by this sort of free association, but it does not explain why the dream occurred.

(Wittgenstein 1978: 51)

But above all, Freud should not have conflated interpretation and scientific explanation. Wittgenstein blames Freud for presenting hypothetical explanations of his own as interpretations of what the analysand said or dreamed, as well as for the opposite mistake, portraying clarifications of meanings as scientific hypotheses.[6] The dangers of psychology are not exhausted, then, by its tendency to reify and mythologize, but extend to serious category mistakes. In this context, Wittgenstein's warnings against psychologism are directed not at mentalistic theories of meaning, or against radical subjectivity, but rather the internal/external confusion. On this point, we can expect conflict with James.

The distinction between description and causal explanation motivates Wittgenstein's central enterprise—providing a "perspicuous representation" of language. The aim of such a representation is to uncover the grid of grammatical connections between various expressions, connections which manifest themselves in competent use of language, but which we tend to ignore or misinterpret in philosophy. Wittgenstein's "critique of language"[7] targets such misinterpretation, and, like other forms of critique, is intended to have a liberating effect. Once we perceive the multitude of grammatical or internal relations, the most stubborn problems of traditional philosophy, such as the nature of necessary truth, intentionality, and the sceptical paradoxes, lose their force. Thus, disclosure of the grid of internal relations not only allows for an adequate conception of language, but, in addition, constitutes a powerful means of emancipation.

In Wittgenstein's writings, the notion of an internal relation, though related to traditional analyticity, is much broader in scope. Thus, it is not normally considered analytic that the expectation that one will see John is fulfilled by, and only by, seeing John. But Wittgenstein wants to solve old puzzles about intentionality by stressing the linguistic character of the intriguing match between intention and what is intended: "It is in language that an expectation and its fulfillment make contact" (Wittgenstein 1972 I: §445) It is precisely because Wittgenstein makes such extensive use of the notion of internal or grammatical relation in his critique of traditional positions, that he so zealously protects the distinction between the internal and the external. Blurring this distinction would undermine what he sees as his greatest achievement.

All this is very far from James's philosophical temperament. Not that he is indifferent to the liberating force of his philosophy: James's pragmatism is no less a critique of traditional fixations than is Wittgenstein's.[8] But the philosophical dichotomies Wittgenstein holds fast to, fact and value, internal and external, causes and reasons, are the very dichotomies James is trying to bridge. Thus, while for Wittgenstein the description of language is the description of its grammatical internal relations, for James the internal and the external, the causal and the linguistic, are ultimately inseparable.

Causes, according to Wittgenstein, should not be conflated with clarifications of meaning, interpretations, and so on. But what about effects? If, as Wittgenstein maintains, causal relations are external relations, while meanings are typically an internal matter, then the conflation of the meaning of an expression with its effects is as misguided as its conflation with its causes. Recall that it was precisely in this respect that James's unpacking of the meaning of the belief in the absolute seemed psychologistic. It appears that even if James does not construe meaning subjectively, and even if his conception of meaning does not reify mental entities (though his psychology may), his deliberate carelessness about the explanation–description distinction will generate a conflict with Wittgenstein.

But this is an oversimplification. Clearly, Wittgenstein does not want to say that clarification of meaning can always be reduced to the uncovering of internal relations. His above-quoted remarks on understanding an utterance in terms of the difference it makes to our lives are incompatible with such a narrow conception. The question we raised at the outset—is an effect-oriented examination of meaning psychologistic?—should perhaps be broken down into a number of questions. Are James and Wittgenstein using the criterion of making a difference to one's life in quite the same way? If they are, we need to ascertain whether this criterion can be used without involving Wittgenstein in the conceptual muddles he deplores. If, however, they are ascribing different meanings to the "making a difference" criterion, further work is needed to pin down the difference between them. Since I am unable to find conclusive answers to these questions in the texts, I can only offer some tentative ones.

One option is to bring James closer to Wittgenstein by questioning the assumption that James's method of interpretation is indeed effect-oriented. It might, after all, be argued that analysis of the absolute in terms of the ability to take a moral holiday is no more effect-oriented than understanding the sentence "he feels grateful to her" in terms of the thankful words he utters, the smile on his face, the gift he presents her with, etc., an understanding Wittgenstein would probably sanction. Wittgenstein would most likely remind us (and James would welcome this reminder) that to understand a belief in terms of the feelings it induces in the believer is not necessarily to understand it in terms of an inner experience, and certainly not always the same type of inner experience. He might go on to remind us that feeling as if we are on a moral holiday is in certain respects different from common-or-garden-variety feeling, asking us to compare "feeling responsible" with "feeling his arm around my shoulder" or "feeling dizzy." Could one say, for example "I stopped feeling responsible five minutes ago and now I feel it again"? Such an interpretation would perhaps make James's analysis more "grammatical" and less psychologistic.

A notable difference, however, between understanding "feeling grateful" in terms of familiar patterns of grateful behaviour and James's analysis of the meaning of the absolute, is the relative normativity of the former in comparison with the latter. A typical member of the community should recognize the former behavior as an expression of gratitude, but would find it much harder to interpret the behavior of the absolutist as an expression of his creed. Thus, Wittgenstein might well construe James as offering an interesting psychological hypothesis regarding the possible connection between belief in the absolute and a certain kind of behavior, while Wittgenstein himself is highlighting ordinary, and, more importantly, normative connections between linguistic expressions and their manifestations in practice. This difference may well be critical, for, as we saw, Wittgenstein's aim is to point to something we already know rather than to come up with daring new hypotheses. The normativity of language is at the heart of Wittgenstein's concerns. It is this normativity that enables him to dismiss sceptical puzzles such as the rule-following paradox, and to ground necessary truth in language rather than in reality. If this is the case, then James's charitable interpretation of belief in the absolute would not necessarily be deemed psychologistic by Wittgenstein, but would nonetheless be considered peripheral to the enterprise of understanding language in general.

Another possibility is to give more weight to those undercurrents in Wittgenstein's writings that bring him closer to James. The "Remarks on Frazer's *Golden Bough*" are a rich source of relevant material. First, these remarks make it quite clear that, for Wittgenstein, as for James, the problem of understanding the other has moral as well as cognitive aspects. He thus criticizes Frazer for lack of respect for, and compassion with, the people whose cultures he studies. Second, when endeavoring to understand the other across a cultural gap, the main vehicle for understanding is *analogy*. By its very nature, such analogical interpretation goes beyond the normative, and is therefore different from the more standard means available to speakers of the same language.[9] Frazer's paternalism is rejected not only because it makes the other look less endowed than the Western individual, but because it blinds Frazer to the similarities between the cultures he describes and his own. Thus, according to Wittgenstein, Frazer misses the simple fact that what arouses horror in members of the foreign culture arouses horror in us, the fact that when he undertakes the translation of foreign beliefs into English, he has the words "ghost" and "soul" ready-made in his language. "Compared to this [the existence of such words in our language], the fact that we do not believe our soul eats and drinks is a trifling matter" (Wittgenstein 1993: 133). If we miss such analogies, if we fail to construct a bridge from the alien to the familiar, we might have to give up on understanding altogether. But since, in drawing such analogies, we cannot fall back on purely normative aspects of language, we must use our creative imagination. Hence, what is peripheral in daily use of language becomes central when we attempt to understand the radically different.

Further, although the comments on Frazer restate the distinctions we have noted, explanation versus description, causal hypothesis versus internal relations, they also drive home the problematic nature of these distinctions. Wittgenstein asks himself, for instance, whether the sinister is an integral part of the rituals connected with the Beltane Fire Festival, or is only related to them through the historical hypothesis that traces the origin of these rituals to human sacrifice. And he replies: "No, the deep and the sinister do not become apparent merely by our coming to know the history of the external action, rather, it is *we* who ascribe them from an inner experience" (Wittgenstein 1993: 147). Wittgenstein, it seems, cannot afford to let go of his distinction. But is it not precisely in such cases that we are unable to distinguish the meaning we ascribe to the ritual from the horrifying effect it has on us? Is it not likely that Wittgenstein himself was somewhat ambivalent about this very point?

This look at the positions of James and Wittgenstein seems to point to conclusions that transcend questions of historical interpretation, and have direct bearing on major issues in the philosophy of language. We may decide to part company with Wittgenstein and conclude that since it is virtually impossible to separate meanings and effects, some effect-oriented clarifications of meaning are perfectly in order. I myself am inclined towards this latter move, though the issues are complex and merit further reflection.

To conclude: psychologism, in the sense of a subjectivist theory of meaning, or the tendency to reify psychological terms of ordinary language, seems convincingly repudiated by Frege and Wittgenstein and such contemporary thinkers as Quine, Putnam, Davidson, and Dummett. It no longer has the grip on our thought that it did when Frege warned against it. Psychologism, in the other sense, that is, the sense that construes meanings and effects as inseparable in some cases, still remains attractive. The outlook for theories of meaning is somewhat friendlier now, with one obstacle out of the way, and reasonable hopes that the other may yet prove innocuous.[10]

NOTES

1 See Bar-Elli (1996: ch. 3) and Dummett (1973) for this point as well as for the above comments on Frege.
2 In fact James says: "What do believers in the Absolute mean by saying that their belief affords them comfort?" But it is clear from the preceding passages, and from the end of the present quotation, that James explicates the meaning of the belief in the Absolute, not just the meaning of the second-order belief that belief in the Absolute affords comfort.
3 See James (1955: 132) for a context in which James approves of a "copy" conception of truth.
4 See also Wittgenstein (1972 I: §250): "Why can't a dog simulate pain? . . . the surroundings which are necessary for this behavior to be real simulation are missing."
5 And see also Wittgenstein (1972 II: 230).
6 Wittgenstein also sees Freud as having created myths, such as that of the unconscious, and that of the repetition of patterns originating in early child-hood, that fascinate us tremendously, but for that very reason are easily mistaken for what they are not—scientific explanations.
7 In the *Tractatus* (1922: 4.0031) Wittgenstein says: "All philosophy is critique of language." I believe this characterization is equally apt regarding his later work.
8 See for example, *Pragmatism* (James 1955: 44).
9 Recall that interpretation is different from standard linguistic understanding: "There is a way of grasping a rule which is not an interpretation", *Philosophical Investigations* (1972 I: §201).
10 Acknowledgment: I am grateful to Hanina Ben-Menahem, Gilad Bar-Elli, and Meir Buzaglo for many helpful suggestions.

BIBLIOGRAPHY

Bar-Elli, G. (1996) *The Sense of Reference*, Berlin: W. de Gruyter.
Dummett, M. (1973) *Frege: Philosophy of Language*, London: Duckworth.
Frege, G. (1884, 1953) *Die Grundlagen der Arithmetik, The Foundations of Arithmetic*, bilingual ed. trans. J. L. Austin, Oxford: Blackwell.
James, W. (1955) *Pragmatism*, Meridian, Cleveland and New York: Meridian.
——(1956) "The Dilemma of Determinism," in *The Will to Believe*, New York: Dover.
Moore, G. E. (1993) "Wittgenstein's Lectures in 1930–33," in J. C. Klagge and A. Nordmann (eds), *Philosophical Occasions*, Indianapolis and Cambridge: Hackett.

Putnam, H. (1975) "The Meaning of Meaning," in *Philosophical Papers II*, Cambridge: Cambridge University Press.

Wittgenstein, L. (1922) *Tractatus Logico-Philosophicus*, trans. C. K. Ogden, London: Routledge and Kegan Paul.

——(1972) *Philosophical Investigations*, trans. G. E. M. Anscombe, Oxford: Blackwell.

——(1976) *Lectures on the Foundations of Mathematics*, C. Diamond (ed.), Ithaca: Cornell University Press.

——(1978) "Conversations on Freud," in C. Barrett (ed.) *Lectures and Conversations*, Oxford: Blackwell.

——(1980a) *Culture and Value*, G. H. von Wright and H. Nyman (eds), trans. P. Winch, Chicago: The University of Chicago Press.

——(1980b) *Remarks on the Philosophy of Psychology I*, G. E. M. Anscombe and G. H. von Wright (eds), trans. G. E. M. Anscombe, Oxford: Blackwell.

——(1993) "Remarks on Frazer's *Golden Bough*," in J. C. Klagge and A. Nordmann (eds), *Philosophical Occasions*, Indianapolis and Cambridge: Hacket.

Part III

Heroes

8 Frege, semantics, and the double definition stroke[1]

Juliet Floyd

I

In 1964, in his introduction to his partial translation of Frege's *Grundgesetze*, Montgomery Furth wrote:

> There is . . . reason for attaching great importance today to Frege's treatment of [his primitive assertions and his sound rules of inference]: that is, Frege's explanation of the primitive basis of his system of logic, and particularly of the primitive symbolism, *is undertaken in terms of a deeply thought-out semantical interpretation*, which in turn *embodies an entire philosophy of language*. The influence of the latter upon *the semantical structure* and even the syntax of the language developed makes itself felt steadily throughout the discussion. This *philosophy of language* is very profound, and possesses great interest quite independent of its origin as the handmaiden of "logicism". *It too is not generally well understood even today.*
>
> (Frege 1893: vi—vii, my emphases)

In a quite different vein, Jean van Heijenoort, in his 1967 paper "Logic as Calculus and Logic as Language," wrote:

> From Frege's writings a certain *picture of logic* emerges, a conception that is perhaps *not discussed explicitly* but nevertheless constantly guides Frege. In referring to this conception I shall speak of the *universality* of logic.
>
>   . . . The universality of logic expresses itself in an important feature of Frege's system. In that system the quantifiers binding individual variables range over all objects . . . . *Frege's universe consists of all that there is, and it is fixed.*
>
>   . . . Another important consequence of the universality of logic is *that nothing can be, or has to be, said outside of the system*. And, in fact, *Frege never raises any metasystematic question* (consistency, independence of axioms, completeness). Frege is indeed fully aware that any formal system requires rules that are not expressed in the system; but these rules are void of any intuitive logic; they are "rules for the use of our signs" (note: Beg §13). In such a manipulation of signs, *from which any argumentative logic has been squeezed out*, Frege sees precisely the advantage of a formal system.
>
>   Since logic is a language, that language has to be learned. Like many languages in many circumstances, the language has to be learned by suggestions and clues. *Frege repeatedly states, when introducing his system, that he is giving*

"hints" to the reader, that the reader has to meet him halfway and should not begrudge him a share of "good will". The problem is to bring the reader to "catch on"; he has to get into the language. (note: Here *the influence of Frege on Wittgenstein is obvious. Also, Frege's refusal to entertain metasystematic questions* explains perhaps why he was not too disturbed by the statement "The concept *Horse* is not a concept". The paradox arises from the fact that, since concepts, being functions, are not objects, we cannot name them, hence we are unable to talk about them. Some statements that are (apparently) about concepts can easily be translated into the system; thus, "the concept $\mathbf{f}(x)$ is realized" becomes "$(Ex\,)\mathbf{f}(x\,)$". *The statements that resist such a translation are, upon examination, metasystematic*; for example, "there are functions" cannot be translated into the system, but we *see*, once we have "caught on", that there are function signs among the signs of the system, hence that there are functions.)

(Van Heijenoort 1985: 12–13, my emphases)

Van Heijenoort insists that for Frege, logic is universal, it cannot pick or choose different universes of discourse, and the formula language (*Begriffsschrift*) that is the formalization of this logic is not subject to differing interpretations.[2] Moreover, when correctly formulated this formula language lays bare the framework within which *all* thought must take place, it lays bare the *limits* of rational discourse, the *limits* of sense. Alluding to the Kerry paradox, van Heijenoort treats the issues raised by "the concept *horse*" problem as paradigmatic for Frege's attitude toward most, if not all "metasystematic" questions. And thus he holds that in the (German) presentation of his formula language Frege takes himself to rely wholly, or at least in large part, upon "suggestions," "clues," and "hints" to help the reader *see* or "catch on" to "rules . . . from which any argumentative logic has been squeezed out." In this way van Heijenoort argues that no "metasystematic questions (consistency, independence of axioms, completeness)" *can* arise for Frege about his formal system, his formula language.

This reading sharply questions Furth's claim that in Frege we find "a deeply thought out semantical interpretation" or "semantical structure" embodying "an entire philosophy of language." For although van Heijenoort wrote in a subsequent paper that for Frege the formula language *elicits the latent and determinate content of ordinary language*[3]—a picture many would call "semantical"[4]—nevertheless van Heijenoort insisted that Frege conceived himself to be uncovering this latent structure of language, namely logic, from *within* the one and only universal language, namely, logic itself. Hence, unlike Furth, van Heijenoort denied that Frege could have adopted any sort of "metatheoretical" or model theoretic stance in so proceeding. (For van Heijenoort, "semantics" always meant model theoretic or set theoretic semantics.) The formula language was, van Heijenoort claimed, intended by Frege to totally *supplant* rather than simply to reflect or to aid natural language. This claim explicitly appears in a later part of "Logic as Calculus and Logic as Language," where van Heijenoort buttresses his reading of Frege by appealing to what he says are parallel lines of thought in Russell:

> Questions about the system are as absent from *Principia mathematica* as they are from Frege's work. *Semantic notions are unknown.* "⊢" is read as " . . . is true", and Russell could hardly have come to add to the notion of provability a notion of validity based on naive set theory. . . . If the question of the semantic completeness of quantification theory did not "at once" arise, it is because of the universality—in the sense that I tried to extricate—of Frege's and Russell's logic. *The universal formal language supplants the natural language, and to preserve, outside of the system, a notion of validity based on intuitive set theory, does not seem to fit into the scientific reconstruction of the language. The only question of completeness that may arise is, to use an expression of Herbrand's, an experimental question. As many theorems as possible are derived in the system.* Can we exhaust the intuitive modes of reasoning actually used in science? To answer this question is the purpose of the Frege–Russell enterprise.
>
> (van Heijenoort 1985: 14, my emphases)

In his 1973 *Frege: Philosophy of Language* Michael Dummett massively articulated the reading of Frege called for by Furth. Hence, in particular, though without explicitly mentioning van Heijenoort, Dummett strongly differed with van Heijenoort's denial of the possibility of metasystematic considerations in Frege:

> Although Frege did not expressly define the two notions—semantic and syntactic—of logical consequence, *they lie ready to hand in his work*: for there, on the one hand, is *the formal system*, with its precisely stated formation rules, axioms and rules of inference and there, on the other, are *the semantic explanations of the sentences of the formalized language*, set out, clearly separated from the formal development, in German in the accompanying text. . . . The sentential fragment of Frege's formalization of logic is complete, and likewise the first-order fragment constitutes the first complete formalization of first-order predicate logic with identity. It was left to Frege's successors to prove this completeness, as also to establish the incompleteness of his, or of any of the effective, formalizations of higher-order logic. *Frege had it to hand to raise these questions*: but he did not do so . . .
>
> (Dummett 1973, 1981: 82, my emphases)

Dummett's reading greatly enhanced the growing interest in Frege by securing Frege's relevance to contemporary philosophy of language and theory of meaning. It has become the dominant reading.

However, Dummett has not gone unchallenged. In his 1979 "Logic in the Twenties: The Nature of the Quantifier," Warren Goldfarb explicitly criticized Dummett[5] and agreed with van Heijenoort about the absence of any "metasystematic" standpoint in Frege. Goldfarb based his argument on a detailed historical assessment of the development of quantification theory and concluded:

[The] lack of intelligibility [of independence questions in logic] may be intrinsic to the logicist program. If the system constitutes the universal logical language, then there can be no external standpoint from which one may view and discuss the system. *Metasystematic considerations are illegitimate rather than simply undesirable.* This is what Harry Sheffer called "the logocentric predicament" (Sheffer, "Review of Whitehead and Russell, *Principia Mathematica*", *Isis* 8: 226–231), and forms a large part, I think, of the motivations behind Wittgenstein's *Tractatus*. (Fn: A similar "logocentricity" may underlie Frege's curious claim that "Only true thoughts can be premises of inferences" (Frege 1971: 425).)

(Goldfarb 1979: 353, my emphasis)

Goldfarb too (1979: 353) buttressed his claim about Frege's "logocentricity" by drawing a parallel between Frege and Russell, pointing out that in §17 of *The Principles of Mathematics* (1903) Russell had written:

Some indemonstrables there must be; and some propositions, such as the syllogism, must be of the number, since no demonstration is possible without them. But concerning others, it may be doubted whether they are indemonstrable or merely undemonstrated; and it should be observed that *the method of supposing an axiom false, and deducing the consequence of this assumption, which has been found admirable in such cases as the axiom of parallels, is here not universally available.* For all our axioms are principles of deduction; and if they are true, the consequences which appear to follow from the employment of an opposite principle will not really follow, so that arguments from the supposition of the falsity of an axiom are here subject to special fallacies.

(Russell 1938: 15, my emphasis)

Thus, though Russell in *one* sense certainly does raise a question about independence, he seems, as Goldfarb says, "not even to see the intelligibility of stepping outside the system to use an intuitive logic in metasystematic arguments" (1979: 353).

Since the 1970s several other philosophers interested in early analytic philosophy have also explicitly differed with Dummett's semantical reading of Frege by offering their own anti-semantical readings.[6] Gordon Baker and Peter Hacker (1984), Cora Diamond (1991a, 1991b), Burton Dreben (1962–6), Jaakko and Merrill Hintikka (1979, 1986), Thomas Ricketts (1985, 1986a, 1986b, 1996a, 1996b, 1997), Hans Sluga (1980, 1987), and Joan Weiner (1982, 1984, 1990, forthcoming), while differing in various ways with each other, all belong to this anti-semantical tradition.[7] Like van Heijenoort they have argued that far from advocating a *theory* of meaning or a semantical *theory*, Frege rejects as nonsense any attempt to account systematically for the nature of logic, the nature of meaning, or the nature of language. Of course, no one denies that Frege uses the notion of the content of a judgment and, later, the notions of *Sinn* and *Bedeutung*. What is questioned is the idea that in using these notions Frege is theorizing about language or meaning in general. In order to question this idea, these philosophers emphasize as crucial Frege's use of what he calls "elucidations," "Erläuterungen" (Sluga 1980: 180–2; Weiner 1990: ch. 6; Weiner forthcoming). Frege tells us that elucidations serve to set forth the way we are to understand certain of his undefinable, i.e. logically primitive, notions (1984: 300, 302; 1979: 207, 214, 235).[8] In one way or another Frege's anti-semantical readers all seem to agree with van Heijenoort's focus on Frege's explicit uses of elucidation, hints, clues, and metaphors in presenting his formula language.[9] Indeed, Weiner goes so far as to maintain that Frege must deny both that our numerals in everyday arithmetic may be said to have *Bedeutungen*, and that our ordinary, pre-analyzed propositions of arithmetic have determinate truth-values (Weiner 1984: 78). While not all the anti-semantical readers go this far, all emphasize the extent to which Frege explicitly emphasizes that at times he is forced to fall back upon hints, metaphor, and indirect suggestion, relying on his reader for cooperation, good will, and guesswork.[10] Such figurative and colorful language indicates, they argue, that Frege has no antecedent or independent theoretical account of semantical notions. Thus elucidations are to be sharply distinguished from judgments, from theory; they do not and are not intended to play anything like the role of theoretical premises in deductive arguments. Furthermore, on the anti-semantical reading all Frege's judgments, i.e. all his genuine theoretical claims, are expressible in the formula language, where proofs are set forth by means of assertions, and assertions are recorded by means of the judgment stroke. As van Heijenoort insisted, Frege does not and cannot so transcribe certain apparently crucial claims about his basic philosophical notions (e.g. *function, concept, object*). It is Frege's conception of logic, these philosophers argue, which leads him to treat such apparently metasystematic and semantical talk as mere pedagogical rhetoric. Thus all such talk must be sharply distinguished from a theory of sense, a theory of meaning, or even a theory of how the truth-values of sentences are determined by semantic features of their constituents.[11]

For example, in "What Does a Concept-Script Do?" (1983), Cora Diamond emphasized, as had van Heijenoort, Frege's treatment of "the concept *Horse*":

> What Frege thinks is that through an inadequacy of ordinary language, we can form sentences in it which are acceptable according to its rules but which are not the expression of any thought. It is possible to become clear about what has happened, if we are led to see how thoughts are expressed in a language more nearly adequate by the standards of logic. In grasping the significance of the distinctions embodied in that language, we do not grasp any ineffable truths. A truth is a truth about something; a true thought (that is) is about

whatever logic may construe it as being about. But the distinctions embodied in the concept-script are not what any thought can be about.

(Diamond 1991a: 140–1)

Ricketts bases his argument for an anti-semantical reading of Frege on what he takes to be Frege's underlying conception of judgment and inference.[12] This conception, he argues, lies behind the way Frege introduces his formula language and is intimately connected with Frege's arguments that truth is indefinable.[13] At best, holds Ricketts, Frege's post-1890 talk of *Sinn* and *Bedeutung* is in "deep tension" with his underlying conception of the universality of logic (Ricketts 1985: 3; 1986a: 172; 1986b: 66–7).

Such readings are almost always buttressed by an appeal to the influence of Frege upon Wittgenstein. In *Tractatus* 4.112 Wittgenstein wrote that:

The aim of philosophy is the logical clarification of thoughts.
Philosophy is not a theory but an activity.
A philosophical work consists essentially of elucidations (Erläuterungen).
The result of philosophy is not a number of "philosophical propositions," but to make propositions clear.

(Wittgenstein 1922: 4.112, cf. 6.54)

The line of descent from Frege appears to be explicit; the anti-semantical tradition sees in Wittgenstein the heir to Frege, and the *Tractatus* show/say distinction is said to have emerged directly from Frege's conception of logic as universal.[14]

Dummett remains unmoved by such claims. Indeed, in his 1981 *The Interpretation of Frege's Philosophy* he explicitly based his semantical reading of Frege on what *he* insisted was Frege's "universal logic":

It is, of course, true that Frege did not attempt to explain his logical notation by giving rules of translation from his formulas into sentences of natural language. Rather, when you grasp the senses of the primitive symbols, you thereby grasp the thoughts expressed by the formulas, which thoughts you are then able to express in any language known to you and capable of expressing them. But it is plain that he did not think that, in the logical notation of *Grundgesetze*, he had devised a language in which thoughts could be expressed that could not be expressed in any other way; the logic of *Grundgesetze* was intended as a *universal logic*, not one peculiar to a special language unconnected with the thoughts we are ordinarily concerned to communicate to one another. *The meaning-theoretical notions used in Part I of Grundgesetze are therefore not to be considered as applying exclusively to Frege's formal system.* They are to be taken as applicable both to it and to natural language, and perhaps as required for any intelligible language; and the *theory of meaning that embodies them accordingly serves both as a theory of sense for natural language and as a foundation for the formal logic* . . .

If these conclusions are correct, there is a substantial body of Frege's theory—*precisely that comprising his philosophy of language*—of which no definitive exposition, comparable to *Grundgesetze*, or even carrying an authority equal to that of *Grundlagen*, exists.... We can do no more than surmise the reason why he never achieved a formulation of his *general theory of philosophical logic.*

(Dummett 1981: 18–19, my emphases)

Dummett admits that Part I of *Grundgesetze*, where Frege explains to the reader how to use his system, contains "no definitive exposition" of a semantical theory. Yet, Dummett argues, since Frege's apparatus of philosophical notions such as *function, object, sense, reference,* and so on are intended to apply to natural language as well as to language regimented in the formula language, there is in Frege's writings a semantical theory which goes far beyond "hints" and "clues" to help the reader "catch on" to the formula language. Dummett takes Frege's conception of the universality of logic to commit Frege to a theory of meaning for his formula language, a theory which simultaneously applies to sentences of natural language. Thus we have Dummett's implicit challenge to the anti-semantical tradition: What is the point of forcing a reading on Frege which *precludes* him from adopting anything like a contemporary metasystematic perspective on his formula language? That is, if we were to imagine Frege living a bit longer than he had, and learning of model-theoretic results, on what grounds and for what purposes can we hold that Frege's conception of logic would have had to shift if he had come to accept those results as illuminative of logic?

Dummett reiterated this challenge in his 1984 review of Baker and Hacker's *Logical Excavations.* Baker and Hacker too had claimed that:

Begriffsschrift contains the first complete axiomatization of the propositional calculus. Of course, Frege did not prove its completeness or its consistency. Indeed, the scorn that he poured on Hilbert's metalogical investigations of axiomatization of geometry he would have turned too against metalogical proofs concerning his own logical system. The only proof of the consistency of a set of axioms is a demonstration of their joint truth, the only demonstration of their independence the compatibility of the denial of one with the joint assertion of the rest (*On the Foundations of Geometry and Formal Theories of Arithmetic,* 15f.,104). Lacking any means of precisely demarcating logical laws apart from their derivation as theorems within his axiomatic system (Cf. *Grundgesetze der Arithmetik* p. xvii, he was not even in a position to frame an exact question about the completeness of his axiomatization.

(Baker and Hacker 1984: 114)

Hence Baker and Hacker concluded that there are "no grounds for asserting that [Frege] advanced ... to any conception that the true business of logicians is a science of language (semantics) ... The hypothesis that [Frege] intended to lay the foundation of logical semantics is implausible" (1984: 248–49).[15] Dummett responded:

The word "semantics" is used in several different ways, but the references to logic and logicians suggest that what [Baker and Hacker] have in mind is a semantic theory for a formal language as conceived in contemporary model theory. If so, their [above-quoted] assertion is very surprising, since Part I of *Grundgesetze* appears to contain a semantic theory for the formal language, clearly separated from the account of its formation rules, axioms and rules of inference: this theory is stated by stipulating what references the primitive symbols are to have, and laying down how the reference of a complex expression is determined from the references of its constituents. In addition, Frege gives a general framework for such a theory, namely an account of the various possible logical types of expression, of their nature and how they are formed, and of what it is to assign a reference to an expression of any one such type; this is likewise clearly separated from the specific stipulations governing the primitive symbols of the system.

One reason why Baker and Hacker do not see the matter in this light is that they conflate a semantic theory with a semantic definition of logical consequence. They are quite right in saying that Frege lacked the latter notion. He lacked it because he did not operate with the conception of a range of possible interpretations of a formal language. . . . *If, however, he had formed this conception, he would have had very little more work to do to arrive at the semantic notion of validity: for the background theory stated in Part I of Grundgesetze would immediately have yielded a formulation of what, in general, any one such interpretation should consist in. It is precisely because of the presence of this background theory, and its close, though not complete, resemblance to the notion used by modern logicians of an interpretation of a formal language within classical two-valued semantics, that Frege's work can be fruitfully compared with that of later logicians.*

(Dummett 1984: 201, my emphasis)

Thus Dummett emphasizes the ease with which Frege's work may be appropriated from a contemporary model-theoretic perspective. And he remains deeply dissatisfied with the notion that Frege's mature philosophy of logic is in tension with model theoretical clarification of logical notions.

Dummett again gave voice to this dissatisfaction in his review of a 1987 essay of Dreben and van Heijenoort (Dummett 1987). In this essay, a commentary on Gödel's dissertation and subsequent publications on the model-theoretic (semantical) completeness of first-order logic, Dreben and van Heijenoort raise the question: Why was it that fifty years elapsed between the publication of Frege's *Begriffsschrift* (1879) and Gödel's proof of the completeness theorem (1929)?[16] Their answer is that in order to frame the question of completeness coherently, the algebra of logic tradition—the tradition which denied the universality of logic and emphasized the notion of varying universes of discourse—needed to be combined with the quite different logicist tradition stemming from Frege and Russell:

For Frege, and then for Russell and Whitehead, logic was universal: within each explicit formulation of logic all deductive reasoning, including all of classical analysis and much of Cantorian set theory, was to be formalized. Hence not only was pure quantification theory never at the center of their attention, but metasystematic questions as such, for example the question of completeness, could not be meaningfully raised. We can give different formulations of logic, formulations that differ with respect to what logical constants are taken as primitive or what formulas are taken as formal axioms, but we have no vantage point from which we can survey a given formalism as a whole, let alone look at logic whole.

(Dreben and van Heijenoort 1986: 44)

Once again, this reading of Frege is buttressed by quoting from Russell:

In the words of Whitehead and Russell 1910 (page 95, or 1925 page 91),

"It is to some extent optional what ideas we take as undefined in mathematics. . . . We know no way of proving that such and such a system of undefined ideas contains as few as will give such and such results. Hence we can only say that such and such ideas are undefined in such and such a system, not that they are indefinable."

We are within logic and cannot look at it from outside. We are subject to what Sheffer called "the logocentric predicament" . . . The only way to approach the problem of what a formal system can do is to derive theorems. *Again to quote Russell and Whitehead, "the chief reason in favor of any theory on the principle of mathematics must always be inductive, i.e., it must lie in the fact that the theory in quetion enables us to deduce ordinary mathematics"* (1910, page v, or 1925, page v). (On this point see van Heijenoort, "Logic as Calculus and Logic as Language" and Goldfarb, "Logic in the Twenties: the nature of the quantifier".)
. . . To raise the question of semantic completeness the Frege–Russell–Whitehead view of logic as all embracing had to be abandoned, and Frege's notion of a formal system had to become itself an object of mathematical inquiry and be subjected to the model-theoretic analyses of the algebraists of logic.

(Dreben and van Heijenoort 1986: 44, my emphasis)[17]

Dreben and van Heijenoort's use of the history of logic to develop an anti-semantical reading of Frege did not convince Dummett:

Dreben and van Heijenoort . . . discuss [a] question, one of the most interesting in conceptual history, why it took so long for the concept of completeness to be framed. . . . The explanation given by Dreben and van Heijenoort is that, in the tradition descending from Boole through Peirce and Schröder, the very notion of a formal system was lacking: in his paper of 1915, for instance, Löwenheim worked with exclusively semantic notions. Frege, on the other hand, had bequeathed the notion of a formal system to the tradition that stemmed from him; but, according to that tradition, logic is all-embracing: since there is only one logic in accordance with which all reasoning must be conducted, we cannot step outside logic in order to formulate theorems *about* rather than *within* it.

However accurate a statement of the views of Russell and Whitehead this may be, it appears to me an oversimplification as applied to Frege. True, he never considered the sentential and first-order fragments of his logic as significantly separable from it; and he had repudiated the traditional conception of variable universes of discourse. But, in his *Grundgesetze*, he did attempt a precise formulation of the semantics of his formal system, clearly distinguished from the specification of its axioms and rules of inference. Indeed, he attempted a proof that every term of the formal system had a unique denotation (and every sentence a unique truth-value), which, if correct, would have constituted a consistency-proof. Moreover, he did not content himself with laying down specific interpretations for the primitive symbols, but stipulated what form the interpretation of an expression of each logical type must, in general, take. *All that he lacked, therefore, for a formulation of the concepts of validity and satisfiability was the conception of variable interpretations* (ironically so close at hand in Hilbert's *Foundations of Geometry*). The mystery of the half-century that elapsed between the invention of mathematical logic and the formulation of its fundamental problem is thus not fully dispelled.

(Dummett 1987: 573–4, my emphases)

In unpublished lectures Dreben has pointed out that in at least two places Frege *did* raise the question of completeness (*Vollständigkeit*). In *Begriffsschrift* Frege wrote,

Since in view of the boundless multitude of laws that can be enunciated we cannot list them all, we cannot achieve completeness (*Vollständigkeit*) except by searching out those that, *by their power*, contain all of them. Now it must be admitted, certainly, that the way followed here is not the only one in which the reduction can be done. That is why not all relations between the laws of thought are set out clearly through the present mode of presentation. There is perhaps another set of judgments from which, when those contained in the rules are added, all laws of thought could likewise be deduced. Still, with the method of reduction presented here such a multitude of relations is exhibited that any other derivation will be much facilitated thereby.

(Frege 1879: §13)

And in "On Mr. Peano's Conceptual Notation and My Own" (1897):

In order to test whether a list of axioms is complete (*vollständig*), we have to try and derive from them all the proofs of the branch of learning to which they relate. And in so doing it is imperative that we draw conclusions only in accordance with purely logical laws, for otherwise something might intrude unobserved which should have been laid down as an axiom.

(Frege 1984: 235; 1967: 221)

However, Dreben argues that these passages confirm the Dreben and van Heijenoort reading of Frege. For in both passages Frege eschews any jump to a metalevel; he operates with what Russell called "inductive" reasoning and what van Heijenoort, following Herbrand, called an "experimental" approach: derive as many theorems as possible *within* the system in order to answer the question of whether the system is complete.

Thus, those questions Dummett holds that Frege *merely* didn't raise, but "had it to hand to raise," others say he didn't raise because he *couldn't* raise, "couldn't" in the sense that he did not have room, within his conception of logic, for the posing of these questions in their metamathematical sense.

In response to a 1992 lecture of Dreben's, Quine expressed scepticism about the anti-semantical reading.[18] Does Dreben mean, asked Quine, that if Frege had seen Gödel's proof of the completeness theorem, Frege wouldn't have been able to understand it? Dreben replied: the Frege of the *Grundgesetze* would have understood it as a piece of mathematics, as showing that a certain set-theoretically definable class is recursively enumerable; but Frege would have questioned whether this set was a proper specification of his notion of logical truth, of logical validity.[19] Naturally, Quine, devoted as he is to Tarski, was not satisfied with this response. Dreben's reply to Quine is also his reply to the suggestions of Heck, Stanley, and Tappenden that since logic is universal, by the techniques of Gödel and Tarski, many metasystematic questions, in particular the completeness theorem, can be carried out *within* the system.[20] Presumably Heck, Stanley, and Tappenden would share Quine's dissatisfaction, as of course would Dummett.

II

My aim in what follows is modest: I wish to slightly shift the scope of the interpretive debate about Frege and semantics. Rather than directly addressing those elements of Frege's conception which have been treated at length in the recent literature, I shall focus on one especially puzzling feature of Frege's *formal* procedure, namely, his use of the double stroke (" $|\vdash$ "), his symbol for explicit definition. Frege's use of this symbol—and his attitude toward his use of it—seem to me to exemplify in an especially perspicuous way how it is that Frege's writings can so easily lend themselves to such radically different interpretations and appropriations of his philosophy. For the double stroke for definitions shows us, I claim, the importance of the fact that at least until 1903 Frege never clearly articulated a distinction between "metalanguage" and "object language," or between a "metasystematic level" and an "object level."[21] It helps us to see that even if we can quite naturally regiment Frege's work by means of the distinction between meta- and object level without appearing to go beyond what is written in his logical system, the deeper philosophical questions about Frege's standpoint still remain. My discussion is not intended to decide or exhaustively characterize the interpretive questions I have canvassed about Frege and semantics. I intend, rather, to emphasize that these questions will not be resolved by any argument resting its case on purely formal or mathematical features of Frege's system. If I am right that there is no way to establish how to read uniquely Frege's use of the double stroke, then the interpretative questions make themselves felt even at the most basic level of Frege's system, in the part of his work one might think is *not* open to philosophical interpretation, viz., in his formal system. This confirms that the debate about how best to read Frege is at root a philosophical one, not amenable to resolution by means of any particular formal or mathematical distinction we may find in Frege.

In contemporary logic and philosophy of logic we may distinguish three different issues surrounding identity statements and definitions. First, we may give a syntactical specification of identity statements and definitions in a particular formal language by making statements in a metalanguage (whether metasyntactic or metasemantic). Second, we may discuss the nature or purpose of definitions and the nature or purpose of identity statements *about* the identity relation. Third, we may give an account of the nature of the identity relation itself, the nature of the truth asserted in a true identity statement.[22]

It is striking that in his 1894 review of Husserl's *Philosophy of Arithmetic*, Frege seems to have conflated these issues. This apparent conflation seems to indicate that Frege did not always sharply distinguish between statements and what statements are about. For in this review Frege forwards the following argument, which purports to show that identity is undefinable: "Since any definition is an identification [*Gleichung*], identity itself [*Gleichheit selbst*] cannot be defined" (Frege 1984: 200; 1967: 184; 1980a: 80).[23]

The argument appears to be this: in order to present a definition, one must *use* the identity sign, and thus there is no way to present an explicit, i.e. eliminative definition of the identity sign itself.[24] Therefore, Frege reasons, identity must be taken as a logical primitive, an undefined— because undefinable, and hence logically simple—notion.[25]

This 1894 argument for the indefinability of identity is simultaneously an argument that the notions of *definability* and of *definition* cannot be defined.[26] For in the *Begriffsschrift* and in the *Grundgesetze*, in order to present a definition Frege must always use, not only the identity sign, but also his special sign for definitions, the double stroke ("$|\!\!\vdash$"). Hence, by Frege's 1894 line of reasoning there is no way to eliminate the sign for definition by means of a definition itself, for in order to frame a definition one must always *use* the double stroke. The plausibility of this reasoning and the parallel argument about identity, thus appear to turn in part upon Frege's not sharply distinguishing between an object level and a metalevel, and in part upon the way in which he handles definitions formally within his logical systems.

However, fourteen years earlier Frege had claimed to be able to define identity, to show, that is, that it is *not* a logically simple notion. Presumably his idea was to use Leibniz's law of the identity of indiscernibles, according to which *a* is identical to *b* if *a* and *b* share all their properties. In "Boole's Logical Calculus and the *Begriffsschrift*" (1880–81) Frege argued that his own formula language is superior to Boole's partly because

> Boole uses a greater number of signs. Indeed I too have an identity sign, but I use it between contents of possible judgment almost exclusively to apply the stipulation of sense of a new designation. Furthermore I now no longer regard it as a primitive sign, but would define [*erklären*] it by means of others. In that case there would be one sign of mine to three of Boole's.
>
> (Frege 1979: 35–6; 1969: 40)

This appears to indicate both that Frege previously regarded identity as a primitive notion, and that he came, at least for a time, to change his mind about this.[27] This may be connected with his doubts about the treatment of identity he propounded in the *Begriffsschrift* (1879). There Frege held that identity is a relation between names and not objects, writing:

> Identity of content differs from conditionality and negation in that it applies to names and not to contents. Whereas in other contexts signs are merely representatives of their content, so that every combination into which they enter expresses only a relation between their respective contents, they suddenly display their own selves when they are combined by means of the sign for identity of content; for it expresses the circumstance that two names have the same content. Hence the introduction of a sign for identity of content necessarily produces a bifurcation in the meaning (*Bedeutung*) of all signs: they stand at times for their content, at time for themselves.
>
> (Frege 1879: §8)

Of course, Frege is aware that it will strike his readers as odd that names come to change their *Bedeutungen* in contexts where the identity sign appears between them. He even raises the spectre of an attitude toward identity later pursued by Wittgenstein in the *Tractatus*:

> At first we have the impression that what we are dealing with pertains merely to the *expression* and *not to the thought*, that we do not need different signs at all for the same content and hence no sign whatsoever for identity of content.
>
> (Frege 1879: §8)

But Frege immediately calls this "an empty illusion" and argues that the sign for identity of content is needed whenever we have two different ways of "determining" a conceptual content, for, "that in a particular case *two ways of determining [the content]* really yield the *same result* is the content of a *judgment*" (1879: §8). He also points out that "a more extrinsic reason for the introduction of a sign for identity of content" is our need for definitions, it being "at times expedient to introduce an abbreviation for a lengthy expression" (1879: §8). But it does not seem that Frege conceives of either definitions or of the shift in the meaning of the names which takes place in identity contexts in terms of a clear distinction between meta and object level. Rather, he treats identity contexts as shifting the *Bedeutungen* of certain names within the very same language.

Frege came to surrender his *Begriffsschrift* theory of identity.[28] By 1890–1 he had divided up his original notion of conceptual content into two aspects, via the notions of *Sinn* and *Bedeutung*, and he used these notions to explain the relation between names and an object in both informative and uninformative truths of identity. Whether or not this is connected with his argument that identity is a logically primitive (undefinable) notion, after 1884 he never again claims that identity can be defined. In the *Grundgesetze* identity is taken to be a logical primitive.[29]

Despite his vacillation about the nature of the identity relation and the nature of our statements about that relation, Frege seems never to have vacillated about how to handle definitions *formally*. However, we shall see that just as there are competing ways of reading Frege's discussions of truth, meaning, and sense, so there are competing ways of reading his use of the double stroke for definitions. I shall focus most closely on the use of the double stroke in the *Grundgesetze*, which, I believe, should be the primary testing ground for any interpretation of Frege.

By closely following Frege's textual divisions in volume I of the *Grundgesetze*, we may and should, at least prima facie, distinguish several different ways in which Frege discusses—and uses—his formula language. First, in his Introduction, he presents, entirely in German, a series of what he calls philosophical arguments about the nature and scope of logic. Second, in Part I, Chapter 1 he introduces his basic logical notions (such as *function, concept, object, value-range,* and *generality*) and presents the primitive signs, the Basic Laws and the formal rules of inference of the formula language. Third, in Chapter 2, Frege discusses the nature of definitions, introduces the double stroke, and then uses it to frame what he calls *besondere*, that is, "special" definitions. These definitions are applied later in proofs through substitutions. Frege also lists the Basic Laws and Basic Rules and "adds a few supplementary points" (1893: §§47–8).

Part II of Volume I, where Frege's proofs occur, falls into two kinds of sections (cf. 1893: §53). On the one hand there are the *Zerlegungen*, or "analyses," where Frege sketches the essential elements of his proofs in a mixture of German, signs of the formula language, and *names* of judgments, that is, (expressions of) judgments surrounded by quotation marks.[30] Each such *Zerlegung* is set off in a separately numbered section, and is immediately followed by another section presenting a precise construction, or *Aufbau*. An *Aufbau* is used to construct proofs. It contains primitive signs of the formula language, indices and markers to help us read the *Aufbau*, and signs that have been explicitly introduced by means of prior definitions. It contains no words of German or of any other natural language. An *Aufbau* always consists of an annotated series of judgments, each prefaced by the judgment stroke, and each one of which either (i) is an identity indexed with a capital Greek letter referring back to an explicit definition given in a prior *Zerlegung*, or else (ii) follows by means of Frege's explicit inference rules from Basic Law(s) or from truths previously asserted in earlier *Aufbauten*. By contrast, the *Zerlegungen* contain no formal proofs. Indeed, the *Zerlegungen* contain no judgments in Frege's special sense, no uses of the judgment stroke to record judgments. *The Zerlegungen contain only words of German, as well as names of judgments and occurrences of identities preceded by the double stroke which are not surrounded by quotation marks.* Writes Frege,

> In connection with the following proofs I emphasize that the implementations which I always mention under the heading "*Zerlegung*" serve only for the ease of the reader; they could fail to appear without lessening the power of the proofs in any way, for that power is to be found only under the heading "*Aufbau*".
>
> (Frege: 1893: §53)

Now what, *precisely*, does Frege say about the use he makes of his double stroke for definitions? We are interested in the bearing this question has on the appropriateness of ascribing to Frege a sharp distinction between his use and his mention of his formula language, between his procedures at what we might naturally call his object level and what we might naturally call his meta level. It is striking that Frege so sharply distinguishes between contexts of formal proof, his *Aufbauten*, and contexts in which he gives definitions and discusses his formula language, his *Zerlegungen*. The anti-semantical tradition would, presumably, deny that the *Zerlegungen* are part of any substantive metatheory for the formula language.[31] I thus ask the following interpretive questions:

1 Is Frege's double stroke a (primitive) sign of his formula language?
2 If it is not a sign used *within* Frege's formula language, but rather a sign *about* the formula language, does Frege's use of the double stroke in his definitions function as *elucidation* of his formula language, or rather as part of a *metatheory* of his formula language?
3 If the double stroke is part of a metatheory, is this a genuine *semantical* theory or just a *metasyntactic* theory?

The answers to these questions, as I shall now try to explain, are not as readily available as one might think.

In both the *Begriffsschrift* and in the *Grundgesetze* the double stroke indicates the operation of defining one sign in terms of others, and this operation always has a double role. Frege's double stroke reflects what he calls the "double-sidedness of formulas" (*Doppelseitigkeit der Formel*) used to express his definitions (cf. 1879: §24). From 1879 on, whenever Frege uses the double stroke to frame a definition, he takes himself to be putting forward a *stipulation*, something that is not a judgment at all (1879: §24). Yet any such stipulation can, he maintains, be "immediately transformed" into a *judgment* of identity and used in logical constructions, in proofs within his system. (In the 1879 *Begriffsschrift* Frege calls these judgments "analytic"— cf. 1879: §24.)[32] And this is how Frege actually proceeds. He frames an explicit definition with the double stroke and then peels away the first of the two vertical strokes in order to assert a corresponding identity judgment in the context of an *Aufbau*.

Thus in its first role, a definition *stipulates* that definiens and definiendum are to share the same content (according to Frege's 1879 view), and the same *Sinn* and *Bedeutung* (according to Frege's post-1890 view). On Frege's early account of identity,

> [A definition is a proposition which] differs from the judgments considered up to now in that it contains signs that have not been defined before; it itself gives the definition. It does not say "The right side of the equation has the same content as the left," but "It is to have the same content." Hence this proposition is not a judgment, and consequently *not a synthetic judgment* either, to use the Kantian expression.
>
> (Frege 1879: §24)

And on Frege's later account of identity,

> [The double stroke of definition] is used in place of the judgment-stroke where something is to be, not judged, but abbreviated by definition. We introduce a new name by means of a *definition* by stipulating that it is to have the same sense [*Sinn*] and the same meaning [*Bedeutung*] as some name composed of signs that are familiar.
>
> (Frege 1893: §27)

In its second role, a definition is immediately "transformed" into a *judgment* in an *Aufbau*. This judgment says *that* the two signs *do* share the same content—or, after 1890, the same *Sinn* and the same *Bedeutung*. Frege conceives of the double stroke as literally picturing this dual aspect of definitions: its first, vertical bar indicates the stipulation; its second vertical bar, which looks just like the judgment stroke, indicates the transition from the stipulation into a judgment of identity. The judgment is only expressed, i.e. asserted, in an *Aufbau*, in proofs where it is prefaced by the judgment stroke. But the transition from a stipulation to a judgment is immediate and unexplained.[33]

How are we to interpret Frege's use of the double stroke? One suggestion is to build on our contemporary distinction between meta- and object language in characterizing Frege's procedures. Then we might hold that the double stroke is *not* a primitive sign of Frege's formula language. After all, it occurs only within the *Zerlegungen*[34], and never within *Aufbauten*. Its role, we might claim, is relegated to a place "outside" the workings of the formula language itself. Furthermore, because an *Aufbau* contains defined terms which are not primitive signs of the formula language, we might also hold that an *Aufbau refers to* the "pure" formula language itself, in which formal derivations are written *solely* with the use of primitive signs of the formula language. Thus I shall call the *metasyntactic* reading of the double stroke.[35]

On this reading Frege is seen to treat the double stroke for definitions as a metasyntactic device: it is *not* part of his formal system. Every use of Frege's double stroke in a *Zerlegung* is coded into a corresponding *Aufbau* through its index, a capital Greek letter. This letter must be written in the margin at every line of an *Aufbau* where the corresponding judgment of identity appears. So, on the metasyntactic reading, the double stroke is an explicit sign of an algorithm which "decodes" every *Aufbau* of the *Grundgesetze* into a proof couched solely in primitive signs of the formula language. (The *Aufbauten* on this view are like "programs" which can be algorithmically carried into an "assembly level language.") In the primitive formula language itself all "definitional" judgments of identity vanish. This might be held to explain why Frege repeatedly remarks that from the perspective of the formula language, definitions are "mere abbreviations," convenient shorthand devices used to make logical constructions, *Aufbauten*, perspicuous. Differently put, Frege's *Zerlegungen*, his analyses, use definitions in order to present his logical constructions in such a way that they can be taken in by us:

> The need of definitions never ceases to be apparent in any attempt of this sort. . . . The definitions do not really create anything, and in my opinion may not do so; they merely introduce abbreviated notations (names), which could be dispensed with were it not that lengthiness would then make for insuperable *external* difficulties.
>
> (1893: Preface, vi, my emphasis)

In the *Begriffsschrift* the same point appears to be made twice:

> A more *extrinsic* reason for the introduction of a sign for identity of content is that it is at times *expedient* to introduce an abbreviation for a lengthy expression . . .
>
> (Frege 1879: §8, my emphasis)

> [A definition] is not a judgment, and consequently *not a synthetic judgment* either, to use the Kantian expression. . . . If [it] were a synthetic judgment, so would be the propositions derived from it. But we can do without the notation introduced by this proposition and hence without the proposition itself as its definition; nothing follows from the proposition that could not also be inferred without it. Our sole purpose in introducing such definitions is to bring about an *extrinsic* simplification by stipulating an abbreviation. They serve besides to

emphasize a particular combination of signs in the multitude of possible ones, so that our faculty of representation can get a firmer grasp of it.

(Frege 1879: §24, my emphasis)

According to the metasyntactic reading, an *Aufbau* of the *Grundgesetze* which is not written exclusively in the primitive formula language *represents* a genuine proof; that is, it presents a precise set of rules telling us how we are to write down a particular proof in primitive signs of the formula language. We can take it in *as* a representation because it uses abbreviations. But we know it successfully represents a genuine proof only insofar as every definitional judgment of identity occurring in it can be eliminated in a mechanical way, with no appeal to elucidations, hints, or guesswork.

Of course, this "metasyntactic" reading of the double stroke cannot wholly sever the signs it speaks of from their *Sinne* and from their *Bedeutungen*. When Frege speaks of a definition as a "stipulation," he does not mean that a definition tells us to substitute one uninterpreted sign for another uninterpreted series of signs. Rather, the stipulation appeals to the *content*, to the *Sinn* and the *Bedeutung*, of the definiens. As he writes in "Function and Concept," "In definition it is always a matter of associating with a sign a sense or a meaning. Where sense and meaning are missing, we cannot properly speak either of a sign or of a definition."

Thus the metasyntactic reading inevitably spills over into some sort of meta*semantical* reading. The double stroke may be said to function as a paradigmatically semantical sign insofar as it tells the reader how to assign *Sinne* and *Bedeutungen* to signs. Nevertheless, even though the assignment of *Sinne* and *Bedeutungen* to newly introduced signs may take place in a metalanguage, the terms of this language have, at least so far, no more, no less and no different semantical content than what is already gotten—directly and immediately—out of the object language. Thus, the question as to whether this metalanguage consists of mere elucidation, as opposed to an articulate semantical or philosophical theory, remains unresolved—and perhaps unresolvable—by this reading.

Moreover, in an unpublished manuscript which further develops his anti-semantical reading of Frege, Ricketts explicitly denies that Frege's double stroke for definitions is in any sense a metasyntactic device.[36] According to Ricketts, just as the judgment stroke uses the formula language to make judgments—something we do *within* language—so the double stroke uses the formula language to define one sign in terms of another—something else we do *within* language. On his view, the double stroke is part of Frege's formula language, and definitions take place within the universal formula language. Thus does Ricketts interpret the immediacy of Frege's transitions from stipulations to judgments of identity.

If Ricketts is correct, then Frege's system has no precise, closed, vocabulary, and there is no set of well-formed formulas given by Frege once and for all. Instead, through the use of the double stroke, the formula language is systematically enlarged in a step-by-step way. This enlargement helps us to work with the formula language more easily, and this is the point of Frege's definitions. On this reading there is no room to view the *Aufbauten* as metasyntactic representations of the primitive formula language, for there is no formula language with a fixed vocabulary. Frege *had* no closed formalism at all! Instead, the *Aufbauten* function by means of the formula language in the context of a carefully regulated, growing vocabulary. The additions of new vocabulary in definitions function like special axioms of identity which are always conservative extensions of Frege's original primitive system—though as Ricketts emphasizes, Frege nowhere attempts to *prove* such a metatheoretic statement. On Ricketts' reading, the uses of the double stroke, though not part of Frege's logical constructions, are formalized in the *Aufbauten* by means of the judgments of identity which are indexed to the explicit definitions given in the *Zerlegungen*. Definitions are set off from *Aufbauten* because they are not judgments, but, rather, stipulations. But they are still "part of the system" in the sense of being framed within the universal formula language, they are not stipulations or abbreviations made from a standpoint external to the system or the language. Thus Ricketts holds that Frege did not have a metasyntactical theory, but only rules for writing proofs down in his formula language.[37]

This shows how deeply the debate between the semantical and the anti-semantical readings of Frege may be said to penetrate our understanding of Frege's philosophy and logic. For we have been told—even by van Heijenoort himself—that Frege was the first to frame precisely the notion of a formal system (1985: 12). If Ricketts is right, then even this understanding of Frege may have to be revised, even if only slightly. My point has been to emphasize the difficulties we face in attempting to extract definitive answers about Frege's overarching enterprise, and even about the structure of his formula language. To read Frege we are constantly thrown back on our own philosophical predilections—even at those points where Frege's procedures may seem most clear.[38]

NOTES

1 This chapter is slated to appear in French in *Frege, Logique Mathématique et Philosophie*, ed. Mathieu Marion and Alain Voizard (Paris: l'Harmattan). I

hereby give my permission for the paper to be printed there and for my rights to it to be transferred to Routledge for the present volume.

I am indebted to the English translations of Frege cited, though I have occasionally altered them when I felt it necessary. Unless otherwise specified, page numbers refer to the original page or section number of Frege's works.

2 Van Heijenoort, "Logic as Calculus and Logic as Language," (1985: 12–13): "Boole has his universe class, and De Morgan his universe of discourse, denoted by '1'. But these have hardly any ontological import. They can be changed at will. The universe of discourse comprehends only what we agree to consider at a certain time, in a certain context. For Frege it cannot be a question of changing universes. One could not even say that he restricts himself to *one* universe. His universe is *the* universe."

3 Van Heijenoort, "Frege and Vagueness," (1985: 95). Van Heijenoort is quoting from Quine's "Facts of the Matter" (1977), and holds, with Quine, that these words accurately describe Frege's conception of his own enterprise. Of course, the whole point of Quine's thought experiment about the indeterminacy of translation is to undercut the view that there is a "latent and determinate content" to be elicited from ordinary language. Compare Burton Dreben, "Putnam, Quine and the Facts" and Hilary Putnam's reply in Hill (ed.) (1992).

4 Compare Michael Dummett, *The Interpretation of Frege's Philosophy* (1981: 13, 17–19).

5 Goldfarb wrote: "Frege has often been read as providing *all* the central notions that constitute our current understanding of quantification. For example, in his recent book on Frege (*Frege: Philosophy of Language*, first edn), Michael Dummett speaks of 'the semantics which [Frege] introduced for formulas of the language of predicate logic.' That is, 'An interpretation of such a formula . . . is obained by assigning entities of suitable kinds to the primitive nonlogical constants occurring in the formula . . . [T]his procedure is exactly the same as the modern semantic treatment of predicate logic' (pp. 89–90). Indeed, 'Frege would therefore have had within his grasp the concepts necessary to frame the notion of the completeness of a formalization of logic as well as its soundness . . . but he did not do so' (p. 82). This common appraisal of Frege's work is, I think, quite misleading" (Goldfarb 1979: 351).

6 I use the term "anti-semantical" as shorthand for "anti-theory of meaning" or "anti-theory of semantics." It should be clear to the reader from what has already been quoted that in a loose or intuitive sense of the term, Frege lives in semantics. My overview of this "anti-semantical" tradition is highly schematic, and obviously cannot do justice to the specifics of each individual member's view of Frege.

7 Others who have discussed and characterized this tradition and its relation to Dummett include Richard Heck (forthcoming); Jason Stanley (forthcoming); and Sanford Shieh (forthcoming). James Conant's article "The Search for Logically Alien Thought: Descartes, Kant, Frege and the *Tractatus*" is replied to by Hilary Putnam (1992). See also Kemp (1995).

8 Note that "Erläuterung" is not systematically translated (Cf. 1969: 224, 232, 254).

9 An especially subtle working out of the sorts of paradoxes Frege faces in introducing his system is contained in de Rouilhan (1988).

10 Passages where Frege calls attention to such ideas occur in "On Sense and Reference" (1980a: 61; 1984: 161; 1967: 145); see also "Concept and Object" (1980a: 54; 1984: 193; 1967: 177; 1980b: 37; 1976: 63; 1893, 1903: Appendix 2, n 1, 1969: 288ff).

11 For example, in "What Nonsense Might Be" (1991a: 97) Cora Diamond explicitly criticized Dummett's reading of Frege, emphasizing that: "On the Frege–Wittgenstein view, if a sentence makes no sense, *no* part of it can be said to mean what it does in some other sentence which does make sense— any more than a word can be said to mean something in isolation. If 'Caesar is a prime number' is nonsense, then 'Caesar' does not mean what it does when it is in use as a proper name, and the last four words do not mean what they do in sentences which make sense" (Diamond 1991a: 100). "I have wanted . . . parallels (between Frege and Wittgenstein) to be suggested. I have . . . wanted to suggest . . . a *distance* between Frege's view and what might be called a Tarskian view" (1991a: 112).

12 All of Ricketts' work is relevant, but see especially 1985 and 1986b.

13 Frege's arguments that truth is indefinable are canvassed by Ricketts in "Objectivity and Objecthood" (1986b), as well as in "Logic and Truth in Frege" (1996a).

14 See Diamond (1991a: ch. 4), Sluga (1980: 182), Ricketts (1985), and Weiner (forthcoming).

15 Like Dreben, Goldfarb and van Heijenoort, Baker and Hacker draw a parallel between Frege and Russell: "It is salutary . . . to remember how modern the semantic conception of validity is. Although Russell acknowledged a profound debt to Frege 'in all questions of logical analysis', *Principia Mathematica* did not formulate a clear distinction between logical truth and provability within its axiom system, and hence it did not envisage the possibility of proofs of consistency, independence, and completeness" (1984: 373).

16 Compare van Heijenoort, "Logic as Calculus and Logic as Language" (1985: 14), and Goldfarb (1979).

17 Compare van Heijenoort, "Logic as Calculus and Logic as Language" (1985: 14). Note that in a footnote on p. 95 of *Principia Mathematica* (1910 edn; p. 91 1925 edn) Russell and Whitehead explicitly refer to the 1903 passage quoted by Goldfarb (see p.144 above). It might be added that even as late as Russell's *Introduction to Mathematical Philosophy* (1919) we find Russell maintaining that "The theory of deduction . . . and the laws for propositions involving 'all' and 'some,' are of the very texture of mathematical reasoning: without them, or something like them, we should not merely not obtain the same results, but we should not obtain any results at all. We cannot use them as hypotheses, and deduce hypothetical consequences, for they are rules of deduction as well as premisses. They must be absolutely true, or else what we deduce according to them does not even follow from the premisses" (Russell 1919, 1920: 191).

18 Dreben, "Frege on Foundations," 4/6/92 lecture to the Boston University Colloquium for the Philosophy of Science. Quine responded as a member of the audience.

19 See, for example, Thomas Ricketts (1996a). Ricketts argues that for Frege truth is not a genuine property, and *truth* not a genuine concept. Hence Frege would not have been able to accept, without significant modification of his standpoint, the Tarskian criterion of material adequacy as relevant to any

truth *definition*. A fortiori, from Frege's point of view the Gödel completeness theorem, formalized in the *Begriffsschrift*, could not give any explanation or account of the notion of "logical truth." Compare Ricketts' "Objectivity and Objecthood" (1986b: 76, especially footnote 18).

20 For an investigation of a similar response, namely Wittgenstein's response to Gödel's first incompleteness result, see my "On Saying What You Really Want to Say: Wittgenstein, Gödel and the Trisection of the Angle" (Floyd 1995).

21 In the very late "Logical Generality" (1923 or later) Frege began to articulate a distinction between what he calls *Hilfssprache* and *Darlegungssprache*, which could be taken to anticipate Tarski's later distinction between metalanguage and object language. See Frege 1979: 260ff., 1969: 287ff.

22 We can also discuss, in set theory, the capacity of a formal theory to define, i.e., to contain, formulas model-theoretically satisfiable by certain relations and sets. Such a discussion would I think be quite foreign to Frege, but I shall not argue this point here.

23 I am grateful to J. Weiner for having pointed this passage out to me in her "Frege and the Origins of Analytic Philosophy" talk.

24 See Frege's review of Husserl (1980a: 80; 1967: 184). Dummett holds that Frege's argument in the Husserl review that identity is a logically primitive notion is "not very convincing" since "it is only possible for Frege to say this because he takes the sign of identity to do duty also for the biconditional, which is in turn possible only because he assimilates sentences to names, viz., of truth-values; and in any case it seems more natural to take a definition as a stipulation of the interchangeability of two expressions, rather than of the truth of a sentence connecting them. . . . [T]he thesis of the indefinability of identity does not seem to play any important role in Frege's philosophy" (Dummett 1981: 543). Frege in one way does and in another way does not countenance a sharp distinction between stipulating interchangeability among (linguistic) expressions and capturing, analyzing, proving, and asserting by means of a *real* definition. Compare Benacerraf, "Frege: the Last Logicist" (1995).

25 What is "logically simple" cannot, according to Frege, be defined (cf. 1903: §146, n. 1; 1980a: 42).

26 Rosalind Carey pointed out to me that in "Insolubilia and Solution by Symbolic Logic" Russell writes that "the notion of definition . . . oddly enough, is not definable, and is indeed not a definite notion at all" (1906 essay, reprinted in Russell 1973: 209). The remark occurs in the context of Russell's treatment of the Richard Paradox and the Vicious Circle principle.

27 Tappenden discusses Frege's paper on Boole's logical calculus, and suggests that between at least 1880 and 1884 Frege developed an interesting and novel account of the fruitfulness of definitions and concepts—albeit a view which came into tension with the later *Sinn/Bedeutung* distinction. Tappenden argues that quantificational complexity in a definiens corresponds to fruitfulness of a definition at this stage of Frege's development. This may be related to Frege's claim to be able to define identity, although I cannot pursue this conjecture here. See Tappenden 1995. Compare Picardi 1988.

28 For an informative account of the difficulties facing Frege's early view, see Mendelsohn 1982.

29 Basic Law III in the *Grundgesetze* formalizes Leibniz's law, but does not purport in any way to be a definition of identity. Section 65 of the *Grundlagen* could be

read as explicitly advocating Leibniz's law as a definition of identity, although even in the Husserl review Frege mentions the law as expressing something important about identity (see Frege 1984: 20). Jan Harald Alnes has persuaded me that it is doubtful that in the *Grundlagen* Frege held that identity could be defined.

30 More precisely, the *Zerlegungen* contain names of judgments which will be made in the corresponding *Aufbau*, and some of these judgments will contain defined terms, as well as primitive terms of the formula language.

31 This denial is quite explicit in Weiner 1990: ch. 6.

32 The word "analytic" does not occur in *Grundgesetze*. However, in 1914 Frege says that the sentence expressing the judgment of identity corresponding to a definition is "a tautology" ("Logic in Mathematics," in 1979: 208). (Presumably he writes this *after* he and young Wittgenstein had spoken.) Jan Harald Alnes has suggested in conversation that sameness of sense on two sides of a true identity statement occurs only when the identity springs from an explicit definition or is an instance of a basic law. This would explain why, even after introducing the Sinn/Bedeutung distinction, Frege holds in "Function and Concept" that the two sides of an instance of Basic Law V "express the same sense, but in a different way," while simultaneously holding that derived truths (such as "2+2=4") involve expressions with differing senses on either side of the identity sign (Frege 1984: 143; 1967: 130).

33 This formal point points toward several unclarities in Frege's attitude toward definitions in the context of his "reduction" of arithmetic to logic. See, in particular, Benacerraf 1995, and the response to Benacerraf by Weiner 1984. See also Picardi 1988, Dummett 1991b (ch. 2), and Tappenden 1995.

34 And, of course, in the section on "special definitions" in *Grundgesetze* Chapter I and in the table of definitions in *Grundgesetze* Appendix.

35 I am aware that there is a long established usage in which the metalanguage is dubbed the "syntax language" of the object language. In this sense what I am calling "metasyntactic" would be called "syntactic."

36 In conversation, correspondence and in Chapter 1 section 3 of his unpublished manuscript on Frege.

37 Further evidence for Ricketts' view, as Ricketts himself has suggested, is *Grundgesetze* §48 #12, labeled "Citation of Definitions." Here, according to Ricketts, Frege sets out the use of the double stroke as a rule of inference of the formula language. A critic of Ricketts' view would have to claim that this section, rather than setting forth a rule of inference, is giving what Frege called in §47 a "supplementary point." Note, however, that in *Grundgesetze* §53, Frege does speak of 'the rules to which I appeal in the *Zerlegungen*" and refers the reader back to 48.

38 I was stimulated to think about Frege's treatment of definitions as a result of responding to papers by Hans Sluga and Joan Weiner at a December 1995 American Philosophical Association symposium on "Frege and the Origins of Analytic Philosophy." Both Sluga and Weiner argued against several widespread interpretations of Frege's distinction between *Sinn* and *Bedeutung*, and their arguments got me to think more carefully than I had about Frege on identity and definitions. Thanks are due to them for their stimulation, both at the symposium and in other published works. I also thank Anat Biletzki and Anat Matar for their enthusiasm and generosity in organizing the January 1996 Tel Aviv conference at which an earlier version of this

paper was read. The audiences at Tel Aviv and at Oslo University in June 1996, contributed helpful suggestions, for which I am grateful.

My understanding of Frege and controversies about how to read him is enormously indebted to Burton Dreben, and I thank him for our many hours of discussing Frege since 1983, and for his sage editorial and philosophical advice at every stage of this paper's composition. Jan Harald Alnes, Rohit Parikh, and Sanford Shieh have also offered helpful comments on drafts of my paper, as has Thomas Ricketts, whose manuscript on Frege's philosophy has been especially instructive, especially its Chapter 1, §3 on Frege on definitions.

BIBLIOGRAPHY

Baker, G. P. and Hacker, P. M. S. (1984) *Logical Excavations*, Oxford: Oxford University Press.

Benacerraf, P. (1995) "Frege: The Last Logicist," in W. Demopoulos (ed.) *Frege's Philosophy of Mathematics*, Cambridge, Mass.: Harvard University Press.

Conant J. (1992) "The Search for Logically Alien Thought: Descartes, Kant, Frege and the *Tractatus*," in Hill, C. (ed.) *Philosophical Topics* 20/1.

de Rouilhan, P. (1988) *Frege: Les Paradoxes de la Représentation*, Paris: Les Editions de Minuit.

Demopoulos, W. (ed.) (1995) *Frege's Philosophy of Mathematics*, Cambridge, Mass.: Harvard University Press.

Diamond, Cora (1991a) *The Realistic Spirit*, Cambridge, Mass.: MIT Press.

——(1991b) "Ethics, Imagination and the Method of Wittgenstein's *Tractatus*," R. Heinrich and H. Vetter (eds) *Bilder der Philosophie, Wiener Reihe 5*, 55–90.

Dreben, B. (1962–96) Unpublished lecture transcriptions.

——"Frege on Foundations," 4/6/92 lecture to the Boston University Colloquium for the Philosophy of Science, unpublished transcription.

——(1992) "Putnam, Quine and the Facts," in Hill, C. (ed.) *Philosophical Topics* 20/1.

Dreben, B. and van Heijenoort, J. (1986) "Introductory note to 1929, 1930 and 1930a," in S. Feferman, J. W. Dawson, Jr, S. C. Kleene, G. H. Moore, R. M. Solovay, J. van Heijenoort (eds) *Kurt Gödel, Collected Papers, I*. New York, Oxford: Clarendon Press.

Dummett, M. (1973, 1981) *Frege: Philosophy of Language*, Cambridge, Mass.: Harvard University Press.

——(1978) *Truth and Other Enigmas*, Cambridge, Mass.: Harvard University Press.

——(1981) *The Interpretation of Frege's Philosophy*, Cambridge, Mass.: Harvard University Press.

——(1984) "An Unsuccessful Dig: Critical Notice of G. Baker and P. Hacker, *Logical Excavations*" in C. Wright (ed.) *Frege: Tradition and Influence*, Oxford: Blackwells.

——(1987) "Review of *Kurt Gödel Collected Works*," *Mind* 96: 570–5.

——(1991a) *The Logical Basis of Metaphysics*, Cambridge, Mass.: Harvard University Press.

——(1991b) *Frege and Other Philosophers*, Oxford: Clarendon Press.

——(1993a) *The Seas of Language*, Oxford: Oxford University Press.

——(1993b) *Origins of Analytic Philosophy*, Cambridge, Mass.: Harvard University Press.

——(1994) *Frege: Philosophy of Mathematics*, Cambridge, Mass.: Harvard University Press.

Floyd, J. (1995) "On Saying What You Really Want to Say," in J. Hintikka (ed.) *From Dedekind to Gödel*, Dordrecht: Kluwer.

Floyd, J. and Shieh, S. (eds) (forthcoming) *Future Pasts*, Cambridge, Mass.: Harvard University Press.

Frege, G. (1879) *Begriffsschrift*, Halle, Verlag von Louis Nebert, second edition, Ignacio Angelelli (ed.) Hildesheim: Georg Olms (1964); trans. J. van Heijenoort (ed.) *From Frege to Gödel: A Sourcebook in Mathematical Logic 1879–1931*.

——(1884) *Die Grundlagen der Arithmetik*, Breslau; trans. J. L. Austin as *The Foundations of Arithmetic* (2nd edition, Oxford, 1953; reprinted by Northwestern University Press, 1980).

——(1893, 1903) *Grundgesetze der Arithmetik*, Vol. I, Vol. II; reprinted by Hildesheim: Georg Olms Verlagsbuchhandlung (1966); partially translated into English (through s.52) as *The Basic Laws of Arithmetic* by M. Furth, Berkeley: University of California Press (1964).

——(1967) *Kleine Schriften*, I. Angelelli (ed.) Hildesheim: Georg Olms Verlagsbuchhandlung.

——(1969) *Nachgelassene Schriften*, H. Hermes, *et al.* (eds) Hamburg: Felix Meiner.

——(1971) *On the Foundations of Geometry and Formal Theories of Arithmetic*, trans. E. Kluge, New Haven: Yale University Press.

——(1976) *Wissenschaftlicher Briefwechsel*, G. Gabriel *et al.* (eds), Hamburg: Felix Meiner.

——(1979) *Posthumous Writings*, Hans Hermes, Friedrich Kambartel, Friedrich Kaulbach (eds), trans. P. Long and R. White, Chicago: University of Chicago Press.

——(1980a) *Translations from the Philosophical Writings of Gottlob Frege*, trans. M. Black and P. Geach (eds), third edition, Totowa, NJ: Rowman and Littlefield.

——(1980b) *Philosophical and Mathematical Correspondence*, G. Gabriel *et al.* (eds), abridged by B. McGuinness, trans. H. Kaal, Chicago: University of Chicago Press.

——(1984) *Collected Papers on Mathematics, Logic and Philosophy*, B. McGuinness (ed.), trans. M. Black *et al.*, Oxford: Blackwell.

Gödel, K. (1986) *Kurt Gödel, Collected Papers, I.*, S. Feferman, J. W. Dawson, Jr., S. C. Kleene, G. H. Moore, R. M. Solovay, J. van Heijenoort (eds) New York: Oxford, Clarendon Press.

Goldfarb, W. (1979) "Logic in the Twenties: the Nature of the Quantifier," *Journal of Symbolic Logic* 44, 3: 351–68.

Heck, R. (forthcoming) "Frege and Semantics," in Ricketts (ed.) *The Cambridge Companion to Frege*, Cambridge: Cambridge University Press.

Hill, C. (ed.) (1992) *Philosophical Topics* 20, 1: 114–80.

Hintikka, J. (1979) "Frege's Hidden Semantics," *Revue Internationale de Philosophie* 33: 716–22.

——and Hintikka, M. (1986) *Investigating Wittgenstein*, Oxford: Blackwell.

Kemp, G. (1995) "Truth in Frege's 'Law of Truth'," *Synthese* 105: 31–51.

Marion, M. and Voizard, A. (eds) (forthcoming) *Frege, Logique Mathématique et Philosophie*, Paris: l'Harmattan.

Mendelsohn, R. (1982) "Frege's *Begriffsschrift* Theory of Identity," *Journal of the History of Philosophy* XX, 3: 279–99.

Picardi, E. (1988) "Frege on Definition and Logical Proof," in *Atti del Congresso Temi e prospettive della logica e della filosofia della scienza contemporanee*, Cesena 7–10 gennaio 1987, Vol. I CLUEB, Bologna Italy: 227–30.

Putnam, Hilary (1992) "Reply to Conant," "Reply to Dreben," in *Philosophical Topics* 20, 1.

Quine, W. V. O. (1977) "Facts of the Matter," in R. W. Shahan and K. R. Merrill (eds) *American Philosophy from Edwards to Quine*, Norman, Ok.: University of Oklahoma Press.

Ricketts, T. (1985) "Frege the *Tractatus*, and the Logocentric Predicament," *Noûs* 9,1: 3–15.

——(1986a) "Generality, Meaning and Sense in Frege," *Pacific Philosophical Quarterly* 67, 3: 172–95.

——(1986b) "Objectivity and Objecthood: Frege's Metaphysics of Judgment," in L. Haaparanta and J. Hintikka (eds) *Frege Synthesized*, Dordrecht: D. Reidel: 65–95.

——(1996a) "Logic and Truth in Frege," *Proceedings of the Aristotelian Society*.

——(1997) "Truth-Values and Courses-of-Value in Frege's *Grundgesetze*," in W. W. Tait (ed.) *Early Analytic Philosophy: Essays in honor of Leonard Linsky*, Chicago: Open Court Press.

——(forthcoming) unpublished manuscript on Frege's philosophy.

Ricketts, T. (ed.) (forthcoming) *The Cambridge Companion to Frege*, Cambridge: Cambridge University Press.

Russell, Bertrand (1903) *The Principles of Mathematics*, Cambridge: Cambridge University Press; second edition (with a new Introduction), New York: W. W. Norton & Company, 1938.

——and Whitehead, Alfred North (1910, 1912) *Principia Mathematica* (2 vols.), Cambridge: Cambridge University Press; second edition, 1925.

——(1919) *Introduction to Mathematical Philosophy*, London: George Allen & Unwin, Ltd; (second edition 1920).

——(1973) *Essays in Analysis*, D. Lackey (ed.) New York: George Braziller.

Shieh, S. (forthcoming) "On Frege's Logic and Semantics," in M. Marion and A. Voizard. (eds.) *Frege, Logique Mathématique et Philosophie*, Paris: l'Harmattan.

Sluga, H. (1980) *Gottlob Frege*, London: Routledge and Kegan Paul.

——(1987) "Frege Against the Booleans," *Notre Dame Journal of Formal Logic* 28 1: 80–98.

Stanley, J. (forthcoming) "Truth and Metatheory in Frege," *Pacific Philosophical Quarterly*.

Tappenden, J. (1995) "Extending Knowledge and 'Fruitful Concepts': Fregean Themes in the Foundations of Mathematics," *Noûs*: 427–67.

van Heijenoort, J. (1985) *Selected Essays*, Naples: Bibliopolis.

van Heijenoort, J. (ed.) (1967) *From Frege to Gödel: A Sourcebook in Mathematical Logic 1879–1931*, Cambridge, Mass.: Harvard University Press.

Weiner, J. (1982) "Putting Frege in Perspective," Ph.D. thesis, Harvard University.

——(1984) "The Philosopher Behind the Last Logicist," in C. Wright (ed.) *Frege Tradition and Influence*, Oxford: Blackwell.

——(1990) *Frege in Perspective*, Ithaca: Cornell University Press.

——(forthcoming)"Theory and Elucidation," in J. Floyd and S. Shieh (eds) *Future Pasts*, Cambridge, Mass.: Harvard University Press.

Wittgenstein, Ludwig (1922) *Tractatus Logico Philosophicus*, with an introduction by Bertrand Russell, trans. C. K. Ogden, London: Routledge and Kegan Paul (corrected edition 1933).

Wright, C. (ed.) (1984) *Frege: Tradition and Influence*, Oxford: Blackwell.

9 Analysis without elimination:
On the philosophical significance of Russell's "On Denoting"

Gilead Bar-Elli

ANALYSIS AND ELIMINATION—SOME CONCEPTIONS

Since its very beginning analytic philosophy—inspired by its great founders, Frege and Russell—has been ontologically oriented. By way of its concerns with ontology it has put language at the center; and this has been done more out of fear than out of love, for the great founders of analytic philosophy were concerned with language mainly because they believed that language can be profoundly misleading. It can mislead ontologically by suggesting unfounded ontological pictures, preconceptions and presumptions, which may have far-reaching philosophical consequences.

Contrary to a common view, the great analytic philosophers were so concerned with language not because they believed that "everything is linguistic" and that "language is the key to truth," but for quite the opposite reason: they believed that language, i.e. natural language, can be profoundly misleading and that we must free ourselves from its bonds. The idea was not that language is misleading in its regular capacity as a tool of communication. The idea was rather that some features of language—particularly logical and grammatical features—may suggest wrong and misleading philosophical (again, mainly ontological) conceptions. And that is how logic came to acquire its central role. Logic was held to be the route to freedom—the means of escaping the misleading bonds of language. This does not mean that we can disregard or eschew language, and get directly at the truths themselves. This is impossible. The fight against the misleading bewitchment of language was held to be so important just because language was held to be so powerful, to reign everywhere, so that we are caught in its bonds at every turn.

But language, it was believed, can be fought against from within, so to speak, by rejecting, correcting, and improving the pictures and preconceptions it suggests. It has often been assumed and asserted by the great champions of analytic philosophy that modern logic, and the logical analysis of language, are the main weapons against this misleading bewitchment by language. Hence, "elimination" in my title is mainly elimination of "coined entities" and spurious ontological misconceptions, and "analysis" is logical analysis of language. This marriage of ontological concerns with logical analysis has turned on two main axes: the logical analysis of the notion of existence (construing it quantificationally in contrast to understanding it as a property of objects), and a detailed examination of the ontic commitments and implications of sorts of talk and expression.

These two ideas are Fregean in origin. This is obvious with regard to the quantificational construal of the notion of existence. But it is also true with respect to the second axis: the paradigm examples are the Fregean idea of contextual definitions and their ontological implication in *Grundlagen*, his reduction of arithmetic to logic, and the various techniques he used for this end, as well as his analyses of various forms of compound sentences (e.g. in "On Sense and Reference"). I will not discuss the Fregean background of this trend in analytic philosophy, but will focus, after some preliminaries, on its manifestation in Russell.

A major trend in analytic philosophy has been to show that certain kinds of entities (dubious entities) are eliminable by means of a logical analysis of the sentences in which the expressions purporting to denote them occur. This has taken either the radical way in which the dubious entities were totally eliminated, or the milder way in which they were shown to be reducible to more respectable kinds of entities. Thus numbers were reduced to concepts and sets (Frege, Russell); and sequences were reduced to sets (Wiener, Kuratowski); and some kinds of intensions were reduced to extensions (Carnap in *Meaning and Necessity*; Lewis on explicating modal operators in possible worlds semantics; see his *Counterfactuals*). All these belong to the mild sort of elimination. I call it "mild" because reducing a certain domain to another, more "respectable" one, may be regarded as legitimating the former domain, just as easily as rejecting it, or eliminating it, in favor of the latter one.

Examples of the more radical sort are analyses of what may seem to be mental talk in terms of extensional contexts about physical objects (sentences; brain processes). One such example is Quine's opposition to mental predicates and certain uses of modal operators, and the ways he and others proposed for analyzing modes of speech (or what is legitimate in them) that seem to be committed to these unwelcome conceptions. Russell's theory of descriptions may appear to belong here too: It shows that certain kinds of entities (denotations) are eliminable in the strong sense that talk, which is purportedly about them, is analyzable as talk in which they do not function at all; or so at least it has been usually taken to show.

I said that the analysis was of the sentences and expressions involved. This, though true in general, is inaccurate in a way, since many of the propounders of analytic philosophy, of whom Russell is a paramount example, regarded the (logical) analysis involved as directed at the facts, propositions and concepts themselves, rather than at their linguistic expressions. G. E. Moore was quite explicit about this (e.g. in his *Replies* in Schilpp, ed., *The Philosophy of G. E. Moore*), and G. Ryle, for example, concluding his discussion in another classic of analytic philosophy, writes:

> Philosophy must then involve the exercise of systematic restatement. . . . Its restatements are transmutations of syntax, . . . controlled . . . by the desire to exhibit the forms of the facts into which philosophy is the inquiry . . . For we can ask what is the real form of the fact recorded when this is concealed . . . by the expression in question. And we can often succeed in stating this fact in a new form of words which does exhibit what the other fail to exhibit. And I am for the present inclined to believe that this is what philosophical analysis is, and that this is the sole and whole function of philosophy.
>
> (Ryle 1931: 36)

Quine seems to share Ryle's appreciation of the possibility of restating a certain phrase in less troublesome terms. He is probably less sympathetic to the realistic spirit in which Ryle speaks of analysis as revealing the true "form of facts"; he is likely to prefer keeping analysis within its linguistic confinements. Thus, in explaining his dictum that "Explication is elimination," Quine cites some exemplary explications (of ordered pairs, definite descriptions, indicative conditionals, quantification) and says:

> In all these cases, problems have been dissolved in the important sense of being shown to be purely verbal, and purely verbal in the important sense of arising from usages that can be avoided in favor of ones that engender no such problems.
>
> (Quine 1960: 261)

Quine gives this way of analysis an explicitly pragmatic turn:

> We have, to begin with, an expression or form of expression that is somehow troublesome. . . . But also it serves certain purposes that are not to be abandoned. Then we find a way of accomplishing those same purposes through other channels, using other and less troublesome forms of expression. The old perplexities are resolved.
>
> (Quine 1960: 260)

Though both Ryle and Quine (like many others) cite Russell and his theory of descriptions as a paradigmatic example for their versions of philosophical analysis, Russell, I believe, had a much "thicker" notion of philosophical and logical analysis—a notion that is more "constructive" and systematic than Ryle's, and less "pragmatic" and more analytical than Quine's. For Russell, analysis does aim at revealing the truth and its ultimate constituents. It consists in "going backwards," in a sort of inductive manner, from conclusions to premises, from intuitively known or believed truths to their ultimate constituents and structure:

> The process of sound philosophizing, to my mind, consists mainly in passing from those obvious, vague, ambiguous things, that we feel quite sure of, to something precise, clear, definite, which by reflection and analysis we find is involved in the vague thing that we start from, and is, so to speak, *the real truth of which that vague thing is a sort of shadow.*
>
> (Russell 1956a: 179–80, my italics)

The motivation in Russell is explicitly epistemological. Analysis ends up in simpler truths and concepts, about which claims to knowledge are less risky. He sums it up himself by saying: "Whenever possible, substitute construction out of known entities for inferences to unknown entities" (1956a: 326). And as examples he mentions there, in addition to numbers and classes, the theory of descriptions (p. 327f.).

Generalizing, and disregarding for the moment these (and other) important differences, we may say that in Quine, Ryle, and Russell, as well as many other philosophers, elimination of a kind of entity is supposed to be attained by logical analysis in the following way:

1 A certain expression seems to suggest a commitment (of some sort) to objects or concepts of a certain type.
2   For some philosophical reasons, this type of object is dubious and problematic.
3 Logical analysis reveals that this mode of expression is superfluous— sentences of this kind can be analyzed or paraphrased by others which do not have these undesirable commitments, without a significant loss in content.
4   The logical analysis concerned reveals the true (logical) form of the "content" in question (proposition, fact, concept).
5 Thus, the "problematic" expression is proved to be unnecessary and unfaithful to the "real" logical form of the content, and the dubious sort of entity to which it is committed is eliminated by logical analysis.

Among the many questions that can (and have) been raised on this issue, a natural one pertains to the constraints about such analyses, and the conditions they must satisfy: When (under what conditions) should we regard an analysis as giving the logical form of the desired fact (or proposition or concept)? This is, of course, a very large question—it is in fact *the* question of analysis. I am not going to discuss it in any comprehensive way. I should like, however, to point out three main approaches to the question; I shall then make a general comment pertaining to all three, and proceed in this light to discuss some features of Russell's theory of descriptions in "On Denoting."

1 The first approach is the pragmatic one, often associated with Carnap's notion of "explication" (also a Fregean notion in origin): a certain form of speech (or a whole "language") is offered in the place of a previous one. The only conditions required here are that the new mode will be in some respect "better" (more precise, well defined) than the old one, and that it will at least match the pragmatic utility of the old one (apply to most of the typical cases of the old one, and satisfy some other pragmatic conditions). Quine's approach, cited above, is very much in this spirit.

2 The second is the "local," intra-linguistic approach—a local, sometimes piecemeal paraphrase. A good example is provided in Ryle's own paper, cited above, with regard to what he calls "quasi-referential" descriptions like "The owl perched at the top of that tree," where the description seems to refer to a definite thing or place, but proper paraphrase may show that no such reference is "really" involved. Similarly, the phrase "the idea of taking a holiday has just occurred to me" is paraphrased so that no Lockean ontology of ideas is presupposed ("I have just thought of taking a holiday"). In these cases, Ryle writes, "Philosophers and others who have to abstract and generalize tend to be misled by the verbal similarity of 'the'-phrases of the one sort with 'the'-phrases of the other into 'coining entities' in order to be able to show to what a given 'the'-phrase refers" (1931: 27). Ryle's main reason for thinking this to be a mistake is that these statements can be easily rephrased in a way that does not suggest any such ontological commitments (1931: 30).

3 The systematic–global approach, where global conditions on the equivalence (or sameness) of contents are proposed (e.g. in terms of truth conditions), and an analysis is shown, in a systematic way, to retain the content, as thus determined, invariant, say, by providing an analysis with the same truth conditions. Analyses of this kind have become very common in logical and semantical studies. It can be called the "classical approach," to which most of the classical analyses offered by Frege, Russell, and many other analytic philosophers belong. Many reductions, in which a certain domain is modeled on another belong here. A relatively simple example is Quine's presentation of the Kuratowski set-theoretic definition of sequences as a paradigm of analysis (1960: 257–62). Here identity conditions of sequences are fixed, and then a set-theoretic formula is proven to satisfy these conditions,

thus providing a set theoretic analysis of the notion of a sequence (or of order). The idea that modeling a certain domain on another one is sufficient for reduction has often been challenged, and many proposals have been offered as to what additional conditions must be satisfied in order for a genuine reduction to occur. A discussion of this, though relevant, would take us too far afield.

I would like to mention, however, one point which pertains, in a greater or lesser degree, to all these approaches. Actually, the point pertains to the very idea of elimination by analysis. A philosophical analysis, one may feel, should aim at more than just offering a way to bypass or avoid a problem. A proper philosophical analysis should, in addition, show or explain how the problem in question arises; what are the concepts, principles, and conceptions whose use or misuse engenders it. It should detect those elements in the concepts and principles involved that are valid and should be respected, and those that need change and correction. Such an analysis, when successful, should not merely point out the fact that we went wrong somewhere, and by a miraculous trick put us at the right place; it should rather explain how we went wrong, and by putting us back on the main road should provide us with the means to get at where we want by our own routes. Philosophical troubles are not eliminated by showing how they could be avoided by taking altogether different routes. Philosophical troubles are eliminated by showing how they should be avoided by proceeding properly and carefully in the same routes that, when taken improperly and uncarefully, led to them.

DENOTATION AND ABOUTNESS IN RUSSELL'S "ON DENOTING"

In light of these general remarks I would like to examine some features of what is perhaps *the* classical paper of analytic philosophy, a paper considered by many to mark its beginning: Russell's "On Denoting" of 1905 (1956b). The theory, I assume, is familiar to everybody and so I shall not repeat its details. Generally, it analyzes what appear to be singular (subject–predicate) statements of the form "The F is G" as quantificational statements of the form "There is an F such that there is no other F and every F is G." The main significance of the theory was formulated by Russell in the doctrine that descriptions (like other denoting phrases) are "incomplete symbols," i.e. they are meaningless in themselves, though they contribute in a systematic way to the meaning of the sentences (propositions) in which they occur.

At a first glance the paper seems to fit nicely both the general characterization of elimination by analysis and the third approach to analysis mentioned above. There are many troubles that descriptive statements may seem to raise, and Russell's theory shows how to handle descriptive statements so as to avoid the troubles. Thus, "The present King of France is bald" seems to be a subject–predicate singular statement that ascribes (perhaps wrongly) baldness to someone, in analogy to the way "The present King of Jordan is bald" seems to be a singular subject–predicate statement that ascribes baldness to King Hussein. But the former statement, as we know, is problematic in many ways: it may even threaten the coherence of our logic, or invite unwelcome creatures such as a subsistent but non-existent King of France. Likewise, "The golden mountain does not exist" seems to deny a property (existence) to something, just as "The Golan mountain is stony" ascribes a property to a mountain. But this again is very problematic in similar ways. Russell's theory, with its quantificational rendering of these sentences, offers nice solutions to these problems—they simply don't arise in Russell's renderings.

In general, then, it appears that the theory provides an analysis of the third type mentioned above: it provides general, systematic prescriptions for formulating sentences of pure quantification theory, with no alleged reference to any dubious entities—sentences which exactly match the content—the truth conditions—of the original sentences "as intuitively understood."[1] In this sense, whatever could be said in terms of the previous "problematic mode" of descriptions can be transformed into the new mode of quantificational theory.

This is good and familiar enough, and Russell's paper would remain a paradigm of analysis if it did only that. But it does much more. This is the main point I want to stress here, for I believe that not only has this "more" escaped the notice of able commentators, but that it is this "more" that includes the main philosophical significance of "On Denoting": the relationship between descriptive reference and its quantificational analysis is not one of simple, one-way reduction, but rather one of revealing inner conceptual interconnections. Descriptive reference is analyzed in terms of the quantificational idiom; but our understanding of quantification involves, and may even depend on, our capacity of descriptive reference. Russell's theory of descriptions in "On Denoting" does not eschew or eliminate descriptive reference altogether; it rather shows how to handle it by connecting it to general referential features of quantificational idiom. By revealing and analyzing the internal interconnections between descriptive reference and quantification theory Russell reveals (discovers) and explains essential features of the very referential, intentionalistic machinery of our language and thought.

I shall mention here some of the most important features of what is thus revealed and explained. The following five points are interconnected: the significance of each should be seen in conjunction with the others.

The role of aboutness

Russell's theory shows how to respect the general intuitive demand that *any meaningful sentence be about something*. Russell, as far as I know, never formulated this principle explicitly, but it exists as a covering principle in the background of whatever he did. Much of *The Principles of Mathematics* of 1903, for instance, is unintelligible without it, although even in that work Russell does not always comply with it. The notion of aboutness is constitutive of the notion of a proposition in the *Principles*: in every proposition something—what he calls assertion—is asserted about something—a term (1903: 39; see also 1903: 44). Saying that the notion of aboutness is thus constitutive of the notion of proposition does not mean that every proposition is about something, any more than saying that the notion of truth is constitutive of that of proposition means that every proposition is true. What it means is rather that we cannot understand what a proposition is without understanding what it is for it to be about an object, just as we cannot understand what a proposition is without understanding what it is for it to be true. The fact that some propositions, like "The golden mountain is in France," appear not to be about anything poses a serious problem for Russell, but in itself it does not disclaim the general conception that aboutness is constitutive of the notion of proposition—it poses a challenge within that conception.[2]

The notion of aboutness is also of vital importance in the *Principles* for delineating a special class of concepts—denoting concepts. In the proposition "I met a man," something is asserted about myself and nothing is asserted about the concept "a man", though it occurs in the proposition. Something, however, is asserted about "some actual biped denoted by the concept" (1903: 47). In chapter V of the *Principles* Russell emphasizes the fundamental character of the notion of denoting and its importance. He elaborates on the previously quoted remark and says: "The fact that description is possible—that we are able by the employment of a concept to designate a thing which is not a concept—is due to logical relations between some concepts and some terms, in virtue of which such concepts inherently and logically denote such terms." And he proceeds in the next paragraph to define: "A concept denotes when, if it occurs in a proposition, the proposition is not about the concept, but about a term connected in a certain peculiar way with the concept" (1903: 53).[3]

As remarked above, a descriptive proposition may contain a denoting concept—the meaning of the description—which does not denote anything, and hence, be about nothing. Russell discusses such propositions in the *Principles*, though he is surprisingly brief here (see, for instance, 1903: 73–4). Some commentators have argued that the theory of denoting concepts in the *Principles* does provide a satisfactory solution to the problem of "empty descriptions" (though Russell may have missed the solution at the time). I believe that this is a mistake: there is no satisfactory solution to the problem in the *Principles*, as Russell rightly thought when he later considered this one of the main reasons to abandon the theory and replace it by the one in "On Denoting."[4] There is therefore a real tension in the *Principles* between the role of aboutness as constitutive of the notion of proposition, and the idea that some descriptive propositions are devoid of denotation and not about anything.

In the new theory of "On Denoting" Russell could maintain the intuitive demand that any proposition be about something by broadening the scope of the aboutness relation. A descriptive proposition—like any proposition—is about its constituents; it is also about its denotation, where it has one. A meaningful proposition is thus never about nothing, and sometimes what it is about is determined by the facts. What makes such a view possible is precisely the fact that denotation is no longer regarded as a primitive logical relation (as it was in the *Principles*), but as determined by the logical structure of the proposition as a whole. There being a denotation for the proposition to be about is thus naturally regarded as an aspect of its truth, determined by the facts.

Objecthood of descriptive statements

Russell's position in "On Denoting" respects the basic intuition that *descriptive statements are "object-oriented"* or "entity-involved," i.e. not only is a descriptive statement about something, it is typically about an object, determined by its description. This is a major point on which I must elaborate, as it goes against the prevalent, almost unanimous, interpretation of Russell's view. The object-directedness I am talking about is the idea that descriptive statements are conceived as typically directed at and being about an object (in which they may fail), rather than purely "universalistic," as their quantificational analysis may suggest.[5] This object-directedness is manifest not only in the very title of "On Denoting," but in three substantial aspects of the theory: (1) the explicit motivation of the theory, in which Russell talks about "reaching objects" by means of denoting phrases (1956b: 41); (2) the need to explain knowledge *about* objects, or knowledge of objects by description (1956b: 41); (3) the definition offered in "On Denoting" for the notion of denotation (1956b: 51).

Russell's theory of descriptions, as can be seen in the title of his classical paper of 1905, is *on denoting*. The problem of denoting was, for Russell, the problem of the capacity of thought and propositions to be *about objects*. Hence, the primary aim of his theory (at least in its original phase) was to reveal and analyze the concepts and mechanisms involved in the relations of a thought or a proposition with the objects it is about. The problem Russell was preoccupied with in "On Denoting" was the problem of *successful descriptions*: How can a descriptive proposition ever be concerned with objects which are not among its constituents? A "universalistic" inter-pretation takes this rendering of the logical form of the proposition as meaning that such propositions, contrary to what they seem to be, are not really about objects.[6] If this were correct as a general interpretation of Russell's main insight, it would render Russell's theory as denying the presumption of the problem of denoting which it was designed to solve. For in rendering such propositions as general or universal we lose an important aspect of their meaning—their being about objects—the denotations involved. One may think that this is merely a superficial and misleading feature of their grammatical structure, which has nothing to do with their meaning. But, my claim is that on Russell's theory this is not the case. In fact, this is a crucial feature which his theory was designed to explain. Naturally, it was an especially reassuring advantage of the theory that it could handle "failures" (sentences with empty descriptions) as well. But focusing exclusively on that feature may detract our attention from the theory's main aim and merit.[7]

As I indicated above, this conception of descriptive reference, and the object-directed approach to descriptive statements are echoed in Russell's notion of knowledge by description, or knowledge about, which is a central notion of his epistemology. Here again, knowledge by description, which was analyzed by Russell in terms of the quantificational rendering of his theory of descriptions, was persistently conceived by him as knowl-edge of objects. A purely universalistic conception of these renderings does not leave room for such a conception and even makes it unintelligible.[8]

Remote intentionality

An important feature of Russell's theory is that it contradicts the (Fregean) "dogma" that what a proposition is about must be explicitly mentioned by one of its constituents (must be the referent of a name). In Russell's theory *a descriptive statement can be about something "external" to it*, that is, not one of its constituents (I call this feature remote intentionality). This again is a major theme on which I can here only make some brief remarks: Frege's theory, and Russell's theories prior to "On Denoting," held that a proposition (sentence, thought) can only be about one (or some) of its constituents (I use the term "constituents" loosely to cover also Frege's referents of the components, or names of a sentence). This is a very important principle in Frege's philosophy, which, in a way, shaped his conception of general statements as about concepts rather than objects.[9] In the *Principles* Russell generally upheld this principle, though the point is debatable. Some commentators would deny this on the basis that denotations—the objects that denoting concepts denote—are not constituents of the proposition. I think there is no evidence for this view in the text, and there is much evidence for the opposite view—that the denotation is a constituent of the proposition.[10] In the *Principles*, denotation is effected in terms of "denoting concepts," and the "peculiar logical" relation they have to objects which are their denotations. Russell never says in the *Principles* that such an object—the denoted term—is not a part or a constituent of the proposition in which it is denoted. Moreover, on various occasions he explicitly says quite the contrary. With regard to "Socrates is a man," for instance, he says that "the proposition contains a term, a relation, and what I shall call a disjunction" (1903: 54; cf. also pp. 44, 46, 47). The disjunction in question is the denoted term of the denoting concept—a man. Russell's view was, therefore, that the denoted term is contained in the proposition in question, and this may be naturally glossed as the view that it is a constituent of the proposition.[11] On the other hand Russell says in the *Principles* that a proposition like "I met a man," when true, is about some "actual biped," which is, supposedly, no constituent of the proposition. It may thus appear that it is unclear in the *Principles* whether a proposition contains its denotation as a constituent. This may cause much trouble in understanding the notion of proposition in the *Principles*, and may well be one of the reasons why Russell found it unsatisfactory.

All this is drastically changed in Russell's theory of "On Denoting," where the principle that a proposition must contain (as a constituent) what it is about is clearly and neatly abandoned: a descriptive proposition, in the new theory, is about its denotation (when it has one) even though the denotation is in no case among its constituents. A much clearer notion of proposition is thus effected: what a proposition contains—what are its constituents—is governed by an epistemic constraint—the principle of acquaintance, according to which all the constituents of a proposition we can understand must be known to us by acquaintance. The notion of proposition is thus construed as distinctly belonging to a theory of understanding and of knowledge.

Intentionality by logical structure

Finally, what is perhaps the most important point is that Russell's theory shows how *denotation and what a statement is about are determined by logical form*, i.e. by the logical form of the whole proposition. King Hussein is the denotation of "The King of Jordan is bald" even though in the analyzed form of that proposition—"There is a King in Jordan such that there is no other King in Jordan and any King in Jordan is bald"—there is no name or expression which has King Hussein as its meaning. Rather, it is determined as the denotation and as what the proposition is about by the structure of the whole proposition. And again, this is a great innovation: no previous theory (as far as I am aware) has claimed or shown that. On all previous conceptions, reference and what a proposition is about are determined "locally" or "lexically," by a certain expression in the sentence, or a certain constituent of the proposition. This is true, with some reservations, even of Frege; for, in his conception a proposition (or a thought) is about the references of its names, and these references are determined solely by the respective senses. "Global" features of the proposition, like its logical form, are irrelevant here. They are important of course for many other things, such as the deducibility power of the proposition, and even for how to understand it. In the *Principles*, denoting was regarded as a primitive "peculiar" logical relation between a denoting concept and an object. But this relation and its marvelous effects remain there completely mysterious, and Russell could say nothing on how it is determined—except as by some mysterious feature of the denoting concept itself.

All this is, of course, completely changed in "On Denoting." Russell's "On Denoting" theory is the first in which the logical structure of the (descriptive) proposition as a whole is regarded as determining the reference (denotation) of terms—or what the proposition is about. And this is an essential feature of Russell's theory: Denotation, or what the proposition is about (when it has a denotation), is not determined "locally" or lexically, but rather by a "global" feature of the proposition as a whole—its logical structure.

Predication

One of the main problems which occupied both Frege and Russell concerns the nature of proposition, or more specifically, the problem of the unity of a proposition—what has been later referred to as the propositional "cement" or "glue." In Russellian terms the problem is what distinguished propositions from other "complexes." Frege dealt with the problem in terms of his distinction between objects, which are complete and "satisfied" entities, and concepts (or functions) which are essentially incomplete and unsatisfied *(ungesättigt)*, and his view that concepts are "essentially predicative." Important differences notwithstanding, Russell's general picture in the *Principles* was similar. We have already mentioned that he explains the peculiar nature of proposition in terms of his distinction between "assertion" and "term," and in ascribing the assertive or predicative force of a proposition to the assertion it contains. (I use "predication" here in a wide sense, including many-place relations.) An important feature common to both these views is that the assertive or predicative force, which is the essence of the propositional "glue," is ascribed to a particular component of the proposition, actually to one of its constituents.

This picture is in fact shattered in the new theory of descriptions in "On Denoting": Here Russell strictly maintained that all the constituents of a (descriptive) proposition are objects, either particular (the meanings of names) or universal (the meanings of predicates or general terms). The predicative force and the propositional "glue" are not ascribed to any of the constituents, but solely to the logical form of the proposition. This revolutionary point is more difficult to appreciate in the case of simple atomic propositions than in descriptive quantified ones. But in fact, as Wittgenstein was later to see in the *Tractatus* (where he pressed this point to its extreme), it applies to all propositions, and effects a revolutionary change in the conception of the nature of a proposition. This then is another point in which Russell's new conception brings logic and logical form to the metaphysical fore

Eliminating a Meinongian ontology of subsistent (non-existent) Kings of France or round squares by means of logical analysis of propositions and expressions that seem to be committed to it is fine and important; doing this extensionally, without appeal to notions like Fregean senses or Russellian denoting concepts, is even more impressive and significant. But there are many philosophical conceptions that are presumed or presupposed along the way—whether explicitly or not. Revealing, explaining, and analyzing them is, I believe, the main philosophical significance of this theory. One very important conception of this sort is the idea of incomplete symbols: the idea that an expression may be meaningful—in the sense of systematically contributing to the meaning of sentences in which it occurs—without having any meaning in isolation. This has been widely discussed, and I have hardly touched on it here. I have tried rather to point out at least five other important philosophical conceptions that are revealed in the theory of "On Denoting," sometimes in a very implicit way. Seen in the light of these, Russell's theory of descriptions in "On

Denoting" is seen not as a suggestion to reduce, or to replace, descriptive idioms by quantificational ones, but as a real analysis that goes deep into essential features of our referential capacity. It is not an analysis that eliminates descriptions or descriptive reference (though it does eliminate bad philosophical concepts and conceptions of it—e.g. in terms of denoting concepts). It is rather an anlysis of some of the basic principles and notions behind our capacity of descriptive reference. The five points I have discussed here are among these basic notions. These points have shaped so much of the concerns and ways of philosophizing in the analytic tradition that bringing them to the fore may, I hope, simultaneously contribute to a clarification of what this tradition is, and to explaining why Russell's "On Denoting" is a paradigm of it.

NOTES

1 I regard it particularly significant that the equivalence between the "problematic" idioms and the "accepted" ones is typically established only in the veridical cases, where the problematic idiom is understood on its face value, without the analysis, but I shall not argue for this here.

2 The notion of aboutness is also constitutive, I believe, of the individuation of propositions in the *Principles*, but I shall not elaborate on this here.

3 This "definition" of denoting raises a problem. The distinctive mark of concepts in general (presumably including denoting concepts) is that they are capable of "that curious twofold use which is involved in human and humanity" in (1): "Socrates is human," and (2): "Humanity belongs to Socrates." We have also seen that the difference between (1) and (2) is that (1) is not about the concept (human). By the definition of denoting concepts quoted above we might conclude that the concept is denoting in (1). But Russell explicitly denies that (1903: 54); it is evidently also not denoting in (2) (where it occurs as Humanity in the subject position). One should perhaps conclude here that a concept is denoting only if whenever it occurs in a proposition the proposition is not about it. Hence, Human is not denoting in (1) because it occurs in (2) and is what (2) is about. Alternatively, one could think of denoting as pertaining only to concepts in the subject position.

4 Hylton, a notable example of these commentators, is right that the fact that a description is empty does not rob the proposition, in the *Principles*, of the appropriate constituent—it still contains the denoting concept as a constituent. But Hylton seems to miss the grave problems this view raises. I shall briefly mention two: A proposition containing an empty description would be a (meaningful) proposition about nothing, which was an appalling idea to Russell. Secondly, denotation and the relation between a denoting concept and what it denotes was regarded as a primitive, logical relation in the *Principles*; this doesn't seem to cohere with the idea of empty denoting concepts, for this idea relies on the view that whether a denoting concept is denoting is an empirical one. See Hylton (1992: 73 and 247).

5 The object-directedness I am talking about is weaker, more general, and abstract than, e.g., Donnellan's "referential" use of descriptions. It does not mean that in uttering a descriptive statement the speaker has a particular

object in mind about which his statement says something, but rather that he conceives of the statement as being or purporting to be about an object.

6 At least, this would be so on a Fregean interpretation of the quantification involved, rendering these propositions second-order predications about concepts. Other interpretations of the quantifiers may call for other formulations (such as "being about an unspecified object"). Although some such formulations occur in Russell, he does not seem to have held any clear conception of the matter.

7 One can justly feel a tension here, but this is a tension in Russell's own thought: Russell was not very clear about the significance of his theory and he toyed with these—seemingly conflicting—views for a very long time. The tension and its significance in Russell's epistemology, as manifested in his notion of knowledge by description, are discussed in Bar-Elli (1989).

8 I have elaborated on this claim and on its philosophical significance in Bar-Elli (1989).

9 I have elaborated on this in Bar-Elli (1996), especially chs 1 and 7.

10 See Hylton (1992). As mentioned in the text I believe Hylton's claim is unfounded. Moreover, it conflicts with Russell's repeated claims in the *Principles* that the "disjunction" (which is the denotation of the denoting concept "a man") in "I met a man" is a constituent of the proposition. This is not a trivial matter of exegesis, for, if I am right, it shows the notion of proposition in the *Principles* to be bogus—it contains constituents to which we don't have direct cognitive access. This is another aspect in which the theory of "On Denoting" is far superior to that of the *Principles*.

11 Hylton's view, according to which the denoted term is not a part of the proposition in which it is denoted is not only unsupported by the text; it also seems to me to make poor explanation of the very phenomenon it is designed to explain, which is the possibility of a proposition to be about an infinite totality. For if, say, an infinite totality is not a part of the proposition in which it is denoted, what proposition is it a part of? If none, what is the ontological complex which constitutes a truth about this totality—a truth we may know?

BIBLIOGRAPHY

Bar-Elli, G. (1989) "Acquaintance, Knowledge, and Description in Russell," *Russell*, 9, 2: 133–56.

——(1996) *The Sense of Reference–Intentionality in Frege*, Berlin: Walter de Gruyter.

Hylton, P. (1992) *Russell, Idealism and the Emergence of Analytic Philosophy*, Oxford: Oxford University Press.

Quine, W. V. O. (1960) *Word and Object*, Cambridge, Mass.: MIT Press.

Russell, B. (1903) *Principles of Mathematics*, London: Allen and Unwin.

——(1956a) "Philosophy of Logical Atomism," reprinted in R. Marsh (ed.) *Logic and Knowledge*, London: Allen and Unwin.

——(1956b) "On Denoting," in R. Marsh (ed.) *Logic and Knowledge*, London: Allen and Unwin.

Ryle, G. (1931) "Systematically Misleading Expressions," *Proceedings of the Aristotelian Society*, reprinted in A. Flew (ed.) *Logic and Language*, Oxford: Blackwell (1953).

10 Perception:
from Moore to Austin

Ruth Anna Putnam

John Austin ended his book *Sense and Sensibilia* with this sentence, "The right policy . . . is to dismantle the whole doctrine before it gets off the ground" (1964). Now, one might say that the doctrine in question—sense-datum theory of one sort or another—begins with the beginnings of modern philosophy, i.e. with Descartes. In one sense, that is surely correct—those who developed the doctrine were in the grip of a picture that they inherited from Descartes, the picture that our knowledge must have an indubitable foundation.[1] But one might also say that the train of philosophical thought that Descartes had set in motion, that developed further in England on a Lockean foundation and culminated on the continent in the work of Kant, had, at the beginning of the twentieth century, in the writings of the great Absolute Idealists—Bradley in England and Royce in America—come to a conclusion. If so, then Moore's "Refutation of Idealism" (1922a) marked a new beginning. Of course, Moore did not single-handedly produce analytic philosophy; Russell, in the preface to *Our Knowledge of the External World* (1926) gives credit to Frege for producing the first complete example of the use of the "logical-analytic method" in philosophy, and that book itself played a seminal role in the development of analytic philosophy of perception. On one reading, a fairly straight path leads from that book to Ayer's phenomenalism (Ayer 1940) and from that to Austin's refutation of it. But by 1921, in *Analysis of Mind* Russell had become convinced by the "radical empiricism" of William James (1976) and rejected Moore's account of perception. Of course, Russell retained the construction of *Our Knowledge of the External World* in its new edition of 1926, but I shall maintain that this construction, given these new elements, cannot be seen as a precursor of phenomenalism. My purpose, then, is twofold. It is to deal with certain major figures in the history of analytic philosophy of perception as historical figures, and it is to argue that while the aim of providing a foundation for empirical knowledge is a chimera, the aim of explaining how it is that we live in a knowable world is in principle achievable.

I

Let us begin, then, with the analysis of sense perception that Moore offers in "Refutation of Idealism" in opposition to what he takes to be the Idealists' account. All sensations, he says, involve two terms: a respect in which they are alike, which he calls "consciousness" or, later, "awareness" and a respect in which they differ, which he calls the "object." For example, an awareness of a blue sky and an awareness of a green meadow are alike in being awarenesses but differ in their objects. Of course, Moore does not speak of blue skies and green meadows, he speaks merely of blue and of green, and he means, I think, that we are aware of the property blue.[2] On the other hand, in his reply to Ducasse in the Schilpp volume (Schilpp 1942), Moore tells us that to say that blue exists is to say that some object that is blue exists; so, to be aware of blue may be to be aware of some blue object, and for all he says in "The Refutation of Idealism" that object may be the sky.

In any case, Moore rejects what he calls the traditional view, the view that both consciousness and blue exist and that blue is the content of the consciousness. Moore understands this to mean that blue is a quality of the sensation, that a sensation of blue is a blue mental image, and this is what he rejects. He sees no reasons for supposing that there are mental images, but holds

> that even if there are mental images, no mental image or sensation or idea is *merely* a thing of this kind: that "blue," even if it is part of the content of the image or sensation or idea of blue, is always *also* related to it in quite another way, and that this other relation, omitted in the traditional analysis, is the *only one which makes the sensation of blue a mental fact at all.*
>
> (Moore 1922a: 24)

Moore emphasizes the last clause, but he needs arguments rather than a mere raising of the voice. For whether all mental facts are intentional, and specifically whether sensing is a case of knowing, is, as we shall see, debatable.

What is the point of Moore's insistence that a sensation of blue consists of three elements: blue, an awareness, and the relation of the awareness to blue? In asserting that sensation has an object, Moore takes himself to have shown that the object sensed is not an inseparable aspect of our minds, that "[m]erely to have a sensation is already to *be* outside that circle," namely, what is according to Moore's opponents, "the circle of our own ideas and sensations" (Moore 1922a: 27). But could one not always be aware of another idea or sensation? Moore takes this to be ruled out by the nature of the peculiar relation that holds between an awareness and its object. Here is his argument. Once we understand that the

peculiar relation which I have called "awareness of anything" . . . is involved
equally in the analysis of *every* experience from the merest sensation to the most
developed perception and reflexion,

and furthermore that

this awareness must be in all cases of such a nature that its object, when we are
aware of it, is precisely what it would be, if we were not aware: then it becomes
plain that the existence of a table in space is related to my experience of *it* in
precisely the same way as the existence of my own experience is related to my
experience of *that*.

(Moore 1922a: 29)

And so, he concludes, we have as little reason to doubt the existence of
material things as we have to doubt the existence of our own sensations.

Fortunately, Moore holds elsewhere that he knows, without need for
argument, that material objects exist; for this argument depends crucially
on two wholly unargued-for premises: that any object of awareness is
precisely what it would be if we were not aware of it, and that the relation
of awareness is the same in all types of experiences. Moore did, in fact
hold, sensibly, that one need not have an argument for all of one's
premises, but surely these premises cry out for reasons (1959b). However,
we must turn to a matter that troubled Moore for the rest of his life.

In "A Defence of Common Sense," Moore makes clear that when he
perceives his hand (and he is quite sure that he knows that he perceives his
hand, hence that his hand exists, hence that a material object exists), then
in another sense of "perceive," he perceives the back of his hand, and he is
also certain that he perceives a sense-datum. If the sense-datum is the part
of the back of his hand that he perceives, then he perceives the sense-
datum in the same sense of "perceive" as that in which he perceives the
back of his hand, otherwise he perceives it in yet another sense of
"perceive."

Moore vacillated throughout his life between the view that visual and
tactual sense-data are parts of the surfaces of material objects, and the
view that they are not. In 1914 in "The Status of Sense-Data" (Moore
1922b), he embraced the latter view because two persons seeing the same
surface of a coin may have quite different sense-data. In 1918, in "Some
Judgments of Perception" (Moore 1922c) he leaned toward the former
view, although, for the reason just given, it requires accepting the possibility that sense-data may seem to be what they are not. In 1925, in "A
Defence of Common Sense," (Moore 1959c) Moore thought that double
vision constituted a fatal objection to the view that sense-data are parts of
the surfaces of material objects. But later he seems to have changed his
mind again. In his replies to his critics, in the Schilpp volume, where one
would hope to receive a final and definitive answer to this question, Moore

turned out to be still ambivalent. Responding to Ducasse, he wrote that he was now (1942) inclined to think that it is as impossible for any sense-datum to exist unperceived as it is for a headache to exist unfelt, and that, therefore, no sense-datum can be a physical surface (Schilpp 1942: 658). But earlier, in responding to Bowsma and Murphy, when he was concerned to argue that there was nothing mysterious about sense-data, that they are simply whatever it is that we directly apprehend, he had expressed a strong inclination to think that our visual sense-data, or at least many of them, are parts of the surfaces of physical objects.[3] And so he confessed, "And this is the truth. I am strongly inclined to take both of these incompatible views. I am completely puzzled about the matter, and only wish I could see any way of settling it" (Schilpp 1942: 659).

Moore claims to know certain propositions about the shape and unperceived persistence of material objects, and that knowledge is said to be "based on" his direct apprehension of sense-data. When he held that visual and tactual sense-data are not parts of the surfaces of material objects, he was attracted by two views concerning relations between a material object and the sense-data on which our knowledge of the object is based: (1) a phenomenalistic view that propositions about physical objects are propositions about sense-data, for the most part hypotheticals about the sense-data that would be had if certain conditions obtained, and (2) the Lockean view that the material object is the source (part of the cause) of the sense-data and that it really has the primary qualities it is said to have. (1), Moore argued, best explains the sense in which our knowledge of physical objects is "based on" our direct apprehension of sense-data, but against (1) he pointed out that propositions about physical objects will turn out to be true only in a Pickwickian sense, that to say something about coins, for example, will be to say something quite different about certain sensibles. Against (2) Moore could see only one objection, namely that if we can ever know that a sense-datum of ours has a source with certain primary qualities, then we "must know *immediately*, in the case of *some* sensibles, both that they have a source and what the shape of this source is" (Moore 1922b: 196). That is, if we can know that the source of the roundness of some sense-datum is a round coin, then we must, in some cases, know this sort of thing *immediately*, i.e. noninferentially and without mediation by categories. Moore thought that this is not a fatal objection to the Lockean view. For, the objection, and with it phenomenalism, "rests wholly on the assumption that there are only certain kinds of facts which I can know immediately." That assumption, he thought, could not be shown not to be a prejudice. Decades later, to the same effect, Moore would question the different assumption that what he called "certain knowledge" had to be either immediately known or be a logical consequence of things so known (see note 1).

For Moore the existence of the external world was not, as for Descartes, a hard-won (if indeed won at all) conclusion. For Moore knew—these are the premises that do not require proof—that, for example, this is a hand. Moore's defense of common sense and his proof of the existence of the external world are ringing affirmations rather than arguments. One wonders why a philosopher who could be so commonsensical introduced sense-data. One wonders in particular since, as we saw, their status constituted for him an insoluble conundrum. Moreover, both Ockham's razor and our inability to speak about sense-data without speaking about material objects seem to counsel against adopting sense-datum theories of perception. Why did a philosopher who intended to defend common sense succumb to the philosophical temptation to introduce an interface between us and the world in which common sense takes us to have our being? We ask the wrong question. Moore did not think of himself as *choosing* sense-data theory, he *knew* that sense-data existed, are characterized by an unanalyzable property, and are neither in physical space nor in the mind.[4] This is not the view of sense-data/sensations as neutral stuff developed in Russell's *Analysis of Mind*, for that view rests on a rejection of Moore's analysis of sensation. But the view is very close to the view Russell held in *The Problems of Philosophy* (1954), where sense-data are said to be physical though not in physical space. In any case, Moore, being entirely truthful and convinced of the existence of sense-data, had no choice but to offer the analysis of perception that he did in fact offer.

II

Unlike Moore, Russell began both in *The Problems of Philosophy* and in *Our Knowledge of the External World* not by asserting such common sense judgments as "here is a hand" but by displaying the sceptical doubts of traditional philosophy, by asking whether the existence of anything other than our hard data can be inferred from them, for

> the real table, if there is one, is not the same as what we immediately experience by sight or touch or hearing. The real table, if there is one, is not *immediately* known to us at all, but must be an inference from what is immediately known.
>
> (Russell [1912] 1954: 11)

For what is immediately known he introduces the term "sense-datum." The "real" table, in contrast, is not a sense-datum but a physical object. So is there a real table? Here I cannot forebear remarking, as John Austin would, that both "immediately" as in "immediately known" and "real" as in "real table" are terms of art, and as philosophical terms of art so often do, they mislead. Russell, I think, is misled, for he points out within a few paragraphs, "The one thing we know about [our familiar table] is that it is not what it seems" ([1912] 1954: 16), to which I am tempted to reply, "If it isn't what it seems, then it isn't our familiar table," but this flippant reply makes it impossible to continue. So let me return to Russell who held that we know the table, as we do all physical objects, by a definite description, namely by the description, 'the physical object which causes such-and-such sense-data" (Russell 1912] 1954: 47). Two years later, in *Our Knowledge of the External World*, Russell rejected this Lockean view because he saw that it could not even be stated unless a world more stable than the world of sense-data had already been constructed. The crucial word here is "construction." In the preface to *Our Knowledge of the External World* Russell credits Whitehead with "the whole conception of the world of physics as a *construction* rather than an *inference*" (8).

What is this distinction between inference and construction? And why is construction to be preferred to inference? Given that the objects known by acquaintance (or immediately) are not the material objects of everyday life nor the objects that physics speaks of, we can take two attitudes towards our everyday or scientific beliefs. Either we take it that we understand what we believe but wonder whether it is true, whether it can be inferred from what we know, or we assume provisionally that our beliefs are true and ask what they mean. The difficulty with the former view is that a principle of inference is required that cannot itself be verified, while on the construction view, the objects of everyday life and physics turn out to be ontologically like the objects of acquaintance—they are logical constructions out of sensibilia, "objects which have the same metaphysical and physical status as sense-data, without necessarily being data to any mind" (Russell 1957: 143). Of course, we continue to depend on inductive inference, but our inferences are now not to in-principle-not-immediately-knowable material objects, but to further sense-data. As Russell puts it succinctly, "this view is the only one which accounts for the empirical verifiability of physics" (Russell 1957: 173).

Because the elements of construction in the first edition of *Our Knowledge of the External World* are sense-data, one may be tempted to confuse Russell's position, which is a consciously metaphysical as well as epistemological position, with A. J. Ayer's phenomenalism, which claims to be anti-metaphysical. The contrast between the two positions becomes clearer after 1921; I want, therefore, to turn immediately to that position.

Under the influence of William James's *Essays in Radical Empiricism*, Russell came to reject the mind–body dualism implicit in the analysis of sensation that he had shared with Moore. He seems to have thought, however, that the construction of the external world would proceed in the same manner whether the elements of construction are thought of as sense-data, or as something else. Russell states this new view succinctly, "The stuff of which the world of our experience is composed is, in my belief, neither mind nor matter, but something more primitive than either" (Russell 1921: 10). What is this stuff?

In *Analysis of Mind* Russell develops his view in contrast to that of Meinong, who held that when one thinks of Kant and when one thinks of Hume, the act (of thinking) is the same in both cases but the contents, i.e. the events/images in one's mind, are different, and so, of course, are the objects. The content is not identical with the object because the content must exist at the moment of thought, while the object need not do so, and the object "need not be mental." (Russell 1921: 14). By 1921, Russell had come to think that the act of thinking is fictitious because the agent who is said to perform that act is itself constructed out of thoughts, hence cannot be a constituent in each thought. This leaves us with content and object, but the relation between these is not an unanalyzable relation of intentionality, rather it consists largely of beliefs; in perceiving these beliefs will be called mnemic accompaniments. If I think of the Knesset, I may have an image, or merely have the word "Knesset" before my mind, but in addition I have certain beliefs: that I would see a certain building if I went to Jerusalem, that I would feel stone if I touched it, that I would see certain other sights on my way, from, say, Rehavia to the Knesset, etc. My awareness of these beliefs, says Russell, constitutes my belief that my thought of the Knesset has an object. Beliefs of this sort are lacking in cases of pure imagination; in imagination we have content without object. What is of more interest to us, however, is Russell's view that "in seeing or hearing it would be less misleading to say that you have object without content, since what you see and hear is actually part of the physical world, though not matter in the sense of physics" (Russell 1921: 19).

What are we to make of this odd statement? For Russell, there is a clear distinction between the causal laws that belong to physics and those that belong to psychology; sensations are "neutral" because they are subject to both kinds of law. In so far as they are subject to the laws of physics, they belong to the physical world. But matter is a construction out of sensations, no single sensation is a piece of matter, just as no single brick is a house. Analogously, minds are constructions out of sensations, but no single sensation is a mind.

How does Russell distinguish between laws of physics and laws of psychology? A thorough answer presupposes Russell's construction of an ordinary physical object, say a table, out of its appearances from different places. Unfortunately, space for even a summary of this is not available to me. Physics takes such constructions to be causal units while psychology is interested in the particulars, the appearances, out of which the physical object is constructed. But the construction presupposes some of the laws of physics, especially those of perspective and reflection. An air of circularity permeates this project (as it did the analogous project of 1914), if it is taken to be an attempt to answer the sceptical question in *The Problems of Philosophy*, "Is there a real table at all?" Russell admits as much when he writes, "[b]elief in the existence of things outside my own biography exists antecedently to evidence . . . from the standpoint of theoretical logic it must be regarded as prejudice" (Russell 1921: 133). Having made this acknowledgment, Russell proposes to continue yielding to the prejudice, and the title—*Analysis of Mind*—is perhaps an indication that the sceptical question "*how* do we know?" has been abandoned in favor of the question "*what* do we know?" What we know is far more complex than we have thought. For example, Russell writes,

Adhering, for the moment, to the standpoint of physics, we may define a "perception" of an object as the appearance of an object from a place where there is a brain (or, in lower animals, some suitable nervous structure), with sense-organs and nerves forming part of the intervening medium. Such appearances of objects are distinguished from appearances in other places by certain peculiarities, namely:

1   They give rise to mnemic phenomena
2   They are affected themselves by mnemic phenomena.

(Russell 1921: 131)

It is thanks to the mnemic accompaniments, we might say, that we make sense of our sensations and that they themselves will shape our subsequent perceptions and behavior. Given the mnemic accompaniments, there is knowledge, but the sensation itself is not knowledge, although it is involved in the cognitions we call "perceptions" (Russell 1921: 142). What Russell appears to have learned from James and the American realists is that one and the same thing can be subject to both psychological and physical laws, hence the Moorean anti-idealist reason to distinguish the act of sensing (as psychical entity) from the object sensed (as physical entity) has vanished.

To summarize, Moore and the early Russell distinguished between the sensation and the object sensed, called sense-datum. For Moore, in some of his moods, the sense-datum would be part of the surface of a physical object. If so, there would be nothing particularly problematic about our knowledge of the external world, for if x is part of the surface of y, and x exists, then so does y, and to know x is to know something about y. But Moore came to be equally inclined to think that sense-data exist if and only if they are sensed. And since he also thought, as do the rest of us, that the surfaces of physical objects exist whether or not they are perceived, he came to be inclined to think that sense-data were not parts of the surfaces of physical objects but *sui generis*. If so, I fail to understand how he was still able to say that he had defended common sense.

But Moore was also inclined to agree with Russell, who, under the influence of Whitehead, came to analyze physical objects as complex constructions out of sensed and unsensed sensibilia. If a physical object is nothing but such a construction, and if I am aware of one, or better yet, several sense-data that belong to such a complex, could I be said to have some reason to believe that the whole complex is present? One might think so, for if I see several bricks related as they would be in a wall, I have reason to think that there is a wall and possibly a building. But Julius Caesar, when he took himself to see a table, could not have understood that his sense-datum was a constituent in a complex that could only be "constructed," i.e. adequately described, by someone who had knowledge of laws of physics that would not be discovered for well over a millennium. Yet Caesar had as much reason to believe in the existence of the table that he saw as Russell and Moore had to believe in the existence of the table that they saw. Here it is important to remember that logical constructions are NOT inferred entities. Neither Caesar nor Russell infer the existence of the table (the logical construct). Rather Caesar's and Russell's confidence that there is an external world and that we know something about it is justified because that whole external world consists simply of more of what we know by acquaintance, though of course arranged in very complex ways.

Having studied the writings of William James and those of such American New Realists as Perry and Holt, Russell came to reject the distinction between the act of sensing and the object sensed. The object (it is actually an event) is subject both to physical laws and to psychological laws; it is a constituent of the constructed table that is seen as well as of the constructed self that sees the table. It is the intersection of the viewer's biography with that of the table. Of course, what we ordinarily consider to be a case of perception is not a pure sensation, but that together with a good deal of conceptualization. So what the newborn sees is quite different from what the adult sees when they look at the same object, just as a physicist sees a positron track where I see a string of water droplets. But I stray. What matters is that in perception understood as it is understood in *Analysis of Mind*, my-sensation-of-the-table belongs to the table as much as it does to me; it is, like a part of the surface of the table and unlike a mind-dependent sense-datum, not an interface that comes between me and the table. I don't infer the table, though my encounter with it sets up a series of expectations that may turn out to be frustrated.

How does this view differ from the earlier view, the view that constructed the external world out of sense-data? The details of the construction are not affected, the external world is in neither case an "inferred entity." The difference is ontological—the elements of construction are different, and that difference carries with it, I believe, an epistemological difference. The elements do not separate the knowing mind from the known matter, rather they are the interactions of entities constructed out of the interactions.

Moore and Russell, if I understand them correctly, are metaphysicians. We need to turn to A. J. Ayer in *The Foundations of Empirical Knowledge* if we want to enjoy the illusion that we have left metaphysics behind.

III

Ayer, because of what philosophers call perceptual illusions, finds it is advisable to introduce a technical vocabulary for philosophizing about perception. He opts for sense-datum language because it has the advantage of "enabling us to refer to the contents of our sense-experiences, without referring to material things" (Ayer 1940: 57). Thus we might say, "I am sensing a yellow sense-datum." But where does the term "yellow" come from? (Russell, as we saw, would also challenge "I.") This supposed example comes from Ayer's own translation of the perfectly ordinary sentence, "I am seeing a brown carpet which looks yellow to me" into "I sense a yellow sense-datum which belongs to a brown carpet" (Ayer 1940: 68–9). Here "brown" and "carpet" refer blatantly to material objects, and I cannot see any reason for claiming that "yellow" in this sentence is a different term from "yellow" in "I see a yellow carpet." One might also wonder how Ayer can distinguish "sensing" from "imagining," or complain with John Austin that "the two terms, 'sense-data' and 'material things', live by taking in each other's washing—what is spurious is not one term of the pair, but the antithesis itself" (Austin 1964: 4).

For the moment, I want to ignore all these difficulties. What makes Ayer's *Foundations of Empirical Knowledge* of historical interest is his claim—a claim that most of us accepted uncritically at the time—that, unlike Moore and Russell, he, A. J. Ayer, was not a metaphysician.

Having introduced the term "sense-datum" in the usual fashion as that of which one is "directly aware," where direct awareness is necessarily veridical, he *decides* (not discovers) that sense-data exist if and only if they are perceived, and that they have all and only the qualities they are perceived to have. He *opts* for this because he wants sense-data to be unlike material objects. So much for the question that agitated Moore for half a century. Finally, he announces,

> The question, therefore, that we must ask is not how sense-data are to be incorporated in the categories of mind or matter, or whereabouts they are to be located in physical space, but rather how our conceptions of "mind" and "material things" and "physical space" are to be analysed in terms of them.
>
> (Ayer 1940: 78)

Here the difference between Moore and Ayer becomes crystal clear: what is to be analyzed is not an independent reality (a proposition or fact) but *our* conceptions.

What motivates Ayer is not a commitment to the ontological priority of sense-data, but a commitment to foundationalism, to a search for the foundations of empirical knowledge. He wants to construct the material world out of sense-data because only this, he believes, will put empirical knowledge on a firm foundation. Here is the argument:

1 Unless some statements other than logical truths are certain, no statement (other than logical truths) can be even probable.
2 We all believe that many of our statements are not just highly probable but virtually certain, though strictly speaking fallible.
Therefore,
3 There must be statements other than logical truths that are certain, i.e. incorrigible and indubitable and knowable by us.

Sense-data statements as defined by Ayer, are supposed to fill the bill. But if sense-data statements are incorrigible then they cannot serve as foundations. Any statement S that is offered as evidence for some statement T risks being refuted if overwhelming evidence refutes T. Yet Ayer seems to think that sense-data reports cannot be false because sense-data have all and only the qualities they appear to have. This seems to be a mistake; a sense-datum report is always based on memory, and memory is fallible. In addition it seems to me highly unlikely that in the normal course of events people are aware, let alone "directly aware," of sense-data, or anything similar to sense-data. In the normal course of events, we perceive things. I do not say material things because I am mindful of Austin's criticism of that term. Things are of various kinds ranging from my kitchen table to the smell of burning potatoes to rainbows and mirror images. And frequently we react to what we perceive without going through any process of forming beliefs and making inferences, as when I yank the pot off the flame when I smell the burning.

Ayer tries to meet something like this last objection when he writes, "The phenomenalist is perfectly free to admit that the sensing of a visual or tactual sense-datum is, in most cases accompanied by the unreflecting assumption of the existence of some material thing." But, he continues, what is being unreflectingly assumed is "the possibility of obtaining further sense-data" (Ayer 1940: 227–8). In contrast, I claim that we do not "assume" the existence of the burning potatoes, we smell them, and we don't assume or infer the possibility of further sense-data. Often what we infer is not even the possibility of further perceptions, but the existence of certain states of affairs.

At this point, someone might ask why I am so much more critical of Ayer's phenomenalism than I am of Russell's constructionism in *Analysis of Mind*? Are these two philosophers not engaged in similar enterprises? There are, it seems to me, significant differences. Russell constructs the world, including ourselves, out of neutral entities of which we are almost never aware, while Ayer constructs the world out of entities which he says are the only things of which we are, strictly speaking, ever aware. I doubt that we are normally aware of sense-data; I see little reason to believe that they exist. On the other hand, I am sure that I interact with my environment, and Russell's neutral entities are just these interactions, though what I am aware of are not the bare interactions but more complex entities. Secondly, Ayer claims that all he talks about is language, that what makes a statement about, say, my kitchen table knowable is that it is equivalent to a statement about my sense-data. But it turns out that only an infinite set of infinite sets of sense-data statements, most of them counterfactuals, corresponds to the simple statement that my kitchen table is covered with bread crumbs. Even if I were aware of sense-data, no finite, and in fact very small, number of sense-data could possibly be good evidence for believing that the members of that huge set are true, even if we had, as we do not, a clear idea of the truth conditions of counterfactuals.

In contrast, Russell's construction, which makes use of all the scientific knowledge available to him, makes it plausible that we can know the world because the world is constructed out of our interactions with it. Interacting with the world is just how we come to know about the world. Mindful that Russell learned about "construction" in this sense from Whitehead, I shall use a Whiteheadian example to clarify my claim. Whitehead constructed mathematical points out of spheres, that is out of familiar, or as we might say "knowable," objects, thereby showing that points are knowable. The project of showing that the world is knowable— though perhaps along a route quite different from Russell's—makes sense to me; the search for foundations, and in particular the project of phenomenalism, does not. Therefore I want to conclude by considering briefly what might have been called "the refutation of phenomenalism." I mean John Austin's *Sense and Sensibilia*.

IV

Austin set himself the task of ridding us of the illusion of the argument from illusion (Austin 1964: 4).

The argument consists of two parts, as follows:

1 If an object x that has quality q appears to have quality q', then there must be something that has the quality q'.
2 In various cases of perceptual illusion, objects appear to have qualities that they do not have.
Therefore,
3 In cases of perceptual illusions something, call it a sense-datum, that has the quality which the material object appears to have but does not have must exist.
4 What we directly perceive in cases of perceptual illusion is not qualitatively different from what we directly perceive in cases of veridical perceptions.
5 Things which are qualitatively alike must be of the same kind.
Therefore,
6 What we perceive in cases of veridical perception is of the same kind as what we perceive in cases of perceptual illusion, i.e. a sense-datum.
Therefore,
7 We never (directly) perceive material things, we only perceive sense-data.

Austin's strategy is to undermine every step in the argument. What philosophers call illusions fall into different classes. A deliberately produced optical illusion, e.g. the headless lady, is quite different from the bent-looking straight stick half immersed in water, and both are quite different from a mirror image, and so on. Many cases of "illusion," for example, the bent stick, do not deceive. We expect the stick to look bent because we see the water as well as the stick! Still, it looks bent. So, by (1) there must be something which is bent. What is this something (which cannot be part of a material thing because there is no bent material thing around)? This question, to which we are to answer "a sense-datum" is, according to Austin, "completely mad" (Austin 1964: 30). We have no reason to accept (1), and if we did, we would have no reason to think that the sort of thing we look for is the same kind of thing in all kinds of illusions.

Furthermore, premise (4) is simply false. The stick half immersed in water does not look like a bent stick in air. A rainbow doesn't look like anything except another rainbow, etc. Even in cases where we are deceived, we need not assume that what we perceive is just like the thing we would be perceiving if our false belief were true. But let us suppose that there are cases "in which 'delusive and veridical perceptions' really are indistinguishable," and let us suppose that we had admitted that in delusive perceptions we perceive sense-data, we would still not need to extend this admission to veridical perception, "[f]or," writes Austin, "why on earth should it *not* be the case that, in some few instances, perceiving one sort of thing is exactly like perceiving another?" (Austin 1964: 52). In other words, Austin sees no reason to accept premise (5). Austin's critique shows not only that the argument from illusion fails to establish the existence of sense-data but that it fails to give good reasons for choosing to speak about sense-data. Nor can Austin discover any other persuasive arguments.

Austin agrees with me that the motivating force behind Ayer's efforts is the "wish to produce a species of statement that will be *incorrigible . . .* " (Austin 1964: 103, his emphasis). But, Austin points out, there are many contexts in which statements of ordinary English are practically incorrigible, that is, "when they are made, the circumstances are such that they are quite certainly, definitely, and unretractably *true*" (Austin 1964: 115, his emphasis). (Here one is reminded of Moore's certain knowledge that this is a hand.) Thus the desire for incorrigibility is no reason to resort to sense-data language. And, as I pointed out above, incorrigibility would be useless.

Thus I agree completely with Austin's remark that the doctrine that empirical knowledge has foundations is "*radically* and *in principle* misconceived" (Austin 1964: 124, his emphasis). But the question, "How do we know?" need not be a sceptical question, and it need not be understood as a search for foundations of knowledge. It may instead be an inquiry into the nature of the world and ourselves; I phrased it earlier as the question, "What do we know?" Austin's refutation of phenomenalism delegitimizes one attempt to respond to the sceptical question, one attempt to provide foundations for empirical knowledge. As matter of fact, I believe, and I think Austin believed, that any attempt to answer the sceptic by "refuting" scepticism is bound to fail. But I do not know whether Austin would have been sympathetic to a response to scepticism that would be content to defend, simply, the belief that we live in a knowable world, which is what I take Russell to have attempted in *Analysis of Mind*.

NOTES

1   Moore was, I think, less in the grip of that picture than Russell and Ayer. In general Moore seems to have been inclined to be more certain of ordinary everyday beliefs than of philosophical doctrines. See, for example, the concluding paragraph of his "Four Forms of Scepticism" (1959a). Although this essay dates from the early 1940s, the position with regard to philosophical doctrines seems to me to have been held by Moore at least since 1903.

2 Peter Hylton (1990:108ff.) has aptly described the views of Moore and Russell at this time as Platonic atomism.
3 "at least many of them" because when one sees double, at least one of the images cannot be part of the surface of the object seen, and also because, in 1942, Moore uses after images as examples of what he means by a sense-datum.
4 It would be an interesting and illuminating exercise to examine the collection of unanalyzable qualities and relations that provide the foundation of Moore's analyses. This is not the occasion for this exercise.

BIBLIOGRAPHY

Austin, J. L. (1964) *Sense and Sensibilia*, London, Oxford, New York: Oxford University Press. Reconstructed from the manuscript notes by G. J. Warnock. First published 1962.

Ayer, A. J. (1940) *The Foundations of Empirical Knowledge*, New York: The Macmillan Company.

Hylton, P. (1990) *Russell, Idealism, and the Emergence of Analytic Philosophy*, Oxford: Clarendon Press.

James, W. (1976) *Essays in Radical Empiricism*, Cambridge, Mass. and London, England: Harvard University Press. First published 1912.

Moore, G. E. (1922a) "The Refutation of Idealism," *Philosophical Studies*, London: Routledge and Kegan Paul. First published in 1903.

——(1922b) "The Status of Sense-Data," *Philosophical Studies*, London: Routledge and Kegan Paul.

——(1922c) "Some Judgments of Perception," *Philosophical Studies*, London: Routledge and Kegan Paul.

——(1959a) "Four Forms of Scepticism," *Philosophical Papers*, London: George Allen and Unwin.

——(1959b) "Proof of an External World," *Philosophical Papers*, London: George Allen and Unwin.

——(1959c) "A Defence of Common Sense," *Philosophical Papers*, London: George Allen and Unwin. First published in 1925.

Russell, Bertrand (1921) *The Analysis of Mind*, London: George Allen and Unwin, and New York: The Macmillan Company.

——(1926) *Our Knowledge of the External World*, revised edition, London: George Allen and Unwin. First published 1914.

——(1954) *The Problems of Philosophy*, London, New York, Toronto: Oxford University Press. First published in 1912.

——(1957) "The Relation of Sense-data to Physics," *Mysticism and Logic*, Garden City, NY.: Doubleday Anchor Books. First published in 1914.

Schilpp, Paul Arthur (1942) *The Philosophy of G. E. Moore*, Evanston and Chicago: Northwestern University.

11 Wittgenstein: analytic philosopher?

Anat Biletzki

I

As many definitions as there are of analytic philosophy—that many answers are there to my question. No—twice as many, at the least. For, given a definition of analytic philosophy, one can proceed to apply it to the early Wittgenstein, and subsequently to check the later Wittgenstein in its light. Unless, of course, one sees the continuities between the early Wittgenstein and the later Wittgenstein as greater than the discrepancies between them; or, perhaps, to put it more subtly, one sees the specific continuity between the two Wittgensteins precisely in their being—both—analytic philosophers. My suggestion, in answer to the question "Was Wittgenstein an analytic philosopher?", is a single-minded "yes" and "no": Yes, the early Wittgenstein was an analytic philosopher, no, the later was not.

An interesting point to notice, at a first glance, is the community's—the analytic community's—deliberation over the question, with answers ranging from denial of his role to warm espousal of his work (either early or later) as an analytic philosopher. I would venture that such diverse philosophical activity attests to a deep significance of this question for that community. My purpose in asking this question goes, therefore, deeper than mere labeling, for it seeks to elaborate on the significance of such variegated attitudes towards a solitary hero within a single community. Accordingly, I will first peruse three representative texts about that community and attempt to mine them for insights that can advance us along in search of an answer. That done, I shall attempt something better than labeling.[1]

Hao Wang, in *Beyond Analytic Philosophy* (1986), refrains, like so many others, from an explicit definition of analytic philosophy. But he does realize that the

> term "analytic philosophy", unfortunately, means quite different things. . . . In the broad (and natural . . .) sense it includes not only the work of Gödel (in

philosophy) and Russell (in its varied aspects), but also . . . for example, the work of Aristotle and Kant. In the narrow (and historically accidental) sense, the most distinguished and least ambiguous representatives would seem to be Carnap and Quine.

(Wang 1986: xi)

Wang mentions Wittgenstein in passing approximately fifteen times throughout the book; that is to say, he mentions (and clearly does not use) Wittgenstein in illustration while pointing to examples and mainstay characteristics of analytic philosophy in all its variants. But, beyond such mention, Wang adopts a most telling strategy: he devotes a full chapter to Wittgenstein—the early Wittgenstein of the *Tractatus*—while calling said chapter a "digression." And he elaborates: "This is a digression in the following sense. Unlike Russell, Carnap, and Quine, Wittgenstein is art centered rather than science centered and seems to have a different underlying motive for his study of philosophy" (Wang 1986: 75). In other words, analytic philosophy does have essentials—made up of a science-centeredness and an underlying motive for studying, perhaps for doing, philosophy. Wittgenstein, in the *Tractatus*, does not live up to either essential, and therefore merits only a digression. One would ask then—perhaps one *should* ask then: given that Wittgenstein does not satisfy the essential criteria for being an analytic philosopher—*why* does he merit such a digression?

A socio-historical answer is as befitting here as are all socio-historical answers in reply to philsophical questions.[2] Wittgenstein was greatly influenced by Frege and Russell, and greatly influenced Carnap. He is thus easily located within an extensional axis which defines analytic philosophy according to its definitive heroes. In this rather superficial manner Wittgenstein gains membership in a club by being where he was, when he was, with whom he was. But an immediate difficulty ensues: In what ways was he influenced? In what ways did he influence? Or better still: What was it about, or in, his, and their, philosophy that can be credited with influence? Or best yet: Where does that two-way influence touch the issues of analytic philosophy?

In Wang's depiction of Wittgenstein's work—as a digressive part of analytic philosophy—the emphasis is, beyond the Russell-connection, on Wittgenstein's conception of logic and on his conception of philosophy. And that is as it should be—for an analytic philosopher. In that very clear, and not unintuitive, sense Wittgenstein is a paradigm of analytic philosophy. Put broadly, logic is at the basis of analysis, and analysis is at the basis of philosophy. It remains to be seen if analytic philosophy demands a *specific* view of logic (which can be at the basis of analysis), and a *specific* definition of analysis (which can be at the basis of philosophy).[3]

Another definitive text is Michael Dummett's *Origins of Analytical*

Philosophy (1994). Whether it be termed a veritable "definition," or merely
a descriptive rendition, of analytic philosophy, it is univocal in its emphasis
on language: "What distinguishes analytical philosophy, in its diverse
manifestations, from other schools is the belief, first, that a philosophical
account of thought can be attained through a philosophical account of
language, and, secondly, that a comprehensive acount can only be so
attained." And Dummett goes on to proclaim, explicitly, and in outright
answer to my question concerning Wittgenstein: "Widely as they differed
from one another, the logical positivists, *Wittgenstein in all phases of his career*,
Oxford 'ordinary language' philosophy and post-Carnapian philosophy in
the United States as represented by Quine and Davidson all adhere to
these twin axioms" (Dummett 1994: 4, my emphasis).[4]

While telling the story of the origins of analytical philosophy,
Dummett indeed brings both the early and the later Wittgenstein to bear
on all arguments grounding his specific story; a story which is based,
constantly, on the definition above. An attempt to deny equal "analyticity"
to the two Wittgensteins would therefore necessitate entry into the intricate arena of "a philosophical account of language" and a convincing
argument that not every philosophical account of language is, by definition, an analytic account of language.[5]

For Wang, Wittgenstein is a digression. For Dummett he is unequivocal
(though sometimes sporadic) evidence. For Peter Hylton, in *Russell, Idealism
and the Emergence of Analytic Philosophy* (1990), he is a complication.[6]
Speaking of the early origins of analytic philosophy, as opposed to
providing us with a definition or characterization of its development, and,
furthermore, addressing specific origins, i.e., the influence and rejection of
idealism in those origins, Hylton chooses to stop his study in 1913. But the
explanation of this decision is intriguing:

> ... any stopping point is to some extent arbitrary. I have chosen 1913 because at
> this point the influence of Wittgenstein on Russell becomes important, which
> greatly complicates the story; and because after this point Russell ceases, for a
> time, to work on the issues which are, by his own acount, philosphically most
> fundamental.
>
> (Hylton 1990: 1)

The reader might infer that not only is Wittgenstein a complication, he
may also be seen as a *destructive* complication for analytic philosophy.

Hylton, like Wang and Dummett, proposes a loose "definition": "In
speaking of analytic philosophy here I have in mind that tradition which
looks for inspiration to the works of Frege, of Russell, and of Carnap"
(1990: 14). One can't help but notice, in this list of heroes, the absence of
Wittgenstein. More important is the claim that

salient features of this tradition are its employment of mathematical logic as a tool, or method, of philosophy; its emphasis on language and meaning; its generally atomistic and empiricist assumptions; and the fact that many of its practitioners have viewed science, especially physics, as a paradigm of human knowledge (and, like many earlier philosophers, have taken knowledge rather than, say, art or human relations or politics to be the paradigmatic field for the exercise of human reason). . . . A distinctive characteristic of the tradition, more narrowly conceived, is the hope that the logic of Frege and Russell would enable us to find an agreed framework or method for philosophy, and that philosophy would thus achieve something like the status of a science.

(Hylton 1990: 14–15)

The length of this quote is intentional, for it serves us well: If one takes Hylton's "definition" to heart, the later Wittgenstein loses all hope of entering the temple of analyticity. The early, I will try to show, is more clearly an analytic philosopher—perhaps with caveats. It is the last remark, concerning the scientific status of philosophy, which explains Hylton's labeling of "complication" onto the early Wittgenstein, especially if one additionally takes to heart Wittgenstein's strictures concerning philosophy itself.[7]

At this point, a tempting, straightforward, and quite facile methodology would be to choose from the list above, or even to creatively adopt, a "definition" of analytic philsophy and apply it to the *Tractatus* and the *Investigations* respectively. I refrain from going this route and choose, at this juncture, to focus on certain key issues—in particular, the definitive three-some, to my mind, of analytic philosophy: language, logic, and metaphilosophy—which are all manifested in the definitions above. This threesome will not be discussed in three separate sections; rather, the first leads inexorably to the second which then necessitates the third, propelling us, in a manner of speaking, to a one-sided answer to the quesion "Was Wittgenstein an analytic philosopher?"

II

It would be a matter of foolhardiness to ignore the place of language as pivotal in analytic philosophy. Not all definitions or views of analytic philosophy have attributed to language equal importance, essentiality, or centrality.[8] But still, had they done so, explicitly or otherwise—would we then be prepared to say that Wittgenstein was an analytic philosopher in virtue of his over-riding interest in language? The *Tractatus* has been almost invariably described as a tract on language, and the *Philosophical Investigations* can be, and is usually, though not always (and less and less so as interpretive time progresses), perceived as such. Furthermore, we have seen, through Dummett's example, that, in the vein of interpretation tying the two Wittgensteins together and insisting on their affinities rather than dissimilarities, it is precisely this focus on language that serves to make them one. But does this emphasis on language make them both, to an equal degree, tracts of analytic philosophy?

Let us answer by asking further, by asking more extremely; let us ask about Nietzsche. What has he to say about language? Not a little. For instance:

> To the extent that [man] believed over long periods of time in the concepts and names of things as if they were *aeternae veritates* . . . : he really did believe that in language he had knowledge of the world . . . and in fact, language is the first stage of scientific effort. Here, too, it is *the belief in found truth* from which the mightiest sources of strength have flowed.
>
> (Nietzsche 1986: 11)

> The learning of many languages is, of course, a necessary *evil*. When it finally reaches an extreme, it will force mankind to find a remedy for it . . . a language of intellectual intercourse generally. . . . Why else would the science of linguistics have studied the laws of language for a century and assessed what is necessary, valuable, and successful about each separate language!
>
> (Nietzsche 1986: 267)

Do Nietzsche's aphorisms on language make him an analytic philosopher? Does the fact that a philosopher views language as pivotal to the human condition in general make him an analytic philosopher? Can there be a more resounding NO!?

What is there, then, in a certain way of doing philosophy of language that makes it more, or less, analytic? A first attempt at an answer here points to logic; i.e., one's philosophy of language has to be "logical," in a sense immediately to be elucidated, in order to function as analytic. The intuition it involves tells us that the early Wittgenstein was analytic, the later was not. But grounding this intuition involves going into logic, or, more precisely, meta-logic.

I shall approach this intuition in a roundabout way by noticing first and foremost that Wittgenstein of the *Tractatus*, besides doing logic, i.e., besides supplying the reader with a "real logic," a formal system of logic, was intent on the status of logic and on the relations between language and logic. So, although "all the propositions of our everyday language, just as they stand, are in perfect logical order" (Wittgenstein 1922: 5.5563), all the same "it very frequently happens that the same word has different modes of signification . . . or that two words that have different modes of signification are employed in propositions in what is superficially the same way . . . " (1922: 3.323). And therefore, seemingly contrary to some commentators' insistence on the early Wittgenstein's acceptance, even admiration, of ordinary language, "[i]n this way the most fundamental confusions are easily produced (the whole of philosophy is full of them)" (1922: 3.324). Famously, "From [everyday language] it is not humanly possible to gather immediately what the logic of language is. Language disguises thought. . . . Most of the propositions and questions of philosophers arise from our failure to understand the *logic of our* language" (1922: 4.002, 4.003, my emphasis).

It is the task of a new philosopher—an analytic philosopher perhaps?—to embark on a "critique of language," precisely by discovering the principles of logic, principles which are accorded the status of a priority and pure generality. But there's the rub: our inability to formulate them in language, while insisting on doing so, leads us into inevitable nonsense (among other varieties of nonsense).[9] It is now a decision, taken by any reader of Wittgenstein, to decide on the essential emphasis of the *Tractatus*: working at discovering those principles, or throwing up one's hands in desperation at the dead-end this will inevitably lead one to. I suggest that the analytic philosopher chooses the former; the mystic (or perhaps the romantic)[10] alights on the latter.

Let us put this somewhat differently. Deep connections have been pointed out between the early and later Wittgenstein—connections that are based on recognition of the ineffable, and identification of the ineffable with the "unconditioned," the "general," the "sublime." I do not deny the recognition, only the identification; and would want to speak of it as being un-analytic, even anti-analytic. Thereby a demarcation may arise between doing logic (for analytic reasons), and realizing the implication of such deeds. The analytic philosopher does logic for the express purpose of uncovering the general form of language (and reality). Evaluating his (own) project by awakening to its consequences and implications is another matter.

A good illustration of this demarcation, and its application by and on Wittgenstein, is his discussion of logic (as opposed to doing logic itself) in general, and of logic as "sublime" in particular. Some telling examples can be unearthed in the *Tractatus*: "What makes logic a priori is the impossibility of illogical thought" (1922: 5.4731). Or: "Logic must look after itself" (1922: 5.4731). Or: "Whenever a question can be decided by logic at all it must be possible to decide it without more ado" (1922: 5.551). Or even: "Logic is transcendental" (1922: 6.13). The list of exemplary ruminations on logic goes on and on. But then, in the *Investigations*, Wittgenstein talks of our "tendency to sublime the logic of our language" (1958: §38) and *asks* "In what sense is logic something sublime?" (1958: §89) His answer: Logic is something sublime in the special sense of that for which we were looking while doing logic in the *Tractatus*.

An almost trite reading of these passages in the *Investigations* has Wittgenstein accusing us, or his earlier self, of thinking of logic as sublime, precisely since we, and his earlier self, were pursuing something "at the bottom of all the sciences . . . the nature of all things" (1958: §89). And this same reading views the later Wittgenstein as bringing us down to earth, enjoining us to *practice* philosophy differently. (I will shortly approach this matter when speaking of meta-philosophy.) But a close reading—of both the *Tractatus* and the *Investigations*— reveals a subtle, yet nevertheless profound difference between the adjectives describing logic in the former and those (like "sublime") in the latter. The analytic Wittgenstein of the *Tractatus* talks of logic as "transcendental" (1922: 6.13), "all-embracing" (1922: 5.511), "a priori" (1922: 5.4541), etc. The later Wittgenstein of the *Investigations* describes it as having "crystaline purity" (1958: §107) but says *that* his former self thought of logic as sublime. Yet that former self did not, himself, describe logic as sublime. The generality, transcendantalism, out-of-this-worldism, etc. that are used to describe logic in the *Tractatus* all get an *analytic grounding* within the Tractarian system. Logic is transcendental, a priori, etc. for good reason; and precisely for that reason it is therefore never sublime. Or never described as sublime. For sublimity, I venture, is a mystical trait, a romantic temptation. And the later Wittgenstein—having given up in despair on ever reaching the end of analysis—which the early advocated—labels the project in romantic terms. Indeed, it is the "craving for generality," which beautifully describes the activity of logic as a basis for philosophy and the activity of logic as a basis for analysis of language (both of which are attempted in the *Tractatus*), that is later denounced.

We have come full circle to the third stopping point—meta-philosophy, or the philosopher's thoughts on his own project. Starting with the focus on language, which seemed to put us in the direction of being analytic, we narrowed the domain of interest: In order to be an analytic philosopher, he who focuses on language must, in some way, relate language to logic. This move to the basis of the analytic in logic pushes us onward to a philosophy of logic; i.e., not merely using logic while analyzing language, but asking of the why and wherefore of that logic. But such questions about the status of logic submit answers which now turn us in the direction of further questions—about the status of generality in general, and, more so, about the craving for generality. Put differently yet again—our talk above of the ineffable led us to ask about logic; it now leads to questions about philosophy itself.

Wittgenstein's strictures on the doing of philosophy, in both the *Tractatus* and the *Investigations*, are too (in)famous to bear repeating at length. But let us glance at them with a different purpose in mind, the purpose of explicit comparison between the two loci. Admittedly, the *Tractatus* demands that we engage in "activity" rather than in "theory," such activity focusing on "elucidations," and resulting in clarifications rather than "philosophical propositions." It is the activity of "critique of language," removed from any of the natural sciences. In parallel fashion (but more sporadically, in various locations, with few centered presentations of "what is philosophy?"), the *Investigations* also talks of the practice of philosophy and points to its ends. These, again, are neither theories nor propositions, but rather results: "the uncovering of one or another piece of plain nonsense" (1958: §119), descriptions, "perspicuous representations" (1958: §122), clear views, and so on and so on. Where, then, is the difference? In the Tractarian method, or perhaps in the illusion of method; such method being conducive to generality; such method being evidence for the "craving for generality."

Two sections of the *Tractatus* bring out this elusive point in an almost hidden manner:

> In our notations there is indeed something arbitrary, but *this* is not arbitrary, namely that *if* we have determined anything arbitrarily, then something else *must* be the case. (This results from the *essence* of the notation.)
>
> (1922: 3:342)

And even more important:

> A particular method of symbolizing may be unimportant, but it is always important that this is a *possible* method of symbolizing. And this happens as a rule in philosophy: The single thing proves over and over again to be unimportant, but the possibility of every single thing reveals something about the nature of the world.
>
> (1922: 3:3421)

Terms of *necessity*, *possibility*, and *essence* are not precluded by the *Tractatus*. On the contary—they are at the end of our search. Therein lies the vast chasm between the *Tractatus* and the *Investigations*: The particular is all that can be achieved, all one would desire to achieve, in the latter. It is, in itself, unimportant, in the former. For the author of the *Tractatus* the particular could be relevant to philosophy only by hiding the general. And logic and analysis, or, more precisely, the analysis of logic, would uncover the general via the particular. The author of the *Investigations* gave up on that illusion.

III

Using Matar's terminology[11]—of romantic and rationalist—one may almost immediately, in light of the last paragraph, label the early Wittgenstein, he of the illusions, a romantic; the later, he of more modest hopes for philosophy, a rationalist.[12] The natural consequence of such

labeling would then pinpoint the later Wittgenstein as the analytic philosopher (and the early as a romantic)—in contradistinction to my hypothesis.
We seem to have come around full-circle to a contradiction. Perhaps more
subtle moves are now called for.

Matar identifies four characteristics of the romantic (and corresponding contra-characteristics of the rationalist): resistance to
generalization, emphasis on the ineffable, denial of the autonomy of
philosophy, and espousal of impermanence. Of these four I shall address
only the first two in order to reinstate the later Wittgenstein as a romantic
and the early as a rationalist. The romantic, for Matar, insists on the
particular, eschewing generalization. That first characteristic is, for my
present purposes, quite sufficient in order to do away with any attempt to
transform the later Wittgenstein into an analytic philosopher.[13] It is the
early Wittgenstein of the *Tractatus* who is tantalizingly fascinating,
seeming, on the one hand, to fit neatly into Matar's second characterization of the romantic as emphasizing the ineffable in philosophy, and
thereby becoming a natural romantic. If that is accompanied, however, by
the craving for generality, by the attempt to present the general (form of
the proposition, form of reality) through analysis, one is confronted, on
the other hand, by a stark rationalist. Should we say then that the early
Wittgenstein both is, and is not, an analytic philosopher?

Though such a response should not be automatically viewed as repug-
nant (we are, after all, in the heyday of contradictions)—it does suggest a
tension which should be alleviated. This is the tension pointed out in
several commentaries on the *Tractatus*: the tension between the main body
of the book and its preface and last few passages; the tension between its
constructive main body and destructive final admonition; the tension
between the classical reading of a discussion with and continuing Frege
and Russell and the more contemporary one emphasizing its
Schopenhauerian roots. At any rate, these are, to my mind, all versions of
the same tension, a tension presented most blatantly by Wittgenstein
himself:

> the truth of the thoughts communicated here seems to me unassailable and
> definitive. I am, therefore, of the opinion that the problems have in essentials
> been finally solved. And if I am not mistaken in this, then the value of this
> work secondly consists in the fact that it shows how little has been done when
> these problems have been solved.
>
> (1922: Preface, 29)

When faced with such tension the only step open to us is an interpretive
move. By "interpretive move" I point to a choice: a choice concerning
emphasis—a decision as to what to emphasize, what to ignore, what to
accept, what to wave away. Commentators like Cora Diamond, or Burton

Dreben, or Eli Friedlander (and the list goes much farther) have decided to emphasize the ineffable in understanding the *whole* of the *Tractatus*, in putting together its main body of *analysis* with its preface and conclusion. The metaphysical, logical, propositional tract which proceeds in a (more or less) systematic manner, building a comprehensively *logical* structure, is seen to lead to nonsense, to the ineffable. And recognition of this end-point by Wittgenstein then provides an explanation for the surrounding halo of that "whereof one cannot speak." By doing so these commentators provide a reading of the *Tractatus*, an interpretation of the *Tractatus*, that seems to ease the tension by explaining a seemingly dual motivation and empha-sizing one side of the duality.

Adopting a different choice of emphasis one could simply ignore those parts of the *Tractatus* that bow to the ineffable, or claim their relative unim-portance to the main body of the work.[14] Such a choice could even be couched in psychologistic terms, pointing out Wittgenstein's mystical lean-ings, ethical proclivities, or religious personality.[15] Such a choice would, however, be superficial—for it is obvious that a "good" reading of the *Tractatus* must address its various, *sincere* comments concerning what cannot be said. Making peace between its two obviously contradicting senti-ments—between what I have called the main body of work and its framework—must explain the presence of a duality rather than shrug it away. In other words, one must, in interpreting the *Tractatus*, differentiate between its two parts while justifying their double presence.

My suggestion involves separating between talk of logic (or of language) and evaluation of such talk (or of philosophy). I submit, accordingly, that the early Wittgenstein is an analytic philosopher in the main body of his work—exclusive of (some of) the preface, the ladder, and the conclusion. Scrutinizing the list of characteristics attributed to analytic philosophy in the definitions encountered above (and I dare say any others we might have chosen) one cannot but notice that, in large part, they pertain to the early Wittgenstein. The *Tractatus* is a paradigm of philosophical work on thought perpetuated through philosophical work on language. It uses logic as a tool of philosophizing. It focuses on questions of meaning. It views science as a paradigm of human knowledge. And it is, contrary to Wang's evaluation, more science centered than art centered (though "centered" is a term deserving further clarification). Where, then, do we encounter the departure from these definitive descriptions of analytic philosophy? In the *Tractatus*' meta-philosophy; in what Wang calls the "motive for studying philosophy," and Hylton terms the "hope . . . that philosophy would . . . achieve something like the status of a science." Wittgenstein's motives and hopes are certainly different, certainly more subtle.

We have, indeed, come around full-circle. Moving from language to logic to meta-philosophy, it was the third that embroiled us in a contradiction. For it was there that Wittgenstein seemed to be both romantic and rationalist, both analytic and mystic. If we separate the main, analytic body of work from its meta-philosophical evaluation (which is part of the work *de facto*, external to it in status), we can countenance their twofold function consistently. The former does philosophical work; the latter functions negatively in pointing out the ineffable character of such work (which is not yet sublime, as it will be in the later Wittgenstein). Put differently, put in his own words, less narrowly and more pessimistically, the early Wittgenstein is an analytic philosopher who sees "how little is achieved" in analytic philosophy.

NOTES

1 A more exhaustive program behooves us to research a large number of texts with their relative attention to Wittgenstein. Beyond historical texts (i.e., those attending the history of analytic philosophy *per se*) there are several introductions (to analytic philosophy, to the philosophy of language, etc.) which make scant mention of Wittgenstein. This is a phenomenon to be reckoned with, but is beyond the scope of the present article.

2 This comment is not meant facetiously but does point to a skepticism concerning the mixture of socio-historical elements with philosophical aspects of a puzzle. I turn here to the socio-historical only in the hope that it may provide needed insights to intriguing questions and not in any "ideological" stance; only philosophical replies can supply truly philosophical understanding.

3 For a detailed inspection of Wittgenstein's "analysis" and its function, understanding, and role within his view of philosophy, see Peter Hylton's contribution to this volume, "Analysis in analytic philosophy," esp. pp. 45–6.

4 See also Dummett's "Can Analytical Philosophy be Systematic, and Ought it to Be?": "we may characterise analytical philosophy as that which follows Frege in accepting that the philosophy of language is the foundation of the rest of the subject" (1978: 441).

5 See Hylton "Analysis in analytic philosophy," above pp. 52–4.

6 In his "Analysis in analytic philosophy" in this volume Hylton moves closer to Wang by describing his own description of analytic history as including a "detour" to Wittgenstein.

7 This is also in keeping with Wang's assertion that (even) the early Wittgenstein was more art centered than science centered.

8 Several articles in this volume show, most explicitly, that early analytic philosophy was devoid of this emphasis. See especially Ben-Menahem (chapter 7), Putnam (chapter 10), and Skorupski (chapter 6).

9 I do not distinguish here between "senselessness" and "nonsense," though it should be admitted that a careful reading of the *Tractatus* cannot ignore the difference, and the unequivocal realization (by Wittgenstein and, hopefully, by the reader) that the truths of logic are not "nonsense" but rather "senseless."

10 See above, Matar's "Analytic philosophy: realism vs. romanticism," chapter

4. In a certain sense my article is a comment on, or perhaps a continuation of, or even an application of Matar's paper. That she would have applied its implications differently is one more piece of evidence of the interpretive quagmire elicited by Wittgenstein.

11 See above, "Analytic philosophy: realism vs. romanticism," chapter 4.

12 This is the reading Matar would give of the "two" Wittgensteins.

13 This point needs much further discussion, particularly in view of the long list of philosophers, generally acknowledged as analytic philosophers, who insist, along with the later Wittgenstein, on the particular. See also Dummett (1978).

14 This interpretive strategy was the one adopted in the traditional, conservative reading of the *Tractatus*.

15 Indeed, Monk (1990: 105–66) attests to Wittgenstein's psychological state of mind—as a "desire to turn into a different person" which was catered to by his participation in the first world war—as precisely the cause of those parts of the *Tractatus* which we may call "mystical," "ethical," etc.

BIBLIOGRAPHY

Dummett, M. (1978) "Can Analytical Philosophy be Systematic, and Ought it to Be?", in *Truth and Other Enigmas*, Cambridge, Mass.: Harvard University Press.

——(1994) *Origins of Analytical Philosophy*, Cambridge, Mass.: Harvard University Press.

Hylton, P. (1990) *Russell, Idealism and the Emergence of Analytic Philosophy*, Oxford: Oxford University Press.

Monk, R. (1990) *Ludwig Wittgenstein: The Duty of Genius*, New York: The Free Press.

Nietzsche, F. W. (1986) *Human, all too Human*, trans. R. J. Hollindale, Cambridge: Cambridge University Press.

Wang, H. (1986) *Beyond Analytic Philosophy*, Cambridge, Mass.: MIT Press.

Wittgenstein, L. (1922) *Tractatus Logico-Philosophicus*, London, Boston and Henley: Routledge and Kegan Paul.

——(1958) *Philosophical Investigations*, New York: Macmillan Publishing Co.

12 Wittgenstein as the forlorn caretaker of language

Yuval Lurie

Reviewing Wittgenstein's *Remarks on Philosophy of Psychology* in 1982, Ian Hacking noted that they provide a "philosophical psychology"—a term in vogue within analytic philosophy during the 1960s and 1970s. He expressed great hopes for a psychology of this sort, remarking that it differs greatly from what cognitive psychologists investigate and say. "There is a legitimate project called philosophical as opposed to cognitive psychology," he proclaimed. "They are different enterprises, of which only the latter could ever be explanatory." In his review Hacking also compared Wittgenstein and Descartes, noting surprising similarities between these two reclusive expatriate philosophers, as well as marked differences in their views regarding the human soul. He then posed a rhetorical question, asking whether Descartes believed in the soul while Wittgenstein did not, and concluded, without saying why, that this is a bad question to ask. In the years that have passed, what should have been discerned at the time has now become obvious: despite the initial interest, philosophical psychology has *not* penetrated into the heart of modern philosophy. Is this due to current views about the soul, philosophy, or both?

I begin this article with Wittgenstein's "grammatical remarks" on the soul. I then turn to why everyday language plays a central role in his philosophy. Finally, I consider why the pursuit of philosophical psychology no longer interests most philosophers.

A BASIC ATTITUDE TOWARDS HUMAN BEINGS

Descartes wrote that he believed he had a soul, and then went on to prove that his belief was both true and certain. Gassendi was impressed, but not convinced. He thought that there are only particles of matter hurling about in empty space, propelled on their way by physical force. In sarcasm, he addressed Descartes as "O Mind." Descartes replied in kind, addressing Gassendi as "O Flesh" (Descartes 1955: 135–233). What does Wittgenstein say about this highly debated and central issue in modern philosophy? Did he believe that human beings have a soul? Did he side with Gassendi or Descartes—on what we have come to call "The Mind–Body Problem"? Did he say anything on this issue?

In point of fact Wittgenstein concerned himself with the concept of soul and also with the question of whether he believes in the soul's existence. But he did so (in his usual manner) by shifting the question in a surprising direction, noting that there is a distinction between *having an attitude towards things* and having *opinions about* them. "My attitude towards him is an attitude towards a soul," he writes. "I am not of the *opinion* that he has a soul" (Wittgenstein 1971: 178).[1] An opinion communicates *ideas* and is entertained through propositions. Opinions often arise in the context of *reasoning*, and may be assessed accordingly as sound or unsound. When we say, for example, that it is too late to go to the movies, we are voicing our opinion about the feasibility of going to the movies. It is possible to exchange opinions with another person, debate them, support them by arguments. Attitudes are somewhat different. They are not comprised of ideas and are not entertained in the mind through propositions. We have an *attitude of concern* over the health of our children, when their health *worries* us. This attitude is replaced by one of *relief* when we find that what concerned us is no longer worrisome. To be *only* of the opinion that they are not healthy is not yet to be concerned about them. This is a point of view which may be held by any observant, uninvolved bystander. Attitudes are related to emotions, to likes and dislikes. They are ways in which we grasp the significance of things which make up our lives in a very basic, immediate, and non-inferential fashion. Attitudes are manifested in how we *relate* to the things which make up our lives: in how we feel about them, react to them and treat them, rather than *how we reason* about them. Our opinions belong to our *intellectual makeup*: to what we *think* is the case. Our attitudes embody our *attachments, cares, and aversions* to things: i.e. how the case *affects* us. This is not to say that attitudes lack content. Attitudes are ways of apprehending both *the nature and significance of things for us*. As such they are rich in content and may be manifested in beliefs, supported by opinions, and accompanied by feelings and thoughts. In rational human beings, attitudes and opinions are often related to one another, with one affecting the other. Opinions may support attitudes and attitudes may be expressed in opinions. When my attitude of *admiration* for someone diminishes, my previous *high opinion* of him diminishes also, and vice versa.[2]

The assertion that we are not of the opinion that human beings have a soul, but rather we have an attitude towards them as to the possessors of a soul, should remind us that we do not interact with human beings by deliberating whether they have a soul and concluding that they do. It should remind us that in many areas of our lives our existence is based on grasping the significance of things in a more fundamental manner than by entertaining ideas, amassing opinions, speculating, reasoning, and reaching conclusions. Following Descartes, philosophers sometimes say that it is possible to think that human beings are only machines—automatons. If Wittgenstein is correct, and our conceptions of human beings are underlain by an entrenched, deeply ingrained, attitude towards them as beings who possess a soul, what does it mean to *think* otherwise? He reflects on this question in the following way:

> But can't I imagine that the people around me are automata, lack consciousness, even though they behave in the same way as usual?—If I imagine it now—alone in my room—I see people with fixed looks (as in a trance) going about their business—the idea is perhaps a little uncanny. But just try to keep hold of this idea in the street, say! Say to yourself, for example: "the children over there are mere automata; all their liveliness is mere automatism." And you will either find these words becoming quite meaningless; or you will produce in yourself some kind of uncanny feeling, or something of the sort.
>
> Seeing a living human being as an automaton is analogous to seeing one figure as a limiting case or variant of another; the cross-pieces of a window as a swastika, for example.
>
> (Wittgenstein 1971: §420)

The last remark is striking, as it relates the concept of an attitude to seeing something *as* this or that. Seeing things as this or that is a way of apprehending things in a very immediate, non-inferential fashion.[3] To bring out both the entrenched nature of our attitude to human beings as to beings possessed of a soul and its significance, Wittgenstein reflects on what it would be like for us *not* to have such an attitude: e.g. *to see human beings as machines* and to react to them and treat them as though they were machines. Norman Malcolm tells how Wittgenstein explored this idea in lectures through his notorious tribe of human beings who have a different conception of things from us.

> In lectures Wittgenstein imagined a tribe of people who had the idea that their slaves had no feelings, no souls—that they were automatons—despite the fact that the slaves had human bodies, behaved like their masters, and even spoke the same language. Wittgenstein undertook to try to give sense to that idea. When a slave injured himself or fell ill or complained of pains, his master would try to heal him. The master would let him rest when he was fatigued, feed him when he was hungry and thirsty, and so on. Furthermore, the masters would apply to the slaves our usual distinctions between genuine complaints and malingering. So what could it mean to say that they had the idea that the slaves were automatons? Well, they would *look* at the slaves in a peculiar way. They would observe and comment on their movements *as if* they were machines. ("Notice how smoothly his limbs move.") They would discard them when they were worn and useless, like machines. If a slave received a mortal

injury and twisted and screamed in agony, no master would avert his gaze in horror or prevent his children from observing the scene, any more than he would if the ceiling fell on a printing press. Here is a difference in "attitude" that is not a matter of believing or expecting different facts.

(Malcolm 1962: 91)

The attempt to describe this difference in attitude is more problematic than is made to seem here. To judge that such a difference obtains we might want to know to what extent they possess psychological concepts, as well as what kind of attitude they have to members of their own tribe. It is difficult to see what it might mean for them to be human beings who possess our wide array of psychological concepts but react to other human beings not as human beings.[4] Nonetheless, the question is to what extent our basic attitudes to human beings may be subverted or enriched by our opinions and ideas. Wittgenstein reflects on the relationship between *ideas and attitudes* about the soul by considering two cases. In the first he imagines an attempt to undermine through political ideology our attitude to someone as to a being who possesses a soul. He writes:

A tribe that we want to enslave. The government and scientists give it out that the people of this tribe have no souls; so they can be used without scruple for any purpose whatever . . .

(1980a: I, 96; 1967: §528)

If anyone among us voices the idea that something must surely be going on *in* these beings, something mental, this is laughed at like stupid superstitions. And if it does happen that the slaves spontaneously form the expression that this or that has taken place *in* them, that strikes us as especially comical.

(1980a: I, §97; 1967: §529)

Here our attitudes to these people as beings who have souls are undermined by political opinions. In the second, contrasting case, religion exploits such an attitude to build on it theological ideas. Wittgenstein asks: "How about religion's teaching that the soul can exist when the body has disintegrated? Do I understand what it teaches? Of course I understand it—I can imagine a lot here. (Pictures of these things have been painted too.)" (1980a: I, §265; 1971: 178). So various ideas can arise in connection with our attitudes to human beings as to creatures possessed of a soul. These ideas may accompany, enhance, or even undermine our attitudes in certain circumstances. But the attitudes from which the concept emerges, its roots, as it were, are not given to us in the form of ideas or opinions. They are more basic. Wittgenstein reminds us of this fact by asking sarcastically: "Do I *believe* in a soul in someone else, when I look into his eyes with astonishment and delight?" (1980a: I, §268). Delight and astonishment are in this case fundamental, non-reason based attitudes through which we apprehend the human soul. This is not to say that the human soul always provokes delight, or that there is something necessarily civilized and refined about it. "Anyone who listens to a child's crying and understands what he hears," he writes, "will know that it harbors dormant psychic forces, terrible forces different from anything commonly assumed. Profound rage, pain and lust for destruction" (1980b: 2).

COLLECTING REMINDERS

The lesson from Wittgenstein's imagined tribe does not derive from the *success or failure* to imagine a situation in which attitudes of human beings to members of their kind are the same as our attitudes to machines. It comes out in the very *attempt* to do so. In *attempting* it we *remind* ourselves of our subsisting attitudes to human beings, and of how they differ from our attitudes to machines. We remind ourselves that our attitudes to human beings are grounded in apprehending human beings first and foremost as *living creatures* and their behavior as *actions*: attitudes which arise in connection with the *behavior and appearance* of human beings and which are manifested in expectations, apprehensions, feelings, and beliefs. "Pity," Wittgenstein writes in this connection, "is a form of conviction that someone else is in pain" (1971: §287). And so, we might add, is cruelty. Sympathy, delight, concern, compassion, loathing, apprehension, malice, indignation, and so forth are all attitudes that relate to the appearance and behavior of living creatures.[5] Such attitudes disclose an inner bond between the meaningful way in which the world is revealed to us and the way in which we respond to it, both of which are evidenced in the use of our everyday concepts. This suggests that the appearance of things coupled to our attitudes to them is the initial, primary *contextual background* for the emergence and use of our non-scientific psychological concepts of living creature, soul, person, sensation, feeling, belief, thought, intention, wish, and the like. Wittgenstein tries to delineate this contextual background when he notes that "only of human beings and what resembles (behaves like) a living human being can one say: it has sensations; it sees; is blind; is deaf; is conscious or unconscious" (1971: 281).

To *try* to apply these concepts against a completely different contextual background is to bring into relief the natural contextual background for our psychological concepts. Thus, in contrast with metaphysical "thought experiments," Wittgenstein engages in "philosophical reminders." He notes the context in which it makes sense to use a concept by removing it and trying to plant it in alien territory.

> Look at a stone and imagine it having sensations.—One says to oneself: How could one so much as get the idea of ascribing a *sensation* to a *thing*? One might as well ascribe it to a *number*! And now look at a wriggling fly and at once

these difficulties vanish and pain seems to be able to get a foothold here, where before everything was, so to speak, too smooth.

(1971: §284)

The smooth ground is the one that breeds metaphysical opinions. The rough is the one which breeds attributes from which our concepts of everyday use emerge. In the way in which we are immune against apprehending a stone as having pains, so with regard to a corpse. "Our attitude to what is alive and what is dead, is not the same," he remarks. "All our reactions are different" (1971: §284). Another way he highlights this point it is by comparing what we say about human beings with what we say about animals: "We do not say that *possibly* a dog talks to itself. Is that because we are so minutely acquainted with its soul? Well, one might say this: If one sees the behavior of a living thing, one sees its soul" (1971: §357). This reminder is condensed into the assertion that "the human body is the best picture of the human soul" (1971: 178; 1980a: I, §281).

In view of this insight, the philosophical attempt to entertain the *idea* that human beings are automatons, lacking a soul, just like the idea that a stone may possess sensations, appears now as a perverted philosophical game. It asks us to turn our back on our basic attitudes to human beings and to *suppose* that these attitudes are misplaced. But basic attitudes are not opinions. They are not built up out of ideas and cannot be undermined by simply acquiring opinions to fill in for them. They can only be overcome by substituting other attitudes in their place—such perhaps as the attitudes we have to machines. It is in this context that Wittgenstein asserts that his "eyes are shut." He is not able to shake off his attitude to human beings as to beings who have a soul, anymore than a person can evoke in himself an attitude of compassion towards a broken down, old washing machine. He sees astonishment and delight in the faces of those around him, but not in the headlights of cars on the road. In short, he perceives human beings in a particular *meaningful* fashion: as living creatures possessed of a soul. He does so despite any *metaphysical or scientific opinion* that may be advanced and entertained about them.

The same point holds for many other psychological concepts. Use of everyday psychological concepts manifests our attitudes to human beings and other living creatures. This is where these concepts acquire their life, as it were, and it is with the purpose of describing and supporting this use that Wittgenstein engages in philosophical psychology. He describes the ways in which psychological phenomena are expressed in everyday concepts, compares different concepts, suggests new ones, remarks on the ways these concepts are grounded in our lives, and reveals their powerful, expressive ways of displaying things. At times, he tries to excuse his fascination with everyday psychological concepts and the phenomena which are revealed through them by claiming that he is only collecting "reminders" for a future puzzlement. However, like any enamored collector, he appears to be fascinated by the specimens themselves. Looked upon as an undertaking which has merit in its own right, what lends philosophical psychology "its purpose" is that it describes psychological concepts which embody *the ways in which we experience and grasp the significance* of things. These concepts disclose both the nature of our attachments and the psychological ways in which these attachments are made: i.e. they reveal what we value and the way in which we experience and apprehend the value of things. Philosophical psychology is no less than a description of human psychology from a very humanly, partial, meaningful, value-laden, perspective.

THE MIRACLES OF NATURE

If we follow Kant, and call the way things are given to us "the phenomenal" and "the aesthetic," or Cavell, and call it "the ordinary," or Scruton, and call it "the surface of things," then our attitudes, reactions, experiences, and perceptions can be seen to arise in connection with the phenomenal, aesthetic, ordinary, surface of things. They are embodied in the expressive character of everyday language, rather than in theoretical discourse in which scientific explanations are formulated and ideas and opinions are entertained. However, given that we are creatures capable of both forming opinions about the nature of things and acquiring attitudes which disclose their significance for us, why concern ourselves only with a language in which we voice the way in which we apprehend the significance of things in our lives and not with a scientific theory which sets out to explain their nature? Why cling only to the ways in which we apprehend the phenomenal, aesthetic, significant, surface of ordinary things?

One answer to this question was that which Johann Georg Hamann gave. The answer was based on a *religious attitude* to things, as it concerned the way in which God's message to human beings is formulated. Like Galilei before him, Hamann also proclaimed that God speaks through nature. Unlike Galilei, however, who claimed in his *Il Saggiatore* that the book of nature is written by God in mathematics, Hamann claimed that nature is "a book, fable or letter" written by God in the language given to us through our immediate aesthetic experience of it through the senses. The Bible, he claimed, provides a key to this fable, and art is another way in which it is revealed. Art, like the Bible, reveals a way of grasping God's message and disclosing truth through a medium which provides insight and knowledge of reality itself.[6] On Hamann's view, which became the initiating ideological stance for German romanticism, God reveals himself through the human senses and passions through which nature is apprehended. Thus *an artistic activity acquires metaphysical significance*, as it manifests ultimate insight into reality itself. Everyday language, being a language of the senses, attitudes, and emotions, and one in which we express and describe what we value and abhore, and in which poetry and literature are written, is an affiliate of this enterprise. It provides a powerful and immediate human expression for the glory of God's Creation, and it stands apart from the language formulated by means of human intellect in the guise of a scientific discourse which aims to explain things.

Like Hamann, Wittgenstein too had strong feelings for the aesthetic manifestation of ordinary things and for our ability to perceive in ordinary, natural events something remarkable: a work of art created by God. When his friend Engelmann wrote to him, saying that sometimes he perceives something wonderful in what he writes about his own life, and as such would like to make these writings available to all, and sometimes he does not perceive it as such, Wittgenstein delineated Engelmann's experience of the wonder in his life in reference to an ability to perceive an ordinary event as something remarkable: as a work of art created by God.

> Nothing could be more remarkable than seeing a man who thinks he is unobserved performing some quite simple everyday activity. Let us imagine a theater; the curtain goes up and we see a man alone in a room, walking up and down, lighting a cigarette, sitting down, etc. so that suddenly we are observing a human being from outside in a way that ordinarily we can never observe ourselves; it would be like watching a chapter of biography with our own eyes—surely this would be uncanny and wonderful at the same time. We should be observing something more wonderful than anything a playwright could arrange to be acted or spoken on the stage: life itself.—But then we do see this every day without its making the slightest impression on us! True enough, but we do not see it from *that* point of view.—Well, when E. looks at what he has written and finds it marvelous (even though he would not care to publish any of the pieces individually), he is seeing his life as a work of art created by God and, as such, it is certainly worth contemplating, as is every life and everything whatever. But only an artist can so represent an individual thing as to make it appear to us like a work of art; it is *right* that those manuscripts should lose their value when looked at singly and especially when regarded *disinterestedly*, i.e. by someone who doesn't feel enthusiastic about them in advance. A work of art forces us—as one might say—to see it in the right perspective. . . .
> But it seems to me that there is a way of capturing the world sub specie aeterni other than through the work of an artist. Thought has such a way—so I believe—it is as though it flies above the world and leaves it as it is—observing it from above, in flight.

(1980b: 4–5)

Three notable philosophical ideas are expressed in this passage. The first is that there is a way of perceiving an ordinary event as something remarkable and wonderful. The second is that art enables us to perceive ordinary, natural events from such an attitude by representing them as a work of art created by God and, thus, as belonging to something lofty and eternal. The third is that a philosophical thought can partake in the attempt to *represent* things from such an attitude by providing *a conceptual overview* of things.[7] Unlike Hamann, however, Wittgenstein does not delude himself into thinking that such an experience is proof of God's existence, not even at this stage in his thinking. "I would like to say," he writes, " 'This book is written to the glory of God', but nowadays that would be chicanery, that is, it would not be rightly understood" (1975: 7). It would not because in the modern period perceiving an ordinary event as something remarkable does not lead human beings to both seeing it as a work of art created by God and worshipping the glory of God—at least not a person such as Wittgenstein. So while he is still capable of experiencing the remarkable nature of things and giving expression to this experience in a philosophical tract, he is incapable of transforming the experience into an attitude of belief in God. Still, the ability to be struck by an ordinary, natural phenomenon as something remarkable, continues to underlie his thinking, albeit without the former allusion to God.

> The miracles of nature.
> One might say: art *shows* us the miracles of nature. It is based on the *concept* of the miracles of nature. (The blossom, just opening out. What is marvelous about it?) We say: "Just look at it opening out!"
>
> (1980b: 56)

What Wittgenstein reminds us here is of our ability to apprehend an ordinary natural event as the occurrence of something remarkable: this time not as belonging to something eternal, but as a *miraculous metamorphosis*. The concept of the miracles of nature which he tries to bring out here is based on a conception of nature that is prior to that which we acquire through science—or, for that matter, through Western religion as "belonging to something eternal." It is a conception of nature which embodies an ability to perceive natural change from an awe-inspired *attitude of wonder*, as a kind of *wondrous becoming*. It is a conception of nature which underlies art, myth, and religion, but is grounded in everyday perceptions and attitudes. It enables us to perceive even in a functional feature of behavior something wonderful, as of an artistic display: e.g. "Piano playing, a dance of human fingers" (1980b: 36). To perceive natural phenomena from this perspective is to perceive the miraculous not as something which contrasts with the course of natural events, but as something which is integral to them. In reminding us that we still posses an ability to perceive natural phenomena as the miracles of nature, Wittgenstein reminds us that despite all our sophisticated, scientific *ideas* and ways of *thinking*, we are still capable of experiencing things from an inspired attitude which in the past has led human beings to worship God. Indeed, we may even experience its loss when we perceive our modern, civilized environment as devoid of anything lofty and eternal.

> It is very *remarkable* that we should be inclined to think of civilization—houses, trees, cars, etc.—as separating man from his origins, from what is lofty and eternal, etc. Our civilized environment, along with trees and plants, strikes us as though it were cheaply wrapped in cellophane and isolated from everything great, from God, as it were. That is a remarkable picture that intrudes on us.
>
> (1980b: 50)

On the insight which Wittgenstein derives form this experience, there is a crucial, spiritual difference between the perspective on things which a modern, scientific, theoretical explanation provides and that which is supported by an attitude of awe through which we perceive the miracles of nature. The approach which underlies scientific explanations may be that of intellectual perplexity and curiosity, but, on the whole, scientific explanations are not a proper venue for expressing and enhancing an *inspired* attitude of wonder at the miracles of nature. Scientific explanations account for the nature of things by means of abstract, lawlike generalizations. They provide understanding by catering to our *intellect*, not our capacity to be *inspired*. The inspired attitude of awe which is enhanced in myth, religion, and art is dissolved in scientific explanations, and the magic is gone. The rupture between these two different attitudes that he tries to expose underlies the historical development of Western culture into *modernity*. It is manifested in the adoption of an intellectual, scientific attitude to things at the expense of the previous inspired attitudes of awe which, among other things, enabled us to perceive the miracles of nature. On his view, by becoming the dominating spiritual attitude in the modern age, a scientific approach to things hinders our ability to be inspired and to experience things from an attitude of wonder. In our day, Wittgenstein asserts, "Man has to awaken to wonder—and so perhaps do people. Science is a way of sending him to sleep again" (1980b: 5).[8] However, he sees an inherent difficulty in rekindling an attitude of wonder to things once we have succumbed to a scientific outlook on things. This conclusion fosters in him a very pessimistic and grave outlook on the spiritual course taken in modernity by Western culture.

> The truly apocalyptic view of the world is that things do *not* repeat themselves. It isn't absurd, e.g., to believe that the age of science and technology is the beginning of the end for humanity: that the idea of great progress is a delusion, along with the idea that the truth will ultimately be known: that there is nothing good or desirable about scientific knowledge and that mankind, in seeking it is falling into a trap. It is by no means obvious that this is not how things are.
>
> (1980b: 56)

On this view, philosophy in the modern period has chosen to affiliate itself with a scientific attitude of intellectual curiosity which promotes explanations that hide the miracles of nature. It prefers, for example, descriptions of human beings which render them into Turing machines, rather than everyday concepts which reveal that they are beings possessed of a soul. In contrast, Wittgenstein strives to affiliate philosophical psychology with our basic attitudes, those which are given expression in everyday language, art, and religion and which are manifested in our ability to perceive the miracles of nature.

TOURING OUR ANCIENT CITY

In a now famous remark Wittgenstein compresses his views on the relationship between our language and our lives into a very insightful simile.

> Our language can be seen as an ancient city: a maze of little streets and squares, of old and new houses, and of houses with additions from various periods; and this surrounded by a multitude of new boroughs with straight regular streets and uniform houses.
>
> (1971: §18)

I want to focus on this simile with the purpose of both bringing out certain features in Wittgenstein's pursuit of philosophical psychology and showing how it differs from what interests most philosophers today. To begin with, to the extent that our language is a city, it is *our* city: i.e., a city in which we live and know our way. Second, to the extent that language is a city, philosophical psychology comprises remarks which are made during a guided tour of the city. In this role Wittgenstein is the devoted caretaker who shows us fascinating features of our own city. (For we are not tourists who are unfamiliar with it. We are citizens of the city, who have taken a day off from their everyday activities and are wandering along with him in various streets to look at what we already know.) Notice, however, that in Wittgenstein's simile our linguistic city is made up of two districts: one "ancient," consisting of "a maze of little streets and squares, of old and new houses . . . with additions from various periods;" another, consisting of "new boroughs with straight regular streets and uniform houses." The first district is where our *home* is made: the place where we take off our shoes and stretch in comfort. This is where *our basic attachments* are created and expressed: where we experience the value of things. The second district may be thought of as that of science. This is not a place where we actually make our home and in which our basic attachments are made and where we experience the value of things in our lives. It is a place where we go to think about things, to entertain ideas, and to procure and fashion sound opinions.

As far as Wittgenstein is concerned the distinction between the districts is underlain by their spiritual value. Although both districts are comprised of houses and streets, Wittgenstein is inspired only by houses and streets that are incorporated in the "ancient city": i.e. by constructions which comprise what he calls *architecture*. He does not consider all buildings as architecture. Architecture is manifested in an innovation such as a building which has some redeeming *expressive feature* which lends it spiritual value. "Architecture is a *gesture*," he writes. "Not every purposeful movement of the human body is a gesture. And no more is every building designed for a purpose architecture" (1980b: 42). One way in which he tries to phrase his thinking on this matter is by the previously mentioned concept of glory. "Architecture immortalizes and glorifies something. Hence there can be no architecture where there is nothing to glorify" (1980b: 69). As may be clear by now, there are no architectural buildings in the new district of science. Everyday language, we might say, is an architectural building of a human form of life. It is a great work of art, which is created over many years by many generations, not unlike monumental constructions of various cultures, such as the pyramids built in Egypt or the European cathedrals built in the middle ages, through which human beings sought to express and glorify their conception of things.[9]

Everyday language, it might be said, is a series of meaningful, glorious, human gestures. It is a language in which we express our intense, inspired, non-intellectual attitudes and deep attachments and aversions to things— and therefore also a language in which poetry is written. The language of science is not. The language of science does not manifest our intense, inspired, non-intellectual attitudes and deep attachments and aversions to things, and it does not express glory. Therefore scientific questions are not captivating for him. "I may find scientific questions interesting," Wittgenstein writes, "but they never really grip me. Only *conceptual* and *aesthetic* questions do that. At bottom I am indifferent to the solution of scientific problems, but not the other sort" (1980b: 79). The linguistic district of science, we might say in line with his simile, is not architecture, and the buildings that are constructed there lack glory: i.e. spiritual value. They are invented, artificially fabricated constructions, not architectural creations which can be added to our ancient homes. Therefore Wittgenstein turns his back on it. His philosophical psychology pertains only to those parts of our linguistic city in which he still experiences glory.

A philosophical tour which Wittgenstein conducts of our linguistic city is pursued with two related goals. One is *critical*, as it aims to dismantle metaphysical constructions of "houses built in the air." The other is *supportive*, as it aims to bring out the glory in a human form of life which everyday language expresses. The two often go together, as a metaphysical construction hides both the miracles of nature and the glory which is expressed through everyday language. In Wittgenstein's insight, unlike a scientific construction which takes all the wonder out of life, a metaphysical construction is like a fairy tale. It is permeated by an attractive air of magic, false magic. (The house is not a real house, only the pretense of a house.) Therefore, philosophical remarks, he contends, must have a certain magic to them as well, to counter the spell of metaphysics: "The solution of philosophical problems can be compared with a gift in a fairy tale: in the magic castle it appears enchanted and if you look at it outside in daylight it is nothing but an ordinary bit of iron (or something of the sort)" (1980b: 11). However, as I have been trying to show, there is also, on his view, another way of pursuing philosophical activity in which there is magic but which does not consist either in building metaphysical constructions or in tearing down houses built in the air. This is a philosophical investigation which sets out to enhance our ability to perceive the miracles of nature, as, for example, they are revealed when we apprehend human beings as having a soul. A language that gives expression to such attitudes and perspectives glorifies human existence, and philosophy ought to cater to it. Philosophical remarks which do so provide what he calls a "perspicuous representation" of the grammar of our language. In this capacity grammatical remarks are comments made during a tour of our ancient city by its devoted citizen and caretaker who seeks to display it in all its glory. They bring out the glory which is encapsulated in everyday language through insightful descriptions of our concepts that bring out their *significance*. Thus, Wittgenstein's assertion that he is not of the opinion that human beings have a soul, but that he has an attitude to them as to beings who have a soul is a grammatical remark which provides a perspicuous representation of this concept. It discloses its significance in our lives by reminding us that it manifests a basic attitude to human beings, as contrasted with things about which we only entertain opinions.

On this view of everyday psychological language, its glory consists in its ability to express, treasure, enhance, intensify, and enrich our human perspectives, attitudes, and experiences, just as art does. When furnishing a perspicuous representation of the grammar of our language, philosophy caters to its glorious achievement as a complimentary aesthetic discipline which serves it. It operates in this capacity as, for example, the art of framing and hanging pictures caters to paintings by enhancing their glory; or as a good commentator on a work of art enables us to appreciate it better by using his remarks to bring into focus significant features. Thus a true philosopher must have an artistic flair as well as an analytic mind, as he must be capable of bringing out what language glorifies through a perspicuous representation of a segment of its grammar. Wittgenstein describes his view of philosophy in connection with this goal by noting that "philosophy ought really to be written only as a *poetic composition*" (1980b: 24). He sees, therefore, a "queer resemblance between a philosophical investigation (perhaps especially in mathematics) and an aesthetic one. (E.g. what is bad about this garment, how it should be, etc.)" (1980b: 25). The goal thus set before philosophy (and philosophical psychology in particular) is very different from that which underlies philosophical tracts in philosophy of mind today.

THE SPECTER OF SCIENCE AND THE GLORY OF EVERYDAY LANGUAGE

Ever since Galilei showed his contemporaries how to explain the dynamics of nature in abstract physical laws, philosophers have tended to display either of two extreme and opposing intellectual attitudes towards scientific explanations. One is exhilaration over the prospects of acquiring what is perceived as enlightenment, progress, and objective knowledge. The other is panic over what is perceived as the infringing of spiritless hordes on our cherished conceptions of human life and its worthiness. The first attitude has motivated some philosophers to try to join in this enterprise by taking on the role of cheerleaders who proclaim a positive attitude towards science and deride all those who fail to voice their enthusiastic support. The second attitude has motivated others to try to shore-up the defenses of our ancient concepts with arguments which aim to show that everyday concepts, particularly psychological ones preclude all theorizing. Initially, either attitude may seem extreme and unwarranted. For why should a scientific explanation be perceived as either a blessing or a curse? The answer, I believe, lies in that both vilified and celebrated philosophical enterprise referred to as *metaphysics*. It is not scientific theory which is the culprit, but the metaphysical goal of delineating through philosophy a *fundamental ontology* (of what there is) which is the cause for either metaphysical exhilaration or panic over science. As sides are drawn across this metaphysical battleground, Wittgenstein finds himself with very few allies. Unlike Hamann, he does not justify his preference for our ordinary, unscientific attitudes, experiences, perceptions, and the concepts in which they are embedded, by an appeal to God's revelation of his presence through the miracles of nature and the glory which is encapsulated in everyday language. He is a modern writer. He notices a cleavage between everyday language and the language of science. But he uses no metaphysical argument to justify his preference for a description of things which enhances his perception of the miracles of nature and the glory of ordinary concepts. God may have spoken to Hamann through the language of art and the senses. However, as Wittgenstein notes, "You can't hear God speak to someone else, you can hear him only if you are being addressed." And though he quickly adds, "That is a grammatical remark," it may safely be surmised that *grammatical* knowledge is all the knowledge he had of this truth (1967: §717). He may still admire the glory which is encapsulated in this conception of God and which he thus strives to display, but he no longer shares in it. In this respect everyday psychological concepts are different. They provide a still viable, meaningful, glorious expression for human life which is incorporated in our lives and in which we all share. Our use of them in ordinary life shows that they have not been undermined by science.

Wittgenstein's tour of our city is restricted to what he values and cherishes in it. He disdains making excursions into the new, scientific districts of the city, as he does not experience any spiritual value in them. The result of this omission on his part is that many philosophers today find his guided tour of the city fascinating, but outdated. For in contrast with his lack of interest, apprehension, and disdain for science, most philosophers today are constantly peeking over their shoulders at what goes on in science. Indeed, some are more inclined to visit the new boroughs of science and to emulate their style of building than they are to visit the ancient ones in which their homes are made. Even when dealing with everyday language, it is important for them to assess its merits in the context of scientific opinion. As though on its own, it lacks sufficient support. Nabokov is reported to have been irritated once by a nagging admirer, who repeatedly praised how well his book reads in translation: "Yes," he is said to have responded finally, "it does lose something in the original." Present philosophers of mind, it might be said, are akin to someone who misses the sarcasm in this remark. They seriously think that the concept of soul loses something in the original. Some express this idea by referring to everyday psychological concepts derogatorily as "folk psychology," suggesting in this way that, for the sake of truth, it would be better to do without them. Others, seeing a practical difficulty in discarding everyday psychological concepts, want to turn them into a *legitimate opinion* which, through their metaphysical translation of it into science, reads better than in the original.

In the context of such metaphysical attempts to either undermine or support our everyday psychological concepts through science, both Wittgenstein's lack of interest and his disdain of scientific explanations of human psychology, coupled with his admiration for the expressive nature of everyday concepts, is *exceptional*. He displays an ability to cherish ordinary human attitudes, experiences, and perceptions of things and the ways they are given a glorious expression in everyday psychological language—despite all the enthusiasm in philosophy about adopting an intellectual, scientific perspective instead. Like a forlorn caretaker of a once prized, but now mostly disregarded great work of art, he is not swayed in his admiration by the disregard of others, as he again and again endeavors to display the glorious ways in which everyday psychological concepts capture the wonder of it all. For those of us who are not satisfied with simply amassing sound opinions on things, this should be reckoned as both a *remarkable personal gesture* and a *wonderful philosophical achievement.*[10]

NOTES

1 The words he uses are *Einstellung* for attitude and *Seele* for soul.
2 Beliefs may express either attitudes or opinions. In *On Certainty* Wittgenstein often tries to describe beliefs as attitudes.
3 The concept of "seeing as" is discussed by Wittgenstein in *Philosophical Investigations*, Part II, xi.
4 As Cavell (1979: 372) has written in this connection, "Many people, and some philosophers, speak disapprovingly of treating others, or regarding them, as things. But it is none too clear what possibility is being envisioned here. *What* might someone be treated as?"
5 In *Nausea*, Jean-Paul Sartre (1949) describes a basic human attitude of disgust which arises at the sight of a tree. He uses it to carve out a fundamental metaphysical division. It is telling that in the pursuit of this project, he bases his ontology upon an attitude, rather than on ideas.
6 I am indebted for these remarks on Hamann to Frederick C. Beiser's discussion of Hamann in *The Fate of Reason: German Philosophy from Kant to Fichte*, as well as to Isaiah Berlin's "Hume and the Sources of German Anti-Rationalism."
7 It is noteworthy in this connection that in his last remarks, Wittgenstein expressed his overview of his own life in the following way: "Tell them I've had a wonderful life!" See Malcolm (1958: 100).
8 Perhaps what Wittgenstein missed most was seeing the world as a work of art created by God.
9 On Wittgenstein's conception of language as a great work of art, see my "Wittgenstein on Culture and Civilization" (Lurie 1989); also my "Culture as a Human Form of Life: A Romantic Reading of Wittgenstein" (Lurie 1992).
10 Many people have made sound criticism of earlier versions of this paper, especially P. Hacker and Z. Kasachkoff. I thank them all.

BIBLIOGRAPHY

Beiser, F. C. (1987) *The Fate of Reason: German Philosophy from Kant to Fichte*, Cambridge, Mass.: Harvard University Press.
Berlin, I. (1981) "Hume and the Sources of German Anti-Rationalism," in H. Hardy (ed.) *Against the Current*, Oxford: Oxford University Press.
Cavell, S. (1979) *The Claim of Reason*, Oxford: Oxford University Press.

Descartes, R. (1955) *The Philosophical Works of Descartes*, Vol. II. rendered into English by E. S. Haldane and G. R. T. Ross, New York: Dover Publications Inc.

Hacking, I. (1982) "Wittgenstein the Psychological," *The New York Review of Books*.

Lurie, Y. (1989) "Wittgenstein on Culture and Civilization," *Inquiry* 32: 375–97.

——(1992) "Culture as a Human Form of Life: A Romantic Reading of Wittgenstein," *International Philosophical Quarterly* XXXII/2: 193–204.

Malcolm, N. (1958) *Wittgenstein. A Memoir*, London: Oxford University Press.

——(1962) "Wittgenstein's Philosophical Investigations" in V. C. Chappell (ed.) *The Philosophy of Mind*, Englewood Cliffs N.J.: Prentice-Hall, Inc.

Sartre, J. P. (1949) *Nausea*, Norfolk, Conn.: New Directions.

Wittgenstein, L. (1967) *Zettel*, G. E. M. Anscombe and G. H. von Wright (eds), trans. G. E. M. Anscombe, Berkeley: University of California Press.

——(1971) *Philosophical Investigations*, trans. G. E. M. Anscombe, New York: The Macmillan Company.

——(1975) *Philosophy Remarks*, R. Rhees (ed.), trans. R. Hargreaves and R. White, Chicago: The University of Chicago Press.

——(1980a) *Remarks on the Philosophy of Psychology*, Vol. I, II, G. E. M. Anscombe and G. H. von Wright (eds), trans. G. E. M. Anscombe, Oxford: Blackwell.

——(1980b) *Culture and Value*, G. H. Von Wright (ed.), trans. P. Winch, Oxford: Blackwell.

——(1993) *Philosophical Occasions, 1912–1951*, J. C. Klagge and A. Nordmann (eds), Cambridge: Hackett Publishing Comp.

13 Heidegger, Carnap, Wittgenstein: much ado about nothing

Eli Friedlander

THE TRIANGLE

The elaboration of the question of the nature of analytic philosophy might benefit from considering the relation of that tradition to what most oppose it. Hegel aside, one can sense that at some stage a confrontation with one's own other is the most fruitful condition of philosophical progress. Thus the future of analytic philosophy might itself be thought of in terms of its relation with so-called continental philosophy. The problem with such a vision is that at present it is hard to start assessing the relation between those two traditions, each being so out of touch with the other. It becomes necessary to search for past encounters and to try to reassess their significance.

One of these encounters occurs in the early 1930s between Carnap, Wittgenstein, and Heidegger. Articulating the relations that form this triangle reveal much more than relations of agreement or disagreement. It reveals a logic or a field of force that underlies and determines each of the positions. Bringing this out requires placing Wittgenstein in such a constellation that naturally presents itself as the confrontation of analytic and continental philosophy, i.e. of Carnap and Heidegger. The possibility of the third man, who is not necessarily a double agent, is what makes this exchange complex and philosophically fruitful.

In his book, *The Logical Syntax of Language*, Rudolf Carnap explicitly acknowledges the influence of Wittgenstein's *Tractatus* on his work; he takes Wittgenstein to have "first exhibited the close connection between the logic of science (or 'philosophy,' as he calls it) and syntax. In particular, he made clear the formal nature of logic and emphasised the fact that the rules and proofs of syntax should have no reference to the meaning of symbols."

The differences Carnap has with Wittgenstein concern primarily Wittgenstein's idea that there is a dimension of language which can only be shown but not said. Carnap takes this to refer to logical syntax as he understands it and finds Wittgenstein plainly mistaken about the impossibility of representing it. Wittgenstein's mistake has to do with not appreciating the possibility of describing syntax in a meta-language which itself can be represented through arithmetization in the object language itself.

The possibility of describing any syntax in an agreed upon language has important consequences for Carnap: *In logic*, he says, "*there are no morals*. Everyone is at liberty to build up his own logic, i.e. his own form of language, as he wishes. All that is required of him is that, if he wishes to discuss it, he must state his methods clearly, and give syntactical rules instead of philosophical arguments" (1937: 52). Most philosophical views then suffer from not distinguishing clearly between the choice of syntax and the claims about the world. Many philosophical claims involve a confusion of the formal and the material modes, and can be recast and tolerated in Carnap's framework.

But tolerance has its limits: Some philosophical views just cannot be translated into any systematic syntax. Carnap thinks there are many examples of plain philosophical nonsense in the history of philosophy, but he selects one "from that metaphysical school which . . . exerts the strongest influence in Germany" (1932: 69) Picking on Heidegger's striking expression "The Nothing nothings" Carnap with a barely maintained straight face proceeds to point out its meaninglessness through an over-meticulous analysis.

If we turn now to Heidegger we see that he places himself at least nominally within the space of a problem that might be relevant to Carnap. Anticipating the latter's criticism he claims that "the question of the nothing . . . pervades the whole of metaphysics, since it forces us to face the problem of the origin of negation, that is, ultimately, to face up to the decision concerning the legitimacy of the rule of 'logic' in metaphysics" (Heidegger 1977: 110). Carnap might not recognize such a problem as his, as one raised by the limits of his own inquiry, since it would seem to him that the very possibility of challenging the hegemony of logic betokens a psychologistic point of view. To raise that challenge differently is Wittgenstein's role in this encounter. Heidegger does not say much about Carnap's criticism, but he seems to view the encounter as significant. In a late paper he characterizes the distinction between his view and Carnap's as the most extreme positions of philosophy. He expresses the differences in terms of diverging attitudes to language:

> Language, in what is most proper to it, is a saying *of* that which reveals itself to human beings in manifold ways and which speaks to human beings insofar as they do not, under the dominion of objectifying thinking, confine themselves to it and close themselves off from what shows itself.
>
> (Heidegger 1976: 29)

In objectifying language, which means for Heidegger at least thinking of language as a means of representation and making language itself an object, what is missed is the dimension of what shows itself. This saying is, if anything, at least striking in its resemblance to Wittgenstein's attempt to maintain a distinction between saying and showing as well as of his rejection of any attempt to overcome that basic distinction by means of a hierarchy of languages.

So, we must now ask about the relation of Wittgenstein to Heidegger. In a letter addressed to Russell and dated 19.8.1919 Wittgenstein writes:

> Now I'm afraid you haven't really got hold of my main contention, to which the whole business of logical propositions is only a corollary. The main point is the theory of what can be expressed by propositions—i.e. by language—(and, which comes to the same, what can be *thought*) and what can not be expressed by propositions, but only shown; which I believe is the cardinal problem of philosophy.
>
> (Wittgenstein 1974: 71)

The question of showing is itself subordinated to what Wittgenstein famously called the ethical point of the *Tractatus*. Instead of Carnap's statement in *The Logical Syntax of Language* to the effect that "*In logic, there are no morals*," we get Wittgenstein's claim that all his work on logic has an ethical point to it. It would be a rather vicious historical circle if it turned out that such a strange conception of ethics bears some affinity to Heidegger's. So, to close the circle, or to establish initially the triangular relation I think of, Wittgenstein had himself a reaction to Heidegger, reported by Waissman:

> To be sure, I can imagine what Heidegger means by being and anxiety. Man feels the urge to run up against the limits of language. Think for example of the astonishment that anything at all exists. This astonishment cannot be expressed in the form of a question, and there is also no answer whatsoever. Anything we might say is *a priori* bound to be mere nonsense. Nevertheless we do run up against the limits of language. Kierkegaard too saw that there is this running up against something and he referred to it in a fairly similar way (as running up against paradox). This running up against the limits of language is *ethics*. I think it is definitely important to put an end to all the claptrap about ethics—whether intuitive knowledge exists, whether values exist, whether the good is definable. In ethics we are always making the attempt to say something that cannot be said, something that does not and never will touch the essence of the matter. It is a priori certain that whatever definition of the good may be given—it will always be merely a misunderstanding to say that the essential thing, that what is really meant, corresponds to what is expressed (Moore). But the inclination, the running up against something, *indicates something*. St. Augustine knew that already when he said: What, you swine, you want not to talk nonsense! Go ahead and talk nonsense, it does not matter!
>
> (Wittgenstein 1979: 68)

It is not just the sense of understanding that Wittgenstein evinces in Heidegger that strikes me as significant. It is also how this is expressed and to whom. Indeed the language that Wittgenstein uses to recapture Heidegger's insight is the language of the end of the *Tractatus*. In his "Lecture on Ethics" Wittgenstein rephrases the claim about Heidegger in the first person: "My whole tendency and I believe the tendency of all men who ever tried to write or talk Ethics or Religion was to run against the boundaries of language. This running against the walls of our cage is perfectly, absolutely, hopeless" (1965: 12). What does Wittgenstein refer to when he speaks of his whole tendency, if not to the tendency of the *Tractatus* as a whole? We might say that running up against paradox so as to point to something beyond what is said is a pretty accurate description of the end of that text. So Wittgenstein is not merely saying here that he can understand Heidegger but associates Heidegger's project with his own. Can it be that a text that openly cultivates the sound of nonsense but aims at the most significant communication says the same, ultimately, as a text that at times seems overly sound and ends up in utter paradox and nonsensicality?

That Wittgenstein expresses his view of Heidegger to the members of the Vienna Circle, around the time that Carnap publishes his "Elimination of Metaphysics" makes it a statement of Wittgenstein's position in the philosophical world that is taking shape. The title of this chapter might suggest that the triangle and the various misidentifications constitutes a comedy of errors but this is far from being the simple explanation of the matter. Nor do I want to suggest that Wittgenstein is here merely squaring accounts with the Vienna Circle. Above all my aim is not to reclassify Wittgenstein as a continental philosopher, but to think fruitfully the possible affinity between his thinking and Heidegger's in the midst of his relation to the logical positivists.

My assumption then is that there is some kind of strange precision in these exchanges. We must ask why does Carnap merely rejects politely Wittgenstein's showing and is so full of animus against Heidegger's revelation of the nothing. It could be that he senses the affinity between those thinkers but instead of distancing himself from Wittgenstein, which is impossible given his positive influence, he redoubles his criticism against Heidegger. That is, the fact that Carnap focuses on the issue of the nothing in Heidegger's essay might mean that he avoids facing that issue in another place much closer to home. For this last claim to be convincing one must realise that the criticism directed at Heidegger is uncannily accurate. Carnap associates Heidegger's "The Nothing nothings" with nonsense but his analysis in this case sounds peculiar. Such analysis might be insightful for such philosophical texts that disguise themselves as sensical statements about the world, but the example chosen is far from being that. Heidegger's text is careful to display its violation of natural syntax for everyone to see it. The comic effect that the sentence "The Nothing nothings" can still provoke, in some circles, is an indirect sign of its overt peculiarity. More importantly, Carnap's account of philosophical nonsense faces through Heidegger's text an important question: What is the source of nonsense? Is it a mere mistake? Why should anyone be tempted to such mistakes? And why are they so stubborn and seem so important? But these are all issues addressed by Wittgenstein's comment concerning Heidegger: The nothing makes itself manifest in the urge to nonsense. The question of the nothing *is* the very question of nonsense when it translates into the terms of the *Tractatus*.

It will not be possible for me to elaborate here the complex relations formed in this triangle. What I will focus on is Wittgenstein's remarks on Heidegger. Wittgenstein has been known to have expressed strange views on a variety of people and things. In order for this remark to have the pertinence I find it to have, it must be shown to bear on our understanding of the *Tractatus* as a whole, and in particular to challenge the reading of that text that ties it so naturally with Carnap's positivism. This is what I will attempt here, pointing at certain junctures of the text and trying to reread them together, subordinating them to the end. I will not propose here a reading of Heidegger's "What is Metaphysics?" But I want my reading of the end of the *Tractatus* to mark my sense of Heidegger's writing about the nothing. This will involve me in a certain bizarre mixing of idioms which seems inevitable, and thus I hope will be excusable, given my aim.

THE SIGNIFICANCE OF NONSENSE

Reading the end of the *Tractatus* requires a view of nonsense. Thinking of that end and the gesture of throwing away the ladder, it is assumed that one can take either of two positions. Some interpreters would argue that Wittgenstein has conveyed some contentful understanding of the world which, on its own terms, cannot be stated properly. That is, strictly speaking we have nonsense but we can see through it or by means of it what picture of the world Wittgenstein is aiming at. According to an influential reading of Cora Diamond nonsense can in no way be informative.[1] There is no such thing as a category mistake, or a supposedly informative form of nonsense. The only possible kind of nonsense occurs when one fails to give meaning to terms in the sentence one utters or writes. This implies that the nonsense the *Tractatus* itself presents cannot be essentially "higher" and the attempt to produce the unsayable truth of this book is indefensible. "Chickening out" is her favourite term of criticism for what too many interpretations of the *Tractatus* are tempted to do faced by the demand to throw away the ladder.

Both views, in trying to explain the *nature* of nonsense, do not seem to me to address enough the issue of the drive to nonsense. Wittgenstein wants to understand the subject through language (he says, obscurely, that the subject is the limits of language). Then it is language that must account for the throwing oneself against those limits which produces nonsense. Dialectical illusion, in Wittgenstein as in Kant, is not external to reason. This means that the account of language must find the possibility of nonsense intrinsic to it. There is, so it seems, a passion or need at the very heart of language which makes us inevitably run up against the limits of language. This running up against the limits of language cannot be explained by positing a subject that stands over and against language, as it were the empirical or psychological subject. For in that case this running up against the limits of language would be utterly uninteresting and surely not what Wittgenstein could possibly call ethics. What we need is a fundamental phenomenology of being in language that exhibits the dimensions of language as fundamental axes of subjectivity.

The preface of the *Tractatus* provides us with a statement of Wittgenstein that bears on that issue:

> Thus the aim of the book is to draw a limit to thought, or rather—not to thought but to the expression of thoughts: for in order to be able to draw a limit to thought, we should have to find both sides of the limit thinkable (i.e. we should have to be able to think what cannot be thought).
>
> It will therefore only be in language that the limit can be drawn, and what lies on the other side of the limit will simply be non-sense.
>
> (Wittgenstein 1961: 3)

What I find significant in this statement is the claim that both sense and nonsense belong to *language*. One could avoid the implications of this claim by saying that when Wittgenstein speaks of nonsense as belonging to language he uses a thin conception of language associated merely with the presence of linguistic signs arranged according to superficially correct syntax. Were we to take the full blown view of language as signs that express a sense then clearly nonsense would not be part of language. This is undeniable; it is even tautological. Clearly nonsense is not some kind of content of language. But this is not to say that the empty manipulation of signs isn't related to the level of sense. Take an analogous issue: what Wittgenstein has to say about the belonging to language of tautologies and contradictions. There we have a case where the syntax allows for constructions that defeat as it were their own attempt to make sense, or result in senselessness. With nonsense we might say that it is the demand made on you by *significant* communication that is connected internally with the possibility of nonsense.

In order to approach that intuition it is crucial not to conceive language as an abstract system but rather as a place in which the subject can manifest itself. Wittgenstein claims that "Everyday language is a part of the human organism and is no less complicated than it." This expresses among other things that such language has a life whose dimensions we must now reconstruct. "Man possesses the ability to construct languages capable of expressing every sense, without having any idea how each word has meaning or what its meaning is—just as people speak without knowing how the individual sounds are produced" (4.002). A crucial dimension of language is the split between the capacity to produce sense, given our means of expression, and the knowledge of the object that can show through our making of sense. Importantly one need not know meanings, i.e. objects, in order to produce sense. But this gap itself seems to be the source of the nonsense produced in philosophy: "Most of the propositions and questions of philosophers arise from our failure to understand the logic of our language" (4.003). This leads to a tension in Wittgenstein's account: On the one hand language as it were takes care of itself; we need not know what the meaning of our words are in order to produce any sense we want. On the other hand this very gap seems to be what produces the nonsense of philosophers. How are those claims to be reconciled?

We might start by pointing out that the problem is not specific to philosophical activity, it results from "our," that is human beings in general, "failure to understand the logic of our language." The split is according to Wittgenstein a feature of human language as such: "It is not *humanly* possible to gather *immediately* from (everyday language) what the logic of language is" (my emphases). This importantly does not mean that the problem has to do with everyday language and would be avoided in an ideal language. Wittgenstein specifically says later on: Everyday language *is* in perfect logical order. The emphasis on the non-immediate relation to meanings, or objects, is, I take it, on the fact that no matter what language we construct, including a so-called ideal language, i.e. a language whose syntactical means of expression will be clearly displayed in the signs, there will be this gap between the making of sense and the recovery of what it is that constitutes our human world.

This means that the level of significant communication as such is impossible to anticipate; it can only be recovered through what shows itself in language.

Here is then my sketch of the *Tractatus* which further expresses this understanding: Wittgenstein's *Tractatus* might be said, non-controversially I think, to empty logic of any content. This though might be taken in various ways. My understanding is that it is subordinated to a shift of perspective; it turns us from a conception of the world described through its facts by means of logic, to a view of the world in which objects are shown and in which all of the logical scaffolding that allows us to manipulate pictures of facts can in principle disappear. The *Tractatus* way of going beyond negation (the determinate negation of logic) aims at thinking positivity and negativity in a new way, beyond the domination of logic and the need for ground. The new positivity is what shows itself in the form of objects. That view of phenomena through its objects is the view of things through what might be called their internal properties. What is most crucial about that level is that it cannot be systematically described once and for all in advance of experience. Recovering the perspective of the object or the internal form of experience depends on bringing out what shows itself in the application of logic. Logic, our means of expression, the only a priori we have, cannot anticipate the showing of the object. It is nevertheless the form of phenomena that is brought out through the objects since they are the grounds of all possible states of affairs. The world shown beyond logic is, to link Wittgenstein and Schopenhauer, a world beyond sufficient reason, or beyond the form of law. The *Tractatus* is aimed primarily at de-systematizing significance, by radically distinguishing it from the mere making of sense. There is only a very thin description of sense as such: "This is how things are." This must be distinguished from the claim "This is what things are"—"Propositions can only say *how* things are, not *what* they are" (3.221). This thin description elaborated characterizes how we can produce sense by manipulating pictures, but the phenomenon of the significance of sense, the unveiling, or showing of what the thing is by itself is thoroughly impossible to anticipate.

"The application of logic decides what elementary propositions there are" (5.557). Make no mistake: this does not mean that the application of logic decides which among all possible elementary propositions are true, but rather it gives the constitution of elementary propositions. Elementary propositions consist of objects and objects are what spans the possibility of our human world and any world we humans can imagine. This means that the grammar of reality, what determines the possibility of our world cannot be given, a priori, once and for all, systematically and in advance of our encounter with experience. The grammar of reality must be recognized without anything to go by but what we are willing and unwilling to say in language. But now this just means that the separation of sense from nonsense is not criterial and depends on the subject taking up language, affirming the form of the world. There is no grounding beyond that to the phenomenon of language.

This is, one might say, precisely the point of the distinction between showing and saying. It is the reason why Wittgenstein expresses distaste for Russell's attempt to do scientific philosophy by constructing experiences out of a given stock of sense data, and similarly why he says to the members of the Vienna Circle that Carnap's anticipation of the form of experience in his *Aufbau* is dogmatic. It is surely the reason why any attempt such as Russell's or Carnap's to introduce a meta-language into the framework of the *Tractatus* is wholly and totally misguided. For showing marks precisely what cannot be anticipated by means of a priori hypothesizing or arbitrary syntactic understandings. Showing means primarily being related to something that you did not do but that expressed itself through what you did and therefore could not have been anticipated.

We might start to characterize this other feature of language by considering how proposition 4.002 revolves around the analogy with the body and the sense of language as part of the human organism. This means that language can be thought of as expressing a will, or it can be seen as purposive. This is I take it the meaning of Wittgenstein's identification of the world, life, and language. The Wittgensteinian subject has a world. Having a world is not merely having a description of all facts by means of language. All descriptions of facts are of equal value, equally insignificant. Rather it is recognizing objects or language as familiar. It is what makes it possible for the claim "The world is my world" in which the subject recognizes itself in the form of the world that is unveiled. It is the peculiar intelligence or significance Wittgenstein finds in language. The entering of significance into language is the possibility of thinking language as presenting us with a human world, and thus of having a subject in language.

It is this condition of language which, I want to claim, is the basis for the impulse to nonsense. It is the fact that one cannot put bounds and that the livelihood and affirmation of human reality depends on the acknowledgment of the subject (on the subject affirming the world as my world) that makes for the original drive to find an absolute ground of sense. It is the source of the fleeing into established meanings as well as the drive to metaphysical absolutism. For metaphysics, through its demand for an ultimate ground, is precisely the denial of this finite view of the subject and of language, it denies the essential dependence of the subject on its language. The precarious condition of language determines the activity at the limits of language. It characterizes the Wittgensteinian subject in language as one that is driven to flee into what can only be nothing and ever in need of returning to what can never be a final ground. Indeed it identifies the subject through those very possibilities.

But how does significance enter language? What is there to say about the way in which the human world forms itself? There is no synthetic activity of a transcendental understanding whose categories constitute the objects of experience. This is the point of Wittgenstein's discussion of the eye, and his emphasis that nothing we find in experience is at the same time a priori. Indeed all systematicity is associated with the possibilities of syntax and such logical syntax, the activity of thinking, is always the manipulation of facts and does not determine the possibility of objects.

So significance itself, the sense of the world or the possibility of calling the world mine, remains unexplained. The original endowment of significance is grounded in nothing and can be recognized only in the subject's recovering of his experience. But this non-ground can manifest itself. Indeed here we speak no more of active saying, the making of pictures, nor of showing of what forms itself as the horizon of our engagement with things, but of passive manifestation or revelation in feelings or moods.

How does the original passion at the heart of language, that passion which accounts for the very formation of a significant world, manifest itself? It can only manifest itself in its excess. I want to say in the drive to ultimate significance, and thereby to nonsense. Significance, the life of language, is internally connected with nonsense, the death of language. We are now in the position to interpret the remark of Wittgenstein concerning Heidegger through a reading of the end of the *Tractatus*.

DEMANDING SILENCE

How must one read the famous last sentence of the *Tractatus*, "What we cannot speak about we must pass over in silence"? At the outset there is a question: Why is that sentence in the form of an imperative? Indeed if something cannot be done then there is no point prohibiting it. There is a redundancy in the demand. This sense of this redundancy itself is expressed earlier in the book in 5.61: "We cannot think what we cannot think; so what we cannot think we cannot say either." This means that here, at the end, something more comes into play.

So isn't the sense of redundancy generated by misconstruing the opposition of speech and silence? For it seems that the impossibility is indeed of making sense beyond the bounds of sense, and that is indeed tautological. But Wittgenstein does not say: "What we cannot speak about we must not speak about" he rather demands silence. The opposite of silence is not necessarily speaking with sense, but rather making noise. Speaking without sense is one way of being noisy. The ending of the *Tractatus* should then be read in conjunction with the epigraph of the book: "Motto: . . . and whatever a man knows, whatever is not mere rumbling and roaring that he has heard, can be said in three words." Being silent means primarily not falling prey to the rumbling and roaring of rumor. The implication is that the noise of empty talk, whether it be nonsense or mere mindlessness in language, is covering up something. It is to be understood as a condition of avoidance.

It is possible then to form a connection between proposition 7, the demand for silence, and proposition 6.53 speaking of the correct method of philosophy, which describes the formative experience of philosophy as precisely being robbed of speech, by being shown repeatedly that one's speech is drawn into meaninglessness:

> The correct method in philosophy would really be the following: to say nothing except what can be said, i.e. propositions of natural science—i.e. something that has nothing to do with philosophy—and then, whenever someone else wanted to say something metaphysical, to demonstrate to him that he had failed to give a meaning to certain signs in his propositions. Although it would not be satisfying to the other person—he would not have the feeling that we were teaching him *philosophy—this* method would be the only strictly correct one.
>
> (Wittgenstein 1961: 6.53)

Thus being robbed of one's speech produces anxiety which is of course what provides the mood that underlies the ending of the book. In that case we might indeed conceive as an imperative the demand to maintain oneself resolutely within this anxiety. This is demanded in the face of the impulse, one can also call it a compulsion, to run up against the limits of language. The lack of satisfaction that the other person would evince in showing the meaninglessness of assertions is a sign that this attempted speaking will be repeated until that repetition itself and its obsessive quality comes to the fore. This is the primary condition of philosophical learning.

But why is this a delimitation of the domain of the ethical? And what is the sense of the imperative, of the "must" which is not quite an "ought"? In his remarks on Heidegger to the Vienna Circle Wittgenstein refers to Augustine's saying with respect to this impulse to run up against the limits of language: "What, you swine, you want not to talk nonsense! Go ahead and talk nonsense, it does not matter!" (1979: 69). The context here is unclear but Wittgenstein returns to this very remark of Augustine in a conversation with Drury. In response to Drury's assertion that "a professor of philosophy had no right to keep silent concerning such an important subject [as religion]" Wittgenstein quotes the same passage from Augustine, this time correcting the translation: "It should be translated 'And woe to those who say nothing concerning thee just because the chatterboxes talk a lot of nonsense.' 'Loquaces' is a term of contempt. I wont refuse to talk to you about God or about religion" (1984: 90–1).

Seen in a certain light what is easier than being silent, it would seem that a demand is out of place regarding such a matter. But then of course such silence would not address the anxiety or the sense that the limits of language place a demand on the subject through which it is revealed. It is as if one has decided in advance of thinking that since what is important is the silence, we might just as well sit back and avoid nonsense by not speaking of anything important. Avoiding nonsense at the outset, Wittgenstein argues, is swinish behavior. Recognizing significance is always a matter of returning from the temptation of nonsense. Wittgenstein takes the very drive to nonsense to be significant or to manifest the ethical dimension. Indeed it is not what one says, but that one can recognize this disintegration of language that is crucial. That disintegration of language is the sign of the bestowal of significance.

This is precisely what it means that for us, human beings, silence manifests itself in the form of a demand. The demand expresses that the source of the significance of speech manifest itself only through the drive to nonsense. The imperative is not something that can be heeded apart from this division. The imperative of listening in silence is, one wants to say, a demand to get rid of the noisy elements of nonsense that surround us, but the imperative just *means* that silence is ever to be achieved through the temptation to noise.

NOTE

1 See "On What Nonsense Might Be" and "Frege and Nonsense" in Diamond 1991.

BIBLIOGRAPHY

Carnap, R. (1932), "The Elimination of Metaphysics Through Logical Analysis of Language," *Erkenntnis* 2; reprinted in A. J. Ayer (ed.) (1959) *Logical Positivism*, New York: The Free Press.
——(1937) *The Logical Syntax of Language*, trans. A. Smeaton, London: Routledge and Kegan Paul.
Diamond, C. (1991) *The Realistic Spirit*, Cambridge, Mass.: MIT Press.
Heidegger, M. (1976), *The Piety of Thinking: Essays by Martin Heidegger*, trans. J. G. Hart and J. C. Maraldo, Bloomington: Indiana University Press.
——(1977), *Basic Writings*, D. F. Krell (ed.), New York: Harper and Row.
Wittgenstein, L. (1961) *Tractatus Logico-Philosophicus*, trans. D. F. Pears and B. F. McGuinness, London: Routledge and Kegan Paul.
——(1965) "A Lecture on Ethics," *The Philosophical Review* 74: 3–12.
——(1974) *Letters to Russell, Keynes and Moore*, G. H. von Wright (ed.), Ithaca: Cornell University Press.
——(1979) *Ludwig Wittgenstein and the Vienna Circle*, Oxford: Blackwell.
——(1984) *Recollections of Wittgenstein*, R. Rhees (ed.), Oxford: Oxford University Press.

Part IV

An eye to the future

14 Kripkean realism and Wittgenstein's realism*

Hilary Putnam

I have chosen a topic for this volume which has already been much discussed in the literature, namely Kripke's interpretation of Wittgenstein's rule-following argument. Many students of Wittgenstein have criticized Kripke for misreading Wittgenstein, and since I agree that Kripke's interpretation is a misreading, it might seem that this chapter is at best superfluous. But I believe that another look at exactly how Kripke has been led to misread Wittgenstein may shed light on some of the deepest tensions within present-day analytic philosophy. For the difference between the direction that I see Wittgenstein as taking and the direction represented by Kripke is the difference between the direction I would wish analytic philosophy to take, and the direction many influential analytic philosophers—including most of Kripke's colleagues in the Princeton philosophy department—are in fact taking. In a sense, then, the issues I shall be considering are momentous for "the future of analytic philosophy." The difference might be described as the difference between commonsense realism and metaphysical realism; but that, of course, is too brief a description to convey *anything*.

To begin to explain myself, then, let me say that (as opposed to metaphysical realism) commonsense realism always seems to ignore (or beg) a philosophical problem rather than respond to it. Consider, for example, commonsense realism about perception. The commonsense answer to a question like "How do you know that Joan has a new car?" might well be "I saw it." But when John Austin writes that the fact that we hear a bird and recognize the bird "by its booming" (1970: 79) is sufficient reason for saying that we know that there is a bittern at the bottom of the garden (or if I say that the fact that we saw it is sufficient reason for saying that we know that our neighbor has a new car), the objection is always that the response has entirely ignored the "problem," namely that perception, after all, only gives us "direct" acquaintance with our own "sensations" (and that "the real problem" is how we are justified in so much as speaking of perceiving material objects, when all we have directly or immediately before the mind is the sensations). And indeed commonsense realism by itself *isn't* a metaphysical position, or even an anti-metaphysical position. The philosophical work that Austin does and that, in my view, Wittgenstein also does, of undermining the picture on which the supposed difficulty rests, the picture of experience as consisting of "sensations" in a private mental theater, still has to be done. But notice the nature of the strategy that I am attributing to both Austin and Wittgenstein, and that I discussed at more length in my Dewey Lectures.[1] The strategy is not to *offer* an alternative to the various theses of the traditional epistemologists. It consists rather in taking seriously our ordinary claims to know about the existence of birds and automobiles and what Austin referred to as "middle-sized dry goods," and our ordinary explanations of how we know those things, and in meeting the objection that these ordinary claims ignore a philosophical problem by challenging the very intelligibility of the supposed problem. If there is a "program" here at all, it is the program of "uncovering of one or another piece of plain nonsense and of bumps that the understanding has got by running its head up against the limits of language. These bumps make us see the value of the discovery" (Wittgenstein 1972: §119).

With this now in mind, let us consider what the parallel dialectic about following a rule might be. Kripke defines a function "quus" by the stipulation that *a quus b* (where *a* and *b* are whole numbers) is 5 when either *a* or *b* is greater than or equal to 57, and is equal to *a* plus *b* otherwise. And he asks us how we can know that we ourselves did not in the past mean "quus" when we said or thought "plus." His aim is to eventually cast doubt on my confidence that I *now* mean anything when I say or think "plus."

Well, if someone were to ask me, how do I know that someone—call her "Joan"—doesn't mean *quus* by "plus"? my response would be that the questioner is using the question as a "ploy" to start a philosophical discussion. (All the more so if the question is not about someone else but about my own past self!) If Joan were an intelligent adult and a fluent speaker of English, I would be at a loss what to say. Perhaps I would just say, "She speaks English." And this seems unresponsive to the philosophical problem, since of course Kripke doesn't deny that in *some* sense that is the right answer to give.

But let me pretend that the question is a serious one. Then I may say that the "hypothesis" that Joan means *quus* by "plus" is one that can, in fact, be empirically refuted, by asking Joan what 2+57 is.[2] To be sure, it is "logically possible" that Joan would still answer the question "What is 2+57?" by saying "59" rather than by giving the answer which is correct on the "quus" interpretation of "plus," namely "5," since Joan might make a mistake in "quadition." The inference from the response "2+57=59" to

"Joan does not mean *quus* by 'plus' " is not a *deductive* inference. But so what? As Austin famously reminded us, "Enough is enough: it doesn't mean everything" (1970: 84).

But Kripke's problem is deeper. Even if we can rule out the particular hypothesis that Joan means *quus* by "plus," we cannot in the same way rule out every possible hypothesis of this kind. Thus, for each n define a function $quus_n$ as follows:

a $quus_n$ b = a+b *if* a,b<n
a $quus_n$ b = *5 if* a *or* b≥n

If what Joan means by "plus" is $quus_N$, for some very large N, Joan's response to the sums we actually encounter will be "normal." Still, if she is mathematically sophisticated, could we not ask her "Is there a number n such that a 'plus' b = 5 whenever either a or b is ≥ N?" If Joan answers "No," does this not show[3] that, whatever Joan may mean by "plus," she *doesn't* mean $quus_n$, for any n whatsoever? At this point we encounter the really *deep* move in Kripke's argument.

Joan, Kripke tells us, might not only understand "plus" in a different way from the rest of us; she might conceivably understand almost every word in the language differently, but in such a way that she speaks exactly like the rest of us in all actual circumstances. She would speak differently from the rest of us if we could utter or write down the number N in decimal notation and ask her, "What is 2+N?", or some such question. But suppose the number N is so large that it is *physically impossible* to write it down?[4] Then there might be no *physically possible* situation in which Joan would speak differently from the rest of us, and yet she would "mean something different" from the rest of us by "plus."

Kripke is right to think that Wittgenstein would dismiss this as unintelligible. The idea that someone might mean something different by a word although the supposed difference in meaning does not show up in any behavior at all, indeed in any possible behavior, linguistic or extra linguistic, is a "possibility" that Wittgenstein would reject. But must Wittgenstein's rejection be based on a community-standards view of what correctness in rule-following consists in? (This is close to Wittgenstein's supposed "skeptical solution," as Kripke interprets him.)

Here I wish to bring out the *distance* between what we know Wittgenstein thought and what Kripke says he thought. All interpreters agree that we know that Wittgenstein thought that we can speak of understanding a word (or of understanding a word one way rather than another) only against the background of a whole system of uses of words, and we know, moreover, that when Wittgenstein speaks of the "use" of words he means also the actions and events with which those uses of words are interwoven. Descriptions of language and descriptions of the world, including what speakers do in the world, are interwoven in Wittgensteinian accounts. Moreover we know that Wittgenstein thinks that this observation—that the notion of simply understanding a word in isolation from anything one might do with the word, or from the presence of an appropriate background of other uses and actions, makes no sense—is itself a "grammatical" one, that is, in some sense a conceptual observation.

According to Kripke, however, Wittgenstein has much more radical beliefs and much more metaphysical beliefs, in addition to these. Specifically, Kripke's Wittgenstein, Kripkenstein, holds that the only condition we possess[5] for the truth of the claim that someone understands a word the way the other members of his linguistic community do is that that someone be disposed to answer correctly certain specific questions, or, more broadly, to give certain specific linguistic responses in certain situations. Giving those responses in those situations, and the other members of the community then saying that he or she has the concept, itself constitutes a kind of metalinguistic language game, which Kripke calls the "concept attributing game."

In addition, Kripke ascribes to Wittgenstein a certain concept of a "fact": *there are no facts about "a person considered in isolation" except (1) physicalistic facts, that is facts about his or her brain-states, and other such materialistic facts, and (2) (possibly) mentalistic facts, that is facts about his or her sensations, mental images, etc. (described without reference to any intentional content we might ascribe to them)*[6]. In short, Kripke assumes—or rather Kripkenstein assumes—that either materialism or a certain limited form of dualism is the only possible account of what a "fact" is. Given this view of what a "fact" is, Kripkenstein goes on to argue that there are no "facts about a person considered in isolation" which *constitute* the fact that that person understands a word the way the way other people in the community do. Of course, there is no textual basis at all for attributing these views about facts, or even for attributing the concept of "a fact about a person considered in isolation," to Wittgenstein as opposed to Kripkenstein.

Now suppose Joan uses the word "plus" and the other arithmetical words and mathematical signs the way the rest of us do. (I don't just mean that Joan gives the same answer to questions of the syntactic form "What does $a+b$ equal?" that the rest of us do, but that she talks *about* addition the way the rest of us do, and that she talks and behaves the way normal people do about matters which involve the *application* of addition. If you are worried about certain science fiction possibilities, assume also that there are no funny "molecular" facts about Joan which would cast the "sincerity" of any of these responses into question—e.g., funny facts about her polygraph results, her blood pressure, her brain waves, etc.[7] If you are worried about the possibility that Joan might be able to conceal her true thoughts even from the polygraph, suppose—with Kripke—that there are no funny facts about her interior monologue as well.) The grammatical remark I ascribe to Wittgenstein is that we cannot understand talk of "meaning something different" by a piece of language when there is no connection between the alleged difference in meaning and anything the person to whom the difference in meaning is ascribed does or says or undergoes or would do or say or undergo. It follows from that "grammatical" observation that in such a case we shouldn't be able to make heads or tails of the suggestion that Joan *really* means something other than plus by the word "plus" or the sign "+". The thesis Kripke ascribes to Wittgenstein, however, is that there are no facts that determine that an arbitrary sentence S's being true under particular circumstances is *incompatible* with the meaning the community assigns to the words except the verdicts the community actually renders or would actually render in the "concept attributing game."

This is a *general* thesis—not only a thesis about the word "plus," but a thesis about every word in the language. Let us consider what Wittgenstein would be committed to if he held that thesis. Let us begin with mathematical examples and move to non-mathematical ones.

First, let a, b, and c be three numbers too large (and two "complicated" considered as sequences of digits) for human beings to actually add, say, strings of more than 2^{64} more or less random digits. Then there will be *no fact that determines that one particular answer to the question "Is it the case that* $a+b=c$?" *is correct,* on Kripke's interpretation. Our communal understanding of the words *is* just our disposition to give certain responses to certain questions, plus the relation of that disposition to the dispositions of the community. Those dispositions *may*, of course, determine that it is *wrong* to say $a+b=c$, even for very large a, b, and c. For example, if we are told that the numbers a and b end with, respectively, 2 and 3, and that the number c does not end with 5, then no matter *how* long a, b, and c are, we can say that $a+b\neq c$. But these negative tests (tests by which we can say on the basis of a limited amount of information about the numbers that $a+b\neq c$) will not suffice to justify a *positive* statement to the effect that $a+b=c$ (or to employ such a statement in considering whether or not a speaker passes the "concept attributing game" in connection with the sign "+"); indeed, nothing will ever justify such a statement if a, b, and c are very long numbers which are not given as values of functional expressions which are short enough to be written down and understood and that we can prove theorems about. For infinitely many triples of numbers a, b, and c, there will be no "fact" as to whether we understand the word "plus" in such a way that a plus b equals c, on Kripke's interpretation of Wittgenstein.[8]

Of course, Kripkenstein's view doesn't imply that we can't *say* things like "No matter how long the numbers *a* and *b* are, there is a number *c* such that *c* is the sum of *a* and *b*." Kripkenstein would say that it is part of the language game we play that we *do* say things like that. But, I think that Kripkenstein would have to say that when we say "There is a number *c*, such that *a+b=c*," what we say doesn't necessarily imply that there is a *fact* as to *which* number *c* is such that "*a+b=c*" is true.

Just to make the point clear: the point I am making is not just the point (which indeed follows immediately from what Kripke writes) that there is nothing about the understanding of any individual considered in isolation that determines the correct answer to all addition problems. It is that when we consider the necessary finiteness of the responses *of a whole community*, Kripkenstein's argument yields the result that *there is no fact about the whole community* which determines the answer to *all* the indefinitely many possible addition problems.

Consider a non-mathematical kind of case which Wittgenstein himself discusses in *Philosophical Investigations*. It can happen that there are disagreements that we are unable to resolve—that is, that the community is unable to resolve—concerning the genuineness of people's expressions of their feelings (1972: 207).[9] I feel that someone's expression of emotion is genuine, but I cannot convince other people. Yet all of us pass the relevant concept-ascribing tests. If the disagreement is about whether someone's avowal of love is sincere, then in the typical case no one would say that some of us lack the concept, or at least no one would say this on the basis of Kripkean criteria. (Of course we do in fact ask whether people really know what love is, but this sort of discussion is one for which Kripke's view seems to leave no room—or perhaps Kripke would say that this is simply a metaphorical way of talking.)

Now Wittgenstein explicitly says that such judgments, judgments on which the community does not come into agreement, are judgments which nevertheless may be right. There are people who are better *Menschenkenner*, people who are better at understanding people, and such people can make "correct judgments." It is true that Wittgenstein says that these better *Menschenkenner* are also, in general, better at making prognoses; but there is nothing in Wittgenstein's text which implies that *each individual correct judgment* of the genuineness of an emotion will eventually be confirmed behaviorally in a way which will command the assent of the whole community. This would be an extraordinary view for Wittgenstein to hold, writing as he does in the same pages, that such judgments are typically made on the basis of "imponderable evidence."

Of course, Kripke has a possible answer here. Kripke ascribes a deflationist account of truth to Wittgenstein, and no doubt he would reply, "Of course, one can say that my judgment or anyone else's judgment of an emotion is correct, or, for that matter, that a judgment concerning the sum of two huge numbers is correct, *meaning by that* simply to endorse, or repeat, the judgment in question. To say that someone is a superior *Menschenkenner* is, thus, simply to endorse that person's verdicts, but it is not to say that there is a fact about that person considered in isolation which is the fact that he is a better *Menschenkenner* than others, and, for that matter, if the community doesn't agree that he is a better *Menschenkenner*, then there isn't even a fact about the community as a whole—or indeed a fact about the universe as a whole—which is the *fact* that the person is a better *Menschenkenner*." In short, Kripkenstein's view is a combination of a "deflationist" account of truth and a metaphysical realist account of fact![10]

But what could have led Kripke to attribute such an extraordinary combination of views to Wittgenstein? One hypothesis—which I am sure is wrong—would be that Kripke himself believes that there are only the two sorts of fact that I mentioned, and that this seems so self-evident to Kripke that he cannot but believe that Wittgenstein thinks this too. But I am sure that this is wrong, because it is quite clear that Kripke himself believes that there is another kind of fact about a person considered in isolation, namely the fact that the person *grasps a certain concept*.[11] What makes Kripke think that Wittgenstein would *deny* that it can be a fact about someone ("considered in isolation") that he or she grasps the concept of addition?

I think that the answer must lie in a peculiar ambiguity in Kripke's cumbersome phrase "a fact about a person considered in isolation." Consider the two statements:

1 Joan means by "plus" what most English speakers mean by the word.
2 Joan has the concept of addition.

Now, on *any* view, philosophical or non-philosophical, (1) does not express "a fact about Joan considered in isolation." What it says is that there is a certain *relation* between Joan's understanding of a word and a particular linguistic community's understanding of that word. But since the fact that there is no fact *about Joan considered in isolation* which is the fact that she grasps the concept "plus" is supposed to be a shocking thesis (Kripke calls it a "skeptical" thesis, and compares it to Hume's celebrated theses about causation, etc.) this cannot be what Kripke means to point out. Evidently, Kripke, or rather Kripkenstein, means to make the surprising claim that (2) is not a fact about Joan considered in isolation. But it is not clear why not, *even on Kripkenstein's view of what is involved in having a concept.*

To see why not, let us suppose that Joan does have those speech dispositions which enable her to pass the "concept attributing game" when the concept ascribed is the concept of addition, or more specifically *plus*, and the people playing the game are the members of the English-speaking linguistic community. Now, that Joan is disposed to make such-and-such responses under particular circumstances would appear to be as much a fact about "Joan considered in isolation" as any dispositional fact about her—say, the fact that she is fond of sweets, or the fact that she despises Eric Segal's *Love Story*, etc. It is true that English speakers wouldn't express that particular fact about Joan by saying that she has the concept of addition if *their* concept of addition were different; but it is equally true that the fact that Joan likes sweets wouldn't be described by English speakers in those words if our concept of *liking sweets* were different.

Indeed, one might wonder why Kripke chose to express his view in this puzzling way, rather than by saying—what he might straightforwardly have said—that, on his interpretation, what Wittgenstein thinks is that having a concept—*addition*, or any other concept—is simply having those linguistic dispositions that enable a speaker to pass the appropriate concept attributing game. Of course, if he had put his interpretation that way, then the interpretation would not have been called a "skeptical" interpretation. Rather, it would have been called a *behaviorist* interpretation. For it amounts to saying that possessing a concept is just possessing a certain behavioral disposition; which disposition being determined by the appropriate concept attributing game.[12]

But I do not mean to suggest that it was just for "packaging" purposes that Kripke expressed his interpretation in the way he did. I think that, rather, the way in which Kripke chose to express his interpretation is an indication of what Kripke's own view must be. On Kripke's own view, I suspect, that I grasp the concept of addition isn't *just* "a fact about me considered in isolation," but it is a very special kind of fact, a fact that is not reducible to facts about my behavior dispositions, or my behavior dispositions cum bodily states, or the sameness and difference of the foregoing from the behavior dispositions and bodily states of others. Kripke, I believe, sees Wittgenstein as *denying that*.

Yet even this isn't enough to explain what is going on here, because it is pretty easy to see that Wittgenstein would not wish to deny that, say, I, or Joan, possess the concept of addition, or understand the word "plus"; and many have seen that Wittgenstein is anti-reductionist, that he would not wish in any way to reduce the statement that I understand the concept *plus* to any set of statements about my behavior dispositions. Kripke, of course, knows this; so why, in the end, does he—if not in those words—ascribe to Wittgenstein a view which makes having a concept come to no more than possessing certain behavior dispositions?[13] The answer, I think, must be this: While Kripke knows that Wittgenstein was concerned to deny being a behaviorist or a reductionist about the possession of concepts, he finds these denials somehow *unsatisfying*. They don't come, as it were, with the right metaphysical emphasis. To have the right metaphysical emphasis, Wittgenstein would have to say that the fact that I grasp a certain concept is a fact about me somehow on the same metaphysical *plane*, with the same metaphysical *reality* as the fact that my neurons do such and such, or the fact that I have such and such a mental image when I think of chocolate ice cream. *That's* what Wittgenstein must be denying. If my guess is right, Kripke speaks of "facts about a person considered in isolation" not because of anything in *Wittgenstein's* writings, but because that is a description of what *Kripke* himself believes in, and because he sees himself as having a disagreement with Wittgenstein.[14]

At the same time, Kripke is obviously honest in telling us that Wittgenstein created a problem for him. This comes out in a remarkable misreading of §195 of the *Investigations* on p. 52 of Kripke's book. Kripke writes, "Yet (§195) 'in a *queer* way' each such case [of the addition table] is in some sense already present." And after ruminating on how "mysterious" a supposed mental state of understanding would have to be (on p. 54 he writes that it would be a "finite object" which contained an infinite amount of information), Kripke quotes "the protest in §195 more fully," *viz.* "But I don't mean that what I do now (in grasping a sense) determines the future use *causally* and as a matter of *experience*, but that in a *queer* way the use is itself somehow present." Not a hint in this that this sentence is set off in quotes in Wittgenstein's text (i.e., that the voice is the voice of an interlocutor), much less a hint of Wittgenstein's brusque response: "Really all that is wrong with what you say is the expression 'in a queer way'. The rest is all right; and the sentence only seems queer when one imagines a different language-game for it from the one in which we actually use it." In short, Kripke takes the voice of the interlocutor to be Wittgenstein's voice, and he cannot hear Wittgenstein's response at all!

It is because he sees Wittgenstein as showing that it is "queer" that we can understand a rule, that Kripke is virtually forced to see him as a skeptic. But if we grant that this is a misreading, then what is it that Wittgenstein fails to do, that Kripke would have him do, other than, as it might be, pound the table when he says that we do grasp concepts and follow rules?

If grasping concepts is (as Kripke hints that he thinks)[15] a matter of special "facts about a person considered in isolation," then we need to be told more about what the causal or other powers of "facts about a person considered in isolation" are supposed to be. It is striking that the alternative to Wittgenstein's view turns out to be *no clear alternative at all*. Indeed, I suspect that it must consist in saying what practically all of us, including

Wittgenstein, would wish to say, but with a special stamp of the foot ("It's *something more* than physical facts and mental imagery" versus "The statement that someone grasps a concept is not replaceable by a set of statements about physical facts and mental imagery"—but what does "something more" add?).

NOTES

* The present chapter is adapted from one section of a much longer paper entitled "Was Wittgenstein *Really* an Antirealist About Mathematics?," a version of which was delivered at the University of Illinois at a conference on The Reception of Wittgenstein's Philosophy in America in October 1995; papers from that conference are to be published in a volume edited by Peter Winch. It also overlaps a paper titled "On Wittgenstein's Philosophy of Mathematics," forthcoming in the *Proceedings of the Aristotelian Society*.

1 See Putnam 1994, especially Lectures II and III.

2 The "right" answer, on the hypothesis that Joan means "quus" by "plus," is, of course, "5."

3 Someone might object that I have misunderstood Kripke's problem, that the problem is just this: the under-determination of, say, a hypothesis about quarks by laboratory evidence is not a problem for us because we grant that there are *facts* about quarks ("considered in isolation," if you please), but that the under-determination of the supposed "fact" that Joan means *plus* by her speech dispositions is an under-determination by "all the facts" that there *are*. This is, of course, just Quine's problem of "the underdetermination of reference"; and perhaps Kripke fails to see that it is only because he thinks Quine's problem turns on behaviorist assumptions rather than on the notion of a "fact of the matter." (See his remarks about Quine in 1982: 57.) However, Kripke's emphasis on the fact that the plus function is defined for infinitely many cases, so that it is (supposedly) puzzling how my "finite mind" can hold it all introduces a different and more interesting line of argument, even if in the end that line too turns on the notion of a "fact," and it is that line of argument that I have tried to reconstruct here.

4 It would also suffice to suppose that N is so large that it is physically impossible for someone with a human brain to calculate with it.

5 However even this condition—the only one we possess—may not actually determine that the claim *is* true, but only that we agree in calling it true: Kripke (1982: 111–12) would have Wittgenstein deny that the community's responses determine the truth of *any* sentence, and say that *all* that the facts about the community's responses determine is that the community does not doubt certain sentences (e.g., does not doubt that $a+b\neq c$). On this interpretation of Wittgenstein there is no fact of the matter as to whether *any* sentence in the language is true or false; and yet Wittgenstein still thinks he is able to employ the notion of a fact!

6 Kripkenstein (Kripke 1982: 52–54) does consider the possibility that there are other sorts of mentalistic facts, but argues that a mental state that determined the value of the plus function in infinitely many cases would be a "finite object" (because we have "finite minds") that could not determine the value of the plus function "in an infinity of cases." I leave it to the reader to judge if

this argument, with its image of the mind as a finite space and its picture of mental states as objects, is Wittgensteinian at all!

7 I take *Philosophical Investigations* §270 "Let us now imagine a use for the entry of the sign S in my diary. I discover that whenever I have a particular sensation a manometer shews that my blood pressure rises . . . " not only to go against the view that, for Wittgenstein, only "criterial" behavior is relevant to the occurrence or non-occurrence of sensations, and, more general, of propositional attitudes, but also to explicitly allow the (possible) relevance of scientific facts about a person (facts about so-called "molecular" behavior). These issues were, of course, much discussed during the controversies about logical behaviorism which took place in the 1950s and 1960s. See, on the latter, my "Brains and Behavior."

8 It seems from certain passages in his *Remarks on the Foundations of Mathematics* that Wittgenstein may have been attracted to the idea that undecidable propositions lack a truth value at various times. Does this not support Kripke's interpretation here? No, for several reasons. First of all, Kripke is interpreting *Philosophical Investigations* (in fact, just the "rule-following discussion" in *Philosophical Investigations*). His interpretation is not supposed to depend on evidence from unpublished writings (Kripke subtitles his book "An Elementary Exposition"). But *Philosophical Investigations* refrains from *mentioning* any controversial views Wittgenstein may have held on undecidable statements in mathematics. Moreover, as I go on to argue above, other discussions in *Philosophical Investigations* are inconsistent with the views Kripke attributes to Wittgenstein.

9 See my *Pragmatism*, Chapter II, for a discussion.

10 It is here that Paul Horwich, who agrees with Kripke in ascribing deflationism about truth to Wittgenstein—and whose view of what constitutes understanding, like Kripke's, implies that there is no determinate right answer to the question *is p true?* in cases in which the community's standards do not require that one say "yes" or "no"—parts company with Kripke. (For references, see my discussion of Horwich's views in my 1994, Lecture III.) Horwich's Wittgenstein is an antirealist about both truth *and* fact. Given the views that Horwich ascribes him, if the community says that "there is a number *c* such that *c* is the sum of *a* and *b*" but the community's standards do not require that one say that any *particular c* is the sum of *a* and b, then—rather than say that there is such a *c* but no *fact* as to which it is (the position that I claim Kripkenstein should hold, given the views ascribed to him by his creator)—Horwichstein should say that there is some particular *c* (which we cannot know) such that $a+b=c$ is true, but no *c* such that $a+b=c$ is *determinately true*. (The idea that statements can be "indeterminately" true—whatever that means!—is introduced by Horwich in *Truth* (cf. e.g., p.114). For a criticism of Horwich's deflationism see my 1994: 497ff. For a criticism of Horwich and Kripke's identification of Wittgenstein's view of truth with contemporary versions of deflationism, see the same Dewey Lecture, pp. 510–16.

11 Kripke confesses that "Personally I can only report that in spite of Wittgenstein's assurances, the 'primitive' interpretation 'that looks for something in my present mental state to differentiate between my meaning addition or quaddition' often sounds rather good to me" (1982: 67).

12 Kripke does argue that (on his interpretation of Wittgenstein) our behavior dispositions do not determine the *truth* and *falsity* of our mathematical claims;

but that is because *there is no fact as to their truth or falsity on this interpretation* (see note 9 above). This does not show that (on the same interpretation) having a concept is either more or less than being able to pass the concept attributing tests.

13 Or alternatively: a view which implies that there is no such fact as the fact that anyone has a concept, it is just that we sometimes talk that way?

14 I know that Kripke insists that it is not his purpose to talk about his agreement or disagreement with Wittgenstein, but he openly ridicules Wittgenstein's claim that the "primitive" interpretation (see the preceding note) is a philosopher's imposition, writing, "Personally I think that such philosophical claims are almost invariably suspect. What the claimant calls a 'misleading philosophical construal' of an ordinary statement is probably the natural and correct understanding" (1982: 65).

15 Is this not the "primitive interpretation" that "looks rather good" to Kripke? (Cf. note 12.)

BIBLIOGRAPHY

Austin, J. (1970) "Other Minds," in *Philosophical Papers*, second edition, Oxford: Oxford University Press.
Horwich, P. (1990) *Truth*, Oxford: Blackwell.
Kripke, S. (1982) *Wittgenstein on Rules and Private Language*, Cambridge, Mass.: Harvard University Press.
Putnam, H.(1975) "Brains and Behavior," in *Mind, Language and Reality; Philosophical Papers, vol. II*, Cambridge, Mass.: Cambridge University Press
——(1994) "The Dewey Lectures 1994: Sense, Nonsense, and the Senses; an Inquiry into the Powers of the Human Mind," *The Journal of Philosophy*, vol. XCI, No. 9.
——(1995) *Pragmatism*, Oxford: Blackwell.
Wittgenstein, L. (1972) *Philosophical Investigations*, Oxford: Blackwell.
——(1978) *Remarks on the Foundations of Mathematics*, Oxford: Blackwell.

15 Who is about to kill analytic philosophy?

Jaakko Hintikka

WAS WITTGENSTEIN THE HAND?

I can introduce my topic, and my approach to it, by reference to Ludwig Wittgenstein and to the perspectives that his thought forces us to face.[1] His philosophy has been interpreted in a variety of ways. For my present purposes, by far the best starting-point for understanding him is what might be called the nihilist interpretation of Wittgenstein. This line of interpretation has been expounded particularly eloquently by Burton Dreben. It takes its clue from the fact that Wittgenstein believed, and said, that traditional philosophical problems are due to confusions and mistakes concerning the way our language works. Those so-called problems cannot be solved, they can only be dissolved.

Accordingly, Wittgenstein had little regard for contemporary academic philosophy, including analytic philosophy, insofar as it is essentially a continuation of a preoccupation of those confusions. It is not surprising that those writers who have proclaimed the end of philosophy have tried to appeal to Wittgenstein. What is ironic is that the same writers have missed Wittgenstein's true motivation. They have mistaken Wittgenstein's rejection of bad argumentation and bad philosophical analysis for a rejection of argumentation and analysis as such. In reality, his alienation from academic philosophy was not an aspect of his distaste, be it social, ideological, or religious distaste, of academia, of its lifestyle and values.[2] It was not a matter of taste, but a matter of intellectual judgment. When Wittgenstein preferred Street and Smith detective magazines to *Mind*, his judgment was not social or aesthetic or moral. It was intellectual. What he was objecting in contemporary philosophical writing is its lack of purpose and seriousness and also the confused thinking and argumentation which it far too often exemplifies. Wittgenstein had a keen sense of the difficulty of those philosophical problems he found important. He applauded when Russell exclaimed, "Logic is hell!" I do not expect ever to hear that kind of exclamation from Richard Rorty.

Clearly Wittgenstein would have judged equally harshly most of the subsequent philosophy, if he had been alive, including the thought of many of his own followers. Wittgenstein once concluded a year's lectures with this sentence: "The only seed that I am likely to sow is a certain jargon."

In view of Wittgenstein's central role in the history of analytic philosophy, I am tempted to highlight this anti-traditional and anti-academic edge of Wittgenstein's thought by applying to him, *mutatis mutandis*, the same remark Bertold Brecht aimed at Wittgenstein's Viennese *Doppelgänger* Karl Kraus: *When analytic philosophy died by its own hand, Wittgenstein was the hand.*[3]

Like Brecht's original remark, this not so *bon mot* is exaggerated and unfair. Yet it has an uncomfortably large element of truth. Of course it needs all sorts of qualifications. For one thing, the suicide attempt in question was not successful. Wittgenstein's critical message has gone largely unheeded. Even the writers who are proclaiming the end of philosophy are doing so by reference to arguments which would have provoked Wittgenstein's notorious ire that he unfailingly directed at misrepresentations of his ideas.

Other aspects of recent philosophy would fall even more obviously under his indictment. For anyone who takes Wittgenstein's thought seriously it is painful to witness the self-inflicted traditional problem of realism become one of the main themes of recent analytic philosophy. And I cannot help considering it an ultimate insult to Wittgenstein's philosophical intellect and integrity to try to interpret the best-known themes of Wittgenstein's later philosophy in terms of one of the oldest and most confused traditional philosophical problem, the so-called problem of skepticism. Wittgenstein's main epistemological point, or, rather, the first half of his main point, is that in our primary language-games with internal sensations, color-concepts, rule-following, etc. the notions of knowledge, doubt, certainty, evidence, rule, and criterion simply do not apply. The second half of his point is that when we move to the secondary language-games in which the notions of knowledge, certainty, and evidence can be accommodated, we do need criteria, but those very criteria will then enable us to answer the kinds of questions that worry a sceptic.[4]

When it comes to the future prospects of analytic philosophy, Wittgenstein's critical message should be taken much more seriously. I do believe that Wittgenstein was right and that much of the current discussion in philosophical journals, too, not only in *Mind* but in other journals, is not on a very high intellectual level. If Wittgenstein is right, the entire status of academic philosophy has to be reconsidered. Wittgenstein discouraged most of his own students from an academic career. Should we perhaps apply the same consideration to philosophy departments instead of, or in addition to, individual philosophers?

QUINE'S INSCRUTABILITIES

It would also be a mistake to dismiss Wittgenstein's denial of the constructive possibilities of specifically philosophical thought as one of his many idiosyncrasies. The same denial is found in a less conspicuous form and with a different ideological twist in a number of other influential thinkers, and not always where one would first expect it. In these days, it is the logical positivists who are habitually blamed for representing an allegedly narrow view of what philosophy can—and should—be. In reality, it is the critics of logical positivism within the analytical tradition who are depriving philosophers of their *métier*. It is not particularly controversial to suggest, at least for the sake of an argument, that the proper study of philosophy is the world of thought, our conceptual world. And it does not need to be much more controversial, for my present purposes, to think of language as *das Haus des Denkens*, the concrete manifestation of that third world of concepts and thought. And if so, rational self-reflective philosophy inevitably involves using language to speak of language. But this is precisely what the universalist tradition in twentieth-century philosophy claims to be impossible. This tradition is examined and found wanting in my recent work.[5] This tradition is represented under different guises by such surprising bedfellows as Frege, Wittgenstein, Heidegger, and Quine.

The last of these gentlemen can serve as the object of a brief case study. In view of Quine's radical assumption of the ineffability of meaning, it is no wonder that he ends up defending the inscrutability of reference. Even if his argumentation is impeccable, he does not prove the indeterminacy of radical translation or the inscrutability of reference from unproblematic assumptions. The tacit premises of Quine's reasoning are in some ways more restrictive than his conclusions. What is striking about Quine's argumentation is not that he proves inscrutability of reference, but that he assumes the ineffability of semantics and much more.[6] Given his tacit restrictive assumptions, it is no surprise that he cannot make sense of such notions as analyticity or necessity. All that is going on here is nonetheless merely an illustration of the great principle of logical argumentation: presuppositions in, presuppositions out.

One reason why the true nature of Quine's philosophy has not been realized is its unreflective character. He is the least Collingwoodian of contemporary philosophers. Like Hume, he does not relate his ideas to their historical context or to their ultimate presuppositions, but presents them as something every good empiricist should obviously appreciate. For instance, only when Quine's work is viewed in a historical perspective, will an essay like "Two Dogmas of Empiricism" be seen for what it is: less a foray into the wilderness of philosophical ideas than a critical review of Carnap's *Meaning and Necessity*. The curse of Quine's followers is that those who cannot acknowledge their assumptions are condemned to reassume them.

One consequence of Quine's assumptions is clear. If we cannot speak of the semantics of our language in that same language, we cannot rationally examine our conceptual world. The most we can do is to approach the semantics of our language in terms of empirical behavioristic psychology. By the same token, the only thing that we can do in epistemology is the scientific study of human cognition and human inferential behavior. Quine has merely had the courage of his conclusions when he has urged the naturalization of epistemology.

I am not saying that Quine is entirely wrong in claiming that epistemology should be naturalized. But what should not be overlooked is that this is a much more lethal way of disposing of philosophy as an independent discipline than any of Wittgenstein's strictures. For—with a few spectacular exceptions—philosophers like Quine do not have the wherewithal to do more than armchair psychology or armchair linguistics. My own first-hand experience of the history of analytic philosophy makes me sensitive to this issue. In particular, the idea of naturalistic epistemology touches a nerve in me. Whenever I hear references to "naturalistic epistemology" I cannot help remembering the brilliant albeit inconclusive work of Eino Kaila, sometime participant in the discussions of the Vienna Circle, who was a fully competent psychologist and could bring his insights from psychology to bear on the nature of human knowledge.[7] His "naturalistic epistemology" is far superior to its recent incarnation.

KUHN'S NEGATIVE PARADIGM

Similar remarks apply far beyond Quine's philosophy. For instance, the "new philosophy of science" launched by Thomas Kuhn is usually presented as an enrichment of our ideas as to what is involved in the actual life of science.[8] But in a critical philosophical perspective, a main source of this tradition is an exceedingly narrow idea of what can be meaningfully said in the language of science and not only shown by means of paradigms. The reason why this is not any more prominent in Kuhn's writings is the same as in Quine. He illustrates very well his own claim of most thinkers' unawareness of their own "paradigm." But when he is pressed, Kuhn will quickly have to resort to restrictive assumptions. For instance, Kuhn's claim that it does not make sense if progress in science depends crucially on his thesis that we cannot meaningfully speak in science of closeness to truth. But if we can speak of truth, it is merely a matter of careful analysis to understand also the idea of closeness to truth.[9] Hence in the last analysis Kuhn has to rely on some version of the ineffability of semantics claim. The thesis of the ineffability of truth has in fact been the focal point of the critics of logical positivism. Recent work nevertheless discourages all claims of the undefinability and inexpressibility claims.[10] We have to take very seriously the possibility that a realistic concept of truth is an inextricable ingredient of our very own *Sprachlogik*.

The same lack of philosophical self-awareness is characteristic of Kuhn's theories as is evidenced by Quine's philosophy of language. The uses that the "new philosophers of science" make of such notions as the theory-ladenness of observations or incommensurability of theories is marked by a singularly shallow level of awareness of what these notions involve. I have shown in effect that neither supports the pessimistic conclusions that they have been used to argue for.[11]

Just as the only honest conclusion from Quine's views of language is to replace serious philosophy of language by behavioristic linguistics, the only reasonable conclusion from an acceptance of Kuhnian ideas, as they are interpreted by his followers, is to turn philosophy of science into history and sociology of science. In my judgment, that would not only put an end to the genuinely philosophical attempts to understand science but it would impoverish immeasurably the history and sociology of science. And it would impoverish our understanding of science itself.

INTUITIONS THAT ARE NOT

A dim view of the prospects of current analytic philosophy is deepened by a look at the methodology and modes of argumentation currently used by analytic philosophers. In this department, a massive malpractice is rampant. If I open at random a paper published in these days in an English-language philosophy journal, more likely than not I will find appeals to intuitions in support of the writer's views. Sometimes the entire task of a philosophical paper or book is said to be the regimentation of our intuitions about the subject matter in question.

I find this practice scandalous. In the past, every major philosopher who appealed to intuitions had a theory or at least an explanation of why it is that we can obtain new knowledge or insight by reflecting on our own ideas. Aristotle found a basis for such appeals to intuition in his theory of thinking as a genuine realization of forms in the thinker's soul. Descartes found it in the theory of innate ideas, and Kant found it in his transcendental theory of mathematical relations as having been imposed on objects by ourselves in the act of sense-perception, which makes them intuitively knowable, that is, recoverable by means of what we would call intuition. But contemporary uses of intuition in philosophy are seldom backed up by any such justification. This is enough to make them highly suspect.

In a historical perspective, it is embarrassingly obvious what happened. Methodologically insecure philosophers began in the 1960s to imitate Chomsky or, rather, to imitate what they took to be Chomsky's methodology. This methodology was perceived as relying heavily on competent speakers' intuitions of the grammaticality of different strings of symbols. Sometimes a grammarian's task was characterized as a regimentation of such intuitions. What the philosophers who imitated Chomsky did not initially realize was that he was a closet Cartesian who did have an implicit backing for his appeals to intuition which at least satisfied him. Alas, the vast majority of the philosophers who in our days appeal to intuitions are not Cartesians and do not have any other theoretical backing for their appeals to intuition. Hence they do not offer us any reasons why we should trust any of their conclusions that are directly or indirectly based on appeals to intuition.

When philosophers' so-called intuitions are analyzed, in most cases they turn out to be derivative knowledge-claims, based in reality on logic, observation, tacit pragmatic reasons, etc. A paradigm case is offered by Sherlock Holmes' "intuition" to the effect that Dr. Watson had recently been to Afghanistan. ("I have a kind of intuition . . . ") Holmes is nevertheless the first one to admit that his "intuition" was a result of a "train of thought" which "ran so swiftly through my mind that I arrived at the conclusion without being conscious of intermediate steps. There were such steps, however." Maybe we have here an illustration of Wittgenstein's reasons for preferring detective stories to philosophy journals.

Be that as it may, a major change is in order in the argumentative practices of analytic philosophers. I am tempted to suggest that there should be a long moratorium on unanalyzed appeals to intuition in philosophical argumentation, except when the writer can provide some further reasons for us to believe in his or her intuitions.

Notice that in this matter I have abstained from imagining the scorn that Wittgenstein would have poured on appeals to intuition in philosophical argumentation. I do not need his authority here. My point is poignant enough even without appeals to Wittgenstein.

ONE-AND-A-HALF TRUTHS ABOUT WITTGENSTEIN

However, the real message I want to convey to you in this chapter is diametrically opposite to pessimism. Once again I can illustrate my point by reference to Wittgenstein. He was a philosophical genius, but he was socially and intellectually a lone wolf who did not assume any responsibility for, or even exhibit interest in, many of the institutions of our society and culture. He was fighting against his private demons, or perhaps more accurately, against the bewitchment of his intellect by the sirens of our language. This fight was for him the true "duty of a genius." (Here is in fact his closest similarity with Karl Kraus.)[12] Wittgenstein rejected many of our institutions with the same passion, not to say hatred, with which he rejected his own family. And this indifference to, and rejection of, much of the best of our culture was not restricted to academic philosophy. Wittgenstein had no sympathy for, or real understanding of, mathematical and physical theorizing. For all his aesthetic sensibilities, he had for instance no feeling for the elegance and power of a real mathematical theory. There are no indications that he had any appreciation of, or even knowledge of, such things as Galois theory, the calculus of residues, Gauss-Riemann surface theory, or the theory of Hilbert spaces. He was likewise supremely disinterested in the genuinely philosophical problems that have come up in contemporary physical theory. Furthermore, logic was for him merely a tool for eliminating private confusions and misunderstanding, not a means of helping mathematicians and scientists in their tasks. According to Keynes,[13] Wittgenstein objected to the "early beliefs" of his Cambridge friends by saying that they lacked reverence "to everything and everyone." But in some walks of life he outdid the Bloomsburies in his nihilist attitude.

All this does not imply the slightest substantial objection to what Wittgenstein in fact did in his philosophy. What it does imply is that in most cases Wittgenstein had absolutely no idea of, or interest in, the constructive possibilities of his own ideas. These possibilities entail a major qualification to the nihilist interpretation mentioned earlier. Admittedly, those constructive possibilities did not interest Wittgenstein, but they are of a crucial importance to our profession in its present situation.

The nihilist interpretation of Wittgenstein should therefore be handled with extreme caution. While it may do justice to Wittgenstein's intentions, it does not do justice to the potentialities of his ideas. In order to appreciate fully the power of his ideas, one often has to develop them further than Wittgenstein did himself and further than he would have been willing to develop them himself.

The simplest and at the same time most significant example of such a constructive use of Wittgenstein's ideas takes off from his famous notion of language-game. As I have shown, all we have to do (after we have figured out what Wittgenstein himself meant by the term) is to take him more literally than he did himself and to apply to his language-games the concepts of the mathematical theory of games. The result is, I have argued, the best available semantical theory both for natural and formal languages.[14]

The failure to use such opportunities can be blamed partly on Wittgenstein's *soi-disant* followers who have failed to use his ideas for constructive purposes. The only excuse I can think of for them is that the exploitation of these Wittgensteinian ideas will take us beyond what Wittgenstein himself said and did. But then they should have realized the truth of Karl Kraus' remark about the one-and-a-half truths that are sometimes needed to overcome half-truths. During his lifetime Wittgenstein's self-appointed followers did not have the courage to stand up to him and to force him to relate his ideas to what was going on in contemporary logic, mathematics, psychology, and physics. Frank Ramsey was probably the only philosopher who could have done so, which makes his premature death a double tragedy.[15] Wittgenstein sacrificed his immense inherited material wealth for his ideals of simple life. It seems to me that he gave away an even greater intellectual wealth in refusing to use his philosophical ideas for constructive purposes.

My main point is that even apart from Wittgenstein's ideas there is an embarrassment of riches in the form of new opportunities available to contemporary analytic philosophy. I strongly believe that the survival of analytic philosophy depends on philosophers' acknowledgment and utilization of these opportunities. The other side of the coin is that we first have to get rid of various mistakes and misconceptions before we can make use of the revolutionary new opportunities.

Indeed, I believe that we have to make a new start in practically all branches of philosophical studies including logic, foundations of mathematics, language theory, epistemology, and philosophical methodology. The rest of this chapter is a survey of some of the new opportunities in these fields. In some cases, though not in others, the new ideas can be thought of as being inspired by Wittgenstein's suggestions.

THE STRATEGY OF STRATEGIES

In doing so, one of the most interesting focal points is offered by the notion of rule and the role it has played in the methodology of recent philosophy and recent linguistics. Here we have a splendid example both of methodological shortcoming and of excellent opportunities of overcoming them. It is not too much of an exaggeration to say that we are all trying to capture a variety of phenomena by finding the rules that govern them. But rules of what kind? A representative example will help to clarify the situation.[16] Goal-directed activities can usually be compared with games of strategy. In such games, we can distinguish two kinds of rules or principles from each other. I have called them definitory rules and strategic rules. The former tell which moves are permissible and which ones are not. They define the game in question. For instance, in chess the definitory rules include specifications as to how chess pieces may be moved on a chessboard. If such a rule is violated, the move is null and void. It is not a part of a game of chess; it has to be taken back.

But if you only know the definitory rules of chess, you cannot yet say that you know how to play chess. Nobody will deign to actually play against you. In order to claim that you know how to play chess, you have to have some grasp of better and worse ways of playing the game. You have to have some idea of what might be called the strategic rules of chess. They cannot be captured by the definitory rules, which merely define what is permitted and what is not permitted. This distinction between definitory and strategic rules can clearly be made quite generally.

One of the most important differences between the two kinds of rules is that definitory rules typically concern individual moves in the game in question, in contradistinction to strategic rules which (as one can learn from the mathematical theory of games) in the last analysis concern entire game strategies. As a game theorist would put it, utilities can be associated without qualification only with entire strategies, not with particular moves. Admittedly in practice we often do also rate moves, but such evaluations can only be made against the background of some assumptions concerning the players' overall strategies.

The methodological shortcoming of recent philosophers (and the associated opportunity for future ones) that I have in mind can now be described concisely. What philosophical analysts are doing is to try to get away by formulating only definitory rules for the different games people play, thus neglecting conceptualizations which turn on strategic rules. This has led them to a variety of dead ends and missed opportunities.

Perhaps the most important cases in point are found in epistemology. There it is generally agreed that we cannot hope to formulate definitory rules for discovery, that is to say, for the acquisition of genuinely new knowledge. From this philosophers have in effect jumped to the conclusion that discovery is inaccessible to rational analysis and that the best that epistemologists and philosophers of science can do is to study "contexts of justification" instead of "contexts of discovery." For instance, we cannot have a theory of which generalizations to make on the basis of limited evidence. The best we can do is to look for possible "warrants" for such steps.

In the light of the observations just made, this conclusion can be seen to be but a huge fallacy. There are in principle no obstacles to setting up strategic rules of discovery.[17] I can even give you a pretty good idea what they are like, in that I have shown that the strategic rules of pure discovery are very closely related to the strategic rules of deduction.[18]

What is more, discovery and justification are of course facets of one and the same process of knowledge acquisition. Strategies of knowledge acquisition involve both elements. And since the only rock-bottom strategic evaluation of knowledge acquisition must involve entire strategies, one cannot study the processes of justification in isolation from the processes of discovery. Not only are processes of discovery a legitimate object of philosophical study. One cannot in the last analysis study justification without also studying discovery.

This point should be obvious. A Sherlock Holmes can typically find a proof of the perpetrator's guilt only by first figuring out who the culprit is and more generally speaking by figuring out (by hook or crook, so to speak) what actually happened. For instance, Sherlock Holmes had to figure out that the stablemaster had stolen the famous racing horse Silver Blaze in order to lame him through a delicate surgical operation before Holmes could try to confirm his "deduction" by seeing whether the devious thief had perhaps first tried out the operation on the innocent sheep grazing nearby.

Since such a process can involve initially reaching the truth on the basis of inconclusive evidence, it might at first sight look like a hypothetico-deductive procedure, until one realizes that its discovery part is also governed by rules, namely, by strategic rules.

Thus the distinction between definitory and strategic rules prompts a major revolution in epistemology where 99 percent of philosophers' recent efforts have been expended on attempts to deal with the process of justification without taking into account its inextricable ties with the process of discovery.

For instance, rules for induction and other forms of so-called scientific inference should be conceived of as strategic rather than definitory rules. Admittedly, some scientists—mostly computer scientists—have realized that the current conception of rule is too restrictive for their purposes. The development of non-monotonic modes of reasoning is a step in the right direction, but it is an insufficient step because non-monotonic rules for non-monotonic reasoning are still definitory rather than strategic rules.

Whether Wittgenstein's thesis of the primacy of entire language-games over their (definitory) rules can be interpreted as calling attention to the strategic aspects of language-games is a question I will raise but not try to answer here.

Moreover, there are dozens of equally direct applications of the distinction between definitory (move-by-move) and strategic rules. If there is a subtly strategic process, it is the interaction of speakers in conversation.

One cannot possibly hope to develop a satisfactory theory of dialogue without emphasizing the strategic angle. And yet philosophers' theories of discourse and dialogue have attempted to do just that.[19] Speech-act theories traffic in the forces attributed to single language-acts, and Grice operates with conversational maxims that apply to utterances one by one. Such approaches will never reach the whole truth about the logic and semantics of dialogues.

In another direction, constructivists like Dummett have tried to implement their ideas by changing the definitory rules of our verification processes. I have shown that a much more interesting way of carrying out constructivistic ideas in logic and the foundations of mathematics is to restrict the set of strategies that are available to the verifier.[20]

CORRECTING FREGE'S FALLACY

But the shortcomings of contemporary analytic philosophers, and the opportunities available by correcting them are not all methodological in origin. For one thing, they have not even got their basic logic right.[21] This ground-floor part of the edifice of logic is nearly universally taken to be the ordinary first-order logic, aka quantification theory. There is nothing wrong with this logic as far as it goes, but it simply is not what it claimed to be: a genuine and comprehensive theory of (first-order) quantifiers. It is truth and nothing but the truth about our basic logic, the logic of quantifiers and connectives, but it simply is not the whole truth. And this failure is not an accidental oversight. It is a consequence of a failure to understand what quantifiers are and how they work. Quantifiers are not higher-order predicates. Their meaning cannot be exhausted by specifying the class of entities they "range over." They do not operate substitutionally.[22] In reality what quantifiers do is to mark certain choices of entities from the extensions of simple or complex predicates. Moreover, and this is the critical point here, these choices may depend on earlier ones. Indeed, the expressive force of first-order languages depends crucially on the use of such dependent quantifiers, as in the sentences of the form $(\forall x)(\exists y)$ $S[x,y]$ expressing functional dependencies.

But as soon as you realize this crucial role of quantifier dependence and independence, you are in a position to see that Frege (or Russell and Whitehead or Hilbert and Ackermann or whoever can be taken to have first formulated the current rules of ordinary first-order logic) committed a howler when he (or they) set up the formation rules of our traditional first-order logic. Their logic does not cover the whole territory it was supposed to cover. The current formulations simply rule out by a fiat certain perfectly possible and interpretable configurations of dependence and independence between quantifiers and by the same token propositional connectives. The best-known cases in point are so-called branching quantifier prefixes, but the phenomenon in question is extremely widespread in the semantics of natural languages. In formal languages, it can be captured by allowing a quantifier (Q_2x) to be independent of another (Q_1y) when it is not according to the old rules. This may be indicated by writing the former (Q_2x/Q_1y). A similar notation can be applied to other logical and non-logical constants. On the first-order level, we obtain in this way a new, stronger logic, which I have called independence-friendly (IF) first-order logic. It has a better claim to being the true basic logic, the unabridged logic of quantifiers. It does not involve any ideas that are not already needed to understand ordinary first-order logic. Yet it calls for a thorough re-evaluation of our ideas about logic and the foundations of mathematics. Here is a major new opportunity for all logicians and philosophers of mathematics, analytic or not. The contributions they can make here are of course not solutions of traditional philosophical problems. But they are contributions which can help logicians and mathematicians to understand better their own enterprise and can otherwise make a substantial difference to what they are doing.[23] In order to give you a sense of what I have in mind, I may perhaps mention that IF logic has prompted me to argue that the most common framework for doing mathematics in these days, axiomatic set theory, is an artificial and distorting medium for mathematical theorizing. It is a veritable "Fraenkelstein's monster" which has begun as it were to impose its own will on us instead of serving the purposes it was created to serve.

Whether my results in this direction can be said to vindicate Wittgenstein's distaste of set theory is a question I prefer to leave for future research to decide.

REFERENCE SYSTEM VS. IDENTIFICATION SYSTEM

Equally striking opportunities are in the offing in other parts of philosophy. A large-scale and many-faceted example is offered by language theory. There what might easily look like the tritest possible perspective in reality provides a key to a large number of live problems. This perspective is simply an emphasis on the distinctions between the different cognitive systems that are involved in the understanding and use of language. This point is related to Wittgenstein's idea of distinguishing between different language-games, but once again Wittgenstein himself stopped far short to offer any real guidelines for actual language theory.

The simplest distinction confronts us as soon as we have to consider more than one scenario (model or "world"), as we have to do in dealing with epistemic and doxastic concepts. Then we obviously have to distinguish between questions of reference and questions of identification. The former concern which entity a term picks out in the several different "worlds" (models), whereas the latter concern the identities of the entities in different worlds. We could call them the reference system and the identification system, although in reality both are complexes of different subsystems. The two systems obviously are conceptually speaking sharply distinguishable from each other. Moreover, a modicum of empirical evidence shows that they are in fact largely independent of each other in our actual linguistic and conceptual practice. For instance, our criteria of *knowing that* do not prejudice our criteria of *knowing who*. The latter can be varied, and are often varied, while the former remain constant.

All these observations look innocent enough. Yet a second thought shows that they have sweeping consequences for recent and current discussion. For it can be seen that the so-called New Theory of Reference is squarely based on nothing but a mistaken assimilation of the identification system to the reference system.[24] Certain expressions of our languages, prominently including quantifiers, rely on the identification system. In other words, they rely on one's knowledge of what counts identical with what in different scenarios. The mistake of the New Theorists of Reference consists in thinking that such knowledge can be explained only by postulating terms which necessarily pick out the same entity in all different worlds. However, in reality there is nothing to accommodate here, for it is simply a mistake to try to account for the identification system in terms of the reference system. Moreover, the specific candidates for the so-called direct or rigid reference are easily seen to be but chimeras.

WHAT VS. WHERE

In a more constructive vein, it turns out that the identification system is in reality two systems operating at the same time in our conceptual system.[25] A distinction between the two is in my view the most important neglected opportunity in recent philosophy. Taking the identification of persons as an example, we have on the one hand the public system in which a person is identified by placing him or her in a definite slot in a public world history. In this enterprise, a role is played by such things as places and dates of birth, parents' names, social security numbers, FBI files and entries in *Who's Who*. But, on the other hand, one can identify persons, objects, events, places, times etc. through one's direct cognitive relations to them, from one's own vantage point. I have called such identification systems perspectival. The simplest case in point is offered by visual cognition where persons and objects can be identified by their coordinates in one's visual space. Such identification can be dramatized by using the only "logically proper names" of English that Russell countenanced, to wit, "this," "that," and "I." Perspectival systems are clearly local, and the problem as to how they are integrated in our thinking into one over-arching public system is a philosophical problem that lies at the bottom of several major philosophical enterprises. For instance, the perspectival system of identification is of course what a horde of philosophers and philosophical logicians have in vain tried to accomplish by postulating so-called indexical reference.[26] Once again, what is involved in such attempts is a confusion between different systems. As little as identification as distin-guished from reference can be conceptualized as a mythical direct reference, as little can perspectival identification be done justice to by means of an alleged special type of reference called indexical reference.

But the main reason why I am speaking of overlooked opportunities is that here my logical and semantical distinction between the two identifica-tion systems is identical with a distinction made by cognitive scientists between two different cognitive systems—or perhaps between two kinds of cognitive systems. Moreover, these systems are distinguished from each other not only functionally but neuro-anatomically.[27] For the first time since Descartes, important philosophical points can be non-trivially related to anatomical discoveries. Different kinds of neurological damage may result in the loss of one of them while the other one remains intact. Such patients offer dramatic examples and illustrations of my conceptual distinction. The patient of Oliver Sacks who mistook his wife for a hat provides me with a far better illustration of a loss of public system in visual cognition than I could ever have dared to invent myself.[28] Neuroscientists know my distinction as one between what-system (public system) and where-system (perspectival system). In cognitive psychology, an analogous distinction is prominent in the form of Endel Tulving's contrast between what he calls semantic memory and episodic memory.[29]

What is remarkable about this identity of my distinction with the neuroscientists' distinction is the bridge it builds between conceptual and empirical studies. John Searle has complained that most of the specula-tions about neural networks and suchlike do not explain consciousness. For that purpose, we need to know more about the hardware (and "wetware") of the brain.[30] The perspectival vs. public distinction is important because it gives a concrete example of a constructive response to Searle's challenge and hence an example of what can—and should—be done in the philos-ophy of cognitive science.

Once again it is possible to find anticipations of the new insights in Wittgenstein's work, especially in the last few pages of *The Blue Book*

(Wittgenstein 1958). Once again, neither Wittgenstein nor his *soi-disant* followers ever developed his insights far enough to bring out their relevance to concrete philosophical and scientific problems. The only commentator who has to my knowledge realized the importance of the identification system (questions of identification) in Wittgenstein is David Pears.

WHO IS ABOUT TO KILL ANALYTIC PHILOSOPHY?

Thus none of the major present preoccupations of analytic philosophers is likely to further their subject significantly nor perhaps even keep it alive. This list of misdirected preoccupations includes the practice of appealing to intuitions, step-by-step conceptualizations as distinguished from strategic ones, the epistemology of knowledge justification as separated from the epistemology of knowledge acquisition ("logic of discovery"), ordinary first-order logic, axiomatic set theory, Kripke–Marcus theory of direct reference, theory of indexical reference, etc. In each case the misdirected theory has prevented contemporary philosophers from utilizing an important opportunity to develop further their own subject matter.

The list of new opportunities can be continued. I am firmly convinced that unless our colleagues make use of them (and/or of similar ones), then it will be true to say that analytic philosophy is dying by its own hand. But that hand is not mine nor is it, I hope that I have demonstrated to you, Ludwig Wittgenstein's hand, even if he would have liked himself to play that role.

NOTES

1 This chapter is a distillation of the consequences of my work in the last several years for the topic of this volume. As far as Wittgenstein is concerned, most of that work is published in Hintikka and Hintikka (1986) or in Hintikka (1996a).
2 For Wittgenstein's personality and life, see Malcolm (1958).
3 Brecht's original line is more general but perhaps not entirely inappropriate in the case of Wittgenstein, either: "Als die Zeit Hand an sich legte, war er diese Hand."
4 See here Hintikka and Hintikka (1986), last chapter; also "Different Language-games in Wittgenstein," essay 15 in Hintikka (1996a).
5 See the essays collected in Hintikka (1996b), especially "Quine as a Member of the Tradition of the Universality of Language."
6 See Hintikka (1997).
7 See Eino Kaila (1979), especially "The Perceptual and Conceptual Components of Everyday Experience."
8 Kuhn (1970).
9 See, e.g., Niiniluoto (1987).

10 See, e.g., Hintikka (1996b), especially the essays "Defining Truth, the Whole Truth and Nothing but the Truth" and "Contemporary Philosophy and the Problem of Truth."

11 See here Hintikka (1988a) and (1992). For instance, it turns out in the former that the vaunted idea of incommensurability of theories can be perfectly well understood in terms of the estrangement of their normal scientific consequences.

12 More generally speaking, the authenticity of language was an imperative for both of them. For Wittgenstein the laws of thinking were ideally rules for language. "The rules of logic are rules of language." For Kraus, moral rules should ideally reduce to rules for language use. "Welch ein Stil des Lebens möchte sich entwickeln, wenn der Deutsche keiner andern Ordnanz gehorsammte als der der Sprache!" Edward Timms (1986: 341–8) compares Kraus with Lichtenberg. A comparison with Wittgenstein would have been more apt.

13 Keynes (1949).

14 See, e.g. Hintikka (1983), Hintikka and Kulas (1985) and Hintikka and Sandu (1997).

15 See here Hintikka, " 'Die Wende der Philosophie': Wittgenstein's New Logic of 1928," in Hintikka (1996c).

16 See here Hintikka (1990a) and (1996c).

17 See, e.g., Hintikka (1985) and (1988b).

18 See Hintikka (1989).

19 See here Hintikka (1986).

20 Hintikka (1996d), ch. 10.

21 See here Hintikka (1995a) and (1996d), chs 3–4.

22 Hintikka (1995d).

23 See here Hintikka (1996d), especially chs 8–9.

24 Hintikka (1995b).

25 Cf. here Hintikka (1990b).

26 See Hintikka (forthcoming).

27 Cf. here Vaina (1990).

28 Sacks (1985), title essay.

29 Tulving (1983).

30 Cf. e.g. Searle (1994: 1–10).

BIBLIOGRAPHY

Hintikka, J. (1983) *The Game of Language*, Dordrecht: D. Reidel.

——(1985) "True and False Logics of Scientific Discovery," *Communication and Cognition* 18, 1–2: 3–14.

——(1986) "Logic of Conversation as a Logic of Dialogue," in Grandy R. and Wagner, R. (eds) *Philosophical Grounds of Rationality*, Oxford: Clarendon Press.

——(1988a) "On the Incommensurability of Theories," *Philosophy of Science* 55: 25–38.

——(1988b) "What Is the Logic of Experimental Inquiry?," *Synthese* 74: 173–90.

——(1989) "The Role of Logic in Argumentation," *The Monist* 72, 1: 3–24.

——(1990a) "Paradigms for Language Theory," *Acta Philosophica Fennica* 49: 181–209.

——(1990b) "Cartesian *cogito*, Epistemic Logic and Neuroscience," *Synthese* 83: 133–57.

——(1992) "Theory-ladenness of Observations as a Test Case of Kuhn's Approach to Scientific Inquiry," in D. Hull, M. Forbes and K. Okruhliki (eds), PSA, 1: 277–86, East Lansing: Philosophy of Science Association.

——(1995a) "What Is Elementary Logic?," in K. Gavroglu *et al.* (eds) *Physics, Philosophy and Scientific Community*, Dordrecht: Kluwer Academic.

——(1995b) "The Fallacies of the New Theory of Reference," *Synthese* 104: 245–83.

——(1996a) *Ludwig Wittgenstein: Half-truths and One-and-a-half-truths*, Dordrecht: Kluwer Academic.

——(1996b) *Lingua Universalis vs. Calculus Ratiocinator*, Dordrecht: Kluwer Academic.

——(1996c) "Strategic Thinking in Argumentation and Argumentation Theory," *Revue Internationale de Philosophie* 50, 2: 307–24.

——(1996d) *The Principles of Mathematics Revisited*, Cambridge: Cambridge University Press.

——(1997) "Three Dogmas of Quine's Empiricism," *Revue Internationale de Philosophie* 50.

——(forthcoming) "Perspectival Identification, Demonstratives and 'Small Worlds.' "

Hintikka, M. B. and Hintikka, J. (1986) *Investigating Wittgenstein*, Oxford: Basil Blackwell.

Hintikka, J. and Kulas, J. (1985) *Anaphora and Definite Descriptions*, Dordrecht: D. Reidel.

Hintikka, J. and Sandu, G. (1997) "Game-theoretical Semantics," in Johan van Benthem and Alice ter Meulen (eds), *Handbook of Logic and Language*, Amsterdam: Elsevier, 361–710.

Kaila, E. (1979) *Reality and Experience*, ed. by Robert S. Cohen, Dordrecht: D. Reidel.

Keynes, J. M. (1949) "My Early Beliefs," in *Two Memoirs*, London: Rupert Hart-Davis.

Kuhn, T. (1970) *The Structure of Scientific Revolutions*, second edition, Chicago: University of Chicago Press.

Malcolm, N. (1958) *Ludwig Wittgenstein: A Memoir*, with a biographical sketch by G. H. von Wright, Oxford: Oxford University Press.

Niiniluoto, I. (1987), *Truthlikeness*, Dordrecht: D. Reidel.

Sacks, O. (1985) *The Man Who Mistook His Wife for a Hat*, New York: Summit Books.

Searle, J. (1994) "The Problem of Consciousness," in R. Casati, B. Smith, and G. White (eds) *Philosophy and the Cognitive Sciences*, Vienna: Hölder–Pichler–Tempsky.

Timms, E. (1986) *Karl Kraus, Apocalyptic Satirist*, New Haven: Yale University Press.

Tulving, E. (1983) *Elements of Episodic Memory*, Oxford: Clarendon Press.

Vaina, L. (1990) " 'What' and 'Where' in the Human Visual System," *Synthese* 83: 49–91.

Wittgenstein, L. (1958) *The Blue and Brown Books*, Oxford: Basil Blackwell.

Index

a posteriori 25, 110
a priori 8, 12, 18, 21, 23, 25, 27, 30, 73,
  108–9, 110–12, 115, 119, 202, 203,
  234, 235
aboutness 174–5, 180
absolutism 6, 75, 126, 127, 134–5, 137,
  234; Absolute Idealists 182
acquaintance 43, 177
aesthetics 74, 215–16, 222, 259
Alnes, J.H. 163, 164
analysis xii, 3, 16, 23, 24, 44–6, 168;
  alternative languages 47–9; clarity
  in 37, 50–1; connective 4, 5, 6, 23,
  110; defined 38; development and
  variety in 51–4; and elimination
  168–72; function and argument
  39–40; genetic 6; local, intra-
  linguistic approach 171, 178; parts
  and wholes 41–4; pragmatic 169,
  171; realism in 51–2; systematic-
  global approach 171–2, 178; see also
  linguistic analysis; logical analysis,
  logico-linguistic analysis
analytic philosophy: characteristics
  3–14, 24, 25; complacency in 25;
  critical/positive tasks of 28–30;
  decline of 27–8; definitions of
  197–200; and elimination of entities
  168–72; future prospects 254–5;
  internal/external perspective xi-xii;
  and logical positivism 21–2; method
  38; nature of 226; origins of xii, 57,
  199; style in 56–69; unity in 24,
  38, 52
analytic/synthetic distinction 25–8, 49,
  50, 51

Anscombe, E. 22, 62
anti-psychologism 6–8, 15, 80–1, 101,
  133; see also psychologism
anti-semantical 155, 160
Aristotle 10, 13, 14, 257
atomism 5, 12, 17, 65, 196
Augustine, St. 228, 236
Austin, J.L. 4, 12, 17, 22, 54, 62, 65, 80,
  86, 182, 186, 194–5, 241–2
autonomy 72, 80–2, 129–30, 205
Ayer, A.J. 4, 17, 60, 63, 182, 187, 191–3

Baker, G.P. and Hacker, P.M.S. 31, 77,
  147, 161
Bar-Elli, G. 137, 181
Bedeutungen 125, 144–5, 153, 154, 158
behaviorism 248–9, 250, 251
Beiser, F.C. 224
Ben-Menahem, H. 137
Benacerraf, P. 162, 163
Bentham, J. 11–12, 13, 16, 28
Bergmann, G. 31
Berkeley, G. 14, 15
Berlin, I. 22, 224
Berlin Society for Scientific
  Philosophy 4
biological structure 103, 105
Black, M. 4
Bolzano, B. 6, 57, 59, 121
Boole, G. 153, 160, 162
Bradley, F.H. 60, 182
Braithwaite, R.B. 4, 20
Brecht, B. 254, 267
Brentano, F.C. 67, 71
Brinton, C. 72
Broad, C.D. 4, 20, 32